**On Both Sides of the Tracks**

# On Both Sides of the Tracks

Social Mobility
in Contemporary
French Literature

Morgane Cadieu

THE UNIVERSITY OF CHICAGO PRESS
CHICAGO AND LONDON

The University of Chicago Press, Chicago 60637
The University of Chicago Press, Ltd., London
© 2024 by The University of Chicago
All rights reserved. No part of this book may be used or reproduced in any manner whatsoever without written permission, except in the case of brief quotations in critical articles and reviews. For more information, contact the University of Chicago Press, 1427 East 60th St., Chicago, IL 60637.
Published 2024
Printed in the United States of America

33 32 31 30 29 28 27 26 25 24    1 2 3 4 5

ISBN-13: 978-0-226-82712-4 (cloth)
ISBN-13: 978-0-226-83036-0 (paper)
ISBN-13: 978-0-226-83035-3 (e-book)
DOI: https://doi.org/10.7208/chicago/9780226830353.001.0001

Published with the assistance of the Frederick W. Hilles Publication Fund of Yale University.

Library of Congress Cataloging-in-Publication Data

Names: Cadieu, Morgane, author.
Title: On both sides of the tracks : social mobility in contemporary French literature / Morgane Cadieu.
Description: Chicago : The University of Chicago Press, 2024. | Includes bibliographical references and index.
Identifiers: LCCN 2023023145 | ISBN 9780226827124 (cloth) | ISBN 9780226830360 (paperback) | ISBN 9780226830353 (ebook)
Subjects: LCSH: French fiction—21st century—History and criticism. | Social mobility in literature.
Classification: LCC PQ630 .C33 2024 | DDC 843/.9209355—dc23/eng/20230802
LC record available at https://lccn.loc.gov/2023023145

*(I realize that I am always searching for the signs of literature in reality.)*

ANNIE ERNAUX, *Journal du dehors*

# Contents

NOTE ON CITATIONS *ix*

Introduction: The Parvenant 1

1. Rastignac Redux 49
2. The Muddy Parvenant, Then and Now 78
3. The Transient Body of the Transclass 102
4. Self-Maid? The Social Mobility of Literary and Cinematic Servants 126
5. A Foot in the Door: Passing on Social Mobility 154
6. Travel Class: From the Ladder to the Train 185
7. From Rastignac to Subutex: The Immobilization of the Fictional Character 210

Conclusion: A Demoted Canon 237

ACKNOWLEDGMENTS 245
NOTES 249
WORKS CITED 291
INDEX 309

## Note on Citations

Unless indicated otherwise in endnotes, the French citations have been translated by Emma Ramadan, who worked with me to keep the translated quotes as close as possible to the original French.

# The Parvenant    Introduction

Readers of twenty-first-century literature face a new critical challenge. Not only are living authors increasingly exploring more than one genre—novels, narratives, short stories, letters, diaries, screenplays, theater scripts—thus forcing literary critics to constantly hone and update their reading skills. Not only are they publishing prefaces, books of interviews, and newspaper articles; composing manifestos; and leaving behind various forms of archives, often available while they are still alive. The important novelty is that writers today contribute to criticism in the making: they offer oral and written interpretations of their books and instructions on how to read them; they are invited as respondents at conferences devoted to their work, which means they can publicly approve or disapprove of a scholar's critical approach; and because many of them are also professors well versed in literary criticism and social sciences, they have the distance and the competence to justify such self-analysis. This phenomenon, by which writers today are regularly adding materials to their corpus and providing user's manuals within their own books, is amplified when they tackle aesthetic *and* societal topics: in that case, they also sign petitions, write opinion pages, and make media appearances to debate nonliterary issues. This way, they have the opportunity to call attention to the political power of their writing in real time before critics can even start formulating hypotheses on their political stances. This critical situation, I contend in this book, radically intensifies when the authors in question are socially mobile precisely because they have become overtrained readers: acute readers of literary signs who have become experts at interpreting texts because they have crossed the social field from one class to another through studying, reading, writing, and teaching; readers of social signs, too, because they have learned to navigate various milieus and often write books with an explicitly sociological lens. These multiclass writers display what Richard Hoggart—a socially mobile sociologist who wrote about the working class—has called "an unusual self-consciousness."[1] As will become clear in this book, social climbers also need more than one format to contain their cross-class trajectories, which obliges critics to ponder their approaches and develop tactical mixed methods to avoid simply rewording the author's commentaries or muddying the waters. An upwardly mobile writer therefore is a borderline case for contemporary critics and a double-edged sword for interdisciplinarity. What remains of literary criticism, political interpretations, and the sociology of literature when the novelists themselves have become rival experts? The media pay a lot of attention to moving education novels and edifying tales of reinvention.[2] Recently published narratives have made the plot of social mobility commonplace but understudied, often reviewed through interviews, summaries, and paraphrasing. *On Both Sides of the Tracks* responds to this growing trend by proposing a more critical examination. In addition to gathering a variegated corpus to address the pressing social issue of class migration, I argue, chapter by chapter, that the figure of the social climber is a compelling entryway into the intricate coordinates of the contemporary social field and literary landscape. It is through the framework of social mobility that this book proposes to apprehend French literature from the 1970s onward while reflecting on the state of criticism.

## Social Mobility Today

The 2008 financial crisis and the 2018 Yellow Vests movement have put social classes back in the spotlight. In response, contemporary thinkers are unceasingly trying to identify the phrases and keywords that would best define our moment. For economist Thomas Piketty in *Le Capital au XXIe siècle* (2013; *Capital in the Twenty-First Century*), France is facing growing inequalities because the gap between capital and revenue is widening. For demographer Emmanuel Todd— who explicitly counters Piketty's framework in *Les Luttes de classes en*

*France au XXIe siècle* (2020; *The Class Struggles in France in the Twenty-First Century*)—class struggle remains a better lens than inequality to describe the structure of French society today.³ Geographer Christophe Guilluy, for his part, foregrounds the "cultural renaissance of ordinary people" at the turn of the twenty-first century.⁴ Social mobility can at times be pushed into the background of a socioeconomic landscape marked by inequality, precarity, and migration, or sidelined in favor of more collective and antagonistic concepts such as class struggle.⁵ Marxists, for example, envision social mobility as an exacerbated form of individualism incompatible with class consciousness.⁶ As Theodor Adorno once wrote, "In the end, glorification of splendid underdogs is nothing other than glorification of the splendid system that makes them so."⁷ Taking social mobility out of its blind spot, out of its status as an ambivalent subtopic, and putting it at the forefront, as this book endeavors to do, is not self-evident. Social science research on class mobility faced a slow start in France in contrast to the United States, and it has a tendency to quickly veer off onto other fields such as taxation, education, or employment.⁸ Often considered a traitor and deserter, the social climber also does not have a good reputation politically. The working class and the bourgeoisie, despite their antagonism, used to commonly fear this representant of social change: the former group aspired to a collective bettering of life while the latter dreaded demotion.⁹ Twenty-first-century scholars agree on two assessments regarding socioeconomic mobility: France is better at it than the United States but less efficient than Scandinavia; and social mobility has been decreasing in France since the 1970s, making the anomaly of the social climber even more exceptional.¹⁰ Within this framework, the Gilets jaunes or Yellow Vests movement (2018–20) could be interpreted as the symptom of a mobility crisis: demonstrators protested a fuel tax raise that would have penalized rural citizens who depend on private modes of transportation; they wore the yellow vests that all French drivers are required by law to keep in their back seats or trunks, ready to put on while they wait for the tow truck next to their broken-down vehicle. The protesters often met on roundabouts, a staple of French infrastructure and a metaphor for circular movement than can either organize traffic or lead to nowhere. On many counts, the Gilets jaunes uprisings are the symbol of arrested social mobility in the contemporary period.

Given the steep decline of class mobility since the late twentieth century, why focus on it today? The reasons are all deeply connected to language and literature. Social climbers publish bestsellers and populate social novels. Fictional or testimonial social mobility is a plot; a touching and uplifting success story; a compact narrative with a clear beginning and end, packed with twists and turns, peopled by intriguing personages who need to learn the social and linguistic code of another crowd. While it can be difficult to identify with precarious characters or with migrants if you have not experienced these conditions yourself, social mobility is a more relatable story. People reading coming-of-age stories have come of age, too, and probably faced various degrees of childhood traumas, dashed hopes, social estrangements, and difficulties fitting into society. However false, misguided, or inappropriate, there is thus a feeling of universalism or collectivity at play in tales of class mobility, especially if we agree with Michel Foucault that "identities are defined by trajectories," not by social positions.[11] Moreover, precarious workers and migrants rarely get the opportunity to tell, not to mention write and publish, their own stories, unlike social climbers who have made it to a privileged stratum of the society. These controversial figures—spotlighted by the proponents of meritocracy or detested because they partake in "liberal storytelling" and symbolize betrayal—possess a dual standpoint that provides readers with a panoptical access to the social field.[12] According to Jennifer Morton in *Moving Up without Losing Your Way* (2019), such social apertures even put climbers "in a unique position to advocate for policy change."[13] Readers who do not envision literature as a site of identification can thus appreciate how narratives of class mobility offer a pocket-size panorama of society, a digest of our political and literary moment. Inequality and class struggle alike can be refracted in the social climber's family and individual trajectory. This is the case with 2022 recipient of the Nobel Prize in Literature, Annie Ernaux, who admits, in a narrative about her mother, "At certain moments, she had in her daughter opposite her, a class enemy."[14] The uncalled-for comma accentuates the class gap. Ernaux even became her own antagonist when, on her way to a conference, she saw herself through the eyes of the underprivileged child she used to be and concluded, "I am an enemy figure."[15] The navel-gazing of autobiographies—accountable for the decline of literature according to some critics—morphs into a formidable eye-opening tool for inquiry when the author has traversed the social field.

Upward mobility is also deeply connected to the history of the European novel at the turn of the nineteenth century: realist writers used to populate their fictions with ambitious climbers. And as literary critics Jerome Hamilton Buckley and Bruce Robbins have shown, a bildungsroman often is a *Künstlerroman* (literally an "artist's novel" and a specific form of apprenticeship novel recounting how one becomes an artist).[16] Through class mobility, *On Both Sides of the Tracks* thus situates today's prose within the history of modern French literature. My narrative fleshes out the main difference between contemporary texts on class mobility and the epitome of the bildungsroman: the nineteenth-century realist novel. With the increasing dominance of autobiography and autofiction, today's characters of parvenus write their own stories in the first person with a style crafted to represent the tension between classes and the meanders of an upward trajectory.

A nineteenth-century arriviste would not declare, like the narrator of J. D. Vance's best-selling 2016 memoir, *Hillbilly Elegy*, "I was upwardly mobile. I had made it. I had achieved the American Dream."[17] Nor would she exclaim, like Ernaux in *La Place* (1983; *The Place*), "now, I am really a bourgeoise."[18] Some literary parvenus have said "I" before the contemporary period but always with a nonnegligible distance: the "I" in question either did not match the author's civil status or was explicitly fictional. This is the case in Balzac's *Le Lys dans la vallée* (1835; *The Lily in the Valley*). Critics have underlined the similarities between the literary life of social climber Félix de Vandenesse and Honoré de Balzac's biography, underscored by the intimate epistolary format of this novel. Yet the disproportionate book-length letter from Vandenesse to his love interest lends weight to fiction over facts. Before Balzac, the lead character of Marivaux's *Le Paysan parvenu* (1735; *The Parvenu Peasant*), Jacob, also said "I." But Marivaux was noble born, unlike his character, the son of poor peasants who starts his social ascent through a position of servant. Marivaux's and Jacob's "I" do not match socially. Strikingly in *Le Paysan parvenu*, the first-person narrator talks about himself in the third person every time he reaches an important rung of the social ladder: "and, my word! when I was dressed up, Jacob presented very well";

"standing here we will see my adventures become more noble and more important, starting here fortune begins: a servant by the name of Jacob, he will now only be known as *monsieur de la Vallée*"; "I had the pleasure of seeing Jacob transformed into a cavalier."[19] An omniscient viewpoint pierces the memoir's screen. The first-person narrative morphs into a third-person account, as if the split generated by social mobility could only be registered through a distant voice.

Today, instead of third-person novels in which the all-knowing narrator zooms in on the consciousness of a socially mobile character, we are reading narratives penned by parvenu authors who, through their "eye" and through their "I," aspire to sweep the entire social world. As Ernaux wrote in the diary that prefaces her complete works, "I've always written simultaneously from me and outside of me, the 'I' that circulates from book to book cannot be assigned a fixed identity and its voice is traversed by the other voices, parental, social, that inhabit us."[20] Certainly. And yet the biographical details of this unmoored "I" are those of the writer.

Such a change of perspective has a significant impact on the representation of social mobility: it reinforces its rarity. While in *Upward Mobility and the Common Good* (2007), Bruce Robbins powerfully demonstrates that networks of characters function as a proto-welfare state in nineteenth-century French and British novels, the narrowing of the focalization today goes hand in hand with our sociopolitical moment: concrete upward mobility is decreasing as more light is shed on the success stories of a few isolated figures.[21] The transition to, and overwhelming presence of, first-person narratives in the contemporary French literary landscape also put more weight on forms and details, as the style of a text is now fully part of a writer's self-fashioning and social conversion. Nineteenth-century characters worried about what to wear and what to say, less about how to say things, because their voices were mediatized, ventriloquized, by the authors who had invented them. The parvenus' faux pas were content based, their blunders metaphorically linguistic. In Balzac's *Splendeurs et misères des courtisanes* (1838–47; *Splendors and Miseries of Courtesans*), for instance, Madame de Nucingen asks, "Am I the type of woman to make such spelling errors in an outfit?"[22] Similarly, Georges Duroy's hesitant lines when he enters the high society of Maupassant's *Bel-Ami* (1885) are narrated, but we do not have access to the exact wording: "Georges Duroy opened his mouth and said, surprised by the sound of his voice, as though he had never heard himself speak before [...]. He spoke with a certain boastful panache [...]. He even mustered up a few colorful words."[23] This type of reported speech would necessarily change if Duroy were to write his own story in the first person.

I have identified a dividing line in the contemporary French literary landscape that explains the arc of my book, from chapter 1, "Rastignac Redux," to chapter 7, "From Rastignac to Subutex." At odds with the nineteenth-century enmeshment of genre (the novel) and class (upward mobility), contemporary novels have swapped the parvenu for the picaro and are now depicting social immobility and precarity (Marie NDiaye, Julia Deck, Michel Houellebecq, Virginie Despentes). To paraphrase Margaret Cohen's own borrowing in *The Sentimental Education of the Novel* (1999), the novel form itself is no longer a "young man of great expectations." We now have to turn to nonfiction and autobiographies to read successful plots of upward mobility (Christine Angot, Maryse Condé, Didier Éribon, Annie Ernaux, Kaoutar Harchi, Édouard Louis, Abdellah Taïa). Bildungsromane have split into narratives of upward mobility and novels of social immobility. Instead of focusing on one author or genre, the following pages track the causes and examine the consequences of this new partition for the portrayal of social mobility in books that are rarely thought about together: experimental texts, form-oriented and plot-oriented novels, best-selling page-turners, and narratives of the self.

French social events (like the Yellow Vests) have received extensive coverage in the United States. The French writers I engage with also make headlines (Michel Houellebecq), have their books translated into English (Virginie Despentes, Annie Ernaux, Marie NDiaye), tour American bookstores and colleges to promote their translations (Christine Angot, Kaoutar Harchi, Abdellah Taïa), teach courses in American universities (Édouard Louis), and are awarded American prizes (Didier Éribon). To further this transatlantic dialogue, so as to clarify the French and American understandings of social mobility, I regularly intersperse my narrative with references to US sources, from economist Alan Krueger's "Great Gatsby Curve" to J. D. Vance and Tara Westover's best-selling memoirs of upward mobility, *Hill-*

*billy Elegy* and *Educated*. Although my primary focus is literature, short analyses of films will also allow me to track the afterlives of literary protagonists and tropes and show how social mobility conflates person and personage, especially in adaptations of books by Marivaux, Mirbeau, Louis, Vance, Flaubert, and Balzac.

## Interdisciplinary Writings, Disciplinary Readings

Paradoxically, the parvenu's knowledge, narratives, and acute reflexive skills do not facilitate the task of criticism. Take Fredric Jameson's groundbreaking interpretative method in *The Political Unconscious* (1981), for instance: "It is in detecting the traces of that uninterrupted narrative [of class struggle], in restoring to the surface of the text the repressed and buried reality of this fundamental history, that the doctrine of a political unconscious finds its function and its necessity."[24] Can a literary critic continue to partake in "the unmasking of cultural artifacts as socially symbolic acts" when socially mobile writers—who embody class struggle in their life as in their prose—also set themselves the task of bringing out the sunken social grid of a given society?[25] At first glance, a contemporary narrative of social mobility could be the best place to find Jameson's *ideologeme*, understood as "the smallest intelligible unit of the essentially antagonistic collective discourses of social classes."[26] These texts are indeed "dialogical," "heterogenous," and "schizophrenic," filled with social "rifts and discontinuities."[27] But a parvenu's literary take on history, politics, and class is no longer buried. In his readings of writers from the long nineteenth century, Jameson tells us that "the social contradiction addressed and 'resolved' by the formal prestidigitation of narrative must, however reconstructed, remain an absent cause, which cannot be directly or immediately conceptualized by the text."[28] Can we continue to detect social traces in contemporary novels and narratives written by detectors in chief? In a way, aren't we now witnessing the very opposite of "the political unconscious," whereby writers explicitly formalize their social positions and political opinions? Facing a different corpus today, my aim in *On Both Sides of the Tracks* is to propose a reading method that registers this literary and critical shift.

For social sciences, taking literature into account to discuss class issues no longer is a methodological stance but a prerequisite. Such widespread interdisciplinarity functions as a swinging door. On the one hand, economists, sociologists, historians, and politicians have annexed the modern French library as yet another database worthy of being used in their respective fields. On the other hand, critics have noted a "return of the social" in literature itself in the wake of the textuality extolled by New Novelists and structuralist thinkers.[29] Nowadays, language is not supposed to be exclusively self-referential. And literature, far from autonomous, is increasingly read against its context and reception. French writers—renowned ones and newcomers alike—intersperse their texts with social portraits, observations, and pleas against inequality; they also actively take sides on class matters in and out of their books. I offer as evidence Nicolas Mathieu's *Leurs enfants après eux* (*Their Children after Them*), a bildungsroman on the social trajectories of three characters in the deindustrialized east of France, which won the Goncourt—France's premium literary prize—in 2018. This prize gave mainstream and institutional visibility to the social thread of French literature in the early twenty-first century. Mathieu—described as "white trash in corduroy" by a fellow writer—is also very active on what a journalist called his "very social media."[30] He uses online platforms to support the Gilets jaunes and lay into neoliberal rhetorics. But while literature and social sciences are constantly intersecting, do they, for all that, meet in the middle? Are they talking about the same thing? To start answering this question, and before laying out how I read contemporary narratives of social mobility, I will survey the fields that propose a sustained conversation with literature: economics, sociology, and history.

Economics books engaging with literature offer refreshing perspectives on the literary field and on the interest of studying humanities beyond the "pleasure of the text." In *Cents and Sensibility* (2017), literary scholar Gary Saul Morson and economist Morton Schapiro combine their competence to read novels by Tolstoy, Dostoevsky, Eliot, Austen, and Balzac. They highlight the capacity of literature to offer "a distinct way of understanding the social world" through cultural, ethical, and cognitive insights.[31] Similarly, in *Literature and Inequality* (2020), tax law scholar Daniel Shaviro surveys nine realist novels, including some by Balzac and Stendhal, to argue that "Narrative fiction can offer qualitative insights about a given society's status conflict—thereby both complementing and informing expressly empirical social science research."[32] In these two books, fiction does not generate but rather supports quantitative research. The list of examples could go on. Thomas Piketty illustrates the conflict between capital and revenue through multiple Balzac quotes in *Le Capital au XXIe siècle*. In *Selling the Story* (2019), former investment banker Jonathan Paine shows how novels by Balzac, Dostoevsky, and Zola reflect the authors' participation in the publishing business of literature. And Robert Shiller recently coined the concept of "narrative economics," which he defines as the "art" and "science" of looking at viral narratives—including the "story of the self-made man"—in order to collect data and create economic forecasts.[33] Despite differences, these works share one characteristic: they apprehend literature as content, as a vessel of knowledge. Close attention to the texture of prose or to details—beyond references to general overarching elements such as the figure of the narrator—is put aside. For Morson and Schapiro, close reading risks "dehumanizing" the reader's experience; for Shiller, it consists in an "unusually heavy use of paragraph-length quotes."[34] In this context, the word *narrative* does not necessarily bridge literature and social sciences: in Shiller's *Narrative Economics* (2019), it points to "databases of personal diaries, sermons, personal letters, psychiatrists' patient notes, and social media."[35] The majority of these books include French examples—especially novels by Balzac, whose preeminence in and out of the nineteenth century I analyze in my first chapter, "Rastignac Redux." More striking is the fact that economists rarely use examples from twenty-first-century literature.[36] What accounts for this absence? Considering the point of view of quantitative research, I would say that contemporary novels and narratives challenge this type of interdisciplinary approach because they do not contain a sufficient quantity of what economists are looking for: empirical evidence. Or rather, the data has changed in nature; it rarely amounts to exact sums of money in different currencies, throughout social groups, and across decades, as it used to in Balzac.[37] As for qualitative research, contemporary literature—because of the importance of first-person narratives and single-character novels—lends itself more easily to microeconomic, indeed microscopic information, than to macroeconomic models. *Houellebecq économiste* (2014; *Houellebecq Economist*) is one notable exception in the landscape of literature-informed economics books. Here Bernard Maris unpacks the author's discourse on late capitalism and economic liberalism, but for him, too, textuality is not central. Critic Jochen Mecke has compellingly pinpointed the game-changing difference between contemporary authors like Houellebecq and nineteenth-century realists like Balzac: if you put Houellebecq's books and interviews side by side, you would not be able to detect a notable dissonance between the writer's and his narrators' voices. As a result, there is no play—or "antagonism," as Jameson would say—between the plot and the author's commentaries.[38] And Houellebecq writes novels; imagine how social autobiographies dramatically accentuate this phenomenon. As a matter of fact, such homogeneity can deter economists *and* literary critics alike: what is there to add, what "qualitative insights" are left to comb, if a writer—learned in economics, politics, and history—has already said it all without any encryption?

The sociology of literature is especially concerned with this question as well. Like economics, the field has a long history of entanglement with the arts, which takes two directions: literature can increasingly be called sociological, while sociology engages more and more with literary works. What is crucial for this book is the fact that postwar social mobility and the figure of the parvenu have further brought these two disciplines together. Many landmark sociologists and cultural theorists are upwardly mobile: Pierre Bourdieu, Richard Hoggart, Carolyn Steedman, Raymond Williams. And the leading literary voices of class mobility—the central authors of this book— have been deeply influenced by Bourdieu: Annie Ernaux, Didier Éribon, Édouard Louis. Their works carry the traces of the sociologist's reflections on domination, distinction, taste, bodies, the school system, and the political engagement of intellectuals to such an extent that there is an "Annie Ernaux" entry in the 2020 *Dictionnaire international Bourdieu* (*Bourdieu International Dictionary*), edited by literary sociologist Gisèle Sapiro.[39]

Two years before the "culturally explosive" publication of his first novel on social mobility, *En finir avec Eddy Bellegueule* (2014; *Ending Eddy Bellegueule*), Louis organized a conference on Bourdieu's legacy, with talks by Ernaux and Éribon among others.[40] Louis and Éribon's social introspections have even been translated into English by a Bourdieusian scholar specializing in Balzac and Proust, Michael

Lucey, which further seals the porosity between literature, criticism, and social sciences when it comes to class mobility.[41] I would argue that Bourdieu's death in 2002, and the posthumous publication of his "intellectual *Bildungsroman*" *Esquisse pour une auto-analyse* (*Sketch for a Self-Analysis*) in 2004, are largely responsible for the renewed interest in social mobility at the turn of the twenty-first century as well as for the now inextricable intertwining of (autobiographical) literature and sociology.[42] Yet I believe that the figure of the parvenu can be a thorn in the sociology of literature's side. In *Pour une sociologie du roman* (1964; *For a Sociology of the Novel*), Lucien Goldmann argues that "the real subjects of cultural creation are social groups and not isolated individuals."[43] Can we consider that social climbers belong to a social group, and if so, to which one: their class of departure, arrival, or transition? And can we bring back to "context" those who strive to decontextualize themselves? If narratives of class mobility are written under the influence of socially mobile sociologists, this book steps away from the sociological circuit of reading, writing, and interpreting.

The sociology of literature faces new challenges today that go well beyond the commonplace feud between text and context: how should we approach the authors who have read social sciences books and embedded sociological remarks in their prose, as is the case with the autobiographers of my corpus? Critics of nineteenth-century literature can write convincing sociological studies on texts published before the age of sociology, before it became a fully constituted and institutionalized field of study. In *The Misfit of the Family: Balzac and the Social Forms of Sexuality* (2003), Michael Lucey unearths how "there is something in the *imaginative form* of Balzac's novels that *is sociological.*"[44] The critic hones in on the way the author engages, literarily, with the Napoleonic Civil Code promulgated in the early nineteenth century to offer new articulations between economics and kinship. Frédérique Giraud for her part, in *Émile Zola, le déclassement et la lutte des places* (2016; *Émile Zola, Demotion, and Place Struggle*), shows how the writer's biography—his upwardly mobile, then demoted father—is mirrored in the multidirectional social mobility of his numerous characters. Lucey and Giraud are Bourdieusian scholars, but Balzac and Zola had not read Bourdieu. What if novels and narratives were constantly interspersed with "sociological stage directions"?[45] What if authors were now practicing a "permanent participant observation" of the social field and of their own place within it?[46] Annie Ernaux, for instance—who makes explicit, strategic use of Bourdieu's sociological insights and concepts— initially titled one of her books *Éléments pour une ethnologie familiale* (*Towards a Familial Ethnology*) and introduces herself, in a narrative called *La Honte* (1997; *The Shame*), as an "ethnologist of myself."[47] Even if we put aside the fields of ethnology and sociology, she remains a peculiar "spectator of myself for reasons of social rupture."[48] Can a Bourdieusian-infused criticism be as revealing, socially, if its main object of study is Bourdieusian-infused too? Would the critic's job be confined to checking that the theory has been correctly transposed? Or as a reader of Ernaux once wrote in her private correspondence with the author, is she simply "the Bourdieu of the novel"?[49]

Bourdieusian sociologist Éric Fassin is well aware of this pitfall. In *Le Sexe politique* (2009; *The Political Sex*), he apprehends sexuality as a "social reality" in the works of authors who also belong to this book's constellation: Christine Angot and Michel Houellebecq.[50] His final literary chapters start with the following assessment: "literature anticipates a sociological reading."[51] Fassin's way of bypassing such sociological awareness is to focus on the tacit pact between writer and reader: "Thus commentary focuses on the way in which literature defies sociological commentary. It's the reader-writer contract that becomes the subject of analysis."[52] Similarly, philosopher Martine Leibovici, in her research on Richard Wright, Assia Djebar, and Albert Memmi as class renegades, opts for the autobiographical pact in order to uncover the knowledge of those who have crossed the social field.[53] However pertinent and generative, this focus on literary pacts also ends up sidelining the text's details. Fassin, for instance, plays down the attention to form: "But let's not go as far as to believe that it would suffice to speak of the 'form' rather than the 'content' [...]. With Christine Angot, literature thus recuses all commentary in advance."[54] Fassin is not the only sociologist to skirt textuality. In *Ce qu'ils vivent, ce qu'ils écrivent* (2011; *What They Live, What They Write*)—an edited volume that includes many chapters on class mobility—Bernard Lahire virulently describes a literary critic's attention to style as a self-serving corporatism aimed at promoting their fields of study at the detriment of literature's "reality" and "content." For him, the "literariness" of texts can well do without "textuality" and "form."⁵⁵ In the preface to the French translation of Richard Hoggart's seminal work on social mobility and the working class, *The Uses of Literacy* (1957), Pierre Bourdieu's frequent coauthor Jean-Claude Passeron also tones down "literary devices" to praise instead "the author's strictly sociological undertaking."⁵⁶ Similarly, Paul Pasquali in *Passer les frontières sociales* (2014; *Crossing Social Frontiers*) argues that literary writers, even when they are socially mobile, are not the best sources for understanding class mobility. Their texts, he argues, are too caricatural (Richard Hoggart, Jack London, Paul Nizan), as well as inconveniently retrospective and filtered by literary creativity (Didier Éribon, Annie Ernaux). To avoid these caveats, Pasquali examines the cover letters written by underprivileged schoolers who apply to the *grandes écoles*—the French elite system of higher education.⁵⁷

In sociology, as in cultural studies, forms, when addressed, end up losing their literariness to become reflections, relays, transpositions, or mediations of social content. For Jameson in *The Political Unconscious*, "the practice of mediation is particularly crucial for any literary or cultural criticism which seeks to avoid imprisonment in the windless closure of the formalisms."⁵⁸ But as he also admits, such "transcoding" has consequences: "What must now be stressed is that at this level 'form' is apprehended as content."⁵⁹ According to Pierre Bourdieu's influential "theory of the field" in *Les Règles de l'art* (1992; *The Rules of Art*), the emphasis should not be on textuality either but on words as "conductive bodies" and "mediums" of the social world.⁶⁰ A text reflects the author's position in the literary field. A novel is a choice between available social postures and literary practices. In this framework, Gustave Flaubert's *L'Éducation sentimentale* (1869; *The Sentimental Education*) amounts to "an attempt at the *objectivation of the self*, of self-analysis, of socioanalysis."⁶¹ The process by which novels mediate or objectivate a collective consciousness and vision of the world is typical of Marxist sociology. One of its representatives, Lucien Goldmann, however opposed to the concept of "reflection" in *Pour une sociologie du roman*, nonetheless foregrounded a *"rigorous homology"* between the *"novel form"* and the *"structure* of the social milieu."⁶² Even Alain Viala, a fervent advocate of style and of the "sociopoetic," joins in this theory of mediation: "A sociology of content, like for example that of Goldmann and of the 'vision of the world,' renders style of secondary importance. A more consequential sociology, using the concept of *habitus*, can at least attempt a mediation between an acquired social characteristic and a way of writing."[63]

All these examples concern fictional and/or noncontemporary literature: Balzac, Flaubert, Sarraute, Robbe-Grillet, Le Clézio. *On Both Sides of the Tracks* expands on the inspiring field of sociopoetics without understanding form as mediation by gathering a contemporary corpus of novels and narratives.

On the other end of the debate, sociology also challenges literature because it no longer solely relies on data (quantitative research) but also on narratives and interviews (qualitative research), on the "biographical approach of 'life stories.'"[64] Sociologist Jules Naudet—a specialist of social mobility in France, India, and the United States—champions the transition from data to discourse when it comes to capturing "the ambivalence and the multiplicity of the effects caused by upward social mobility."[65] Two competing corpuses are now able to provide proximate information on labor, precarity, and classes: novels and narratives of upward mobility published by acclaimed authors, and autobiographies written or uttered by a representative sample of social climbers, by the anonymous respondents to qualitative social inquiries. Writers have morphed into wild, untrained sociologists of themselves, and sociological case studies have become the unpublished authors of their own stories. French writer of rurality Pierre Bergounioux once wrote that "it's in the absence of sociology that the nineteenth-century novelist was able to believe himself omniscient."[66] In the twenty-first century, now that sociology has become a separate, scientific social science, we could transpose this analysis and say that "in the presence of sociology, the twenty-first-century novelist has lost his omniscience." Sociology forces social literature to reassess its singularity. The central question of this book thus cannot be *what* does literature tell us about class mobility that the media, the politicians, and the social scientists versed in qualitative research cannot but *how*. Otherwise, the answer might well be nothing. As I will show throughout the chapters and lay out in the remaining paragraphs of this introduction, the attention to form, detail, nuance, and style can get us out of this catch-22.

Like sociology, the field of history challenges the uniqueness of social literature and calls for an interdisciplinarity that aligns very well with the hybrid narratives of my corpus. In his manifesto *L'Histoire est une littérature contemporaine* (2014; *History Is a Contemporary Literature*), Ivan Jablonka proposes to abandon two nineteenth-century conceptions of history: as a novel or as a science. Instead, he places at the forefront the epistemological strength of hybrid forms of nonfiction he alternatively calls "text-investigation," "*creative history*," "postrealism," and "literature of the real."[67] To him, such texts are historical *and* literary insofar as their authors seek the truth while using first-person pronouns to narrate the steps of their historical inquiry. Such hybridity, he argues, is also coterminous with a process of "democratization," that is, with a greater attention paid to modest people.[68] Jablonka—the author of a nonfiction on his grandparents—includes himself in the list of practitioners alongside many of the authors discussed in this book: Annie Ernaux, Didier Éribon, Georges Perec, Richard Wright, Richard Hoggart, Florence Aubenas, and François Maspero. He also supervises the publication of sociological and economics books for the publishing house Le Seuil. His coeditor, historian Pierre Rosanvallon, shares his call for blending literature with social sciences and for using fiction in order to represent social entities, such as "the people."[69] Rosanvallon created his own short-lived collection, "Raconter la Vie" (2014–17), in which professional and nonprofessional writers were given a platform to share their life stories with a focus on either trades or settings. But unless they were penned by renowned figures—like Ernaux, who analyzes supermarkets in *Regarde les lumières, mon amour* (2014; *Look at the Lights, My Love*)—these short texts were most often published online (eight hundred digital narratives versus twenty-eight printed volumes) or written by someone else.[70] Jablonka, for instance, became the temporary voice of estheticians in *Le Corps des autres* (2015; *The Body of Others*). As the title of Rosanvallon's collection suggests, the literary focus of these volumes resides in the process of "narrating." Similarly, although he praises literary writing as a powerful tool for historical inquiry, Jablonka ends up shrinking the definition of literature by vehemently opposing the linguistic turn, decrying its relativism as "postmodern nihilo-dandyism."[71] He does not engage with the works of Paul de Man and Jacques Derrida but pushes against Gérard Genette and Roland Barthes's conceptions of all fields of knowledge—including history—as "a discursive construction like any other."[72] Conversely, in my book, instead of envisioning literature from the standpoint of social sciences, we immerse ourselves in diction, and follow in Barthes's much-commented maxim, "a little bit of formalism takes us away from History, but a lot brings us back to it."[73] The contemporary period is often presented as the age of return: of the self, of narratives, of story and history.[74] In *Beyond Return: Genre and Cultural Politics in Contemporary French Fiction* (2019), Lucas Hollister warns readers that "in many instances the discourse of return names precisely an effort to forget the 'Age of Suspicion,' and it is obvious that coming after a literature or a theoretical current is in no way tantamount to assimilating its lessons or building on its innovation."[75] *On Both Sides of the Tracks* capitalizes on the productive hybridity of contemporary social literature as well as on the stimulating postwar care for language. In order to appreciate the literary works of neo-Balzacs who have not forgotten the lessons of the New Novel, we need the toolboxes of both the referential and the linguistic turn.

In *Realizing Capital: Financial and Psychic Economies in Victorian Form* (2014), what Anna Kornbluh's calls her "social close reading" and "financial formalism" originate in her object of study: capitalism and its own fictitiousness.[76] She underlines "the historically specific fact that, for the Victorians, capital was no simple referent amenable to mimetic index. The rendering of capital in realism therefore entails less reference—to brokers, to laws, to new instruments readers must learn about—and more aestheticization, crafting forms that engage the formal logic of capital."[77] From capital to class, my methodology adapts to the "formal logic" of social mobility today. As I will show in the next section, my attention to form is not (only) the fruit of a critical preference; it stems from my very object of study—the contemporary parvenu.

## The Poetics of Social Mobility

Narratives of social mobility are a double threat: a threat to disciplinarity, as they unsettle the neat demarcations between literature, economics, history, and sociology; and a threat to interdisciplinarity, from the point of view of critics, because socially mobile writers rival social scientists. Qualitative researchers open the critics' eyes to literature as a social field, from creation to publication and prizes; they replace texts within a longer history, broaden their relevance, and evaluate their political and epistemological potency. But in the same way that literary critics can object to collecting data, social scientists often step over literariness. Literary critics, even those who are the most attentive to style, also tend to delegate their critical voice to the writers when they discuss sociological content. In an essay titled "Annie Ernaux, une politique de la forme," Jérôme Meizoz, who specializes in literature and sociology, compellingly zooms in on microelements of Ernaux's prose and unearths, through selected details, the social implications of her use of orality and patois. Surprisingly, once he adopts a more explicitly sociological prism, as in "Posture de l'auteure en sociologue," Ernaux's own theorizations—on writing, on sociology—supersede the critic's voice.[78] Indeed, why focus on a verb tense or a punctuation mark? Why split hairs when the author is already providing you with intimate details, qualitative insights, a plot, and a user's manual on how the book was written and how you should read it? In this section, I make the case for another reading of bildungsromane, one that does not isolate fields but puts poetics, rhetorics, and stylistics first.

The originality of this book lies in its attention to the formal details of sociologically relevant texts *contra* the emphasis on "mediation" supported by historical, economic, and sociological approaches and *contra* antiformalist criticism. *On Both Sides of the Tracks* demonstrates that a rejuvenated, socially conscious reading of forms is capable of going beyond what authors explicitly formulate, beyond their biographical experience and social expertise so as to avoid relying on summary, paraphrase, contextualization, and metacomments. Instead, the following seven chapters put forward Roland Barthes's objection to Lucien Goldmann's sociology of literature: "the level at which Goldmann positions himself is essentially ideological: what happens, in this macro-critique, to the verbal *surface* of the work, this perfectly coherent body of formal phenomena [...], writings, rhetorics, modes of narration, techniques of perception, notation criteria, which also *make up* the novel? Goldmann's 'form' paradoxically seems to bypass 'forms.'"[79] Unlike Barthes though, my examination of forms is not restricted to novels but encompasses all the utterances of contemporary authors: fiction, nonfiction, interviews, petitions, and theoretical texts. By poetics and formalism, I do not mean to sever literature from social inputs to practice stylistics for stylistics' sake. Neither do I solely focus on plot, genre, and macroelements, such as the figure of the narrator, for such perspective lets isolated details and telling microelements fall by the wayside. Instead, this book finds meaning in trifles and minutiae, requires patience and care on the part of the reader, and refocuses the scale and pace of our attention. To take only a couple of examples, *On Both Sides of the Tracks* asks, How can a verb tense capture a cross-class romance? Why do journalists name-drop literary characters in their articles on social classes? What does the motif of the door tell us about rites of passages from one class to another? How is an abundant use of italics indicative of a writer's view on the working class? Why should we care about the "social ladder" as a metaphor? Even though I do capitalize on sociology's contributions, it is a text's poetics that orients my forays into other domains (economics and politics in chap. 1; cultural studies in chap. 2) and my exploration of interpretative methods (media studies in chap. 4; editorial strategies in chap. 6). Conversely, the most text-oriented chapters of this book (chaps. 3, 5, and 7) ask and answer social questions that are relevant for the twenty-first century. For instance, in chapter 5, do social climbers emancipate others in return?

Why reject mediation to put texts under a microscope, beyond a taste for stylistics and the conviction that interpretations only emerge from details? First of all, because it has become customary—and condescending—to do the very opposite and consider that "outsider" writers are interesting only insofar as their literature is testimonial. Working-class authors crafting rags to riches narratives could not access the filters of fiction and style, qualities innately available to those destined for the arts. Against such a stereotype, Réda Bensmaïa in *Experimental Nations* (2003) argues in favor of another reading of marginalized authors, postcolonial francophone writers in his case:

> What has long struck me was the nonchalance with which the work of these writers was analyzed. Whenever these novels were studied, they were almost inevitably reduced to anthropological or cultural

case studies. Their literariness was rarely taken seriously. And once they were finally integrated into the deconstructed canon of world literature, they were made to serve as tools for political or ideological agendas. This kind of reading resulted more often than not in their being reduced to mere signifiers of other signifiers, with a total disregard for what makes them literary works *in and of themselves*.[80]

Bensmaïa does not radically disconnect the text from its context for all that. Through his readings of works by Nabil Farès and Kateb Yacine, among others, he focuses on "the originality of the *literary* strategies deployed by postcolonial Marghrebi writers to reappropriate their national cultural heritage, to regain their idioms, and to reconfigure their history, territory, and community."[81] Like *Experimental Nations*, *On Both Sides of the Tracks* informs readers about the state of social mobility in contemporary France but puts literariness first, from reported speech to sonority, from intertextuality to punctuation.

Second, and this is the cornerstone of my argument: mediation (forms as the transposition of a social content) is not necessary today when it comes to social climbing because the parvenu's world is already literary, the way capital, in Kornbluh's analysis, is fictitious. Why should we continue to connect social narratives to their context—the very point of sociology—when the context itself is literature? The epigraph from Ernaux that I chose for this book points in this direction: "(I realize that I am always searching for the signs of literature in reality.)"[82] The social climber's eye and insights are irremediably tied to textuality, not simply to writing books in general but to detecting literary "signs." Many other groups are good at reading signs, but since parvenus also climb the ladder through literature, reading and decoding constitute the core of their experience. In *Retour à Reims* (2009; *Return to Reims*), Éribon's mother underlines her son's class mobility by stating, "you talk like a book."[83] The reading voraciousness social climbers often confess is at the origin of their life choices and vision of the society: "We choose to interpret our lives—or even to live—according to books."[84] Ernaux here equates life to interpretation. "To live" is even embedded between dashes as between "interpret" and "books," which brings to mind Tom Eyers's argument in *Speculative Formalism: Literature, Theory, and the Critical*

*Present* (2016): texts, even when they are nonmimetic and reflexive, are not sealed from their context as the realms of history, sociology, and politics are "vivid folds in literary form as such."[85] When Ernaux reread Charlotte Brontë's *Jane Eye* as an adult, many years after a memorable discovery at the age of twelve, she was amazed by the performative, world-shaping power that the book had had on her life: "I conceived of the world through the entire text of *Jane Eyre*, even though I was convinced that I had only been captivated, moved by the story of Jane as a child, in the repugnant Blackhurts's boarding house. [...] I really looked for everything in my readings. And then, writing took over."[86] This excerpt underlines the totalizing effect of reading, from "the world" to "the entire book" to "everything." Ernaux—a paper parvenu—will read her whole life: in order to study, to teach, to write.

Literature not only appears as a socially marked choice between available pastimes but as the very location of her cross-class trajectory. In her first novel, *Les Armoires vides* (1974; *The Empty Cupboards*), the narrator considers literature to be "a symptom of poverty, the classic means of fleeing one's milieu."[87] But then a couple of years later in *La Femme gelée* (1981; *The Frozen Woman*), a college major in literature becomes "statistically a girl's choice and, the icing on the cake, a petty bourgeois girl's choice."[88] From poverty to bourgeoisie, from reading for pleasure to reading for diplomas, books accompany the author's class mobility. Although she renounces fiction after the publication of her first three novels, this generic modification does not coincide with an impoverishment but with a renewed exploration of forms: "A horizon appeared at the same time as I was rejecting fiction, all possible forms opened up."[89] The author transitions from the novel form (Bourdieu, Goldmann, Jameson) to forms in the plural (Barthes). Her texts are particularly attentive to vernacular languages: "(In Norman, 'ambition' means the pain of being separated, a dog can die of ambition.)"[90] Here, as with the epigraph to this book, Ernaux uses parentheses to embed the metacommentaries that define her uniqueness: looking at the world through literary glasses, through etymology, semiology, and linguistics.[91] Textuality guarantees the authenticity of her social and autobiographical narratives.

Ernaux is unable to narrate the same event twice for this very reason: "I cannot describe those moments because I already did so in another book, which is to say that there will never be another possible narrative, with other words, with sentences in another order."[92] Her father's death exists as a single, specific ordering of words. Literature is the sieve through which she apprehends this event; she realizes, while reading Simone de Beauvoir's *Les Mandarins* (1954; *The Mandarins*), that "on a certain page of this book, quite thick, my father would no longer live."[93] Twice in her literary career, Ernaux also published chunks of her diary—*Se perdre* (2001; *Getting Lost*); *"Je ne suis pas sortie de ma nuit"* (1997; *"I Have Not Emerged from My Night"*)—but not out of egotism or exhibitionism; Ernaux had already penned and published the corresponding narrative versions in *Passion simple* (1991; *Simple Passion*) and *Une femme* (1987; *A Woman*). She explains this original practice as follows: "It seems to me that I couldn't publish any part of my diary that doesn't correspond to a published narrative. As if only the latter would *authorize me* to do it, as if life had to become 'form,' concerted literary form, with a degree of generality, for me to then present it in its immediacy, its formless nature."[94] Life is a matter of form. The narrative takes precedence over the diary; a carefully selected language precedes the raw exposition of life. What Ernaux calls a "degree of generality" is at the core of her artistic and social project. Diving into her subjectivity and into her past is relevant insofar as autobiographical details can lead to insights about the social world: "I needed for my personal reality to become literature: only in becoming literature would it become 'true' and something other than an individual experience."[95] Details seal a text's pertinence: the more personal, the more socially relevant.

This is why Ernaux is constantly trying different strategies to arrive at an "impersonal form" or "transpersonal form" in what she calls her "auto-socio-biographies" and "external diaries."[96] As she often explains during interviews, whether she uses the "I" or alternates between various personal pronouns, she aims to decenter herself, to find history and community within the singular details of her biography. This is how I interpret the title of her Proustian literary summa, *Les Années* (2008; *The Years*), which retraces the life of a woman from the 1940s to today: *Années*, with a capital A, is the plural and transpersonal form of Ernaux's first name, *Annie*.[97] This interpretation is accentuated in English: Annie becomes *any*. In *On Both Sides of the Tracks*, I derive my reading method from Ernaux's formal and bookwormy inclination, from the literary grid with which she combs through the social world. I, too, believe that it is through details that one can best apprehend our social moment and especially the place of class mobility in contemporary France. My book foregrounds a poetics of class mobility attentive to formal details so as to capture the contemporary routes of emancipation: literature and education. Although Ernaux adheres to Bourdieu's sociology, I find the reverse to be quite debatable. Bourdieu would not have appreciated Ernaux's apology for literature. In *Les Règles de l'art*, readers have to go through four quotes before hearing the sociologist's voice: two epigraphs by Raymond Queneau, one by Gustave Flaubert, and the preface starts with a fourth quote whose author is not mentioned in the body of the text:

> "Will we allow the social sciences to reduce the literary experience, the most elevated experience we can have, along with love, to surveys about our leisure activities, when literature is about the meaning of our lives?" Such a sentence, taken from one of the countless, timeless, and authorless appeals in favor of reading, and of culture, would have without fail unleashed the furious elation that the narrow-minded commonplaces inspired in Flaubert. And what to say of the hackneyed "topos" of the pedantic culture of the Book, or Heideggerian-Hölderlinian revelations worthy of enriching the "Bouvardo-Péchuchetian compendium" (this phrase is borrowed from Queneau ...): "To read is above all to be wrested from oneself, and from one's world"; "it is no longer possible to be in the world without the help of books"; "in literature, the essence is revealed all at once, it is presented with its truth, in its truth, like the very truth of the being that reveals itself."[98]

Unlike Queneau and Flaubert, the author whose quotes are mocked does not deserve to be mentioned outside of a footnote: "D. Sallenave, *Le Don des mots*." The sole initial D. does not inform readers that the author in question is a woman, Danièle. Bourdieu does not mention (or maybe he does not know) that Sallenave is, like him, socially mobile. While the quote is allegedly "timeless and nameless," it is neither genderless nor classless. Therefore, what Bourdieu considers a "commonplace" (the apology of reading and education) was on the contrary Sallenave's tool to climb the social ladder. The phrase "to read is above all to be wrested from oneself, and from one's world'" can of course, out of context, sound clichéd; but in fact, it was Sallenave's (and Ernaux's) strategy to change social classes.[99] Unlike *Les Règles de l'art*, my book does not deride the apology for literature, for it is at the core of class mobility.

Literary critics have recently developed a methodology that consists in broadening the meaning of forms without losing their textuality. Forms, according to this fascinating trend, are capable of overflowing literature to have effects on life, emotions, and perceptions. Caroline Levine's *Forms: Whole, Rhythm, Hierarchy, Network* (2015) "makes a case for expanding our usual definition of form in literary studies to include patterns of sociopolitical experience."[100] Marielle Macé advocates for a stylistics of the everyday and the "the ability to continue a literary style in one's own life."[101] She traces the genealogy of a stylistic turn from the "stylistic moment" of the nineteenth century—Balzac's dandyism and distinction—to the "stylistic strength" of the lower classes in the works of Rancière and de Certeau to forms as social manners in the critical sociology of Bourdieu and Hoggart.[102] In *Spoiled Distinctions: Aesthetics and the Ordinary in French Modernism* (2015), Hannah Freed-Thall excavates from Marcel Proust, Francis Ponge, and Nathalie Sarraute a mode of "too-close reading" that does away with distinction, prestige, and social hierarchy by focusing on nuances and ordinary environmental objects such as a cloud, a flower, and a patch of light.[103] Macé apprehends reading "less as an active task of deciphering than as a certain kind of conduct."[104] Similarly, for Freed-Thall, "nuance is not a symptom or a clue," and her "Proust diffuses and redirects the potentially paranoid, clue-seeking energies of close reading."[105] One of her emblematic examples is the description of the hawthorns, which "offer the perceiver not an object to penetrate, consume, or expose, but a multisensory rhythmic texture."[106]

However persuasive this approach, the authors of my corpus do let me sideline their active social deciphering of the world. Ernaux loves Proust, and she twice commented on the hawthorns passage. But to her, the description of the hedge is "paltry" and "mawkish."[107]

Similarly, although she admires Sarraute's social project, she finds her writing as "tedious" as Proust's hawthorns.[108] Ernaux's social mobility equipped her with a social "filter" and "hyperconscience" that prevent her from acknowledging, like Proust, "the volatility of signs of distinction" in everyday events and sensations.[109] As I will show in my fifth chapter, her writing can be read as "a distinction-flattening experience."[110] But not her reading and perception of the world. Interestingly, she historicizes this social unveiling through nature too: "to replace the gentle topography of memories, all made up of impressions, colors, images (the villa Edelin! the blue wisteria! the blackberry bushes of Champ-de-Courses!), with another made up of harsh lines that disenchant it, but whose evident truth is not disputable by remembrance itself."[111] In Freed-Thall's powerful reading, Proust uses the hawthorns to undo social hierarchies by describing a sensation accessible to the greatest number of walkers. On the contrary, Ernaux's social trajectory led her away from wisteria and blackberry to confront, head on, the hard texture of social class.[112] She wishes to expose what Marcel Proust, from his privileged position, wanted to undo. I believe Ernaux's very first book, *Du soleil à cinq heures* (*Sun at Five O'clock*), could have been part of this lineage of writers and characters who fell for "aesthetic disorientation" and delved into nuances: "It's a period that I called after the fact that of 'the smear of light on a wall,' in which the ideal consisted for me in expressing in the entirety of a novel that sensation evoked by the contemplation of a trace of sun in the evening on the wall of a bedroom."[113] But this first text—written under the influence of the New Novel—never found a publisher.

In *Esquisse pour une auto-analyse*, Bourdieu contextualizes his career and position: "I must, using a proper method, first examine the state of the field at the moment when I entered it."[114] To clarify my reading method from another angle, I would like to reflect on this book's institutional context, that is to say on my current position as associate professor of French at Yale (a "ladder" faculty). The university has long been associated with the theory of deconstruction practiced by "Yale Critics" Paul de Man and Jacques Derrida, among others—scholars for whom language is radically reflective, metaphorical, and ultimately undecidable. As Marc Redfield put it in *Theory at Yale*, the Ivy League institution was the "metonym for 'theory' in the 1970s."[115] If you think about Yale and literature today, another trend will come to mind, that of Yale graduates who publish memoirs about their social mobility through the institution: *Hillbilly Elegy*, the bestseller written by J. D. Vance, who attended Yale Law School in the 2010s; *There Will Be No Miracles Here* (part of NPR's and *The New York Times*' "best books of 2018" lists) by Casey Gerald, who completed a BA in political science, played varsity football, and cofounded the Yale Black Men's Union; and *The Short and Tragic Life of Robert Peace* (*New York Times* best book of the year 2015) by Jeff Hobbs about the author's Yale roommate who majored in molecular biophysics and biochemistry.[116] Despite significant differences (sexual orientation, skin color, geographical region, political opinions, fields of study), the three young men shared an underprivileged childhood plagued by addiction and climbed the social ladder through a college degree—all signposts for the through line of this book: education. Recently, a report from the American Talent Initiative also described Yale as "an institution that has 'led the way toward enrolling and graduating lower-income students.'"[117] Moreover, Didier Éribon's *Retour à Reims* originates in a lecture he gave at Yale in 2008, "The Dissenting Child."[118]

Writing a book on social mobility at Yale, in New Haven, means I am holding together two different intellectual legacies: novel and memoir, life and theory, contextualized and decontextualized interpretative practices. Ernaux, and later Bourdieu, have theorized this ambivalent approach. Ernaux writes about "the desire to upend literary and social hierarchies by writing the same way about 'topics' considered unworthy of literature, for example supermarkets, the RER, abortion, and about other, more 'noble' topics, such as the workings of memory, the sensation of time, etc., and by associating them."[119] Bourdieu describes "[investing] great theoretical ambition into empirical objects that often seem trivial at first glance" and "the attention paid to humble objects."[120] Paying close attention to literary forms is commonly associated with prestigious genres such as lyric poetry.[121] In turn, *On Both Sides of the Tracks* showcases a form of interpretative reading that I would mischievously call "morganatic." As in a "morganatic marriage" that unites spouses from opposed social statuses, my book proposes to explore the misalliance of antagonistic objects, corpuses, and methodologies.

## One Telling Detail: The Subtitle

In order to lay out the stakes and scope of my attention to details, I would like to turn to one further example. In May 2017 the *New York Times* published a review of Édouard Louis's debut novel, translated into English as *The End of Eddy*. The book pictures the village and childhood of Eddy Bellegueule (Louis's name before an official change), a childhood marked by precarity and homophobia. Louis sold more than three hundred thousand copies of his first book, thus drawing the attention of the press and symbolizing the return of the social novel since Ernaux—a major reference for Louis. *New York Times* journalist Jennifer Senior opens her article with the following comparison: "It took a few dozen pages to see it, but once I did, it was very hard to unsee: Édouard Louis's *The End of Eddy* is the *Hillbilly Elegy* of France."[122] She uses multiple examples to underline how Vance's Ohio resembles Louis's Picardy in terms of poverty, rurality, and violence: "the distinguishing features of poverty do not vary all that much from place to place." And according to her, the only differences between the two texts lie in Louis's homosexuality and in the largesse of the French welfare state. But she doesn't acknowledge other crucial differences: Louis and Vance are on the opposite sides of the political spectrum, and more importantly, *Hillbilly Elegy* presents itself as "a memoir." The blurbs of praise featured on the first pages of the paperback edition make no mistake about it, calling the book a "sociological analysis," "a fiercely astute social critic," "a work of cultural criticism," and "the memoir of the political moment" depicting "the real people who are kept out of sight by academic abstractions." *The End of Eddy*, for its part, is subtitled "A Novel." Admittedly, Louis blurs the line between fact and fiction. And in the French context, subtitling a book "novel" can be part of a marketing strategy: the most prestigious literary prizes are awarded to novels, and the majority of readers favor this genre. However, the distinction between novel and memoir is entirely ignored by the *New York Times* journalist, who states that Louis's text is "deeply autobiographical" and "a novel in name only." Her article ends with advice to readers: "For anyone interested in learning about the white underclass that's helped power the populist movements of Europe, it is an excellent and accessible place to begin." She is right; *The End of Eddy* is filled with social and political insights, and I, too, am in favor of broadening the scope and relevance of literary texts, as the title of her article suggests: "*The End of Eddy* Captures a Savage Childhood and a Global Movement." This article raises an important question for this book's critical framework: is it necessary to favor interdisciplinarity over textual details? Would the journalist arrive at the same synthesis if she had not conflated novel and memoir, writer and narrator? On the other side of the Atlantic, social geographer Christophe Guilluy fell into a similar trap. He, too, brought Vance's and Louis's texts together in *Le Temps des gens ordinaires* (2020; *The Time of Ordinary People*), for they both unearth working-class culture and the thought process behind voting.[123] Contrary to Senior, Guilluy displays a French bias and reads the American text as an "autobiographical novel."[124] This way, he completely misses Vance's subtitle, "A Memoir of a Family and Culture in Crisis," which indicates something much broader than autobiography but also not as fictional as a novel. What would we learn about social mobility through literature if we were to switch from macro to micro? Are broader claims on society incompatible with the conclusions drawn from tiny textual elements?

It makes a lot of sense to compare, in the vein of Senior and Guilluy, French and American tales of social mobility. My corpus of parvenus is replete with comparisons to anglophone literature: *Gone with the Wind* and *Jane Eyre* for Annie Ernaux; novels by William Faulkner, Toni Morrison, James Baldwin, and Zadie Smith for Édouard Louis; by John Edgar Wideman for Didier Éribon.[125] Foreign literature seems capable of reflecting the social climbers' estrangement from their family culture and class. They might find commonality with what Homi Bhabha—reading Morrison's *Beloved*—calls "vernacular cosmopolitans of a kind, moving in-between cultural traditions, and revealing hybrid forms of life and art."[126] But Louis read American *novels*, not *memoirs*.

The impulse to compare is simply too tempting when it comes to narratives of upward mobility, whether they are told orally from friend to friend or published in memoirs and novels. These stories have a lot in common. In her sociological memoir *Se ressaisir: Enquête autobiographique d'une transfuge de classe féministe* (2021; *Pulling Oneself Together: Autobiographical Investigation of a Feminist Class Defector*), published in the wake of this renewed interest for cross-class trajectories, Rose-Marie Lagrave initially admits, "When I rewind my journey and compare it to those of other class *transfuges*, nothing utterly exceptional appears."[127] Likewise, it would not be hard to compare Tara Westover's best-selling memoir *Educated* (2018) to Louis's *The End of Eddy*. Acting was an important step of these authors' social mobility, and they both describe how their reluctant fathers always alternated between shaming and supporting them: "Nearly every night he said he was going to put a stop to my going, that one evening he'd just show up at Worm Creek and haul me home. But each time a play opened he was there, in the front row"; "It hadn't been easy to convince my father to drive me to the train station the day of the audition *Waste gas on your theater bullshit, honestly it's just not worth it.* [...] For several days he assured me that he would not be driving me and that it was no use getting my hopes up. On the last night he changed his mind *Tomorrow don't forget to set your alarm, I'm driving you to the station.*"[128] The descriptions are almost identical and could easily be substituted—except, precisely, for the form of the text and the polyphonic use of italics, which I study in depth in chapter 5. There are also striking similarities between Westover's and Ernaux's displaced affects: both feel shame, not primarily because their parents were poor but because they were violent. Actually, the very point of Westover's book is to be universal, as announced on the back cover: "*Educated* is an account of the struggle for self-invention. It is a tale of fierce family loyalty, and of the grief that comes of severing one's closest ties. With the acute insight that distinguishes all great writers, Westover has crafted a universal coming-of-age story that gets to the heart of what an education is and what it offers: the perspective to see one's life through new eyes, and the will to change it." These stories are universal; that is why they sell. The summary describes not "her" but "one's closest ties" and "one's life." The word choice points to a memoir—account, tale, insight, story—not to a novel, which makes the comparison between Louis and Westover, like the one between Louis and Vance, lopsided.

Vance and Westover are equally obsessed with telling a true story, to the point where it sounds like they're giving an oath: "Though I sometimes change the names of people to protect their privacy, this story is, to the best of my recollection, a fully accurate portrait of the world I've witnessed. There are no composite characters and no narrative shortcuts. Where possible, I corroborated the details with documentation—report cards, handwritten letters, notes on photographs—but I am sure this story is as fallible as any human memory. [...] I think there is something to learn in how I've organized the events in my own mind."[129] According to Vance, readers can learn things from the organization of his *mind*, not of his *text*. Similarly, Westover doubts her diary and uses asterisk and italics to indicate conflicting memories and paraphrases. She even goes as far as to thank her fact-checker: "Special thanks are owed to Ben Phelan, who was given the difficult task of fact-checking this book, and who did so rigorously but with great sensitivity and professionalism."[130]

This acknowledgment is drastically different from Louis. When a journalist fact-checked *En finir avec Eddy Bellegueule* to make sure his family was as poor as he claimed, Louis did not thank him but denounced his classism.[131] This anecdote points to a major difference between contemporary French and American narratives of social mobility. Even when the person who writes and narrates the book are one and the same, the French want to keep the narrator at a distance. I would argue that this gap is the result of social mobility: there is a class difference at play between the parvenu author and the young, modest boy described in *En finir avec Eddy Bellegueule*. The name of Louis's French publisher, Le Seuil, literally "The Threshold," underscores this distance. Journalist and social climber Rokhaya Diallo in *Ne reste pas à ta place!* (2019; *Don't Stay in Your Place!*) surprisingly considers her memoir to be a "partially autobiographical narrative."[132] Despite the obvious testimonial tone of the book, she, too, wishes to retain a fictional portion. Following critic Caren Kaplan, we could thus say that a book—novel or memoir—written by a parvenu is an "autobiographical out-law genre."[133] Social trajectories twist literary formats. Annie Ernaux also acknowledges a distancing effect. She describes the "feeling of unreality that transfuges feel" when they study and start their acculturation process.[134] Readers face a similar detachment in Pierre Bourdieu's social and intellectual autobiography, *Esquisse pour une auto-analyse*. The book opens with the epigraph "This is not an autobiography." Yet the sentence is not borrowed from another author but signed by Bourdieu himself, which is very uncommon, and suggests a great internal split. Against this backdrop, Louis's subtitle, "A Novel," is not anodyne. It could even suggest that in our times of precarity, inequality, and impeded social mobility, any narrative of upward success becomes a fiction, even when it has happened to you.

## The Conceptual Characters of Class Mobility

Naming and renaming are decisive steps within cross-class trajectories—the first word choice or literary device of parvenus.[135] To ratify his upward mobility, Édouard Louis swapped his working-class first name Eddy for the bourgeois Édouard and his family name Bellegueule—typical of the deindustrialized north—for another first name, Louis. Hence the title of his first book, *En finir avec Eddy Bellegueule*. This reinvention was "the confluence of literature and friendship:" Louis is the middle name of his friend and mentor, the sociologist Didier Éribon, and the name of the lead character in Jean-Luc Lagarce's *Juste la fin du monde* (1990; *Just the End of the World*), a play on a socially estranged son returning home to announce his imminent death. Louis also considered the last name Sorel, at the crossroad between literature (Stendhal's parvenu from *Le Rouge et le Noir*) and life (the name of a locality near his birthplace).[136] Similarly, Annie Duchesne became the author known as Annie Ernaux after a marriage that, along with diplomas, officialized her entry into the bourgeoisie. Christine Schwartz became Christine Angot when her upper-class, cultivated father finally agreed to acknowledge the paternity of a child he had with a woman from more modest class origins. A human resources manager in the luxury industry and a transclass writer, Hamid Aït-Taleb changed his name to Xavier Le Clerc to put an end to the employment discriminations he had been facing after graduation. Retracing the life of his father in *Un homme sans titre* (2022; *A Man without a Title*), alongside his own trajectory from Kabylia to Normandy, Le Clerc reflects on the importance of the capital letter in his new first name: X is a crossroads, the cross of his illiterate father's signature, the symbol of children born to an unidentified mother (*né sous X*).[137] The name change can also occur within novels: as we will see in chapter 3, Marie NDiaye's social climber character in *Ladivine* (2013), Malinka, renames herself Clarisse. These examples bring to mind another case of class mobility through names: Honoré de Balzac, born Honoré Balzac, son of

Bernard-François Balssa. But in comparison, contemporary parvenus do not add a fake "de" (the French particle) to sound like aristocratic writers; their name change preceded their entry into literature. As writers, Louis, Ernaux, Angot, and Le Clerc choose to align themselves with their working-class roots.

Besides literary and official names, Anglophone speakers are spoiled for choice when it comes to describing those who change class, depending on what aspect of upward mobility one wants to highlight: arriviste, upstart, pariah, parvenu, *nouveau riche*, wannabe, opportunist, autodidact, social climber, outsider, transplant, jumped-up, bastard, careerist, uprooted, and yuppie (for young upwardly mobile professional). In academic circles, sociologists and literary critics chart social mobility by naming those who change milieus—intellectuals with working-class roots, in particular. The nonexhaustive list of "sociological characters" includes stranger in paradise, miracle oblate, plural actor, striver, uneasy hybrid, scholarship student, problematic hero, consoling exception, and third culture kid.[138] Among this crowd, one term has proven particularly stimulating recently: the *transclasse*, coined in French by philosopher Chantal Jaquet in *Les Transclasses ou la non-reproduction* (2014; *The Transclasses or Non-reproduction*), a Spinoza-infused philosophical reflection on the affects of social climbers, from Stendhal's Julien Sorel to the "auto-socio-biographies" of Bourdieu, Éribon, and Ernaux.[139] The success of her book confirms the necessity to linger on this protagonist. With *transclasse*, Jaquet wanted to find a rigorous, far-reaching, and nonderogatory term to encapsulate upward and downward social trajectories.[140] In *Les Transclasses*, as in her subsequent coedited volume *La Fabrique des transclasses* (2018; *The Fabrication of Transclasses*), she strategically uses the word to disconnect social mobility from betrayal and to debunk the concept of merit that pits citizens deserving of upward mobility against their lazy fellows.[141] Like *transsexual*, *transclass* emphasizes the prefix *trans-* so as to capture the process of climbing the ladder instead of the successful arrival.[142] The noun conveniently works as an adjective in English. Jaquet at times also employs the word *passe-classe*, modeled on racial and class passing, as well as on the figure of the *passe-blanc*, the French Creole of color who passed as white in Louisiana.

A transclass is the positive and affective version of the French word *transfuge*, which underlines disloyalty. Before elaborating on the word I will use throughout this book, the *parvenant*, I would like to make the case for *transfuge* instead of *transclasse* or even *transfuge de classe*. *Transfuge* is a deverbal noun from the Latin verb *fugio* (to flee) and the prefix *trans*. A *transfuge* is a social traitor who flees an army, a class, an opinion, a religion, or a political party to join the ranks of the enemy by going *through* and *beyond*, as its prefix suggests. The word itself is in transit: it went from a verb to a noun; it oscillates between movement and stasis. Until the eighteenth century, one could even carry out a "transfuite" and become a "transfugitif." To my ear, *transclasse* and *passe-classe* resonate too much with the neoliberal discourse of flexibility. It is almost as if the persons in question could easily navigate various social spheres at all times and in all directions. The betrayal implied by *transfuge*, however, underlines a resistance and a tearing that suits the social tugging at play in the narratives of my corpus. Despite originating in other identities (gender, race), *transclasse* also singles out class while *transfuge* can refer to various forms of transition. Similarly for Michael Lucey, instead of *queer*, the sexual and social term *misfit* allows him to not "consider sexuality in isolation from other social categories."[143] This indeterminacy proves useful in my book, first, because in contemporary literature, class always intersects with other embodied subjectivities. Édouard Louis, for instance, often uses his position of *transfuge de classe* to reverberate other marginalized identities—social, racial, gendered—through lists. Second, it is useful because my focus on social mobility is not aimed at providing an identitarian reading grid but at destabilizing identity further. Writer and theorist Monique Wittig uses the word *escapee* in English, *transfuge* in French, precisely to designate the subjects who escape "the class of women" to reject sexual difference.[144] This is exactly why the word *transfuge* appeals to me: a *transfuge* flees but never fully arrives. She deserts and yet she never makes it to the group opposed to the one she renounced. She lives her life in between, on both sides of the tracks. She feels "this slightly dizzy sense of still being on the ladder," identified by transclass sociologist Richard Hoggart.[145] "Must I arrive somewhere, once and for all?" asks Franco-Moroccan transclass journalist Nesrine Slaoui, who also declares, in her social memoir, *Illégitimes* (2021; *Illegitimate*), "There was no before-after, only that *in-between* in which I float and remain suspended."[146] *Transfuge* thereby belongs to what Annabel Kim calls "unbecoming language" in her book on Nathalie Sarraute, Monique Wittig, and Anne Garréta: "Unbecoming is thus an act of erosion (eroding those categories we ostensibly correspond to and are contained by) and of excess (becoming more than our identitarian limits would have us be, spilling out past the contours that used to delimit us). [...] Unbecoming is the process by which one attains this nonidentitarian state of plurality and possibility, and it passes through an encounter or relationship with language."[147] Having exceptionally escaped the social order, the parvenus shed their (class) identity to inhabit the transition. In *Les Transfuges de sexe* (2021; *The Sex Defectors*), sociologist Emmanuel Beaubatie uses *trans'* instead of *transsexual* or *transgender* to connect trans identities to the *transfuge*, to think, via Bourdieu, the sexual field as a social field, and to reveal the importance of class mobility—demotion and distinction alike—in trans trajectories: "Changing sex is rarely considered a *transfuge* experience although it is indeed a passing through a social boarder: FTMs experience an upgrade and MTFs are downgraded."[148] Within this framework, Beaubatie is able to originally compare Annie Ernaux's upward trajectory to the trans' men "caught in that same tension, the one caused by joining a group that was formerly the embodiment of the oppressor."[149] Likewise, writer and philosopher Paul B. Preciado recently declared himself a trans man and a "transfuge."[150]

In my view, Guy de Montlaur titled his 1955 translation of Richard Wright's *The Outsider* into French *Le Transfuge* for comparable reasons. The French title underlines the lead character's change of social position from philosophy student to post office worker, and his change in identity from Cross Damon to Lionel Lane in the aftermath of a subway crash. The title echoes Wright's own transition, too, from Communism to Existentialism (*transfuge* in this context would mean "defector"), and from the United States to France. *Le Transfuge* is the only published translation by cubist painter Guy de Montlaur, who had spent two years in the United States. The interlocking points of view of a cubist portrait seem, indeed, particularly suited to render the transient and multifaceted subjectivities of those who change milieus.

While the word *transclasse* was coined by a philosopher, the word *transfuge* is more closely connected to literature. A literary magazine in France is called *Transfuge* and subtitled *Choisissez le camp de la culture*

(*Choose the Camp of Culture*). Canadian critic Richard Saint-Gelais calls novels that display a form of transfictionality connecting fictional universes "transfuge fictions."[151] And as we will see throughout this book—which gives prominence to intertextuality and rewriting—my corpus belongs to Saint-Gelais's library of transfuge fictions. When he received the Goncourt for *Leurs enfants après eux*, Nicolas Mathieu qualified his writing as "a transfuge's style." This remark points out the defining approach of my book: the formal representation of class mobility through the figure of the parvenu. A whole section of Annie Ernaux's book-length interview *L'Écriture comme un couteau* (2003; *Writing as a Knife*) is titled "Transfuge," too, and the betrayal subtext of this word is crucial to her writing.[152] She uses an epigraph from Jean Genet on this very topic in her landmark 1983 narrative of social mobility, *La Place*: "I venture an explanation: writing is the last recourse when we have betrayed." Writing is an antidote to betrayal, but the two go hand in hand. For me to focus on the poetics of social mobility, I need to keep the traitor, the *transfuge*, a term better suited to study the literary life of those who moved from one class to another but continue to inhabit the social ladder.

Although some translators equate it to a traitor, a deserter, a renegade or escapee, *transfuge*—a borrowing from the French—is obsolete and untranslatable in English. I could use it nonetheless, the same way the French say "self-made man" in English because there is no equivalent. Instead, I would like to name my object of study the "parvenant." This neologism first and foremost emphasizes textuality, from the past participle *parvenu* to the present participle *parvenant*, thus reflecting the contemporary framework—formal and literary—of social mobility. While it is easy to imagine a *transclasse* answering a survey or a sociological questionnaire, the parvenant is a storyteller. The parvenant—in its literary guise and writing practice—will function as an entryway into the French landscape and literary field.

Contemporary tales of class mobility have diversified the trajectories of their social climbers since the nineteenth-century bildungsroman: today, we can read narratives of arrival, departure, and return that mix upward and downward mobility. Although this book is mostly concerned with upward mobility, I also use contrapuntal examples of voluntary downward mobility in chapter 3 to reflect on the bodies of those who live between classes. And for writer Abdellah Taïa, discussed in chapter 6, upward mobility passes through demotion when he, a Moroccan Masters student, arrives penniless in Switzerland and lodges at the Salvation Army. The conceptual character of the parvenant thus effectively captures the disorientation of social mobility, like the oxymoronic phrases "downgraded upwards" (Bourdieu) and "immigrant from the inside" (Ernaux).[153] Parvenants, unlike parvenus, have not arrived yet, are always arriving, or might as well return.[154] In *Retour à Reims*, Éribon plays with the verb *parvenir*: "the city where I made it [*parvins*], at the cost of one thousand and one difficulties, possible to become gay."[155] *Parvenir* can be transitive and intransitive, a double verbal property underlined by the comma. In English, the phrase "the city where I made it" has meaning in and of itself but, like *parvenir*, could also use an object: "the city where I made it possible to become gay." Parvenants move up the ladder but also come back and give back: "Is writing not a way of giving," asks Annie Ernaux.[156] It is the round trip that matters today; the two-way trajectory, not only the achievement. Parvenants are two-faced: they write fiction and nonfiction, literature and sociology; they are authors and narrators; they arrive and find ways to return. For Ernaux, parvenants are no longer working class: "At a certain point, Madelin [a French politician] brandishes his origins, 'my father was a skilled worker, I know about paystubs.' As if he were **the same** as the little boy of times past, in a working-class neighborhood."[157] And yet, they don't feel they have entirely made it either: "The French teacher at the high school in A., in the North, who teaches an 'underprivileged' class, drives a Mercedes, jewels, chic scarf, blonde discretion. Whether she was born in a working-class milieu, as she proclaims, doesn't change anything for the students: she is *now* a bourgeoise."[158] Although the latter quote is written with a certain distance, the teacher could well be Ernaux, who regularly calls herself a "narrator-prof-transfuge" and a "schizo-prof [me]."[159] In these two excerpts from her "extimate diary" *La Vie extérieure* (2000; *The External Life*), she offers a provocative reflection on temporality: can social mobility last forever? How long does one remain transclass? Both sentences display lose connections between their phrases: "my father was a skilled worker, I know about paystubs;" "drives a Mercedes, jewels, chic scarf, blonde discretion." Causality crumbles. Right-wing politician Alain Madelin brandishes his origins like a weapon, like something concrete that could be touched by the hand. But whatever these parvenants "show off" or "proclaim," they have left their disadvantaged childhood. Here, the temporal metamorphosis of class mobility is signaled by the typography: bold (**the same**), quotation marks ("underprivileged"), and italics (*now*). Social class is a paper identity. It is through the text's materiality that parvenants like Ernaux offer not a testimonial but a formal portrayal of those who live in the middle of the tracks.

The parvenant is a servant. In chapters 4 and 6, we will see how the characters of maids and cleaners function as foils to social climbers, as a first step of a transclass trajectory.

The parvenant is a *passant*, "the ultimate passerby [...], someone passing through, a passenger," according to Chantal Jaquet.[160] The authors and characters in my corpus had to cross the social field, and this book uncovers the contemporary spaces of social mobility, mapped out by forms and words: the muddy streets of Paris (chap. 2); doors as symbolic transit zones (chap. 5); the metaphor of the train (chap. 6); and the supermarket as a meeting point of consumerism and class (chap. 7).

The parvenant is a *revenant*.[161] My book is concerned with many returns: of characters (Rastignac in chaps. 1 and 7; maids in chap. 4) and tropes (mud in chap. 2 and the train in chap. 6). Because of this splitting, parvenants appear socially uncanny—a psychological experience described by Sigmund Freud as follows:

> I was sitting alone in my sleeping compartment when the train lurched violently. The door of the adjacent toilet swung open and an elderly gentleman in a dressing gown and travelling cap entered my compartment. I assumed that on leaving the toilet, which was located between the two compartments, he had turned the wrong way and entered mine by mistake. I jumped up to put him right, but soon realized to my astonishment that the intruder was my own image, reflected in the mirror on the connecting door. I can still recall that I found his appearance thoroughly unpleasant.[162]

The train has a central place in my argument (chap. 6), for it replaces the "social ladder." In motion between two destinations, it also carries the parvenant's split personality, his uncanny social double, his ghostly past and haunted future.

The parvenant is an *interpretant*. In *Reading in Detail* (1987), Naomi Schor identifies this new character in what she calls the "fiction-as-interpretation/interpretation-as-fiction" of Henry James, Marcel Proust, and Franz Kafka.[163] Unlike the interpreter—an interpreting reader—the interpretant is an interpreting character mirroring the critic's role. Social climbers, because they are overtrained readers and interpreters of signs, could also be apprehended as interpretants, constantly having to decode behaviors, to run with the hare and hunt with the hounds to fit in.[164]

The parvenant is an *apprenant* (in French) or a *s'apprenant* (in Canadian French), terms that designate learners and self-learners in pedagogy. Even when social climbers have become writers and teachers, they continue to learn, like Ernaux: "I don't think I was a good teacher, [...] I mainly learned for myself, used a critical mind, linguistic knowledge for my own literary research."[165] The writer never ceases to acquire social and critical skills.

The parvenant is a *migrant*. The two figures share the "present participle of ongoing action."[166] Immigrants leaving or returning to a foreign country and writers who shuttle from the provinces to Paris usually do not focus on social classes in the same way.[167] In this book, I assemble a corpus where questions of class and race merge so as to consider migration and social mobility together (esp. in chaps. 5 and 6).[168] According to Salman Rushdie, "the migrant, is, perhaps, the central or defining figure of the twentieth century."[169] In this book, I show that the parvenant is an important protagonist of twenty-first-century France.

To conclude, I would like to propose two illustrations of the parvenant that also encapsulate the work of this book. André Kertész's 1955 photograph *Disappearing Act* (fig. 1) centers our attention on a decontextualized upward movement. The framing erases the structure of the building. The setting is devoid of any referential point since the background is both empty and overexposed. The head is missing on account of the way the image has been cropped: we see only a section of the staircase, thus emphasizing the movement, the legs, and their disconnection from the person they belong to. The climber is barefoot and wears bottoms that could either be a skirt

**Figure 1.** André Kertész, *Disappearing Act, New York* (August 29, 1955). © Estate of André Kertész. Photograph: Courtesy of the Stephen Bulger Gallery.

or a pair of khaki shorts. The backlighting also makes the skin color (or is that pantyhose?) hard to fathom. The vertical, horizontal, and diagonal lines accentuate the effect of disorientation: they can point to multiple directions and metaphorical staircases or ladders. Everything seems ethereal: the tips of the toes; the thin cable; the sandy background. And yet, the wide and dark horizontal stripe blocks the view. These legs here are captured in a forever unachieved upward movement, fleeing but caged. Viewers cannot determine whom they are looking at, and the destination is postponed, indefinitely. The stairs of this snapshot turn into a habitat. In *Disappearing Act*, as in the works in my corpus, the social potential of a work of art originates not in facts and affects but in (visual and verbal) forms: namely, here, the artificial displacement and repetition of the staircase's infrastructure. I read this photograph as a figuration of our social and literary moment: like the cut-in-half silhouette climbing an improbable flight of stairs, social mobility is impeded today.

For the few isolated figures who still make it individually, upward movement is no longer a synonym of arrival but of suspension and in-betweenness. Parvenants neither fully arrive nor arrive in full. I see Kertész's unlocalizable staircase as a "phantom ladder." Phantom because I show in this book that the ghostly avatars of nineteenth-century literary climbers come back, as revenants, in contemporary prose (chaps. 1 and 7); because parvenants can feel the nagging of a social "phantom limb" (chap. 3). In one of her published diaries, Annie Ernaux writes, "I am condemned to be, to place myself, between that staircase, terrible, and the one that was. To wander, I wanted to say."[170] Ernaux never left the steps where she learned her lessons and discovered literature. She will forever dwell in the liminal space of her childhood home, caught between a concrete staircase and the one reconstructed by memory and writing.

Throughout the book, I pay attention to each parvenant's background: working class or middle class; one dimensional or intersectional; working as shopkeepers or cleaners; civil status as citizens or immigrants. But their "social ladders" overlay through the shared feeling of inhabiting the in-between.

In one of his luminous articles on photography, Hervé Guibert commented on Kertész's work as follows: "We can only have a direct relation to these photographs, as Kertész had a direct relation to life.

Introduction 41

His entire body of work is a look into life. Kertész said: 'I see what exists.' It's not naivety. It takes imagination to see reality."[171] Indeed, if I had to summarize, in one sentence, my aim in *On Both Sides of the Tracks*, I, too, would say that to look at (social) realities, one needs imagination, but also interpretation, an attention to forms, and a literary eye.

Following the same logic, we will see in chapter 6 that the idiom of the "social ladder" has been replaced by the metaphor of the train in literature and cinema. A 1925 photograph by Alexander Rodchenko captures this reversal. Through form again (the camera angle), the ladder of this *Fire Escape* (fig. 2) morphs into train tracks. Viewers are unsure whether they are looking at a man scaling a building or horizontally crossing a courtyard, at a man looking up or down at us. The beginning and the end of this row of rungs vanish in the perspective and are left out of the frame. The feet point in opposed directions; forward and sidewise. The climber is suspended in the air on this shapeshifting ladder, caught between bricks and clouds, as if between destinations. Similarly, the literary parvenants of this book are characters who shuttle between social groups; writers who have reached the shore of another class but devise literary and formal ways to come back, constantly undoing any fixed social affiliation.

## Chapter Summaries

From chapter 1 to chapter 7, the character of Rastignac serves as a bookend. The rest of the chapters are organized according to the definition of the parvenant: a first group on settings and environments, including embodiment (chap. 2, "The Muddy Parvenant, Then and Now"; and chap. 3 "The Transient Body of the Transclass"); and a second group on movements and the in-betweenness of transclass journeys (chap. 4,: "Self-Maid? The Social Mobility of Literary and Cinematic Servants"; chap. 5, "A Foot in the Door: Passing on Social Mobility"; and chap. 6 "Travel Class: From the Ladder to the Train"). In my conclusion, I show that the bildungsroman has morphed into the *Künstlerroman*. I also put to the forefront a corpus of younger, lesser-known contemporary authors who have published updated rewrites of canonical nineteenth-century novels by demoting the plot of social mobility (Aurélien Bellanger, Sophie Divry, Thomas

**Figure 2.** Alexander Rodchenko, *Fire Escape* (1925). From the series House on Myanitskaya. Printed in 1994 by Alexander Lavrentiev. © 2022 Estate of Alexander Rodchenko / UPRAVIS, Moscow / Artists Rights Society, New York. Photograph: Yale University Art Gallery (Stephen Carlton Clark, B.A. 1903, Fund).

Flahaut, Célia Levi, Nicolas Mathieu, Emmanuelle Richard). If literature is an important tool for parvenants to change class, in return, stories of social mobility are a structuring force in the literary field. Parvenants help us understand the partition and social potency of genres (fiction and nonfiction, bildungsroman and *Künstlerroman*). Operating at the junction between two literary traditions (social literature and reflexive experiments), they teach us how these tracks intersect and provide us with a broad view of the literary field.

Eugène de Rastignac—invented by Balzac in the 1830s—is the literary archetype of social mobility: we now say *a* rastignac in French to designate upwardly mobile persons and arrivistes of all kinds. Chapter 1, "Rastignac Redux," examines the literary life and afterlives of Rastignac in an eclectic set of materials: novels, narratives, manuscripts, a tweet, a television miniseries, newspaper articles and interviews, a management textbook, presidential campaign reports, political discourses, and economics books. I argue that this mixed-method approach is necessary to portray our current understanding of upward mobility. And yet, given how the representation of social classes in France is dependent on the literary canon, this chapter also makes the case that we not consider literature as unfiltered data but rather build social knowledge through literary history, genres, forms, and intertexts. Using research on characters and the history of realism (Margaret Cohen, Alex Woloch), I explain how Balzac turned Rastignac into a shapeshifting archetype endowed with a dual social class. I track how Rastignac resurfaces in the works of Gustave Flaubert, Michel Déon, Maurice Barrès, Paul Nizan, Simone de Beauvoir, and Jean-Paul Sartre, as well as in the events of May 68. Then I examine the name-dropping of Rastignac in contemporary France. I debate Thomas Piketty's use of Balzac in his *Le Capital au XXIe siècle*, in contrast to Alan Krueger's "Great Gatsby Curve" and Karl Marx's references to Eugène Sue. I show how Rastignac is used as a shorthand in the conservative press to express anxiety about the rise of the underprivileged. I explain how an altercation on social media between Emmanuel Macron and Édouard Louis—two public figures on the opposite sides of the political spectrum who are nonetheless both called Rastignac—demonstrates the current misunderstanding of what social emancipation truly means. I finally turn to authors and characters who are called Rastignac (Virginie Despentes), call themselves Rastignac (Abdellah Taïa), and refer to *Le Père Goriot* in their texts (Annie Ernaux, Dai Sijie). What emerges from my reading is that Rastignac—a banker, a politician, a socialite—is remembered as a student, and *Le Père Goriot* has become a textbook, thus pointing to the contemporary location of social mobility: the school system.

Chapter 2, "The Muddy Parvenant, Then and Now," offers a semiotic study of mud as the archetypal attribute of provincial characters who plot their social climbing through perambulations and have to traverse the mucky social field of Paris without being able to yet afford a clean mode of transportation. Mud stains thereby invert the motif of the earth, which is no longer the sign of a rooting but of a displacement. Drawing on major studies of realism and cultural histories of dirt (Alain Corbin, Kristin Ross), I track the literal and metaphorical uses of ductile materials in Balzac against the backdrop of Stendhal's canonical definition of the novel as a "mirror going along a muddy road." This series of detailed close readings opens onto a broader debate: is literature alone capable of historicizing the social issue of upward mobility? On the one hand, focusing on the mire allows us to uncover a decisive shift: from the early to the late nineteenth century, mud transitions from being a social mark on a character's clothes for Balzac to standing as a metaphor for language and knowledge in the works of Jules Vallès. Literary mud therefore dates the very displacement of class mobility itineraries from money and networks to the acquisition of a cultural capital. Vallès's modulations on mud also underscore his own generic trajectory from fiction to journalism and his participation in the Paris Commune. But on the other hand, I also show how the social meaning of mud is carried from one generation of authors to the next. In Annie Ernaux's interviews and Édouard Louis's novels, mud rises up as a surprisingly stable sign of social mobility for authors and characters who do not stay in their place. Militant writers Vallès and Louis, more than a hundred years apart, also display a comparable rejection of the novel in favor of tracts. Mud can thus offer sociohistorical contexts *and* decontextualize characters from their classes and centuries.

What happens to the body of those who change their social milieu? On the one hand, writers and characters experiencing social demotion—especially the May 68 intellectuals who voluntarily went to work in factories—describe at length how difficult it was to attune their muscles to the pace of an assembly line. But on the other hand, despite the appearances, the bodily apprenticeship of upwardly mobile characters is strikingly absent from contemporary literature. Chapter 3, "The Transient Body of the Transclass," theorizes what I call the "trance" of social climbers: a certain unrest and unease, a malaise or nausea, when it comes to describing the reconfiguration of voices, gestures, and postures induced by upward trajectories. Marie NDiaye's parvenus, for instance, apprehend their emancipation as racial passing, not as class mobility. Annie Ernaux also deflects the prevalence of the class factor, in her case toward gender, sexuality, and the experience of a backstreet abortion. Édouard Louis for his part singles out homosexuality as the reason behind his cross-class trajectory. The way transclass writers describe their own bodies is also indicative of their stance on the debate between essentialism and constructivism: is the embodiment of class innate or acquired? Is one born or does one become a social climber? Through the body, I want to show that the novel form alone is no longer sufficient to capture the corporeal tension at the core of class mobility; to fully understand parvenant writers, we must look at their fiction, nonfiction, interviews, and articles side by side so as to embrace their contradictions.

Chapter 4, "Self-Maid? The Social Mobility of Literary and Cinematic Servants," is interested in the return of domestic service in the contemporary French job market as well as in prose, plays, and cinema. First, through a brief survey of canonical servants (from Stendhal to Marcel Proust and Jean Genet) and of philosophical, historical, and literary takes on service (by Franco Moretti and Bruce Robbins, among others), I focus less on the precarity of maids than on their ambivalent social status between classes and their roles as foils to the characters of parvenus. With this framework in mind, and through a series of microreadings, we then see how literary domestics appear in literature as concrete and symbolic, at times formal entryways into the upper class in the works of authors as different as Albert Camus, Maryse Condé, Fatou Diome, Annie Ernaux, Faïza Guène, and Marie NDiaye. These examples help debunk the myth of a spontaneous and instant self-*maid* person to uncover a more patient fabrication of the social self in families, across regions and generations (from metropolitan and Caribbean France to Senegal and the Maghreb). Contemporary literature thereby enjoins us to apprehend maids as intersectional figures at the interplay between race and class, between social mobility and migration. After focusing on the servant as the phantom rung of an upward trajectory, I travel down the ladder to look at authors and actors who temporarily experience the lower class by "playing the maid." This includes artist Sophie Calle and journalist Florence Aubenas's account of their voluntary social demotion as cleaners. I also home in on Abdellatif Kechiche's film adaptations of Marivaux's plays and Benoît Jacquot's 2015 version of Mirbeau's 1900 novel, *Le Journal d'une femme de chambre*. Since servant characters are prone to breaking the referential illusion by talking to the audience, I ask what happens when the wealthy social class of an actor surfaces behind the role of a subaltern. More precisely, I examine the unsettling "theatrical asides" of a maid played by Léa Seydoux—the acclaimed French actress and James Bond girl. I conclude that in the case of Kechiche and Jacquot's maids, we are witnessing a swap by which the temporary downward mobility of actresses replaces the upward mobility of characters and nonprofessional actors.

Chapter 5, "A Foot in the Door: Passing on Social Mobility," uncovers the innovative metaphors and literary strategies used by writers to convey a socially mobile journey. To that end, I focus on the symbolism of doors as transit zones between classes. I also look at how transclass writers introduce the voices of those left behind through intangible discursive thresholds. Such an attention to form leads me to answer a pressing question on transmission: can social climbers become revolving doors, that is to say, agents of mobility capable of emancipating others in return, or do they remain miraculous, dead-end exceptions? I start by surveying the montage of reported speech in the works of Édouard Louis. Despite the presence of multiple voices and forms of discourses, I conclude that his novels fail to be polyphonic: the writer creates a complicity with the educated reader by distinguishing the voice of his relative (in italics) from literary excerpts (in quotation marks). Then I turn to Annie Ernaux and her now famous "flat writing," an egalitarian writing style, a potential vector of social mobility, and a contemporary version of Roland Barthes's "blank writing." In contrast to the works of Flaubert (as interpreted by Fredric Jameson, Pierre Bourdieu, and Jacques Rancière), Ernaux's free indirect discourse, I argue, powerfully levels social classes. In the third section, on Christine Angot, the discussion turns to romance, kinship, and sexual abuse. In *Un amour impossible* (2015), she describes the incest she suffered as a social revenge on the part of a father who came from a much higher class than her mother and wanted to undo his mésalliance. In *Le Marché des amants* (2008), she recounts her transclass and transrace relationship with a Guadeloupean rapper. By working with her manuscripts, I flesh out Angot's idiosyncratic version of the imperfect verb tense as a means to capture her transclass heritage and interclass encounters. The chapter ends with writer and sociologist Kaoutar Harchi, born into a modest family of Moroccan immigrants. Her memoir *Comme nous existons* (2021) compellingly merges issues of social mobility and migration, what she calls "postcolonial and proletarian existences." I show how she strives to mitigate class distance through the strategic use of dashes, present participles, and a labyrinthine syntax, as well as through the final scene of the text, which unfolds on a doorstep.

Literature and social sciences frequently have recourse to spatial imagery to describe class mobility: the social ladder and the social elevator are the most common idioms in English and in French. Modes of public transportation, too, from the omnibus to the commuter rail, have a long history of being places of compartmentalization, social negotiations, and cross-class encounters from Émile Zola to François Maspero and Leïla Sebbar. By bringing together a curated corpus of nineteenth- to twenty-first-century narratives and films, chapter 6, "Travel Class: From the Ladder to the Train," demonstrates that the train has become the leading metaphor for upward trajectories. Such a shift, I argue, registers the transformation of social mobility from one-way success stories of arrival to ongoing processes of pendular movements. Contrary to ladders and elevators, trains do not travel upward and suppose a return ticket: passengers are under the threat of a return trip; commuters go through different neighborhoods without settling in a new place. At the same time, the railroad offers social climbers a way home, a means to reconnect with their past so as to mitigate their social estrangement. Tracks can even represent unwanted class mobility in novels by Paul Nizan and Georges Perec, as well as in Laurent Cantet's films on late-capitalist labor that display what Lauren Berlant calls "lateral and sideways mobility." In positive tales of emancipation, the railway is often used as a framing device that bookends a plot of social mobility and as an editorial strategy that puts locomotives on book covers to illustrate the social thread of a film or memoir. In the central section, I pick up on Michel de Certeau's etymological parallel between metaphors and means of transportation to study the coupling between railroad trips and formal elements: stemming from Roland Barthes's reading of Balbec's slow trains, I show how Marcel Proust turns the machine into a vehicle of intertextuality and a rhetorical device and how Abdellah Taïa combines trains and punctuation to represent his social mobility from Morocco to France by way of Switzerland.

While the previous chapters are mostly concerned with autobiographies of success, chapter 7, "From Rastignac to Subutex: The Immobilization of the Fictional Character," documents how twenty-first-century novels are no longer places of upward mobility but of social immobility and downgrading. I start by showing how Alain Robbe-Grillet and Nathalie Sarraute did not kill but demoted the Balzacian character in their manifestos. As a result, if formalist writers today (Julia Deck in my case study) want to both adhere to the New Novel legacy and address contemporary social issues, they are condemned to craft precarious characters. Second, I turn to Michel Houellebecq and his portrayal of the middle class. However successful, his characters of parvenus, managers, and billionaires—who often compare themselves to Balzac's social climbers—always end up stuck in the middle of the ascent or struggle to renounce their middle-class mentality. Virginie Despentes, too, explicitly emulates Balzac in *Vernon Subutex* (2015–17). But with her trilogy she makes the novel form transition from bildungsroman to picaresque. Subutex is a broke and homeless version of Rastignac who goes places without making it anywhere, who lives on a hillock but refuses to climb the ladder. He stands as the literary emblem of social mobility brought to a standstill at the turn of the twenty-first century. Along the way, this chapter also pinpoints the new literary spaces of social novels, notably harbor cities as social interfaces and supermarkets as places to think class through consumerism.

# Rastignac Redux  1

Literature is a factory of words and archetypes. Many fictional names have made it into the dictionary as nouns (Figaro) or adjectives (gargantuesque, rocambolesque). Before the medieval cycle known as *Roman de Renart*, a "fox" in French was not *un renard* but *un goupil*. Similarly, Molière created a synonym for "hypocrite" and "impostor" in the person of Tartuffe. This chapter focuses on yet another antonomasia, this figure of speech that literally means *to rename* and consists in turning a proper name into a common name "to express a general idea."[1] It considers the case of Balzac's protagonist Eugène de Rastignac, who has become the literary archetype of social mobility. We now say *a* rastignac, in French *un rastignac*, with lowercase *r*, to designate upwardly mobile persons, arrivistes of all kinds, and scheming, power-hungry personalities.[2]

Throughout the volumes of *La Comédie humaine* (1829–48; *The Human Comedy*), Honoré de Balzac tells the story of Eugène de Rastignac, a provincial who wants to make it in Paris. With the help of a well-connected relative and thanks to his success with women, the law student achieves his ambitious goal, enters high society, and becomes a banker, then a cabinet minister. Rastignac is the serial protagonist par excellence, especially as Balzac portrays him in *Le Père Goriot* (1835; *Old Man Goriot*), the novel in which he starts to systematize the use of recurring characters.[3] In the 2021 *Dictionnaire Balzac*—which, as it happens, does not list characters—Rastignac is nonetheless given an entry because his name is now considered a synonym of "ambition" and "arrivisme."[4] He is also the first character portrayed in Peter Brooks's 2020 collection of nine fictional biographies, *Balzac's Lives*.

If Rastignac made it in Paris, the popularity of this "extraordinary character," according to Georges Simenon, bursts the banks of the nineteenth-century novel.[5] In his published 2009–2010 diary *L'Autofictif père et fils* (*The Autofictional, Father and Son*), French writer Éric Chevillard schemes to "make the character Rastignac briefly appear in future reprints of my novels, which would allow me to link all my works to *The Human Comedy* and in this way secure them a less unpredictable posterity."[6] In French studies, there is now a significant body of work on Balzac's continuous comeback in the prose of writers as different as Maurice Barrès and Jean Echenoz as well as in New Wave films made by "the Young Rastignacs of cinematography."[7] But this research either stops in 2000 or sidelines the representation of class mobility. And while many have also noted a "character turn" in twenty-first-century literary criticism, this chapter centers on the *return of one character*.[8]

I have gathered an eclectic set of materials to examine Rastignac's posterity. This bric-à-brac or "bardadrac" (to use the neological title of Gérard Genette's autobiographical dictionary) goes from literary narratives to a tweet, from a management textbook to newspaper articles, from presidential campaign reports and political discourses to a best-selling economics book.[9] What has happened to Rastignac since Balzac? What does it mean to name-drop *Le Père Goriot* today? Why and how does Rastignac leap off the page to produce contrasted avatars in twentieth- and twenty-first-century France? The persistence of this family name first signals the importance of education and of literary references (or *culture générale*) in France. Rastignac will also allow me to portray our current understanding of upward mobility while pinning down the ways that contemporary literature engages with nineteenth-century classics.

### Why Rastignac?

The foreword to the *Dictionnaire des personnages populaires* (*Dictionary of Popular Characters*) published by Les Éditions du Seuil in 2010 opens on the following exclamation: "Quel Rastignac!"[10] Balzac's character is so famous he can disrupt the alphabetical order and be listed first, before dictionary entrees. Because of the final exclamation point, "Quel Rastignac!" means "What a Rastignac!" But if you delete the punctuation, the phrase could be translated as "Which Rastignac," that is to say, which one? Is he the naive, hesitant, and clumsy social climber of *Le Père Goriot*, or the manipulative arriviste of *Illusions perdues* (1837–43; *Lost Illusions*) and *La Maison Nucingen* (1838; *The Nucingen House*)? If Rastignac is an emblematic novelistic character, critics do not agree on his literary function. For some, he simply is a character, not a type, because there are many other *ambitieux* in Balzac's novels. For others, Rastignac becomes an empty archetype in the course of *La Comédie humaine*, what critic Marta Figlerowicz calls a "flat protagonist."[11] It has become proverbial to remember the latter incarnation of Rastignac and to use his last name as a synonym of cynicism and capitalism. To me, the tension between Rastignac young and old is precisely what makes tracking his surfacing relevant. Rastignac is a magnifier, a developing bath to understand our sociopolitical moment in its intertwining with literature.

The simplest way to explain the return of Rastignac when it comes to discussing social mobility is that he succeeds and does not die—unlike Lucien de Rubempré, Emma Bovary, and Julien Sorel, he can more easily represent lasting success. Rastignac also benefits from Balzac's poetics: the author encourages more permeability between literary characters and real-life persons than his peers, from the declaration "All is true" at the beginning of *Le Père Goriot* to Horace Bianchon's remark in *La Muse du département* (1843; *The Muse of the Department*): "the inventions of novelists and playwrights jump as often from their books and their plays into real life as real-life events appear in the theater and bask in books. I watched the comedy of *Tartuffe* take place before my eyes."[12] Although it has never been confirmed, Balzac is supposed to have lamented, on his deathbed, the absence of the fictional doctor he had invented: "I need Bianchon!" Even one of Balzac's models for Rastignac—the first president of the Third Republic Adolphe Thiers (1797–1877)—is categorized as a "character, even more Balzacian than Rastignac" by one of his biographers.[13] And as Marcel Proust wrote in a 1920 letter, "Balzac, who is regarded as a great painter of society, painted it from his bedroom, but the next generation, enamored with his books, was swiftly populated with Rastignac, with Rubempré, whom he invented but who already existed."[14] Other emblematic transclass characters from nineteenth-century novels do not allow the same blurring of life and literature.

Dressed-up to enter the upper class for the first time, Georges Duroy in Guy de Maupassant's *Bel-Ami* (1885) does not recognize himself in the mirror at first and greets his reflection "as one greets important figures."[15] Similarly, "Lucien had thus become almost a character" in Balzac's *Splendeurs et misères des courtisanes* (1838–47; *Splendors and Miseries of Courtesans*), and in Stendhal's *Le Rouge et le Noir* (1830; *The Red and the Black*), Julien Sorel judges his life to be a "novel."[16] Word choices here confine Julien, Lucien, and Georges to their diegetic roles as novelistic characters, thus hindering their capacity to break the fourth wall.

Rastignac also keeps coming back because he has a special relationship to crowds and the ability to distinguish himself within groups of characters. In *The Sentimental Education of the Novel* (1999), Margaret Cohen underlines that "a protagonist possessing the two-syllable name starting with a vowel," like Rastignac's first name, Eugène, "often designates sentimental heroes like Eugène de Rothelin, Adolphe, and Oswald. But in the treacherous world of realism, no community guarantees the stability of the signifier; Eugène de Rastignac is not one in a substitutable chain of virtuous protagonists, despite his name."[17] And as Alex Woloch shows in his book on characterization, *The One vs. The Many* (2003), "The name 'Rastignac' is first buried in a crowd of recurring characters and then gets transferred onto the protagonist who observes this crowd."[18] Conversely, while Rastignac emerges from a crowd in *Le Père Goriot*, he reenters literature through crowded lists after Balzac. To take only two examples: in Georges Bernanos's *Monsieur Ouine* (1943) and *Un mauvais rêve* (1951; *A Bad Dream*), we can read enumerations such as "Rastignac, or Marsay or Julien Sorel." Robert Louis Stevenson for his part piles Rastignac, Marcas, Lousteau, and Maxime de Trailles in the same sentence of *The Wrecker* (1892) to describe Paris's Latin Quarter.[19] Such lists can also be confined to manuscripts. In *L'Éducation sentimentale* (1869; *The Sentimental Education*), Moreau tells Deslauriers, "Remember Rastignac in *The Human Comedy*! You will succeed, I'm sure of it!"[20] The names of Vautrin and Rubempré initially were in the margins of the manuscript but did not make it to the final version.[21] Rastignac is what Roland Barthes calls the "sweeping sign" of a social milieu.[22] Either in a list or as the last remnant of a drafted enumeration, this last name ends up fusing all the nineteenth-century bildungsroman's characters of arrivistes and parvenus, even in the words of Balzac's narrator, who describes, in *Le Père Goriot*, "two or three men who exist in a young Parisian man."[23] With this in mind, Rastignac's famous exclamation at the end of the novel, "À nous deux!" (You and me!), could be read as a gesture toward the character's many facets. Benoît Duteurtre's 2012 coming-of-age novel, *À nous deux, Paris!* takes its title from Rastignac's final words, but the young protagonist, who wants to make it in 1980s Paris, reads Flaubert instead, as he takes "a modern literature course that would break down *The Sentimental Education* over six months, while Jérôme felt as though he were living out this novel in his day-to-day."[24] Duteurtre alternates references to Flaubert and Balzac, yet he situates his fiction, through its Balzacian title, under the aegis of Rastignac's landmark phrase.

Critic Véronique Bui singled out the "powerful sound" of Balzac's own patronym to explain why it features in so many book titles: Delphine de Girardin's *La Canne de Monsieur Balzac* (1836; *Balzac's Cane*), Léon Gozlan's *Balzac en pantoufles* (1856; *Balzac in Slippers*), and Octave Mirbeau's *La Mort de Balzac* (1907; *The Death of Balzac*).[25] In her 1844 novel *Une fausse position* (*A False Position*), Caroline Marbouty portrays Balzac as "Ulric," thus keeping the landmark final consonant. Rastignac sounds like Balzac, and like earlier versions of the character (Massiac, Chastignac). It possesses the prosody, three syllables, and pronounced final consonant of mysterious protagonists—Ferragus, Fantômas, Rocambole, Rouletabille, Cyrano de Bergerac—and of shapeshifting characters such as Franz Kafka's Odrakek and Éric Chevillard's Palafox. To me, the sonority and etymology of Rastignac play an important role in the persistence of this last name and of its social connotation.[26] Rastignac is connected to the upper class via his cousin Madame de Beauséant, and yet he gains entry into this milieu through another relative: Madame de Marcillac. The [ak] sound is a rung on his social ladder. In Rastignac, we hear *race*, a term that used to refer to social status. It starts like *rastaquouère*, which originates in *rasta-cueros*, "parvenus" in Spanish. A French reader today would also hear *gnaque* in Rastignac, a colloquial word that means "biting" in Occitan and is fitting for ambitious characters, often called "young wolves" in Balzac's works. In French, "to have long teeth" and "teeth that scratch the floor," like wolves, are idioms that designate someone who aims high and has a fierce desire for success. "Avoir la niaque" is the slangy equivalent of being competitive in the workplace. Asked in 2008 about the book that changed his life, Franco-Moroccan humorist Yassine Belattar picked *Le Père Goriot*: "Old man Goriot is not old man Momo [short for Mohamed]," but with some updating, "Rastignac could have been named Rachid and grown up in Les Mureaux [a Parisian suburb]."[27] Any youngster can identify with Rastignac who is, according to the humorist, a true *caillera* (the backward slang of *racaille*, riffraff in French). Here, too, sonorities are fundamental: Belattar's identification relies on rhymes and alliterations—Goriot, Momo, Mureaux—and on chiasmus and anadiplosis: Rastignac, caillera, Rachid. A 2009 management textbook whose author, Brigitte Méra, understood the catchiness of Rastignac's name, was even titled *La Méthode Rastignac* and subtitled: *La Comédie humaine, une culture d'entreprise* (*The Rastignac Method: The Human Comedy, an Entrepreneurial Education*). Méra considers Balzac's multivolume collection as "a genuine manual for personal development." About *Le Père Goriot*, she notes that Rastignac "the salesman" barely speaks to his "client" Madame de Beauséant and concludes, "The key to persuasion is thus in speaking little and listening well."[28] *La Méthode Rastignac* is filled with marketing interpretations and advice of this sort, often based on close reading (the breakdown of speech time in this case).

The gripping power of "ac" existed before Rastignac. In one of Molière's *comédies-ballets*, a character exclaims, "Monsieur de Pourceaugnac's very name provoked a terrible rage in me."[29] The antagonizing suffix also had a marked social meaning before Balzac was even born. One of Voltaire's philosophical letters on commerce, published at the beginning of the eighteenth century, praises the bourgeois tradesman over the aristocratic rentier as follows: "In France anyone can claim to be a marquis; and whoever arrives in Paris from a far-flung province with money to spend and a name ending in *ac* or *ille* can say 'a man like me, a man of my status,' and sovereignly scorn a businessman."[30] A character with "a name ending in *ac*" was fated to designate an illegitimate provincial wanting to make it in Paris. The connotation persisted in Émile Zola's novel *La Curée* (1872; *The Mad Rush*), published forty years after *Le Père Goriot*. From Provence to Paris, social climber Aristide Rougon becomes Aristide Saccard, whose double c possesses "the brutality of two rakes gathering gold"; "there is money in that name; it sounds like counting hundred sous coins."[31] Critic Philippe Hamon interpreted the [a] and [k] sounds as important "phonetic agents" in Zola's novels, present in the main family name—Rougon-*Macquart*—as well as in the first name of "Jacques" Lantier in *La Bête humaine* (1890; *The Human Beast*), initially called Dulac.[32] Same phoneme and phenomenon in Théophile Gautier's *Capitaine Fracasse* (1863), published after *Le Père Goriot* but set in seventeenth-century France, in which the baron de Sigognac goes up to the capital by joining a theater company as "CApitaine frACasse." Rastignac's name even traveled to another language: Raskolnikov in *Crime and Punishment* (1866) was inspired by Balzac's character and rearranges its letters: the [a] and [k], the opening [Ras], and the sonorous final consonant. Rastignac and Raskolnikov are both socially and geographically ambiguous. In French, the suffix -*ac* can designate wealth and ownership, that of the "Rastignac estate," but we tend to sideline the aristocratic particle by saying Rastignac instead of "de" Rastignac, thus smoothing the name's social edges. The ending—typical of southeastern patronyms and toponyms—rejects the character outside of Paris. Similarly, the suffix -*ov* in Dostoevsky's character indicates a belonging but the prefix *ras*- a dispersion. Both names encapsulate the disorienting and defamiliarizing trajectory of the social climber from a provincial rooting to a scattering.

Rastignac also sounds like Telemachus in French—Télémaque—whose adventures are painted on the wallpaper of the Maison Vauquer's dining room, the first setting described in *Le Père Goriot*. Right before his death, Goriot formulates a dream of social mobility as follows: "I'll go make starch in Odessa. [...] I'll make millions."[33] While Old Goriot's horizon is Odessa, Rastignac's backdrop is the *Odyssey*. Critic Alexander Fischler identified an epic loop in this first scene, from penniless lodgers dining in front of Télémaque to *Le Père Goriot*'s finale in which Rastignac is about to have a splendid dinner at Madame de Nucingen's.[34] The mythological name of Ulysses and Penelope's son only appears once, in italics. This detail accentuates the resonance with Rastignac but makes it difficult for the reader to decide whether the reference comes from Homer's *Odyssey* or from the didactic novel *Les Aventures de Télémaque* (1699; *The Adventures of Telemachus*), published at the very end of the seventeenth century by Fénelon, whose full name is François de Salignac. Such a genealogy again places tremendous importance on sonority, from Télémaque to Salignac to Rastignac. *Les Aventures de Télémaque* is at the core of the teaching philosophy of a French pedagogue from the first half of the nineteenth century, Joseph Jacotot. Unable to speak Flemish but asked to teach French to Belgian students, he used a bilingual edition of Fénelon's novel as a textbook. This method is discussed at length by Jacques Rancière in *Le Maître ignorant: Cinq leçons sur l'émancipation intellectuelle* (1987; *The Ignorant Schoolmaster: Five Lessons on Intellectual Emancipation*) as a way to advocate for the innate equality of intelligences. However, Rancière concludes, "The book—*Telemachus* or another."[35] Similarly, Fischler considers that the borrowing from Homer and Fénelon in *Le Père Goriot* is "negligible."[36] But to better situate Rastignac, the name "Télémaque" is on the contrary determining, and strategically inserted in the opening scene of *Le Père Goriot*:

> This room, rather poorly boarded, has panels on the lower half of the wall. The upper half is decorated with varnished paper depicting the central scenes of Telemachus, featuring the classical characters in full color. The panel between the barred casement windows displays for the boarders the painting of the banquet thrown by Calypso for the son of Ulysses. For forty years, this painting has provoked the amusement of the young boarders, who act superior by mocking the dinner to which poverty condemns them.[37]

This description is all about social class: the floor is uneven, poorly boarded or equalized, a detail that metaphorizes the precarity of the Maison Vauquer. Boarders are reminded of the blatant distance between their mediocre meal and the banquet painted on the wall. Many consider the first four books of the *Odyssey*—those on Telemachus—to be a bildungsroman, which resonates with Rastignac's social trajectory from Vauquer to Nucingen.[38] I would also argue that the reference to Fénelon signals a social and generic shift. While Homer's *Odysseus* is an epic in verse, Fénelon's *Les Aventures de Télémaque* is an epic in prose. To me, Balzac hints at this downgrading of genres when he writes that the dining room in *Le Père Goriot* was "poverty without poetry."³⁹ The fact that Fénelon disconnects Telemachus from his father Ulysses to bring him closer to a character named Mentor reflects Rastignac's moral conflict between the father figure of Goriot and Vautrin's mentorship. Fénelon's *Les Aventures de Télémaque* is also a didactic novel, written to educate one of Louis XIV's grandsons. By referring to Fénelon, Balzac encircles Rastignac in a literary tradition *and* an educational conversation that erases the character's financial and political career. Finally, *Les Aventures de Télémaque* is a classic, one of the most republished texts between the end of the seventeenth century and the beginning of the twentieth, a fact that resonates with the fame of Balzac's character in and out of the nineteenth century and places Rastignac in a string of canonical masterpieces.⁴⁰ Fénelon, Balzac, and Rancière—through Telemachus—point to the social emancipation of a character from his family, from his class, and from his primary text.

## Rastignac's Social Class in Literature and Politics

Determining Rastignac's social class is not as easy as it seems, which reflects the "blurred and reasserted class boundaries" of the Restoration period.⁴¹ Some readers would argue, rightfully, that he is not really socially mobile because he comes from a privileged background (although impoverished) and has relatives in the upper class. Like Lucien de Rubempré, Eugène de Rastignac is "at least in part, noble born."⁴² Others would not hesitate to call him a "poor relative."⁴³ Thomas Piketty's best-selling economics book *Le Capital au XXIe siècle* (2013; *Capital in the Twenty-First Century*) is the perfect example of the troubled perception of Rastignac's social status. Quoting figures and currencies, Piketty demonstrates that Balzac considers the average income in the 1820s (550 francs) to be "the most absolute poverty."⁴⁴ The land owned by Rastignac's parents generates revenue six times greater, "3,000 francs per year."⁴⁵ Despite these financial details, in the same section of the book, Piketty calls Rastignac a "young penniless noble come from his province to study law in Paris. Full of ambition, scarred by his poverty."⁴⁶ While Rastignac does not, economically speaking, qualify as poor, his ambition and the Parisian context turn him into an impoverished and underprivileged literary character. Three thousand francs per year is barely enough to pursue, humbly, a law degree, and simply insufficient to become a member of the Parisian elite. His stay at the stale Vauquer Pension—where he interacts with lodgers poorer than him—functions as a reset button for his social class. Erich Auerbach and Pierre Bourdieu indirectly confirm my reading: the latter describes Balzac's boarding house as one incarnation of the "unifying" habitus; the former reads it as an emblem of Balzac's "atmospheric realism" and of "the 'stylistic unity' of the milieu."[47] Incidentally, Auerbach shows that the Maison Vauquer houses another dual character, Madame Vauquer herself: "she seems poor, but, as we are later told, she has a very tidy little fortune."[48] The fictional place levels the social condition of its lodgers. Rastignac's class is further confused by the fact that he is portrayed in a novel titled after Jean-Joachim Goriot, who experiences the opposite trajectory. Like the -*ac* suffix discussed in the previous section, the proximity between Rastignac and his "co-protagonist" mixes social demotion with upward mobility.[49]

Rastignac's social class is not even stable at the scale of *La Comédie humaine*. Critic Jean Pommier identified a "dynasty" of Rastignacs by contrasting his first appearance in *La Peau de chagrin* (1831; *The Shagreen*) to his later portraits.[50] Although *Le Père Goriot* was published after *La Peau de chagrin*, its plot unfolds ten years earlier. In the 1831 novel, Rastignac surprisingly appears as a "commoner" without a particle in his name: "One spins around the social ladder, while the other had already nimbly climbed many of its rungs, the most difficult ones."[51] There is a similar fluctuation within *Le Père Goriot*. Critic Jeannine Guichardet studied its manuscripts, more precisely the different versions of the final line that follows the "À nous deux maintenant!" ("It's down to the two of us now!") exclamation. At first, there was only an additional phrase in the same sentence: "and he walked back down rue d'Artois." Then a separate sentence: "Then he walked back down rue d'Artois and went to dinner at Madame de Nucingen's." Finally, in the published version, the detour by the dilapidated Vauquer house has been erased: "And for his first act of rebellion against society, Rastignac went to dinner at Madame de Nucingen's."[52] Rastignac's social mobility occurs at the level of Balzac's creative process.

How is Rastignac used in the twenty-first century to depict social mobility, and what remains of his dual social class in contemporary

France? At times, the dropping of this iconic name just sounds like a convenient idiomatic expression to plant in a literary context. This is the case, to my mind, with the novel *Les Parisiens* (2016; *The Parisians*), written by the director of the Avignon Festival Olivier Py, in which the name Rastignac simply captions the trajectory of a character from Dijon to Paris.[53] But however trite, Rastignac can also be revealing when used on the mediatic arena, both as an insult and a model. To review Virginie Despentes's 1998 novel *Les Jolies Choses* (*Pretty Things*) on the arrival of twin sisters in Paris, *L'Express* magazine called the writer and her heroine Pauline "Rastignacs in underskirts." In a less mocking but still unkind article in *Le Figaro*, Pauline is a "postmodern Rastignac." Critic Shirley Jordan adds that the publisher's advance for *Les Jolies Choses* allowed Despentes to buy an apartment in Paris, which furthers the comparison between the author and her protagonists.[54] Putting aside misogyny and the anachronism of underskirts in 1990s Paris, the nickname "Rastignac" in this context sounds like a judgment of the author's *arrivisme*, a way to express suspicion at her merit. Conversely, Moroccan writer Abdellah Taïa keeps comparing himself to Rastignac in interviews to describe his social trajectory from Morocco to France by way of Switzerland. In *Libération*, he asks: "*How did I, the poorest of the poor in France, managed to end up in Paris like some kind of Rastignac?*"[55] Interviewed for an academic journal a couple of years before, he already compared his desire to make it in Paris to Balzac's character: "Like Rastignac: he arrives in Paris, he studies the world around him, he understands what he needs to keep and what he needs to let go. Without reading Balzac, intuitively I understood the sociology of the world I was living in. When I arrived at the Université Mohammed V, I saw there were rich, arrogant students from the French schools in Morocco. Compared to them, everything about me seemed poor. Then I thought: I will crush them."[56]

To understand these two mediatic examples and the recourse to Rastignac in interviews and book reviews, it is useful to briefly mention the 2001 mainstream miniseries *Rastignac ou les ambitieux* (*Rastignac or the Ambitious Ones*).[57] Eugène de Rastignac (Génie) and Lucien de Rubempré (Lulu) are childhood best friends. The series adds to these the character of a lawyer, Elsa, the only protagonist who does not come from a wealthy family: her father is a French foreman and her mother a Moroccan housewife. Rubempré—a graduate from the National School of Administration (École nationale d'administration [ENA])—becomes a congressman and the protégé of the Freemason Vautrin. Rastignac is a risqué radio host and dance club owner who drives a red Ferrari; he is a celebrity with messy hairdo, big sneakers, oversized jogger pants, flashy shirts with pulled-up collars, and unbuttoned cuffs under suit jackets. The miniseries redistributes Rastignac's traits—celebrity, law school, politics, social mobility—in the trio of characters.

This tacky television adaptation of *La Comédie humaine* is nonetheless spot on when it comes to the professional reconversion of Rastignac. At the turn of the twenty-first century, he is both a journalist *and* a journalistic gimmick, an "evergreen content" that signals, to readers and viewers, an upcoming discussion on social class.[58] In Simone de Beauvoir's *Les Mandarins* (1954; *The Mandarins*), a journalist portrays the character of Henri Perron as a "parvenu" in a press article. Perron—the fictional version of transclass writer Albert Camus—comments on this social characterization by saying that the reporter made him into a "Rastignac-light for schoolgirls [sous-Rastignac pour midinettes]."[59] Rastignac thus appears to be a reflex, a handy journalistic shorthand to discuss upward mobility then and now. Journalist Adrien Naselli name-drops Rastignac in his book-length interviews of social climbers' parents.[60] More broadly, the media (especially the press and the radio) are quick to use Balzac to report on politics: because of Marine Le Pen's conflicted relationship with her father, some compared him to "le père Goriot"; Jean-Luc Mélenchon confided he had his first political emotion when reading *Histoire de la Révolution,* a book written by one of the models for Rastignac, Adolphe Thiers; Nicolas Sarkozy's socially mobile minister of justice Rachida Dati was called a "Rastignac in underskirts."[61] Finally, when François Hollande's former partner—the transclass journalist Valérie Trierweiler—claimed he called the poor "the toothless" (*les sans-dents*) and mocked her family (a father on disability allowance; a mother cashier at a skating ring), philosopher Michel Onfray dismissed her comments as that of a "vengeful," "jealous," and "mean" "Rastignac" who used her "libido" to climb the ladder.[62]

I would like to continue examining what it means to be called "a rastignac" today by focusing on a politician and a writer. The title of the aforementioned management textbook—*The Rastignac Method: An Entrepreneurial Education*—could be the slogan of Emmanuel Macron's presidency (2017–27). References to Rastignac are overwhelming when it comes to him because of his provincial origin (Amiens in northern France), his position as an outsider (unelected, without a political party), and his career as a banker (at Rothschild & Co).[63] In his 2008 article "Rastignac Is among Us," historian Max Gallo portrays Balzac's character as "a handsome young man of 177 years old" who, today, would be a student at HEC (École des hautes études commerciales, a business school in Paris) and ENA or a trader.[64] Having graduated from ENA and worked in investment banking, Macron fits the description. Not to mention the presence of Rastignac's [ak] phoneme at the beginning of his last name.

François Hollande, who helped Macron get a foot in the political door, said he was "Rastignac with no relationship to anyone, except himself."[65] Macron did not marry Balzac's *Femme de trente ans* (1842; *Woman of Thirty*) but a woman twenty-five years older than him, his former high school teacher Brigitte Trogneux. In order to avoid the scandal of him dating, at age fifteen, a forty-year-old married woman and mother of three, he was sent to Paris to finish high school. One of Macron's friends, the novelist Philippe Besson, published a book about his presidential campaign, *Un personnage de roman* (2017; *A Character from A Novel*), in which he wonders whether the president should be compared to Frédéric Moreau, Adolphe, Julien Sorel, Fabrice del Dongo, or Eugène de Rastignac: "A banker, like him. Liberal, like him. But he doesn't seem prepared to do anything to achieve his goals, nor to share his cynicism."[66] Besson also reports Macron's comment about a meeting with elected officials in Besançon, Julien Sorel's land: "It's *The Human Comedy*. Without the literature."[67] In an interview for the *NRF*, Macron, asked whether there was still something "novel-like" in today's politics, compared his encounter with "the [French] people" to Stendhal's "crystallization," and quoted a passage from *Le Rouge et le Noir* on the bodily apprenticeship of the social climber.[68] In his memoir *Révolution*, published just before the presidential elections, he admits to being "carried away by the all-consuming ambition of Balzac's opportunists [literally, young wolves]," yet he does not call himself Rastignac.[69] This way, he keeps his distance from both a manipulative character and his previous position as a banker. Like Besson, writer Patrick Rambaud adopted the literary framework of nineteenth-century bildungsromane to write a satirical chronicle of Macron's presidency, *Emmanuel Le Magnifique: Chronique d'un règne* (2019; *Emmanuel The Magnificent: Chronicle of a Reign*).[70] Even Macron's staffer Alexandre Benalla, a social climber caught in a police brutality scandal, was called a "modern Rastignac" by the press; one Rastignac had thus hired another Rastignac.[71] And when French businessman and politician Bernard Tapie, who once recorded a song called "Réussir sa vie" (Making It in Life), died in 2021, the Elysée's press release praised his ambition by calling him "this young Rastignac."[72]

In 2014 Édouard Louis became a best-selling author with his first novel, *En Finir avec Eddy Bellegueule* (*Ending Eddy Bellegueule*). A *transfuge* from an underprivileged family of the northern French region of Picardy, he was called an "overnight Rastignac" by the book section of *L'Obs*, in a disdainful article meant to fact-check the real extent of his poverty.[73] With his third book, *Qui a tué mon père* (2018; *Who Killed My Father*), he earned the name of "meta-Rastignac," which shows how reception builds on previous articles to perpetuate "sardonic nicknames."[74] More recently though, with the publication of *Changer: Méthode* (2021; *Change: Method*), Louis has started portraying Rastignac in a positive light by reconnecting him to his fictional universe: "Yet he is the only one who takes care of old man Goriot, in the end."[75] Journalist Hervé Algalarrondo peppers his joint biography of Louis and Macron, *Deux jeunesses françaises* (2021; *Two French Youths*), with references to Sorel and Rubempré, but when it comes to summarizing the book on its back cover, it is "Rastignac" whose name appears.[76]

Louis's *Qui a tué mon père* accuses policies, including those of Macron, of having a direct impact on the working class and on his father's body: "Emmanuel Macron takes the food out of your mouth."[77] Following its publication, a journalist wrote that the president had been advised to read Louis's book. His staff even suggested, on social media, that Macron and Louis shared the same goal: emancipation. Louis—who is in absolute opposition to Macron's politics—was furious. He replied, via Twitter, that he and Macron had nothing in common, that his book was aimed at shaming the political actions of the government.[78] This interlocking of literature and politics, this altercation between a political writer and a lettered president, is more than a trivial anecdote. It testifies to the dual return of Rastignac. It showcases the encounter between two aspects of the archetype and reveals the distance between Balzac's Eugène de Rastignac and *rastignac* lowercase *r*. Today's Rastignac redux attests to the elasticity of Balzac's protagonist. Both Macron and Louis come from the north; both are ambitious and succeed, but they clearly don't rise from the same backgrounds nor to the same milieu. While Louis comes from a poor working-class family of factory workers, Macron was born to a wealthy family of doctors, although he clings to the proximity with his grandmother, a schoolteacher of modest origins.[79] There has been so much decontextualization and emphasis on mobility per se that in the media, Rastignac can now designate two political opponents coming from the opposite sides of the social spectrum. Each version of Rastignac could tell the other what the character says in *La Peau de chagrin*, in this order or not: "you're talking about poetry, when this is a matter of business."[80]

I have found a comparable confrontation in Michel Déon's reactionary *Lettre à un jeune Rastignac* (1956; *Letter to a Young Rastignac*). The postwar author from the literary right laments the new competition faced by "the Rastignacs of 1956":

> For some time now, nonliterary celebrities have flourished: a novel by a café waiter, by a miner, poems by a seven-year-old girl, a philosophical essay by a trucker, a lyrical meditation by a metro ticket inspector. These are the formidable outsiders whose peculiarity considerably helps with publicity, while a good, ordinary writer [...] offers hardly anything to attract fame.[81]

In order to portray the opposite of "a good, ordinary writer," Déon jumbles various manual workers and a single child in a mocking list that goes from "novel" to "lyrical meditation." As we have seen, journalists from the conservative written press (*L'Express, L'Obs, Le Figaro*) are quick to use Rastignac when reviewing coming-of-age stories. Didier Éribon—a socially mobile author of the cultural-political left—criticizes such venues in *Retour à Reims* (2009; *Return to Reims*), an autobiographical essay that had a decisive influence on Édouard Louis.[82] To paraphrase Éribon, what performative speech act is "Rastignac"? What "social verdict" does he deliver?[83] I would say that this name-dropping denotes an anxiety toward the rise of the unentitled, a belief that the meritocratic system (and the literary scene) should reward those who were already born on the right side of the tracks. The legitimate Rastignacs, whose mobility is preordained since they move from one position to another within a privileged class (Macron), are now confronted with "nonliterary" trailblazing parvenus (Louis). Through Rastignac, we can conclude that the "social" of "social mobility" no longer rigorously refers to social class but to a broader understanding of the social sphere. If Louis is a Rastignac because he makes it out of precariat, Macron is a Rastignac, too, simply because his parents were not the presidents of France.

Michael Lucey has translated into English both Édouard Louis's *En Finir avec Eddy Bellegueule* (*The End of Eddy*) and Didier Éribon's *Retour à Reims* (*Returning to Reims*). In his critical book *The Misfit of the Family: Balzac and the Social Forms of Sexuality* (2003), he, too, traces the popularity of Balzac's characters beyond *La Comédie humaine*. "Lucien's popularity has proved enduring" in the examples of Gustave Flaubert and Oscar Wilde, for instance.[84] But the afterlives of Rubempré and Vautrin do not reach the literary twenty-first century. Similarly, Vautrin's "fans" and "progeny" seem to run out in the 1920s with Marcel Proust. In the sections titled "'A Rubempré,'" "The Value of Beauty," and "Vautrin's Fans," most of the examples list Lucien and Vautrin alongside Eugène. Gustave Flaubert: "it is Rastignac or Lucien de Rubempré"; D. A. Miller: "a Rastignac or Lucien"; Charles Baudelaire: "ô Vautrin, ô Rastignac, ô Birotteau."[85] Lucey sidelines Rastignac because his book distinguishes the queer kinship of Lucien and Vautrin from Rastignac's homophobia and "reneged queer openness to Vautrin."[86] In this critic's perspective, the fact that Rastignac and Rubempré used to be listed together but that only the first persisted could be interpreted as a straightwashing of Balzac's forms of family.[87] Yet like Lucien, Rastignac can generate a gay panic or innuendo. It is no coincidence that the nickname is used by and for homosexual writers such as Édouard Louis, Abdellah Taïa, and Olivier Py, not to mention the rumors surrounding Macron's homosexual affair with former CEO of Radio France Mathieu Gallet, a "modern Rastignac" according to some tabloids.[88]

Rubempré made a spectacular comeback in fall 2021. Polemist and far-right presidential candidate Éric Zemmour's latest book, *La France n'a pas dit son dernier mot* (*France Hasn't Said Its Last Word*), is distributed via his self-publishing platform called Rubempré.[89] It is only logical for the author of *Le Suicide français* (2014; *The French Suicide*) to use the name of a protagonist who committed suicide. But it also shows how today, Balzac's characters are the unmoored signifiers of upward or downward mobility, as in the case of Zemmour's obsession with demotion and decline.

### The Economics of Gatsby and Rastignac

Critic Sotirios Paraschas considers Balzac's recurring characters as "an aesthetic device which functions as a means of filling a gap in literary property legislation."[90] To counter the unauthorized stage adaptations of his novels, he argues, Balzac started implementing reappearing characters to claim intellectual property not only on the protagonists but on their potential reutilization, on their posterity. The nineteenth-century writer adopted this "commercial attitude" in *Le Père Goriot*, a novel itself considered to be "a middle-class pirated version" of William Shakespeare's *King Lear*, among other borrowings.[91] Rastignac's return, today as during Balzac's lifetime, can thus be apprehended through an economic lens.[92]

Rastignac has also come back into the spotlight because of Thomas Piketty's *Le Capital au XXIe siècle*. In this international bestseller—more than three million copies sold at this point—the French economist traces the imbalance between income and patrimony in the Global North from the Industrial Revolution to today. As inheritance is now the greatest factor of inequality, we are returning, he argues, to the nineteenth-century society of annuitants in which the productivity of capital surpassed the value of work by and large. In such imbalanced societies, meritocracy is rigged and social mobility limited to a bare minimum or to exceptions and miracles. Piketty peppers his book with literary examples. Through Egyptian writer Naguib Mahfouz and Turkish novelist Orhan Pamuk, he shows how post–World War I literature no longer uses currencies, especially when it comes to representing estates and unearned income.[93] Jane Austen's wealthy characters—who do not even consider working—

illustrate for him how marrying was the only profitable option for the prosperous class of nineteenth-century England.[94] Early in the book, Piketty also quotes Vautrin's discourse to Rastignac in *Le Père Goriot*. What Piketty calls "Rastignac's dilemma" is the choice, exposed by Vautrin, between killing his fellow lodger Victorine Taillefer's brother and marrying her so that she can inherit from her father and transform this capital into a dowry, or else slowly climbing the social ladder through a career in law—a path that is uncertain and will, in any case, lead him to a much smaller fortune than marriage would. Piketty turned this literary dilemma into a graph (fig. 3).[95]

Piketty uses other elements from *Le Père Goriot* to interweave literature, economics, and politics, as in the following footnote: "A son of a former president of the Republic, studying law in Paris, has apparently, according to the press, recently married the heiress to the Darty chain; he probably did not meet her at the Vauquer boarding house."[96] Rastignac's name—and that of Nicolas Sarkozy's son—are not even mentioned. What matters here is the means by which one acquires wealth, that is, the conflict between work (law school) and patrimony (marriage).

While Piketty clearly identifies his book as jointly historical and

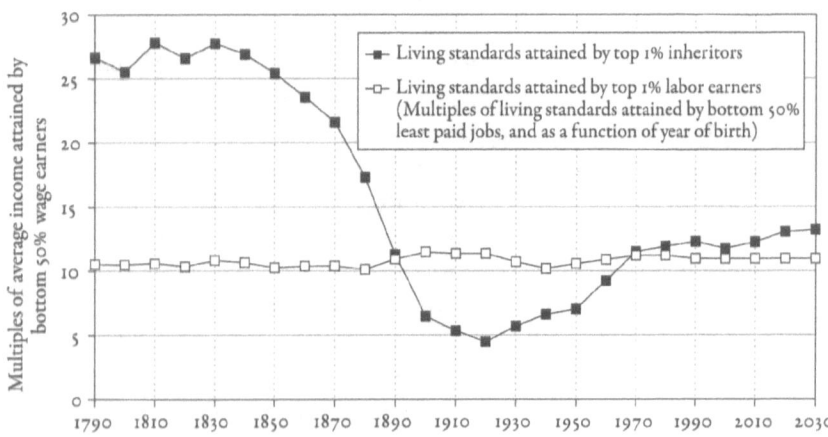

**Figure 3.** "The Dilemma of Rastignac." From *Capital in the Twenty-First Century* by Thomas Piketty, translated by Arthur Goldhammer (Cambridge, MA: Belknap Press of Harvard University Press, 2014). Copyright © 2014 by the President and Fellows of Harvard College. Used by permission. All rights reserved.

economic, he does not introduce himself as a literary critic. "Vautrin's speech is the perfect expression of companies of property owners," he writes in the sequel to his 2013 bestseller, *Capital et idéologie* (2019; *Capital and Ideology*), a statement that does not rely on the labors of literature or even acknowledge the location of this speech in the context of a fiction.[97] His remarks on *Le Père Goriot* are rushed and lapidary: Vautrin simply is "profoundly bad and cynical."[98] As for much-commented phrases, they become unequivocal: "But as soon as he leaves the Père-Lachaise cemetery, captivated by the sight of Paris's riches stretching into the distance along the Seine, he decides to conquer the capital: 'It's down to you and me now!' His sentimental and social education is over, from now on he too will be merciless."[99] The French economist reads "the classic 19th-century novel" as "succession archives" and considers Goriot's two daughters as real-life persons and believable representatives of their socioprofessional category.[100] Balzac certainly encourages such an approach. Judith Lyon-Caen, in *La Lecture et la Vie* (2006; *Reading and Life*) has demonstrated that the July Monarchy (1830–48) gave a tremendous importance to "truth" in literature. The "rage of novels" combined with "the fever of social analysis" turned published prose into a "hybrid object."[101] But while Lyon-Caen's archives are letters sent to Balzac and Eugène Sue, Piketty treats literature as unfiltered data. About *Le Père Goriot*, for instance, he notes that "these two forms of inheritance—land and public debt—pose very different questions, and should certainly not be lumped together as simply as 19th-century novelists do for the convenience of their stories."[102] The economic prevails over the literary.

Piketty's Balzac resonates with two other couplings of literature and economics: F. Scott Fitzgerald and Alan Krueger; and Karl Marx and Eugène Sue. In his 2012 speech "The Rise and Consequences of Inequality in the US" at the Center for American Progress, Krueger introduced what he calls the "Great Gatsby Curve," an economic tool meant to correlate inequality and the lack of social mobility.[103] The economist had thus far refused to use the word *inequality*, but, as he admitted in his speech, the "income dispersion" was now so great, there was just no other word to name it. Focusing on wages and the connection between social backgrounds and job market opportunities, Krueger demonstrates that the share of income disproportionately benefits the ultrarich at levels comparable not to the French 1830s but to the American Roaring Twenties. Hence his reference to F. Scott Fitzgerald's novel, published in 1925.

Although a hundred years apart, Gatsby and Rastignac share some common features: their stories are not told by themselves but by narrators, and both characters abandon the school system (St. Olaf College for the former, a Parisian law school for the latter). They also both live in a world that sharply opposes income and patrimony, as exemplified by Vautrin's discourse to Rastignac and Gatsby's self-fashioning. "It took me just three years to earn the money that bought it [his mansion]," he says to his neighbor and narrator Nick Carraway, who retorts, "I thought you inherited your money."[104] But unlike *Le Père Goriot*, the American classic tells the story of a self-made man, driven solely by ambition and determination, a proof that someone's will to succeed suffices to climb the ladder through hard work, however shady: "The truth was that Jay Gatsby of West Egg, Long Island, sprang from his Platonic conception of himself."[105] Gatsby is carefully and doubly devoid of patrimony by the author: "James Gatz of North Dakota" did not inherit from his parents, who are described as "shiftless and unsuccessful farm people."[106] And even after meeting, by chance, and working with the American version of Vautrin, Dan Cody, he is robbed of his share by the man's widow. By contrast, Rastignac is not self-made: he receives money from his parents and sisters, benefits from a family connection in the upper class, and climbs the ladder through friendship, mentorship, and courtship. He is part of what Bruce Robbins has described as the nineteenth-century proto-welfare state in *Upward Mobility and the Common Good* (2007), in which "narrative claims to hardy independence [...] turn out to be stories of reliance on others."[107]

*The Great Gatsby* and *Le Père Goriot* display two unsatisfactory forms of upward mobility. In the American version, Gatsby is the willful exception that confirms the rule: "young men didn't—at least in my provincial inexperience I believed they didn't—drift coolly out of nowhere and buy a palace on Long Island Sound."[108] In the French version, society rewards Rastignac, whose family was already six times wealthier than the average citizen. Not only are Piketty's and Krueger's examples different; they also do not use literature in the same way. Piketty's coined phrase "Rastignac's dilemma" is limpid:

Vautrin, in direct discourse, exposes a clear choice between income and inheritance. But a discourse is not literary in and of itself; Vautrin's speech is much closer to a real utterance—an archived speech, letter, will, or diary entry—than to a plot. By contrast, Krueger's curve is not named after Gatsby but after the title of Fitzgerald's novel—Gatsby is only "great" in the book's title. Krueger's economic model emphasizes the overall narrative over a scene or speech. The "Great Gatsby Curve" is indeed hard to grasp without context, that is to say, without knowing the novel: paradoxically, it is through the story of a successful social climber that Krueger means to explain how inequality prevents upward mobility. By using a book title instead of the name of a character or an excerpted discourse, Krueger ties the understanding of his economic concept to a work of art, to the process of reading, and to the slack between readers' interpretations. Piketty uses Balzac's character to quickly encapsulate, through the household name of Rastignac, the return of an antiquated, and therefore intolerable, state of inequality. But by not calling his graph the "Old Man Goriot's Dilemma," for instance, he privileges his economic thesis over the literary fiction. His decontextualization of Rastignac sidelines the singular work of literature.

Because of his corpus and reading method, Piketty also echoes Friedrich Engels's remark on how Balzac taught him more about society than "professed historians, economists, and statisticians."[109] And with the word "Capital" in his title, the reference to Karl Marx is unmistakable. In *The Holy Family*, Engels and Marx engage with Eugène Sue's *Les Mystères de Paris* (*The Mysteries of Paris*) to condemn the "paternalist socialism" promoted by the author and commentators.[110] Piketty and Marx focus on comparable characters insofar as they are socially mobile: Marx on Rodolphe, a wealthy baron who passes in working-class neighborhoods; Piketty on Rastignac, who climbs the social ladder. But there is one notable difference. *The Holy Family* dates from 1845 and *Les Mystères de Paris* was published in installments between 1842 and 1843, which means that Marx quoted contemporary literature. Conversely, the only French novel Piketty refers to was published in the first half of the nineteenth century. If today's data match an 1835 novel, why talk about "the Rastignacs born in the 1940s and 1950s" and not quote a more recent text? And since Piketty argues that novels display fewer numbers than in the past, where do we find the data in today's literature?[111] Annie Ernaux's writing offers a powerful answer to this question.

## Balzac's Social Mobility in Contemporary Literature

French writer Annie Ernaux has been documenting her upward mobility in novels, narratives, and diaries since the 1970s. She, too, refers to Balzac and other nineteenth-century novelists within her texts, which allows me to confront the use of literature by an economist and by an author. Ernaux shares Piketty's interdisciplinarity. About the genre of *Une femme* (*A Woman*)—the 1987 narrative about her mother—she writes, "This is not a biography, or a novel naturally, perhaps something in between literature, sociology, and history."[112] Literature is a measuring tool for them both. While Piketty observes that "in Austen and Balzac's time, less than 10% of the global population had access to elementary school," Ernaux explicitly compares the dining room at the "Pension Vauquer" to the absence of such space in her childhood home and concludes, "ten times more terrible than in Balzac, worse than Maupassant."[113] Balzac is especially important for her too. In addition to the name of the author, Ernaux strategically uses the titles of his novels, as in *Ce qu'ils disent ou rien* (1977; *What They Say or Nothing*): "I saw a title at a newspaper kiosk, *Lost Illusions*, I flipped through it, unreadable—must not be the same illusions as mine."[114] She also planted the title of *Le Père Goriot* in the first page of her landmark 1983 narrative, *La Place* (*The Place*), which won the Renaudot prize, had a lasting influence on narratives of social mobility, and functions as a turning point in her writing. It is the first book on her family that does not adopt the disguise of fiction or the scathing and vengeful tone of her first texts. In *La Place*, the narrator's father dies during one of her visits to Normandy, an event that triggers a set of reflections on her emancipation and the distance generated by social mobility from a family of peasants, workers, and shopkeepers to her position as a high school and later university professor of French. *La Place* is, like *Le Père Goriot*, a literary text on social mobility in light of the death of a father figure. In the first scene, the narrator officializes her upward mobility as follows: "In front of a class of eleventh grade, math wizards, I explained twenty-five lines— they had to be numbered—from Balzac's *Old Man Goriot*."[115] "Eleventh," "math," "twenty-five," "numbered": she saturates the sentence with references to numbers before mentioning the book title. Piketty would be right not to consider these numbers as "data," and yet they show the predominance of the numeric over the linguistic. Could this opening scene be a way for Ernaux to conjure up her social background? Her modest parents were on a budget; they counted pennies the way Ernaux numbers the lines of a literary excerpt. As shopkeepers, they also spent their days counting (to buy and sell products; to give change). To me, this intertextual opening scene shows how numbers (as money, capital, or lack thereof) constrain one's access to education and culture. Ernaux flees her milieu by teaching Balzac's 1835 novel during the oral examination required to become a high school instructor in France. She and Balzac also use a similar rhetorical strategy. Both plant character's names as book titles in their texts: *Le Père Goriot* and *Télémaque*. Both inscribe the Rastignac plot of social mobility within the school system. Visually, Ernaux's text resembles Balzac's *Le Père Goriot*, where italics indicate words from different registers.[116] But Ernaux introduces a pivotal shift: her italics single out a book title. While Rastignac left law school and climbed in society through marriage, network, banking, and politics, Ernaux's social mobility required reading, teaching, and writing.[117]

In the introduction to his essay on nineteenth-century Paris, Christopher Prendergast imagines Emma Bovary reading *Le Père Goriot*.[118] In Ernaux's autobiographical version, Balzac's novel is read in a classroom and in the context of a teaching examination within a twentieth-century French school system where *Le Père Goriot* has become a textbook.[119] Literature is thus not an unfiltered archive, but through lexical field and intertextuality, it showcases the transformation of *Le Père Goriot*. Literature is also an indicator of social class. In *Une femme*, Ernaux's mother follows in the literary steps of her transclass daughter. She changes because she reads, moving from Delly and Pierre l'Émile to Bernanos, Mauriac, and Colette: "she recounted the war years like a novel;" and she uses "comparisons she felt were literary."[120] One critic compared Ernaux to Emma Bovary writing her own story.[121] Indeed in *La Femme gelée* (1981; *The Frozen Woman*), Ernaux refers to "Bovary, my big sister" and self-identifies as one of the "neighborhood Bovaries" because of her childhood investment in reading.[122] But the reference to Flaubert and Bovarysm should be coupled with Balzac and social classes as well; it is by teaching, and then by planting *Le Père Goriot* in *La Place*, that Ernaux concretely and officially moves upward. The educational circle is complete because Ernaux's landmark narrative of class mobility, *La Place*—which opens with a reference to *Le Père Goriot*—became itself a classic textbook in schools.[123]

Critic Lydie Moudileno often compares the works of another important writer in this book—Marie NDiaye—to Balzac and Flaubert's novels of manners. In her reading of *Rosie Carpe* (2001), Moudileno wrestles with a striking dissonance between NDiaye's sophisticated writing style and the daily life of her lower-middle-class characters. Within this framework, she notices that the author downplays the central character's education: "although Rosie finished high school and even spent a year at the university, she never makes the slightest reference to canonical French authors or any French cultural phenomenon that might reflect that education (one could, for example, imagine her quoting certain proverbs, or comparing herself to Emma Bovary, to Rastignac, or to a creature from La Fontaine's *Fables*)."[124] Mentioning these names *because* they are absent testifies to the importance of Rastignac and Bovary as academic signifiers of class issues.

Based on interviews, we know that Ernaux had read *Le Père Goriot* when she was fifteen, in the Classiques Hatier edition, a truncated version designed as a pedagogical tool for students.[125] In the last reprint of the 1950 edition, I have noticed that the erased and summarized passages are particularly significant: "He makes his debut at a ball"; " Rastignac receives sums of money from his mother and sister that he asked for in order to keep his rank in the world"; "Rastignac leads a social life that is more and more glamorous ... and costly"; "Rastignac, back home from the ball, replaces Bianchon on Goriot's bedside."[126] The cuts erase or shorten Rastignac's society life and dependence on his family. They tighten the plot around Goriot and the Vauquer house, thus portraying Eugène as a student, not a socialite.

There is a striking parallel between Margaret Cohen's historicization of "the French novel's transformation from polite entertainment into ambitious social analysis" and Annie Ernaux's own literary trajectory, from reading sentimental novels to teaching realist ones.[127] In her 1999 book *The Sentimental Education of the Novel*, Cohen demonstrates how Balzac and Stendhal, despite claiming otherwise, owe their style and realism not to the influence of a political event (namely the French Revolution) but to "a hostile takeover" of the best-selling sentimental novels written by women at the beginning of the nineteenth century.[128] Unlike these authors, Ernaux does not hide the fact that her first readings were sentimental novels bought by her mother: "Everything I liked seems provincial to me now, Luis Mariano, the novels of Marie-Anne Desmarets, Daniel Gray."[129] Cohen's phrase "the sentimental education of the novel" equally applies to the genesis of Balzac's novel and to Ernaux's social and literary trajectory.

Émile Zola is another tutelary figure for Ernaux. In *La Place*, the narrator explains that those who did not know her parents perceived their café/grocery store as an "assommoir," that is to say a pub or a watering hole and the name of Zola's 1877 novel on work and alcoholism (often translated as *The Drinking Den*) and on the social mobility then demotion of Gervaise Macquart.[130] Similarly, the narrator of Ernaux's first novel *Les Armoires vides* (1974; *The Empty Cupboards*), whose parents are also shopkeepers, is named Denise Lesur, most probably, I would argue, after Denise Baudu in *Au Bonheur des dames*, Zola's 1883 novel on the birth of the Parisian department store—a place considered as a "palace for parvenus" by historians.[131] Both Denises are provincials who climb the ladder through work and marriage; both favor malls over small shops.[132] Zola is kept at a distance by fiction (the narrator is Denise, not Annie) and by punctuation (the "assommoir" is put in quotation marks), whereas *Le Père Goriot* is italicized to make sure the name is recognized as the title of a book and textbook, as the novel at the core of Ernaux's social trajectory.

What happened between Balzac and Ernaux? In the following chapters, I will expand on two steppingstones: Jules Vallès in chapter 2 and Marcel Proust in chapter 6. But here, I want to briefly bring together a couple of very different examples to show how Rastignac, despite his career in banking and politics, is being remembered and mobilized as a student figure. Such truncating of Rastignac's résumé constitutes a major shift: in today's literary landscape, we have access to tales of social mobility insofar as they are linked to schools and books.

In Maurice Barrès's multiple nods to Balzac, Rastignac is the archetypical high school graduate (*le bachelier*): he regrets the influence of these "too numerous, too unrealistic rogues" in his 1887 article "La Contagion des Rastignac" ("The Contagion of Rastignacs") but also models his student character François Sturel in *Les Déracinés* (1897; *The Uprooted Ones*) after Rastignac.[133] And as critic François Proulx has argued, Barrès expresses anxiety toward social demotion and school reforms in "Enfin Balzac a vieilli" ("Finally Balzac Has Aged"), his article on the 1894 bombing at the Café Terminus in Paris perpetrated by an anarchist scholarship student.[134] In 1960 Jean-Paul Sartre wrote a foreword to the republication of Paul Nizan's 1931 *Aden Arabie*. The two writers were in the same class at the École normale supérieure, and Sartre recounts an afternoon with Nizan, who told him, once they were near the Sacré Coeur, "Hey! Hey! Rastignac."[135] This Balzacian reference underlines their ambition, seals their school friendship, and crowns their climbing of the Butte Montmartre.

A couple of years later, in 1968, if we adopt a sociological view of the protests, university and high school students, fearing social demotion, rebel against the false promise of social mobility and education (among many other demands). At the end of "Les Trente Glorieuses" (1945–75), there are indeed more students than good jobs.[136] Critic Dominique Viart reminds us of a May 68 slogan, Be Balzacian!, a phrase that means *Soyez Rastignac* for French writer and 1968 militant Leslie Kaplan.[137] May 68's "établissement en usine"—the voluntary and often temporary social demotion of university students who worked in factories—was inspired by the Maoist cultural revolution (1966–67). The Franco-Chinese author Dai Sijie was sent to rural Sichuan to be reeducated through labor (the mirrored trajectory of Rastignac), a story he used for his novel *Balzac et la petite tailleuse chinoise* (2000; *Balzac and the Little Chinese Seamstress*). In this text, a character named Luo reads passages of *Old Man Goriot* (*Old Go* in Chinese) to educate a young illiterate girl. Sijie's novel—the bestseller of year 2000—connects education, reeducation, Balzac and 68; it ratifies the persistence of Rastignac in contemporary France through an educational framework.[138]

Like the characters studied by Michael Sprinker in *History and Ideology in Proust* (1994), Rastignac, too, is "the carrier of certain values and [...] the site for historically significant ideological conflicts."[139] Since the nineteenth century, Rastignac is read and imitated, then taught; the archetype of the high school graduate (Barrès) emulated by his student readers (Nizan, Sartre) becomes a character in a textbook assigned by professors (Sijie, Ernaux).[140] A couple of years before *Balzac et la petite tailleuse chinoise*, Ernaux had thus initiated a pivotal transition from reading *Le Père Goriot* when she was a teenager to teaching it in *La Place* as a way to represent her social trajectory through literature, intertextuality, and the school system. Admittedly, Pierre Drieu La Rochelle had already turned *Le Père Goriot* into a textbook. His 1937 novel *Rêveuse Bourgeoisie* (*Dreamy Bourgeoisie*) puts on the same plane and in the same list "his history textbooks, The Red and the Black, the adventures of Rastignac and Rubempré."[141] But Ernaux literalizes the metaphor of the nineteenth-century bildungsroman as a "textbook" by using it in the classroom.

## A Studious Rastignac

In *Les Transclasses ou la non-reproduction* (2014; *The Transclasses or Non-reproduction*), French philosopher Chantal Jaquet uses a nineteenth-century realist character, too—Julien Sorel—to reflect on the contemporary "auto-socio-biographical narratives" of Annie Ernaux and Didier Éribon, with some additional references to Jules Michelet, Albert Camus, Paul Nizan, and Jack London. Her various examples are stitched together philosophically via remarks from Spinoza and Bourdieu. She mentions once Eugène de Rastignac and Julien Sorel together as figures of ambition and nonreproduction, but later she focuses solely on Stendhal's character, because she is particularly interested in the intersection of social class and imitation (that of Napoleon by Sorel).[142] At times she directly compares the nineteenth to the twenty-first century: the importance of friendship for Sorel and Éribon; the geosocial trajectories of Ernaux and Sorel.[143] What happens if instead of using a character as a point of comparison, we track his afterlives in literature and society? Historian Camille Robcis has analyzed, for instance, how the protesters at French antigay marriage demonstrations in the 2010s wildly quoted Judith Butler, dressed their children as Gavroche, and used the title of Marcel Pagnol's *La Gloire de mon père* (1957; *My Father's Glory*) to oppose parenting reforms and inclusive language.[144] Titles, authors, and characters freely circulate in everyday life outside of book covers. My goal in this chapter was not to build an altar for Rastignac—like Antoine Doisnel did for Balzac in François Truffaut's film, *Les 400 Coups* (1959; *The 400 Blows*)—but to question why this ambiguous last name sticks, why it comes back, in what context and to what end. What is the relevance of such a dense maze of name-dropping?

In the 2017 *Cambridge Companion to Balzac*, French writer Éric Jourdan concluded that "Amongst the prolific writers of the twentieth century—the Jules Romains, the Duhamels and the Martin du Gards of this world and those treading the murky waters of the twenty-first—Balzac's example has become sterile and pathetically imitative."[145] Jourdan would probably alter his assessment if instead of Balzac he were to focus on the representation of upward mobility through Rastignac. Balzac's character never left the literary scene: you can find his last name in texts as different as André Gide's *Journal* (1939; *Diary*), Jean-Paul Sartre's *La Nausée* (1938; *The Nausea*), and Georges Perec's *La Disparition* (1969; *A Void*—Rastignac is a convenient word in a novel written without the letter *e*). But unlike Julien Sorel or Lucien de Rubempré, Eugène de Rastignac made it in twenty-first-century France. "If Rastignac is here tonight, it's because he jumped over the wall of the Vauquer boarding house," writes Julien Gracq in *Un beau ténébreux* (1945; *A Beautiful Dark One*) about Jacques, a character whose name rhymes with both Gracq and Rastignac.[146] The latter is now mobilized to describe a broad range of authors and characters: those who are called Rastignac (Virginie Despentes, Édouard Louis), those who call themselves Rastignac (Abdellah Taïa), and those who refer to Balzac's *Le Père Goriot* within their texts (Annie Ernaux, Dai Sijie). What emerges clearly is that Rastignac is remembered as a student and mobilized in plots and scenes that have to do with the school system. In contemporary narratives of social mobility, the neo-Rastignac and neo-Gatsby are no longer dropouts.

As readers and commentators of Pierre Bourdieu, writers such as Annie Ernaux, Didier Éribon, and Édouard Louis are not naive about the school system either; they unanimously denounce its social hierarchy and the falsity of its meritocracy. Yet one way or another, it is through education that we have access to these stories of upward mobility: "Only my studies allowed me a complete escape," confesses Louis in his second novel, *Histoire de la violence* (2016; *History of Violence*).[147] Authors either climb by way of diplomas, become professors, organize conferences, or write academic books. And in every case, they use schools and universities as pivotal settings in their social trajectories. These climbers manifest what Bourdieu calls a "Rastignacian ambition," that is, an exception in the school system, a case of not seeing the forest (of social reproduction) for the trees (of upward mobility).[148] Besides theory, the sociologist also summons the Balzacian bildungsroman in his autobiography: "As a young hypokhâgne student in total awe of Paris, where literary reminiscences became reality, I identified naively with Balzac (stupefying first encounter with his statue, at the Vavin intersection!)."[149] Today, the paradoxically lively yet petrified "literary reminiscences" described by Bourdieu are no longer confined to the names of authors and characters; my corpus has awakened this immobile statue. Balzac and Rastignac have also imprinted Paris's pavement and the representation of class mobility in urban settings. Prolonging the dialogue between the nineteenth century and today, the next chapter will continue tracking — through the trope of mud and of the muddy parvenants who people bildungsromane — how the Rastignac plot of social mobility now gives prominence to education and the acquisition of culture.

# The Muddy Parvenant, Then and Now

2

In *Fast Cars, Clean Bodies: Decolonization and the Reordering of French Culture* (1995), Kristin Ross analyzes "The striking prevalence of the ideologeme of cleanliness" in post–World War II France as a way for the nation to rebuild itself in the aftermath of war and decolonization.[1] She especially engages with Roland Barthes's take on cleanliness in consumerist discourses as well as in literature: "The New Novel, for Barthes, was successful only to the extent that it hygienically purged itself of a lengthening list of dark enemies—themes, characters, motivations, plot, diachronic agency."[2] What the New Novel cleans away is the Balzacian novel. Conversely, this chapter tells the social story of uncleanliness. If for Barthes, cleansing amounts to "a desire to immobilize time, to step outside of history," what mobility does dirtiness allow us to historicize?[3] Following in the footsteps of chapter 1's attention to Rastignac's name, class, and afterlives, chapter 2 zooms in on yet another attribute of Balzac's character: his muddy attire, the omnipresence of mud in the literary environment of social climbers, and the reverberations of this detail in contemporary bildungsromane. To carry out a semiotic study of mud, I start by tracking its literal and metaphorical uses in several of Balzac's novels. In a second part, a comparison with Jules Vallès's autobiographical novels on class mobility will allow me to show how mud is alternatively a social mark on a character's clothes and a metaphor for language and knowledge. Finally, although class structure, modes of social mobility, and city sanitation have significantly changed since the nineteenth century, we will see that the figure of the muddy parvenu persists in contemporary literature, notably in the works of two socially mobile writers: Annie Ernaux and Édouard

Louis. Such persistence will give us the occasion to reflect on the historicization and contextualization of social tropes, from the nineteenth century to today.

## The Plot of Mud

Before Rambuteau and Haussmann's renovations, Paris was a quagmire. The streets were mudholes and open-air sewers, most of them without sidewalks. A channel in the middle of the road collected dirt, water, and waste of all kinds, even more so when the cesspits overflowed. The 1832 cholera pandemic further exposed two interconnected phenomena: insalubrity and overpopulation.[4] The capital would progressively be sanitized through the development of a network of covered sewers and the systematic implementation of sidewalks. The reconstruction and sanitizing of the city took on symbolic meaning with the opening of the boulevards: cutting through Old Paris, they were meant not only to aerate its narrow medieval streets but also to impede the construction of barricades in the aftermath of the 1830 and 1848 revolutions, and to avoid the cohabitation of different social classes by relocating low-income tenants away from the city center.[5]

Owing to this context, bogs and quagmires are commonplaces for describing urban settings in eighteenth- and nineteenth-century literature. But authors have used this trope with very different political agendas, some to express a moral judgment, like Louis-Sébastien Mercier in *Tableau de Paris* (1781–88; *Panorama of Paris*): "Oh, if only the garbage collector could use his shovel for all those muddy souls infesting society," others to denounce the precarity of the lower classes.[6] In the section of *Les Misérables* (1862) titled "Mud, But the Soul," Jean Valjean flees the police by going down into the sewers, and is thus covered in muck when he meets Thénardier there. In this context, mud stands as a material sign of the characters' "unequal conditions."[7]

In this chapter I focus on yet another use of mud in nineteenth-century realist and naturalist novels: its presence in portraits of parvenant characters. If the muddiness of Paris was a result of the city's high population density and inward development caused by mass migration from the provinces, conversely, mud clings to the literary figure of the provincial who muddies his boots and pants in an attempt at making it in Paris (Eugène de Rastignac's mud-crusted attire is the most canonical example of this topos). Interpretations of these literary mud stains, often offered up in passing, vary greatly from one critic to another. For Christopher Prendergast in *Paris and the Nineteenth Century* (1992), *Le Père Goriot*'s mud functions as "a structural device for the forging of a plot of 'connections' binding all classes, high and low, to the moral implications of the metaphor [of the mud and filth of the Parisian streets]."[8] On the other hand, "mud signifies poverty" and "moral turpitude" in David Bellos's study of Balzac's 1835 novel.[9] I will not consider mud as a metaphor of class leveling nor as a metonymy of poverty but as an urban sign of social mobility. Boots and pants are mud coated in novels because their owners have to walk and traverse the social "field," from one class to another, without being able to afford a clean mode of transportation.

Contrary to what one might think, encrustation with mud in nineteenth-century fictional portraits of class defectors does not signal a provincial childhood but rather an arrival in Paris. This interpretation requires us to look more closely at the characteristics of the substance itself. Mud is not merely an inert and unchanging matter made of a single component but a combination of earth, water, and refuse. Alain Corbin describes its heteroclite nature in *Le Miasme et la Jonquille: L'Odorat et l'imaginaire social* (1982; *The Miasma and the Daffodil: The Sense of Smell and the Social Imagination*): "The mud of Paris forms a complex mixture of sand that has seeped between the cobblestones, nauseating waste, stagnant water, and manure; car wheels knead it, spread it, splash the stench onto the bottoms of walls and passersby."[10] Because it is a mixture, mud can be used by writers as a metonymy for socially mixed characters.[11] Neither the trace of an origin nor a simple baggage, mud is a ductile material, amenable to signaling a process of shaping and reinvention. Such a positive vision of mud can be found in Gaston Bachelard's *La Terre et les rêveries de la volonté* (1948; *The Earth and the Reveries of Will*): "We are demiurges before the kneading trough. We determine the fate of matter."[12] Hence the possibility for the pliability of mud to serve as metaphor for the self-fashioning of ambitious protagonists. In *Les Chiffonniers de Paris* (2017; *The Rag-Pickers of Paris*), Antoine Compagnon underlines another positive aspect of mud in the nineteenth century: it has value in itself when used as manure in the fields.[13] Far from being exclusively a useless waste product, muck can thus also be a catalyst for growth. This recycling accentuates the instability of mud, its pendular movement between the country and the city. Mud stains on socially mobile characters thereby invert the motif of the earth, which is no longer the trace of a rooting but the sign of a displacement. While Sarah Sasson argues, in her book on French and German parvenus, that "the insistence on mud and grease [in *Le Père Goriot*] reveals the concrete and fundamental importance of purity and authenticity," here I will explore the imagery and signification of mud in and of itself, not as the opposite side of cleanliness.[14]

This chapter is interested in the features of the nineteenth-century plot of upward mobility and more precisely in the polysemy of "plot" in this context. The word should be understood in all its usages, in French as well as in English: the outline or main story of a novel; a machination (in the case of Rastignac, a secret plan or a scheme to make it in Paris); or, in one of the French meanings of *intrigue*, a love affair (often the most efficient social ladder in nineteenth-century novels). Peter Brooks starts his book *Reading for the Plot* (1984) by underlining the original meaning of plot as "A small piece of ground, generally used for a specific purpose" and "A measured area of land; lot."[15] In the rest of the text, he uses this "measuring" as a metaphor for what he calls a narrative's "plottedness": "There may be a subterranean logic connecting these heterogeneous meanings. Common to the original sense of the word is the idea of boundedness, demarcation, the drawing of lines to mark off and order. This easily extends to the chart or diagram of the demarcated area, which in turn modulates to the outline of the literary work."[16] My goal is to flesh out a social and material meaning of this plot in bildungsromane: that of a patch of ground or piece of land.

Brooks also explains, "Ambition provides not only a typical novelistic theme, but also a dominant dynamic of plot," especially in *Le Rouge et le Noir* (1830; *The Red and the Black*), where the storyline operates as a "figure of displacement, desire leading to change of position."[17] The plot of ground (understood as pieces of mud) and the plot of class mobility also overlap in Stendhal's novel, starting with its hackneyed description of realism:

> Well, Monsieur, a novel is a mirror that walks along a highway. Sometimes it reflects the azure of the skies to your eyes, sometimes the muck of the mires on the road. And you accuse the man who carries the mirror in his sack of being immoral! His mirror shows the muck, and you blame the mirror! You should instead blame the road

where the mire is, and even more the road inspector who allows the water to stagnate and the mire to form.[18]

Authors need to get their hands dirty (or their mirrors, for that matter) in order to write novels that mirror all aspects of nineteenth-century reality. In this excerpt, the looking glass functions as a transitional object between high and low, the mud and the sky. It reflects the muck and resembles Stendhal's muddy parvenu himself:

> In fact, Julien remembered the king of \*\*\*'s entrance, in Verrières, and thought he rode his horse exceptionally well. But, returning from the Bois de Boulogne, right in the middle of the rue du Bac, he fell as he abruptly tried to avoid colliding with a cabriolet and was covered in mud. It was a good thing he had brought two outfits.[19]

Stendhal underlines the importance of mud (*boue*) with the scansion of its first consonant: *Bois, Boulogne, beau* ("right" in English), *Bac, tomba* (fell), *brusquement* (abruptly), *cabriolet* (cabriolet), *bien* (good), and *habits* (clothing). The evocation of mud is immediately followed by a short note about Sorel's two outfits: it could be interpreted as a reference to the title (the red clothes of the army, the black clothes of the clergy) but also as an anticipation of Sorel's upward mobility and split social status. Thus, in these two passages from *Le Rouge et le Noir*, mud binds realism, perambulation, and emancipation together. The aforementioned citations from Stendhal use *fange* (muck), *bourbier* (mire) and *boue* (mud). These three terms can all, by extension, designate the lower class as well as a moral stain or an abject situation. Although they are often presented as synonyms in dictionaries, "un bourbier" is a pool of mud and "la fange" is a thick mud. The mire and quagmire are more often associated with misery because they are deep or heavy and confined to the ground like silt, while mud, more volatile, not primarily associated with marshes and fields but present in both rural paths and urban streets, can stand in as a symbol of socially mobile characters in the novel.[20]

### The "Crottorama" of Social Mobility

In a 2009 article, critic Alex Lascar gathers together the occurrences of mud and characterizes them as "a hallmark of the Balzacian oeuvre."²¹ Balzac's emphasis on this substance is intentional, he argues, because the word is sometimes added only at the proof stage. It is notably the case for the first occurrence of *boue* in *Le Père Goriot* (1835; *Old Man Goriot*): "streams black with mud" in the final version but only "streams" in the manuscript.²² Lascar unearths another characteristic of Balzac's mud: it is mostly Parisian. In *Les Paysans* (1855; *The Peasants*) for instance, the sludge is only associated with characters connected to the capital: "'These Parisian *Arminacs* should stay in their Paris muds...,' said the guard."²³ The final consonant of Arminac is reminiscent of Rastignac, and "muds" (*boues*) denote the standpoint of a rural character: the plural (nonidiomatic in English) does not designate the Parisian sludge but the matter used for mud bath treatments in spa towns. In a footnote, Lascar explains his methodology as follows: "Here mud is strictly considered as matter. Linguistic imagery, comparisons, and metaphors about mud are not taken into account."²⁴ Conversely, Wolfgang Matzat shows how Balzac's descriptions of Paris are not detailed or concrete but rather moral and rhetorical, notably when it comes to the mire: "The image [...] of the mire is not announced through the evocation of the filth in the streets."²⁵ But how might we understand the specific role of muck in the representation of class mobility? Connecting matter to metaphor will authorize a social interpretation of the mire in modern and contemporary plots.

In Balzac's novels, mud often covers various clothes and body parts of the characters, from Vautrin's hand to Raphaël's waistcoat and Eugène's legs: "[Rastignac] saw the world as an ocean of mud in which a man would sink up to his neck, if he were to dip his foot in."²⁶ In this passage, Balzac describes the Parisian society with a hyperbolic comparison to an ocean, then turns the simile into a metaphor with an idiomatic expression ("up to his neck") before ending on the evocation of soiled feet. The figure of speech takes precedence over the matter, rejected at the end of the sentence, only as a possibility. The first occurrence of dung in *Le Père Goriot* is its negation in the description of "a girl [...] wearing cashmere ankle boots that were not muddied."²⁷ Dirt is so significant that a social object, such as a piece of cloth, must be defined in relation to its presence or absence.

Characters are not the only muddy literary elements in Balzac's prose. Mud also clings to the description of houses and stairsteps, notably in the famous opening of *La Fille aux yeux d'or* (1834; *The*

*Girl with the Golden Eyes*): "the forty thousand houses of that major city bathe their feet in filth."[28] And in *César Birotteau* (1837), stairs are "covered in a layer of hard or soft mud."[29] But this topography is turned upside down when it comes to using the house as a metaphor for a social climber's trajectory. This is the case in the following excerpt from *Illusions perdues* (1837–43; *Lost Illusions*), part of a letter from Lucien to Mme de Bargeton:

> Now that you have pointed out such beautiful hope to me in the sky, I see the reality of misfortune in the mud of Paris. While you will move, brilliant and beloved, through the greatness of this world, on the threshold where you led me, I will shiver in the wretched garret where you threw me.[30]

Using syntactic parallelism, Balzac superimposes the topographies of Paris and of a domestic space. These two sentences—connected by a notion both concrete and abstract: the threshold—form a chiasmus. On the one hand, Balzac designates the privileged classes by a figurative but coherent vocabulary. "Sky" and "greatness" point to the same space: higher, superior, and inaccessible. On the other hand, Lucien flounders in the concrete but also in a contradictory space, both downstairs (the gutters) and upstairs (the garret, where he is paradoxically thrown). Understood as matter, mud fills the space, from the cobblestones to the roof. As a metaphor, it signals the promise of an ascent, not up into the garrets but into high society. Facing such an "Escherian stairwell" in *Le Père Goriot*, that is to say a spiral staircase that gives the illusion of an indefinite up-and-down movement, Rastignac summons his courage with these terms: "Crawl [*Rampe*], endure everything."[31] The imperative in French creates a parallel between to crawl (*ramper*) and climbing the stairs, of which the handrail (*la rampe*) goes up the successive floors. Such a polysemy further suggests that mud is not a sign of precarity but of social mobility. The description of the Maison Vauquer follows the same narrative strategy: "The details of that scene, full of observations and local colors, can only be appreciated between the hills of Montmartre and the heights of Montrouge, in that illustrious valley with plaster always on the verge of falling and streams black with mud."[32] The periphrasis "between the hills of Montmartre and the heights of Montrouge" alludes to the inferiority and insalubrity of Paris. Yet the surroundings of the pension are not muddy: "There, the cobblestones are dry, the streams are empty of mud and water, grass grows along the walls."[33] From the beginning, we thus understand that *Le Père Goriot* takes place in a valley filled, concretely and symbolically, with mud. In addition, the novel is framed by two references to the land, from "the small grounds of Rastignac" to Goriot's enterrement: "[Rastignac] stared at the tomb and buried in it his final tear as a young man, [...] one of those tears that fall to the earth only to splash all the way back up to the sky."[34] Between the land of origins and the ground of the grave, between "the hills of Montmartre and the heights of Montrouge," lies the interstitial, muddy space of class mobility.

The lodging house also stands out because of its "local colors," its brown and yellow hues:

> Rue Neuve-Sainte-Geneviève especially is like a bronze frame, the only one that suits this narrative, for which our minds must be prepared with brown hues, with solemn ideas.
>
> The facade, three stories high and topped with garrets, is built from rubble stones and smeared with that yellow color that gives nearly all the houses of Paris their foul appearance.[35]

The frame is made of bronze: a yellowish-brown metal, a burnished alloy of copper and tin; the house's facade is built with rubble stones, the color of which ranges from beige to brown, daubed with yellow paint; the juxtaposition of "brown hues" and "solemn ideas" suggests that the color is not so much brown as dark and murky. Quoting *Les Chouans* (1829; *The Chouans*), Lascar explains that urban mud is black, while it is yellow in the fields. In his reading of *Le Père Goriot*'s topography, David Bell shows how "the Rue-Neuve-Sainte-Geneviève is a sort of border space between the city and its outside."[36] The color coding of the neighborhood reinforces the liminality of the Pension Vauquer: an emancipation chamber between the provinces and the city.

The alternation of valleys and mountains in *Le Père Goriot*'s description of Paris echoes the V-shaped structure of medieval streets built to collect the wastewater. The richest people walked on the side of the pavement, forcing the others to get muddy or to zigzag, literally to try to maintain the upper hand, *tenir le haut du pavé* in French.[37] We see the same structure in *Illusions perdues*: "feet hit with mountains and valleys of hardened mud."[38] In *Le Père Goriot*, Madame de Langeais exclaims, "The world is a mire, we must try to remain above it."[39] Madame de Restaud's last name (*reste haut* or "remain above") encapsulates this metaphor, as well as the character of Madame de Beauséant, who fears her name might be dragged through the mud: "I give you my name, like Ariadne's thread, to enter this labyrinth. [...] Return it to me unsullied."[40] Balzac's spatial imagery also explains the joke made by another resident (the medical student Horace Bianchon) during a meal at the Maison Vauquer: "Here is his Excellency the Marquis de Rastignac, Doctor of Law-Breaking [*droit-travers*]."[41] Balzac plays here on the polysemy of the French word *droit*, which means "law" (as a noun) and "straight" (as an adjective), whose antonym would be crooked (*de travers*). Rastignac's mother wants him to keep studying law because "tortuous paths do not lead to anything great."[42] But Rastignac needs to veer off in order to climb up: "My options are to either forge my path or stay stuck in the mud."[43] Rastignac gets dirty not because he walks straightforwardly in the wastewater stream located in the middle of the road but because he oscillates between two spaces, two classes. The prefix *par* (in *par*-venu as in *par*-venant) underlines the necessity of a spatial movement, a crossing, a deviation.

To plot his social climbing, Rastignac relies on perambulation: "As he made his way on foot, [...] Eugène fell into deep contemplation;" "The law student's long walk was rather solemn. In a way, he roamed through every corner of his conscience."; "Eugène went back to the Maison Vauquer on foot. It was humid and cold. His education was nearly complete."[44] Throughout *Le Père Goriot*, Balzac superimposes an urban itinerary and a social trajectory. Rastignac constantly regrets not being able to travel by carriage:

> Eugène walked, taking great care not to dirty himself, but he walked thinking of what he was going to say to Madame de Restaud, he garnered his wit, he invented repartees for an imaginary conversation, he prepared his clever words, his phrases à la Talleyrand, imagining favorable circumstances for the declaration that would decide

his future. The student muddied himself, he was forced to have his boots polished and his trousers brushed at the Palais-Royal. "If I were rich," he said as he changed the thirty-sous coin that he had brought with him *in case of emergency*, "I would have gone by car, and I could have pondered at my leisure."[45]

This passage starts with a narrated discourse in the third person, used to list the benefits of walking, and Rastignac's frustration is subsequently expressed through direct speech. The expression "dirtied himself" is located at the pivotal moment between these two forms of reported speech but also between the parvenu's perambulation and his linguistic strategy. In this context, the reflexive verb "to muddy oneself" (*se crotter*) is not only synonymous with the fact of getting dirty but also with the process of inventing sentences. As Bell points out, "A carriage might have spared his shoes and pants, but it would not have allowed him to fill in essential details to the indispensable map of the city he is formulating by experience."[46] Walking the muddy streets of Paris is akin to a spatial and verbal "formulation." Balzac often plays on the double meanings allowed by the lexical field of mud in its connection to blunders: "After getting bogged down at Madame de Restaud [...], only Eugène could recommence his profession as a cowherd, presenting himself at Madame de Beauséant."[47] Mud and the first syllable of cowherd sound the same in French (*boue* and *bouvier*). In English as in French, the first verb means both to get stuck and to get bogged down in the mud, that is to say to make a faux pas during a discussion with the upper class.

In the long aforementioned passage from *Le Père Goriot*, mud connects two different forms of reported speech. Likewise in his essay on characterization, Alex Woloch identifies two turning points in the nineteenth-century European novel, two moments or descriptions when "the protagonist's thoughts have come to occupy such a central space in the narrative universe, and how they converge with the omniscient voice," one passage full of exclamation points describing Rastignac's ambition in Balzac's *Le Père Goriot*, and one "purely unplotted moment" in Jane Austen's *Pride and Prejudice* (1813): "In Meryton they parted; the two youngest repaired to the lodgings of one of the officers' wives, and Elizabeth continued her walk alone, crossing field after field at a quick pace, jumping over stiles and springing over puddles with impatient activity, and finding herself at last within view of the house, with weary ankles, dirty stockings, and a face glowing with the warmth of exercise."[48] For both writers, mud signals an emancipation (from the determinism of social classes, from the rigidity of a plotted novel).

In this "crottorama" of social mobility, I have been focusing thus far on male characters, as there seems to be a tendency in the nineteenth-century novel, especially in Balzac, to spatter them with mud, whereas for women protagonists, mud is often turned into a personal attribute or a flaw, as in *Splendeurs et misères des courtisanes* (1838–47; *Splendors and Miseries of Courtesans*): "But you, [Carlos Herrera] said to Esther, you whom I pulled out of the mud and whom I lathered, soul and body, you do not have the pretension to stand in Lucien's way?..."[49] In this context, mud is a euphemism for prostitution. Émile Zola employs a similar image for Nana, whose face ends up covered with pustules "gray as mud, already taking the appearance of rotting earth."[50] Mud is thus not only different from but worse than soil, a spoiled version of it. Despite her status as a "marquise of the streets" (literally of *high sidewalks* in French), Nana cannot escape muck.[51] But mud does not always distinguish men from women in novels, particularly if we take into account Franco Moretti's remark in a footnote of the new edition of *The Way of the World: The Bildungsroman in European Culture* ([1985] 2000). Moretti explains that the literary equivalent of a bildungsroman for women characters is "the novel of adultery," such as *Madame Bovary* (1856).[52] Mud signals indeed Emma's deviation from the social norm of marriage: Gustave Flaubert describes "Emma's shoes, all coated in dirt—the dirt of rendez-vous."[53] In Zola's *Au bonheur des dames* (1883), Denise Baudu's mobility is symbolized by mud, too: the Parisian megastore *Au bonheur des dames* stands in front of her uncle's antiquated little shop, *Au vieil Elbeuf*, but such a crossing entails a walk through "a thick mud."[54] Unlike Balzac's Eugène however, Zola's Denise does not muddy herself. She contemplates mud from afar; she is kept at a distance, at first, from her eventual class mobility.

### From Street to School: Balzac's Mud in the Works of Vallès

Eugène de Rastignac gets dirty on foot, Lucien de Rubempré by carriage: "Having gone off in Madame de Bargeton's horse-drawn carriage sitting next to her, he came back behind it!"[55] In this episode from *Illusions perdues*, the aspiring parvenu is not muddy but "covered in dust."[56] The author retains only one of the components of mud—the dust—like in this other scene: "There you will find all the poetical Essays, the Inspirations, the Elevations, the Hymns, the Songs, the Ballads, the Odes, all the clutches hatched in the last seven years, muses covered in dust, splattered by hackney cabs."[57] Balzac spatters Lucien, the books, and the muses, with dust. One can understand this distinction as a means to differentiate the intellectual ascent of Lucien (dust and the cultural capital of the poet) from the financial rise of Rastignac (mud and the economic capital of the banker). Mud is indeed connected to money in *La Comédie humaine* (1829–48; *The Human Comedy*). As Lascar shows, it symbolizes the threat of bankruptcy in Balzac's novel *Gobseck* (1830), notably when the eponymous usurer leaves the house of a debtor: "And I leave, marking my presence on the rug that covers the tiles of the staircase. I like to muddy a rich man's rug."[58] Another writer, greatly influenced by Balzac, distinguishes between mud and dust: Jules Vallès.[59] In *L'Enfant* (1979; *The Child*), a diligence arrives in town "whipping up dust or throwing muddy stars."[60] The car whips up the dust (which was lying on the ground), while it throws mud (up to the sky). If we carry this metaphor further to read Balzac's bildungsromane, then mud leads to advancement (Rastignac's success), while dust quickly settles once again (Lucien's failed attempt at social climbing). In his trilogy *L'Enfant*, *Le Bachelier* (1881; *The High School Graduate*), and *L'Insurgé* (1886; *The Insurgent*), Vallès recounts an involuntary trajectory of social mobility imposed on him by his parents. The author and his narrator Vingtras favor the land and soil of their childhood over the school's "lumps of mud."[61] In *L'Enfant* he expresses his distaste for school by turning the Vauquer house into a boarding school, parodically called "Legnagna," which could be translated into English as "Theblahblah." Despite his hatred of the bourgeoisie and the parallels between Rubempré and Vingtras as two aspiring writers, Vallès does not center his attention on dust but on mud. Comparing *La Comédie humaine* to Vallès's trilogy will reveal the persistence of Balzac's muck in narratives of social mobility.

Balzac and Vallès both suggest a comparison between journalism, dirt, and dung. The print shop smells like manure in *L'Enfant*, and in *Illusions perdues*, "the mud of the newspaper" stands in the middle of a tripartite list, between "the pit of misfortune" and "the marshes of publishing."[62] In *Illusions perdues* and *Le Bachelier*, ink replaces mud:

> —My dear, Étienne Lousteau said sternly upon seeing the toe of Lucien's boots, which he'd brought from Angoulême and was finishing to wear out, I implore you to blacken your boots with your ink in order to spare your shoeshine.[63]

> I didn't have the money to take a car, of course. I had to walk and jump to avoid the puddles: I jumped from the Latin Quarter to the Hippodrome. My black trousers drag in the mud. I'm forced to wipe them with my handkerchief.
> My boots are also filthy; I rub at them with the various papers I find in my pockets, including letters that are important to me, but I can't arrive dirty like this![64]

The transition from muddied to inked boots could be easily understood as the result of an attempt at saving money on a shoeshine, at escaping the stigma of muddy clothes, or as the irrefutable proof of a successful upward mobility. But Vallès complicates the motif of the mud by extending the metaphor in *Le Bachelier*: "feet lame like the ones of those *dipped in Latin* who—in shoes riddled with holes walked all the way here, on an empty stomach"; "my head and what it contains: translations, speeches, piled up like dirty laundry in a basket!"[65] The imagery was already in place in *L'Enfant*:

> My *Alexandre* has chewed corners; I gnawed them in a fit of rage, and now its leather is in my stomach.
> All this Latin, this Greek, seems baroque and barbaric to me; I gorge myself on it, I swallow it like mud.

> Very nice buskins with clots of mud and manure gilding.
> I always roam around the stable near our house [...] before going to class, and I don't have mud only on my feet, it must also be in my books.

> "I hope we have a nice topic here!" the professor said, running his tongue over his lips—a yellow tongue, dirty lips.[66]

The first two quotes stress the presence of mud (*boue*) and dirt (*crotte*) by the use of alliterations: "baroque" (*baroque*), "barbaric" (*barbare*), and "gorge" (*bourre*) on the one hand; "buskins" (*cothurnes*), "clots" (*caillots*), "stable" (*écurie*), and "class" (*classe*) on the other. The rare word *buskins*, first used by a professor then mocked by the narrator, reinforces the association between shoes, ancient languages, and art: tragic actors wore cothurns in Greek plays. In these three excerpts, lips, linens, books, heads, and shoes are coated with knowledge, pejoratively described as dirty. Even before arriving in Paris, the young narrator of *L'Enfant* detects mud, by anticipation, in the books he is reading, as they will lead him to stroll the muddy streets of the capital in order to further his education. Mud in this context functions as a metonymy of school and knowledge, of reading books and writing articles, possibly alluding to the fact that mud in French also designates the sediment at the bottom of an inkpot. The substance is thus fully connected to "class," understood as a category, a social rank, as well as a lesson and a group of students.

In comparison, the metaphor of a muddied mouth in *Le Père Goriot* does not serve the same purpose: "Madame de Nucingen would lap up all the mud that lies between rue Saint-Lazare and rue de Grenelle in order to enter my salon."[67] Mud here represents the acquisition of a network, not of a literary or linguistic knowledge. I interpret the modification of the trope of mud from Balzac's stains to Vallès's education the same way I read Annie Ernaux's portrayal of Rastignac as a student and *Le Père Goriot* as a textbook: as a sign of the displacement of social mobility itself from climbing to a position in banking and politics to climbing through the school system. This change, already present in the nineteenth century, is crucial to understand the imagery of mud in contemporary plots of social mobility.

Vallès is also important to study the posterity of Balzac's protagonists. Half a century after *Le Père Goriot*, the narrator of *Le Bachelier* measures up to Balzac's social climbers:

> I've read my Balzac, and I recall that Lucien de Rubempré lived on rue des Cordiers at the Hôtel Jean-Jacques Rousseau. [...]
> Balzac, no doubt, chose the hotel that seemed best suited to the ambition and character of his hero. [...]
> I am chilled by the miserable appearance of that house. My win-

dow has a view of a wall. I cannot look upon Paris and shake my fist at the city like Rastignac! I do not see Paris. There is only the wall opposite, covered in bird droppings."[68]

Vallès combines the protagonists and settings of *La Comédie humaine* in two different ways. On the one hand, he starts to mention the hotel described in *La Peau de chagrin* (1831; *The Shagreen*), then turns to the final scene of *Le Père Goriot*. On the other hand, a comparison between the final version of *Le Bachelier* and its autograph manuscript at the Bibliothèque nationale de France reveals how Vallès made a synthesis: in the first sentence of this passage, he struck out "Lucien de Rubempré or Rastignac or another" (most probably Raphaël de Valentin, who lives on Rue des Cordiers in *La Peau de chagrin*) to keep only two distinct references to Lucien and Eugène.[69] Similarly, Vallès sidelined Rubempré by deleting the phrase "where so many Luciens must have signed their names" when describing the hotel's logbook.[70] The motif of dirt comes along with the name "dropping" of Balzac's protagonists: the wall in front of Vallès narrator is covered in bird "droppings." Stripped of their original differences, Balzacian parvenu characters appear as decontextualized and interchangeable symbols of social emancipation. This amalgamation continues in *L'Insurgé*: "*The Human Comedy* is often the tragedy of a difficult life."[71] The narrator indistinctly calls Rastignac, Rubempré, and Séchard his "brothers in ambition and anguish!"[72] As we will now see, Vallès's conflation of characters, along with his use of the motif of dirt, is the vehicle by which Rastignac's mud is carried on from one generation of authors to the next notwithstanding the differences between the two authors' social backgrounds and political intentions.

### The Persistence of Mud in Contemporary Literature

In *Le Miasme et la Jonquille*, Corbin historicizes the perception of mud as a vector of smells and miasmas in the 1750 to 1880 period, before Pasteur's theories. He underlines a significant shift from the idea of an undifferentiated muddy crowd to the association between lower classes and "social odors."[73] In *Les Chiffonniers de Paris*, Compagnon extends Corbin's work by underlining the material difference between nineteenth- and twenty-first-century mud: "For that 19th-century Parisian mud was nothing like ours, which is a blend of earth and water, a sticky but relatively clean and mineral combination [...]. In the middle of the 19th century, the mud of Paris was a mixture of waste kneaded with earth and water and deposited near kilometer markers and in the stream flowing through the middle of the street."[74] If the matter, its perception, and its social signification have changed over time, I now want to examine how literary mud has remained surprisingly stable as a sign of social mobility. In *The Way of the World*, Moretti surveys European bildungsromane by focusing on "*plot differences*."[75] Conversely, I will turn to contemporary literature to show how the "plot of ground" is precisely that which does not change.

As we have seen in chapter 1, the incipit of Annie Ernaux's 1983 seminal emancipation narrative *La Place* (*The Place*) showcases Balzac. References to nineteenth-century authors (Balzac, Hugo, Maupassant) and novels (*Illusions perdues, Notre-Dame de Paris*) are numerous in her narratives and interviews.[76] To reflect on her literary debut (the publication of *Les Armoires vides*—*The Empty Cupboards*—in 1974), Ernaux uses the lexical field of mud as a way to designate the gray zone between two social classes: "I entered literature 'badly,' in a way that was incorrect, muddy, with a text that rejected literary values, spat on everything, and would go on to offend my mother."[77] *Les Armoires vides* is a scathing novel mocking a fictional version of her parents. Ernaux's first book amounts to a double betrayal, vis-à-vis her social class of origin and her new class, as the text is full of argot, patois, and vernacular slurs. The adjective *muddy* (in the feminine in French, *boueuse*), isolated between commas, agrees with both "way" (*façon*) and Ernaux. Thereby the author rhetorically underlines the similarities between mud as a substance (on herself) and as a figurative matter (in her writing style). Through mud, Ernaux also finds a way to stay in touch with her parents and what is described in *Les Armoires vides* as their "store covered in muddy footprints."[78]

A year before Ernaux's muddy entrance onto the literary scene, Inès Cagnati's debut novel—a bildungsroman titled *Le Jour de congé* (1973; *The Day Off*)—portrays a young girl shuttling between home and school on a bike: "The mud accumulates and then, my bicycle stops moving and I have to either clean it or carry it."[79] The coated mudguard symbolizes the vicissitudes of her social journey.

Zola uses the same adjective to similar effect in *Thérèse Raquin* (1867); a variation on the [ak] sound. While the eponymous protagonist is tied to the soil, "happy to sink her fingers into earth," her lover Laurent is on the side of mud because he ventures to paint: "his peasant's eye perceived nature in a clumsy and filthy way; his canvases, muddy, poorly constructed, grimacing, defied all criticism."[80] Mud, also highlighted by the use of commas, leaves a mark on those who escape social reproduction by way of art. Similarly in Octave Mirbeau's 1900 *Le Journal d'une femme de chambre* (*The Diary of a Chambermaid*), mud appears when an informal register returns in an elite context: "Often, in her quarrels with Monsieur, she would lose control of herself and scream: 'Shit!' In those moments, her anger would stir up the persistent familial muck lingering in the depths of her being, not yet fully cleansed by her recently acquired luxury."[81] Here again, mud signals a spatial, social, and temporal displacement; it points to people who do not stay in their place, thus echoing Mary Douglas's phrase, often attributed to Sigmund Freud, "Dirt is matter in the wrong place."

Édouard Louis is a transclass writer greatly influenced by Ernaux, born to an underprivileged family of factory workers and caregivers qualifying for welfare payments. He became a writer after studying at the École normale supérieure. In his 2014 best-selling debut coming-of-age novel, *En finir avec Eddy Bellegueule* (*Ending Eddy Bellegueule*), he recounts his attempts at overcoming social determinism and the difficulty of growing up gay in the countryside of northern France. He, too, reactivates the "plot" of upward mobility:

> I was part of a theater group started by my French professor: My father, out of his depth faced with my interest in theater, was extremely annoyed by this and often refused to take the car to pick me up after class, muttering *No one is forcing you to do this theater crap*. On foot I would travel the fifteen kilometers that separated me from my house, walking across fields for hours, mud and dirt accumulating beneath my shoes until they weighed several pounds.[82]

The retrospective narrative is influenced by the arrival of Bellegueule in the capital and in the upper class: like Vallès's Vingtras, the narrator is muddy in advance because the practice of theater has already started to emancipate him. The transition from the countryside to the city, and from one social class to another, is visible three times in this passage: mud is still associated with soil; both materials weigh the shoes down, thus hindering the return trip; yet mud is still hidden "beneath my shoes." In Louis's second novel *Histoire de la violence* (2016; *History of Violence*), the narrator wanders in Paris:

> The place de la République was under construction, and the ground was covered in mud; or rather, the ground was mud, there was nothing else, the roads had been destroyed so that the workers could pour cement and lay new slabs of concrete for the pedestrianization of the place, and every day I got filthy crossing it, I returned home with gritty dirt along the bottom of my pants. It wasn't the reddish-brown mud of my childhood in the countryside, the mud that gives off an odor of fresh earth, gleaming like clay, which we would gladly spread over our faces because it seemed so healthy, beneficial, but that gray mud, austere and lumpy, typical of city building sites. [...]
>
> So: Christmas day, I'm walking in the dark, I'm crossing the place de la République, chaotic, shoes covered in mud and small grayish splashes, droplets along the bottom of my pants, as though a filthy rain was falling not from the sky but from the ground, Nietzsche and Simon under my arms.[83]

From the first to the second quote, dirt goes from brown and red to grayish, from sand and earth ("gritty dirt") to mud. In comparison with the aforementioned passage from *En finir avec Eddy Bellegueule*, the dirty matter is now fully visible: it covers the shoes entirely as if, according to the narrator, rain was falling in the opposite direction. Mud has not just replaced the soil of his childhood fields but also the ground of Paris itself. The substance is thus not only associated with the city but with an urban construction site: "the ground was covered in mud; or rather, the ground was mud, there was nothing else, the roads had been destroyed." All these elements highlight the narrator's metamorphosis and separation from the territory of his childhood. Crossing a space, appropriately called "La Place de la République," is thus akin to experiencing upward social mobility. The place is at the edge of the Marais neighborhood, an important detail on three counts. First, because the swampy district was regularly flooded by the Seine river, the literal meaning of "Marais" is "Marsh," which reinforces the muddiness of the place. Second, it is known today as the center of Paris's LGBT cultures, and Louis's work examines the intersection between class mobility and homosexuality. Finally, although Le Marais is "le vieux Paris," that is to say one of the few neighborhoods that avoided Haussmannization, the Place de la République has regularly been remodeled.[84] This location, as liminal as Balzac's Pension Vauquer, puts the narrator at the crossroads of several different symbols and temporalities.

Moreover, the narrator is not only muddy literally because he walks but also metaphorically because he reads. In the second aforementioned quote, the phrase "Nietzsche and Simon under my arms" is apposed at the end of the sentence in a way that does not elicit its connection to the other elements of the scene. Although the third chapter spells out the full names of Friedrich Nietzsche and Claude Simon, this isolated phrase at the beginning of the fourth chapter is polysemic. Could "Simon" be a friend and not just the last name of the New Novel writer? To my ear, the name Claude Simon can be understood as two first names, thereby echoing the author's social mobility, ratified by his legal name change from Eddy Bellegueule to his nom de plume: the two first names Édouard Louis. The narrator's sister incidentally proposes a connection between walking, reading, and social climbing when she says, "I'm sure that as he walked, as he advanced, he was thinking something like: This is one hell of a road I've traveled."[85]

In *Histoire de la violence*, the author uses italics to distinguish between the class renegade's voice and his sister's overarching narrative:

> *You had moved to Paris, this was four years ago, and foolishly you wanted to appear bourgeois to bury what you considered your poor, provincial origins* [...], *but your idea of the bourgeoisie was outdated by a hundred years, precisely because of the distance between you and that world, and you had bought that ascot and a three-piece suit that you wore on every occasion, often with a tie, even to go to the supermarket or to the university. You donned your anachronistic clothing every morning, revealing through your anguished attitude the past you were attempting to inearth.*[86]

To bury (*enfouir* in the original version) means both to put underground and to cover with earth. Paradoxically then, at the very moment the narrator endeavors to inearth (*enterrer*) his past by wearing formal clothes, he is precisely "unearthing" his social origin and connection to a rural area. In this passage the author distances himself from the anachronistic project of a nineteenth- or early twentieth-century cosplaying by using italics and the second person "you." The figurative soil on a suit contrasts with the mud on a pair of shoes, which stands as a sign of a successful upward mobility by way of literature. Although Ernaux and Louis come from the north of France, the trace of mud is not so much an indication of their underprivileged upbringing in the countryside, as of their status as parvenants, adrift between two social classes. We find a similar tension in their texts between the concrete (walking, publishing) and the abstract (writing). Paris is no longer the city of mud, but the literary Paris of social mobility remains muddy, notably when those who climb the ladder are students, professors, authors, and readers.

Despite significant differences in the socioeconomic backgrounds of characters and in the meaning of *parvenir* in the works of Balzac, Vallès, Ernaux, and Louis, the origin of the "muddy parvenant" in today's literature can be traced to the nineteenth-century realist novel. The trope even extends beyond the French corpus. There are many paradigmatic examples from the 1860s. Charles Dickens's *Great Expectations* is full of literal and figurative mudbanks. In Horatio Alger's most famous narrative of upward mobility, *Ragged Dick*, the parvenu used to be a shoe shiner. And in Dostoevsky's *Crime and Punishment*, Raskolnikov (whose name and moral conflicts are modeled on Rastignac) is confronted with the same revelatory power of soiled clothes: muddy for Rastignac, because he wanders the dirty streets of Paris; bloody for Raskolnikov, when he wonders whether the blood stains at the bottom of his pants could betray him and reveal his two murders.[87] From the literal mud on Rastignac's clothes to the figurative mud of books and knowledge in Vallès's autobiographical novels, there is thus a decisive shift in the literary representation of dirt since Balzac: in literary texts after Vallès, upward mobility is no longer primarily achieved through money and business but rather through education and culture.

The matter of mud paradoxically unsettles the historicization of social issues. On the one hand, in Bourdieusian terms, sludgy dirt is capable of signaling a pivotal transformation whereby narratives of upward mobility after Balzac and Stendhal appear to focus on the acquisition of cultural capital rather than on the acquisition of economic and social capital. But on the other hand, mud is not only a mover of class but an autonomous, semiotic agent endowed with its own form of mobility, capable of infiltrating the contemporary novel as signifier and signified, always working on levels metaphorical and literal, even when its presence in the streets of Paris is all but allegorical. Mud appears as a veritable *terre meuble*, that is to say a loose and movable soil or footing. To say it differently: literature has bestowed mud with a new metaphor from Balzac to Vallès, from the early to the late nineteenth century (that of education and literary knowledge), but mud also continues to signal class mobility in the works of Louis more than a century after the death of Vallès.

Footprints in the mire, soiled trousers, and mud-crusted shoes are central in Sherlock Holmes's investigations.[88] These types of trace evidence put the victims and the suspects back in their contexts. But throughout the examples of mud encrustations I have gathered here, we can also see how muddy literary matters tend to stymie the author's (and the critic's) attempt at accounting for the historical specificity of a narrative or trope. Mud denotes at once the decontextualization of characters from their social class and of a literary plot from its century and historical background.

## Communal Mud

In their articles "Partage de l'insolence" ("Distribution of Insolence") and "Polar Chaos," writer Nathalie Quintane and critic Kristin Ross track references to the Paris Commune in twenty-first-century social spaces. Ross, who apprehends the Commune, in its contemporary reappropriation, as "a kind of usable archive of legacy ideas and practices," focuses on the provinces—Notre-Dame-des-Landes's ZAD, for *Zone à défendre* (Zone to Defend), and the Gilets jaunes' occupied traffic circles.[89] Quintane, who is more interested in the 2016 Parisian social movement Nuit Debout, acknowledges the influence of Communard Jules Vallès on the form of her social writing: "Vallès! Carriage returns, cuts, presents, blanks, short, short!"[90] Indeed, the last volume of Vallès's trilogy, whose full title is *L'Insurgé—1871*, combines a depiction of the Commune with a reflection on form and genre. As critic Sylvia Disegni notes, "Vallès does not recount how to become a writer but how to become a journalist and an insurgent."[91] Toward the end of the novel, the narrator incidentally declares: "Journalists! Are you looking for one? ... Here I am."[92] The final, brief chapter is particularly telling, too, as Vallès multiplies personal pronouns to arrive at a communal form of discourse, from "you" to "I" to "he," and finally to "one."[93]

This shift from fiction to journalism and revolt turns on a reference to Balzac. At the beginning of *L'Insurgé*, the narrator describes a conference he gave on Balzac during which he praised the importance of the novel form.[94] Vallès himself gave a talk on the same topic in 1865, that is to say twenty years before publishing *L'Insurgé*. Yet during the fictional account of the lecture, the orator quickly sidelines Balzac in order to address politics and revolution: "I forget about dead Balzac and talk about the living."[95] Then after publishing his first book, narrator Jacques Vingtras admits, "I felt more emotion at my talk; I was moved differently, on the days when I was able to speak to the people."[96] Thus, despite the defense and illustration of Balzac throughout the works of Vallès, the Communard author and narrator of *L'Insurgé* transitions to a more public, direct, and daily form of discourse.

The trope of mud accompanies this shift. In a section of *Les Réfractaires* (*The Resistors*) titled "Les Victimes du livre" ("The Victims of the Book"), published the same year as the conference on Balzac, Vallès connects the realist author to mud and struggles:

> Ah! under the footsteps of this giant, nothing but crushed consciences, nothing but mud, but blood! [...]
> How many have lost their ways, have *sunk*, who were waving above the mire where they would die, a page torn from a volume of *The Human Comedy*.
> They, along with Rastignac, in a garret or standing on the Pont des Arts, shook their fist at life and screamed at the world: *It's down to you and me now!* swearing, on *Old Man Goriot* or the volume next to it, to carve out their place with strikes of the sword.[97]

Balzac encourages readers to fight (blood, sword, fist) in order to succeed, but such a use of literature can also lead to mire, poverty, and death. Twenty years later, in the article "La Littérature sociale" ("Social Literature") written after the Commune, Vallès still detects mud in Balzac, but its connotation has changed:

> By revealing the workings of modern fatality to his readers, the hefty coins stained with blood and mud, [Balzac] started the Revolution in publishing and on the stage, he delivered theater and the novel to the revolt!
> [...] But he didn't take it all the way. Although he wrote forcefully about the tragedy of money, he gave some of his heroes a halo of political glory and a gleam of great life, making fortune bow down before their audacity and their genius. The realist was a romantic in that sense, and that is why he was not despised by the people for whom the appearance of the de Marsays and Rastignacs stood as a consolation for the company of *down-to-earth* figures who are in fact the real, powerful characters of this oeuvre.[98]

Mud and blood come back to describe capitalism ("the tragedy of money") as well as to oppose mud to dirt, romantic genius to realist fatality, and the rich and successful Rastignac to less prosperous "*down-to-earth*" protagonists. Vallès, for his part, will "go all the way." In *L'Insurgé*, he seems to renounce Balzac's characters: Rastignac is mentioned at the very beginning of the novel (chap. 4), but then he disappears and gives his seat to one of Rastignac's models, Adolphe Thiers, the Commune gravedigger (chaps. 24 and 33). If the narrator of *L'Insurgé* was ready to burn the Sainte-Geneviève Library during the uprisings of May 1871's "Bloody Week," Vallès did burn it figuratively. Throughout the three novels of the Vingtras trilogy, mud goes from reading and learning (*L'Enfant*) to journalism (*Le Bachelier*), and is finally replaced in *L'Insurgé* with the mud of rebellion: "For an hour, their stomachs in the mud, their noses soiled, their clothes slick with muck, they shoot through the arrow slit at ground level and inflict cruel pain on the enemy."[99] This scene takes places on the last day of the Paris Commune.

As in Vallès, mud is becoming more political in Louis's latest texts. In *Changer: Méthode* (2021; *Change: Method*), the narrator's shoes are muddied because he is roaming the unpaved streets of his village to gather signatures for a petition against the firing of a librarian.[100] We can also discern a comparable generic trajectory in the works of Vallès and Louis. Although the latter's first two books are deeply autobiographical, both are subtitled as novels, as the author considers that writing transforms life into fiction. Starting with *Qui a tué mon père* (*Who Killed My Father*) in 2018, the "novel" subtitle disappears from the book cover. Fellow contemporary writer Sophie Divry, whom I will be discussing in the last chapter of this book, underlined this change by lambasting Louis's book: "We see this with Édouard Louis's third book. Everyone says it must have been written with his feet, and that he should have stuck to doing opinion pieces for *Libération*, for which he is well suited—[...] he is absolutely not a writer."[101] Louis repeatedly proclaimed that fiction and the novel were dead, that autobiographies and first-person narratives are more politically efficient to denounce oppression and to fight it, that writing a book on his mother means he has to "write against literature."[102] As he said in an interview, "*The time when Zola wrote about factory workers to reveal their conditions is over now*."[103] Louis replaces Zola, and Thiers replaces Rastignac. No more intermediary writer carrying a mirror along a muddy road. Today, mire no longer needs a mirror. Or rather, human beings have become the reflecting surfaces of reality. But what do their bodies look like under this intertextual layer of mud? After the analysis of names, attires, and settings in chapters 1 and 2, chapter 3 will continue the exploration of the parvenant's environment through its most immediate manifestation: the body and the conflicted embodiment of class mobility.

# The Transient Body of the Transclass

3

The Mouvement des gilets jaunes (or Yellow Vests movement) started in fall 2018 and lasted until the spring 2020 lockdown put in place in France to control the pandemic of COVID-19. Without the help of unions or political groups—those traditional organizers of strikes—people from the countryside and from the suburbs gathered via Facebook to protest the rise of fuel taxes and more broadly to denounce the high cost of living. They wore the high-visibility vests required in cars in case of an accident; they occupied roundabouts and blocked roads; on Saturdays, they took to the (muddy) streets of cities, including Paris. In *Jojo, le Gilet jaune* (2019), writer and member of the French Academy Danièle Sallenave analyzes the protests as a "return of the social" that sheds light on inequality, precarity, and the lack of class mobility.[1] She mentions an official report from the Organization for Economic Co-Operation stating that the poor now need six generations to reach the middle class. The title of her short essay sounds derogatory, but her intent was to denounce the elite's contempt toward the movement by quoting one of Emmanuel Macron's disdainful remarks. As the President of France lamented, "Jojo in his yellow vest has the same status [in the media] as a minister or an MP!"[2] "Jojo" is a nickname (for Jonathan or José, for instance), but it also means "rascal" or "scallywag" in French. Conversely, as daughter of schoolteachers and granddaughter of artisans, farm laborers, and factory workers, Sallenave explains that the transclass trajectory of her family allows her to understand and empathize with the movement, to experience a certain "complicity" with its demands. Other parvenant writers have repeatedly voiced their support for the Gilets jaunes, as if their history and liminal social status give them a privileged access to the protesters, a way to get beyond the stereotypical and condescending account of the movement in the media.

One element kept coming back in the public interventions of transclass writers on the Gilets jaunes: the body. The column "Yellow, Green, Red, and Pink Vests—Unite!," published in *Libération* in December 2018 and signed among others by two writers—Annie Ernaux and Patrick Chamoiseau—insisted on the strenuousness of working-class jobs: "On a construction site, André's arm was crushed. René's two fingers were amputated by his machinery. Samia, a cashier, goes home at night with her back aching."[3] Interviewed on public radio, Ernaux said that even though the Gilets jaunes are not used to public speaking, they can vividly express their bodily sensations. She mentioned, for instance, the reaction of a worker facing the closure of his factory interviewed on the radio: "It makes my stomach hurt."[4] Édouard Louis published an essay in *Les Inrockuptibles* to support the movement and to identify with the protesters:

> It's hard for me to describe the shock I felt when I saw the first images of the *gilets jaunes*. In the photos accompanying the articles I saw bodies who almost never appear in the public and media space—suffering bodies ravaged by work, by fatigue, by hunger, by the permanent humiliation of the dominated by the dominant, by social and geographical exclusion. I saw tired bodies and tired hands, broken backs, and exhausted faces. The reason I was so overwhelmed was, of course, my loathing of the violence of the social world and of inequality. But also, and perhaps especially, it was because the bodies that I saw in the photos looked like my father's, my brother's, my aunts' ...[5]

Louis also lingers over these off-camera bodies in interviews, such as here in the *New Yorker*: "I recognized, suddenly, a *body*, in the noblest sense of the term. A body that I'm not used to seeing in the media. And I felt that these images were crying out to me. There was the emergence of the kind of body that we never see, and, along with it, the kinds of words that we never hear. [...] Maybe you have to really come from that world to immediately identify it. Actually, when

I started to write books, it was because I had the impression that these kinds of bodies were never depicted."[6] The Yellow Vests' bodies jolt the parvenant writer ("shock," "overwhelmed"). They bring him back to his origins and urge him to increase their visibility in literary prose.

The attention to the body can also be explained by the violence of some protesters and of the police. If the Gilets jaunes put working-class bodies in the spotlight, these bodies were severely put back in their place by the forces of order. The United Nations even asked France to investigate the use of excessive force during the Yellow Vests' marches.[7] Sophie Divry—a French writer who has published books on precarity and middle-class melancholy, including the noteworthy *La Condition pavillonnaire* in 2014, translated into English as *Madame Bovary of the Suburbs*—gathered the testimonies of five protesters who lost their right hand because of the sting-ball grenades used by the police. In *Cinq mains coupées* (2020; *Five Severed Hands*), she compiled and edited the men's sentences together like a "chorus," a re-membering of the lost body parts. In a separate afterword, she lists an astonishing number of wounds and mutilations: "Officially: 2,500 wounded, 12,000 arrested. 314 people afflicted with head injuries caused by a Flash-Ball, including 24 people who lost an eye, Madame Redouane killed after a tear gas grenade was thrown into her window and, of course, 5 severed hands."[8] Divry's book is surprising; along with Aurélien Delsaux and Denis Michelis, she had coauthored a manifesto against testimonial and historical literature in 2018, arguing that "to tell of our monstrous era, we need monstrous novels. Deformed novels."[9] *Cinq mains coupées* is not a novel, but according to Divry, the pressing historical events of the Yellow Vest marches and mutilations, as well as the necessity to put the protesters' words and bodies to the forefront, called for a polyphonic form of nonfictional testimony.

In addition to exhausted working-class bodies and mutilated demonstrators, the Yellow Vests movement also furthered the visibility of black bodies in France. Ernaux signed a column in *Libération* in favor of the Gilets noirs (Black Vests), a movement aimed at helping undocumented workers from Africa.[10] The Gilets jaunes and the "Truth for Adama Committee" also converged to denounce the death of Adama Traoré during his arrest by the police in 2016.[11] Among others,

Édouard Louis—"a writer from the yellow-vest world," according to fellow novelist Aurélien Bellanger—has been a vocal supporter of both movements.[12]

Since Ernaux and Louis focus on bodies when it comes to the Gilets jaunes, conversely, I want to question their portrayal of the cross-class body. On the opposite side of the political spectrum, American transclass writer J. D. Vance wrote in his memoir *Hillbilly Elegy* (2016), at times compared to Louis's *En finir avec Eddy Bellegueule* (2014; *Ending Eddy Bellegueule*), "I didn't know these things because I read something that someone else had written down. I knew these things because I saw them with my own two eyes and felt them in my bones."[13] On the contrary, contemporary French narratives of upward mobility are often silent on the modalities of the *trans*ition: what is the bodily knowledge of *transfuges*? How do they reconfigure their voice, accent, and gestures to "pass" from one class to another? How do fictions of upward mobility represent the apprenticeship of new postures? Are there any involuntary corporeal movements (Frantz Fanon would say "muscular spams") that could reveal their social origin despite the acquisition of new behaviors?[14] Where are the literary spasms of the *transfuge* and how does literature today depict a "transfleeing" body?

## Muscles on the Assembly Line

Parvenant writers and characters only seem to have a fathomable body when the social mobility in question is not upward but downward. Narratives of voluntary social demotion written in the wake of May 68 recount how a number of French intellectuals (especially Maoists) decided to work in factories in order to better understand the working class and create an uprising from within. The practice goes by the name of *établissement*, and these temporary workers were called *établis*. The many-faceted word designates a person and a workbench; it refers to the revolutionary practice of choosing a precarious employment *and* to people who have settled for good in a favorable social condition. The landmark example of the *établi* narrative is *L'Établi* (1978) written by Robert Linhart, a university professor of sociology who tells the story of his work experience in a car factory in the south of Paris. The car in question—the Citroën

2CV—becomes the symbol of his factory experience: the 2CV, that is to say the two steam horsepower of the machine, are also Linhart's two CVs as doctor of sociology and menial worker.

The body is a class marker in *L'Établi*. In the first pages of the text, the narrator keeps underlining essential corporeal differences between himself and professional laborers: "His gestures seem so natural! What do his hands possess, that mine lack? Why do his arms and his fingers know how to work, and mine do not? A car's bodywork: tin, blowtorch, palette strike, and, where the metallic curvature was cracked, there is now a perfectly smooth surface. Why does he know how to work and I do not?"[15] Hands are autonomous tools here, detached from the person who shapes their seeming natural movements. The sentence describing the work does not even have a subject, as if the body was not in the way of the employee's gestures. The task in question—smoothing a surface—aptly symbolizes how the worker's body has to disappear behind its function. Linhart progressively deconstructs his first impression: "I think: the intellectual's ineptitude for physical effort. Naivety. It's not only about physical effort. The first factory day is terrifying for everyone, many people will talk to me about it later, often with anxiety."[16] Even here, in this attempt at putting him and the workers on the same level so as to de-essentialize class, Linhart isolates his body: workers too are terrified on their first day, but not for physical reasons, he says. Impeded by his clumsiness, the narrator spends a good amount of time narrating his difficulties adapting to the rhythm of manual work: "However, the three thousand seven hundred and fifty daily button pushes made the blood rush to my thumb, and, in the evening, my hand felt so heavy and swollen than it took me a good hour after the end of work to regain more or less normal usage."[17] The adaptation is slow and uncertain. Bodily skills have to be twice acquired: the hand—a tool that can build and write—has to adapt to the repetition of the same gesture *and* to the return to normal. In the end, Linhart finds some commonality with the workers through a parallel between work and word: "[Mouloud] speaks like he works: with precision and regularity. No superfluous gestures. No superfluous words."[18] If Linhart's body never adapts to the assembly line, his way of assembling words can at least near the rhythm, precision, and economy of blue collar work, as in the subjectless sentence previously quoted: "A car's bodywork: tin, blowtorch, palette strike, and, where the metallic curvature was cracked, there is now a perfectly smooth surface."

Like Linhart, Leslie Kaplan was a graduate and 1968 *établie*, first in a crispbread factory in the suburbs of Paris, then in a washing machine factory in Lyon. In the prose poem *L'Excès-l'usine* (1982; *The Excess-The Factory*), she, too, describes her bodily disintegration: "We [*On*] are inside, in the great factory universe, the one that breathes for you."[19] The use of the subject pronoun *on*, here as everywhere in the text, melds her subjectivity with that of the professional workers. The all-encompassing factory supplements a semi-automatic function of the body: breathing.

Claire Etcherelli's 1967 factory novel *Élise, ou la vraie vie* (*Élise, or Real Life*), set during the Algerian War of Independence, also lingers on the body and its fitness on the assembly line: "The muscles, at first refractory, now obeyed, but if an unexpected movement changed the mechanical sequence, they squealed like old pulleys. The good worker is the one who controls his movements and does not make any unnecessary ones."[20] The body of the good worker is neither muscle nor machine, neither moody nor creaky, but a set of precise gestures and postures, especially since the sentence does not start with "my" but with the general "the muscles." The opposite movement—not entering but leaving the factory—is more uncertain in *Élise, ou la vraie vie*: "One day, this will be real life, [*on*] we will do everything we want to do. [...] Lucien affirmed. Yes, [*nous*] we would achieve our dreams, we would join those who trembled like us. Our spirits had already stirred, our bodies would soon follow."[21] The passage from future to conditional, and from *on* to *nous*, reduces the probability of the escape. Workers stir and tread water without going forward, in transit between two bodily functions, between two apprenticeships, between a mind that has already started to move and a body that has more trouble getting out of the factory.

## A Transclass Malaise

The working-class relatives depicted by socially mobile writers do have a body as well. To support this remark, I will take three examples (Éribon, Louis, Ernaux) and gather three different forms of discourses (essay, interview, narrative) in order to signal how contemporary texts on social mobility call for a multigeneric approach, especially because parvenant authors weave declarative discourses, often sociological, within literary prose. In *Retours à Reims* (2009; *Return to Reims*) Didier Éribon compares his childhood to Raymond Aron's and concludes, "You feel in your flesh a sense of class belonging when you're the child of a worker."[22] In a 2016 interview Édouard Louis explained that his social mobility allowed him to dodge a certain use of the body: "The lack of love saved my life. If not for that, it would have been much more painful, because I wouldn't have tried to flee. I would have either had hands destroyed behind the supermarket cash register or a back destroyed in the factory or sweeping the streets."[23] In this interview as in his books, Louis hammers home the argument that working-class bodies are the direct victims of public policies—cuts in welfare benefits can hamper the access to food and health care—while the body of well-off citizens are not as affected by the political choices of the state. When Annie Ernaux looks at pictures of her working-class father in *La Place* (1983; *The Place*), she sees his body first: "Just the clear signs of time, a bit of belly, black hair thinning at the temples, and those, more discreet, of social status, those arms protruding from the body, the bathroom and the laundry room that a petty bourgeois eye would not have chosen as the background for the photo."[24] The body and its surroundings are one and the same. Ernaux also remembers her father through the gestures of others: "It was in the way people sit and get bored in waiting rooms, shout at their children, do their goodbyes on train platforms that I sought the figure of my father."[25] The father's social body is not static or photographic but a set of interchangeable gestures. By contrast, the body of Ernaux's bourgeois husband in *La Place* clashes with that of his in-laws: "My husband arrived in the evening, tanned, embarrassed by a loss that was not his own. More than ever, he seemed out of place here."[26] She underlines the class gap by juxtaposing "embarrassed" with "tanned," an adjective whose incongruity during a wake and in the context of Ernaux's family (neither farmers working in the fields nor beachgoers) is accentuated by its isolation between commas.

We have seen that the *établis* and the members of the working class have a body, however ill-adapted or aching, in literature. What about the body of parvenants themselves? Is there such thing as a corporeal bildungsroman? I perceive a malaise when it comes to these questions throughout my corpus of transclass texts. In a short 2008 article for the newspaper *Libération*, Christine Angot explained that for her, social class had nothing to do with the body: "But the feeling of class, which is nevertheless independent of our will, like every other feeling, is purely cerebral, physically we feel nothing, or very little, small twinges that translated into annoyances so unproductive that we cannot speak of them seriously."[27] First of all, the antonym to "physical" inserted here, "cerebral," directly refers to the brain and is thus more bodily incarnated than adjectives like "mental" or "psychological." Second of all, despite this statement, Angot will continue listing these "very little things" or "twinges" in the rest of her article: "a way of positioning the shoulders," "the span of a step," "a way of going down the stairs," "how you carry your head." She concludes: "Personally, I preferred to tear myself away from the feeling of class. [...] Socially my pedigree branched off in too many directions, [...] it always came down to sideways glances." The author cannot miss that her vocabulary is bodily, from "tear ... away" to the "sideways glances." The strong heterogeneity between what Angot claims and how she peppers her argumentation with bodily examples pertains to what I call the "trance" of the transclass; a certain unrest and unease when it comes to describing the transient body of those who change milieus. Similarly, in *Retour à Reims*, Didier Éribon felt "an awkwardness difficult to discern and describe" and a "malaise produced by the belonging to two different worlds" that "crops up into consciousness."[28] Every time he starts describing the body, though, the narration quickly returns to the central concern of his memoir: the acquisition of new cultural references.[29] Pierre Bourdieu—one of Éribon's mentors—experienced "a terrible unease, tied more to a feeling of blunder than of transgression," when he gave his inaugural lecture at the Collège de France.[30] Éribon reproaches Bourdieu for having silenced the steps of his social metamorphosis, but one could make the same remark about Éribon and his parvenant peers who insist on their social and cultural transformation, rarely on the body itself. If Bourdieu said that "*sociologists always forget that social agents have a body*," I would argue that sociological literature often forgets that transclass characters have to touch up their bodies and behave differently.[31]

In Marie NDiaye's novel *Ladivine* (2013), the narrator's upward mobility is ratified by a change of first name from Malinka to Clarisse. Critic Thangam Ravindranathan shows how "examples abound, particularly in the first pages of the novel, of sentences featuring both 'Malinka' and 'Clarisse Rivière,' as if the very (all-consuming) task of language had become to keep these apart: 'Of Clarisse Rivière, Malinka's mother knew nothing.'"[32] *Ladivine* opens with the description of a diffuse bodily discomfort when the young protagonist, who escaped her class or origin, returns home to visit her mother, a cleaner:

> Seated on the train, eyes riveted to the window, to the specks and small scratches on the glass that her gaze did not see past, so that she would have had a hard time describing the landscape that she'd been flitting through in one direction in the morning, in the other at night once a month for years and years, she trembled with dread imagining herself having to compose a judicious attitude in the event that someone called her Malinka.
>
> Then her thoughts drifted, little by little she forgot the motive for her trembling even though the trembling persisted and she didn't know how to make it stop and she ended up vaguely attributing it to the movement of the train which chanted under her feet, in her muscles, in her tired head, the name that she loved and loathed, that inspired fear and compassion in her at the same time, Malinka, Malinka, Malinka.[33]

The name change results in a corporeal anxiety. Brought back to her dual social status, Clarisse/Malinka fears being unmasked. The uninterrupted shaking anticipates the possibility of having to code-switch and to compose an attitude that would fit with her original social class. But the narrative veers off from explicitly locating the movement within Clarisse's body. "Her trembling" becomes "the trembling," that of the body or the train. The narrator first attributes the shiver to the machine, then she displaces it: the shaking is felt "under her feet"; then briefly internalized "in her muscles"; then it occurs in an imprecise space, half-literal, half-figurative, "her tired head." It is finally transformed into a rhythm, a scansion, with the ternary repetition of Malinka on the page. The prose, the birth name, and the return train share the same sounds and rhythm; they provoke a comparable shaking when the protagonist crosses social spaces.

The distance between Malinka and Ladivine is also racial: the daughter passes as white and renames herself Clarisse, a name that means "bright," so as to underline her fair skin. The mother, Ladivine, is black, but this information—mentioned only rapidly fifty pages after the beginning of the text—is delayed by the author to cast doubt on the daughter's skin color. NDiaye found another literary strategy to complicate the parvenant body by having race supplant class in *Ladivine*:

> In the region where Malinka's mother was born, where Clarisse Rivière had never gone and would never go though she had furtively, with a sensation of deep malaise, looked at a few images of it on the internet, everyone had the same features [...].
> And that her mother had thus inherited the physical characteristics from all the progeny, then had passed them on to her daughter (the features, the arms, the length of the silhouette and, thank God, that was all) had once dazed Clarisse Rivière with anger, for how to escape permanently if you were thus marked, how to claim not to be what you didn't want to be, what you in fact had every right to not want to be?[34]

The shaking has become a more acute malaise or dizziness. NDiaye multiplies the periphrases to circumvent the narrator's inherited blackness: "that was all" implicitly refers to the mother's skin color; the region she never went to is never named, but readers can recognize West African landscapes. Malinka does not fashion her working-class body but the color of her skin: "At fifteen years old, Malinka accentuated the natural pallor of her face with light makeup."[35] The class promotion and legacy at the core of *Ladivine*'s plot is expressed through whiteness. The distance between Malinka Sylla and Clarisse Rivière is diverted from social mobility to racial passing. Such a deflection resembles the trajectory of the word *race* itself: it used to refer not to skin color and ethnicity but to family, lineage, and blue-blooded aristocracy. In her attempt at self-fashioning, NDiaye's compartmentalizing character concentrates on her most visible heritage (her name, her features), thus suggesting that class alone is not passed on as easily through the body.

Ernaux too deflects the bodily apprenticeship of the social climber from class to something else in her first novel *Les Armoires vides* (1974; *The Empty Cupboards*); sex and gender to be precise:

The window display of new arrivals, an unexpected mirror, and I see myself, hair disheveled, smile wide, mouth vicious, almost *mauvais genre*. The other girls have a certain grace, an ease in their bodies and movements, they laugh, run, and rise to answer questions, without thinking about it. My body is always cumbersome, before the eyes of these girls, like someone disabled learning to walk again, haunted by a fall, a misstep. I thought I was nothing like my parents, naturally I walked like my mother and I put my hand in front of my mouth when I laughed like the neighborhood girls. I tugged sharply on my skirt to free it from the chair. At home, I moved without thinking, as soon as I am through the door, outside, I curse my manners but I don't know how to act. [...] And yet, I feel that I possess a hidden grace, a paralyzed dance rhythm, the heroine of novels ready to live...

One day, at last, a boy from school said about me, "she's so relaxed, that girl," which pleased me a hundred times more than a 20 out of 20 in math. Relaxed, no one says that about hicks [...]. It had taken me nearly two years to attain this glory, to be relaxed like the other girls, to swing my briefcase at the end of my arms, to speak the schoolkid slang, to know The Platters, Paul Anka, and Albinoni's Adagio. The rest would surely soon follow, a "flirt" that would take me completely out of myself and my milieu.[36]

Social mobility constrains the narrator (Denise Lesur alias Annie Ernaux) to be aware of the features of her face and of a body she cannot use naturally without thinking about it, whether it is to laugh, run, rise, walk, tug, or swing. The body has to molt under social pressure, but it leaves behind more than just a skin: it is too much, like a surplus. A boyfriend would help the narrator "get out" of herself. The last enumeration levels the body with other markers of class mobility: vocabulary and knowledge. The details of the modifications are silenced; it is time and a hypothetically forthcoming "flirt"—in English and between quotation marks in the French—that will crown her performance. Bodily changes are not under the narrator's control: the clumsiness is attributed to a temporary disability and to the influence of her mother and neighborhood, while the success lies in the hidden (and innate) talent of dancing. The setting of Ernaux's realization is important too: the door symbolizes the social threshold of the emancipated parvenant. As for the shopping window where she glimpses her reflection, it enacts the transition from the parents' little grocery store to the city's megastores. In Ernaux's *Les Armoires vides*, as in NDiaye's *Ladivine*, gender, sexuality, and race override class when it comes to describing a body that endeavors to climb the social ladder.[37]

Successful or not, the transformation is uncomfortable for Ernaux's protagonist: "Books turn my stomach. I play student, I take notes, I try to listen, I am in transit."[38] The transition of parvenants has a physical consequence: it leads NDiaye's Malinka to a disturbing malaise and Ernaux's Denise to nausea, which means that the incorporated knowledge has difficulties staying in. The transclass are at risk of transplant rejection: "It was all fake, a system of passwords to enter into another milieu. It didn't stay in the body."[39] The last sentence could also be translated as "it didn't stick to the ribs." Using fancy vocabulary words as "passwords" (words to pass in the upper class) creates a dissonance with her body. *Les Armoires vides* alternates chapters on two experiences: social mobility and backstreet abortion, which explains the repeated description of a nausea and a foreign body. Two chiasmatic trajectories merge here: on the one hand, Ernaux wants the fetus to leave her body; on the other hand, she would like to incorporate new knowledge (vocabulary) and practices (reading), but they do not stick to her ribs either.

*Les Armoires vides* (Ernaux's first published text) is a novel. Her 2000 autobiographical narrative, *L'Événement* (*The Event*), will link abortion and social mobility more explicitly:

> I was confusedly establishing a link between my social class of origin and what was happening to me. The first to pursue higher education in a family of workers and shopkeepers, I had escaped the factory and the register. But neither my high school nor my college literature degree had managed to divert the inevitability of the transmission of a certain kind of poverty that the pregnant girl, like the alcoholic, was emblematic of. My ass has caught up with me and what was growing in me was, in a way, social failure.[40]

However elliptic, "what was growing in [her]" could be both the fetus and the return of what she strived to avoid: a working-class body, a productive and reproductive body. By inserting the word *ass*, Ernaux turns sex into a bodily feature, more susceptible to being inherited than sex understood as a bodily practice. She thought a flirt would "take her out of herself," but instead it put something "inside" her body and brought her back to one of the archetypes of her working-class neighborhood: the "fille-mère" (the unwed mother, literally the "girl-mother"). Ernaux thereby formulates a certain form of determinism: she was spared a difficult usage of the body at work, but the pregnancy and the painful backstreet abortion compensate for this infraction to social reproduction. In French, "to get pregnant" is literally to "fall pregnant" (*tomber enceinte*), as if the event were a tumble, a demotion. Biological reproduction is a tipping point in Ernaux's biography, halfway between emancipation and return. It also puts her studies at risk, as the abortion prevents her from working on her thesis: "I had stopped being 'intellectual.' [...] (I still often feel that I do not go far enough in my exploration of things, as if I were held back by something very ancient, tied to the world of manual laborers I come from that feared 'the racking of the brain,' or to my body, to that memory in my body.)"[41] Again here, the memory of the working-class body is a diffuse "something" that resists the "racking" of the brain.

As we will see in chapter 6, the train is a powerful metaphor of class mobility, especially in the works of Ernaux. In *Les Armoires vides*, abortion endangers her upward mobility and could cause the derailment of the narrator's "social train": "The black mare, she derailed, lying there, belly in the air, awaiting the contractions to vomit up guts and entrails."[42] By repeating the subjects, by writing "the black mare, she derailed" instead of "the black mare derailed," Ernaux creates a distance between the animal and the machine. But as in the episode of Cinderella's pumpkin coach, the train is always at risk of becoming a horse again. The abortion provokes a derailment of Ernaux's social trajectory that, as a result, makes the messy body reappear (belly, guts, entrails). The unwanted and mysterious pregnancy in Marie NDiaye's *Mon cœur à l'étroit* (2007; *My Heart Hemmed In*) partakes in a similar logic. Transclass protagonist Nadia did everything she could to leave her social milieu behind and erase all bodily traces of her education (traits, diction, postures).[43] But she is brought back to her past and Maghrebi descent first through the name of her granddaughter, Souhar. Then she gives birth to a fuzzy creature she has difficulty describing but whose main characteristic is to be "black."[44] Here's the moral of this fantastical story: chase class out the door, and race will come back through the window.

In her contribution to a volume on Pierre Bourdieu edited by Édouard Louis, Annie Ernaux relies on *La Distinction* (1979; *The Distinction*) to formulate the bodily consequences of her mobility: "The habitus is the embodied relationship to class [...]. Turmoil, unease, awareness appear when there is dissonance between the habitus and the field, when, for example, bourgeois city-dwellers find themselves at a table of peasants, or a student from a working-class background is by chance invited to a bourgeois soirée."[45] According to Bourdieu, the habitus is a set of conditionings, perceptions, judgments, and behaviors so typical of one's social group and acquired so early on that they appear innate.[46] When the corporeal habitus (or *hexis*) changes, parvenants are "uncomfortable in their place and also, as they say, 'in their skin.'"[47] Their "split habitus" generates a malaise, that is, "(a feeling of) vague, non-specific physical discomfort."[48] The French definition also mentions confusion, anxiety, and a loss of consciousness. The disorder is hard to locate, physically and temporally. It lingers when the working-class student takes a seat for good at the table of the bourgeoisie.

Forty years after *Les Armoires vides*, in *Mémoire de fille* (2016; *Girl's Memory*), Ernaux will come back to the necessary steps of her bodily transformation, but the list will again veer from class to gender:

> It was an absolute project for perfection with goals recorded in my lost diary and that I can reproduce all the more easily because they were all put into practice. Targets:
> bodily transformations: lose weight, become as blonde as the blonde from S
> intellectual progress: [...]
> the acquisition of knowledge intended to make up for my social backwardness and my ignorance—learn to swim, to dance [...]
> In reviewing the months of the one who is no longer the girl from S but the girl from Ernemont, I risked stumbling continuously, like a historian with a character, over the jumble of factors affecting my behavior at any given moment—of having to question the chronological order of these factors—and thus the order of my narrative.[49]

The program is intellectual, corporeal, and social. There is a great generic hybridity at play here to recover the body: within an autobiographical narrative, the narrator portrays herself as a historian looking for a character while referring to a diary. The profusion of tools and genres in Ernaux's archival research allows her to access a transformation that was twice erased: the diary has disappeared, and the body molted. After this excerpt, the adjustment or improvement becomes "an envisaged conversion of the entire being, physical, intellectual, and social."[50] If the author claims an entanglement of factors, the conclusion of this section and the title itself (*Mémoire de fille*) irrevocably deflect the "social ignorance" and the "social conversion" toward gender: "It is a different shame from that of being the daughter of grocers-café owners. [...] It's a girl's shame."[51] At the beginning of *Mémoire de fille*, Ernaux remembers a pun on her first name: "Annie what does your body say [*Annie qu'est-ce que ton corps dit*]?"[52] Annie Cordy ("corps dit") was a famous Belgian actress and singer, known for her popular and festive songs. Ernaux's "body says" that the main factor of bodily transformation is gender. Or rather, inscribing upward mobility within a text dilutes and erases the prevalence of the class factor. Through weaving together social mobility and abortion, and the metaphors it engenders, Ernaux tells us that despite the social climber's effort at changing voluntarily, embodiment causes a problem, a conundrum: it tends toward (biological and social) reproduction. The transclass malaise (in Ernaux as in NDiaye) points to the unwanted essentialism at play in upward mobility and to the ways in which the "classed" body—clouded by other identities—slips through the writer's fingers.

Here lies the main difference between Ernaux and Linhart, to whom she refers explicitly in her diary *L'Atelier noir* (2011; *The Dark Workshop*): "The other pitfall is life, life itself, the document of it. I've never done it. Like *L'Établi*. We need another kind of writing, one that calls things into question."[53] Linhart was able to describe his downwardly mobile body in detail as it adapted to the factory; on the contrary, Ernaux's literary forms complicate the access to the bodily archive of her social trajectory. Unlike their family or the *établis*, parvenants no longer have to endure the hardship of physical labor; they access the "life" described above through "writing." The working body gives way to mental activities that, although they certainly do occur in a body (the brain, the nervous system), do not generate the same sensations or the same fatigue of muscles and joints. The social ponderousness of bodies detected by Ernaux in the specific case of her (fated) pregnancy becomes at odds with this unmooring of class mobility, with the elevation of the mind away from worldly considerations. Socially mobile authors, in an attempt at climbing the ladder, thus seem promptly to free themselves from their most immediate environment—their body. Contra Bourdieu's emphasis on corporeal inertia, literature can at first give the illusion that you can extricate yourself from the embodiment of class. But by taking a closer look, we could also come to the conclusion that social class is an unretrievable black box and that you can only attempt to modify it tangentially, through other forms of embodied subjectivities, such as gender and race.

## Being and Becoming

What does Eddy's body say? Do his youth and narratives of departure, not of return like those of Ernaux and Éribon, have an influence on the perception of his body? How does he couple class with questions of gender normativity and sexual orientation? The narrator of *En finir avec Eddy Bellegueule* deconstructs behaviors or judgments deemed innate and unavoidable, especially when it comes to health issues: "The dentist was too expensive and the lack of money always ended up turning into a choice."[54] Louis's community cannot afford to care about this part of their bodies, so they decide that dental hygiene does not matter. The same pattern—what sociologist Luc Boltanski called the "somatic culture" of a social group—is at play when Louis discusses the aching working body: "My mother who would say (also) *The back problems that run in the family, they're genetic and then with the factory it's hard* without realizing that these problems were not the cause, but the consequence of the debilitating nature of factory work."[55] At each and every turn, Louis shows how his family—unable to act on their bodies by paying the dentist or choosing a less arduous job—reverses causality to turn a constraint into a choice, thereby masking the direct influence of class and labor. Louis himself oscillates between innate and acquired when he describes working-class children: "these bodies, already marked by their social class, revealing already, beneath a child's fair, milky skin, the adult musculature to come, developed through helping fathers to chop and store wood, through physical activity."[56] There is a tension in this sentence between the two adverbs *already* and the acknowledgment that bodies are being *developed* by physical activity.

Contrary to his relatives, Louis decides to act on his body, not to change his social manners but to teach himself to desire differently. He notably forces himself to kiss a girl: "I felt desire: a desire that was manifesting physically, impossible to imitate [...]. I saw it as the completion of my project: my body had bowed before my desire. We don't stop playing roles but there is a truth to masks. [...] I told myself that perhaps the body transformed suddenly, perhaps my body suddenly had become that of a brute, like that of my brothers."[57] The possibility of changing one's body is considered only as a sudden metamorphosis (the adverb *suddenly* is repeated twice), which sheds doubts on the possibility of an apprenticeship, be it sexual or social. The modification is as swift as it is temporary, since the narrator will not be able to reproduce such desire: "I wanted, I ordered myself to reach orgasm all while knowing, for I knew very early on, very young, and I could even say that I had always known, that never had the contrary even crossed my mind, that it was the sight of a man's body that stirred me."[58] The realization that it will be impossible to modify the body's inclination is visible in the very structure of the sentence. Before saying what he knows, Louis uses successive and retrospective rectifications to show that this corporeal knowledge was already there, "for I knew." As an assiduous reader of Bourdieu, Louis is aware that the body is a "social product," but that doesn't mean one can easily control it: "The body [...] is, of all the manifestations of the 'person,' the one that is the *least easily* modified, temporarily or even less so definitively, and, at the same time, the one that is *socially relied upon* to signify the most adequately—because it is outside of any signifying intention—the 'essence,' the 'nature' of the 'person.'"[59] Louis's literary attempt at denaturalizing himself—which, in this context, paradoxically, means disciplining the body into being straight and normatively masculine—falters over the same roadblock: the body.

Like Ernaux, Louis portrays the aching bodies of his working-class parents, but instead of addressing class frontally, he deflects the social considerations on, and possible modifications of, his classed body toward sexuality. The most troubling element of *En finir avec Eddy Bellegueule* is the equivalence between bourgeoisie and homosexuality. In the chapter titled "Manners" for instance, Louis plays on the double meaning of the term: to have good manners and to be mannered. The text opens with a bodily diagnosis: "It seems that I was born this way, no one ever understood the origin, the genesis, where that unknown force came from, that had taken hold of me at birth, that made me a prisoner of my own body. When I started to express myself, to learn language, my voice spontaneously took on feminine intonations. [...] Each time I spoke my hands would twitch frenetically, in every direction, contort, stir the air. [...] [My parents] thought that I had chosen to be effeminate."[60] The intersectionality at play in *En finir avec Eddy Bellegueule* complicates Louis's discussion about the classed body because the narrator has to combine multiple innate and acquired experiences: gender expression, sexual desire, and social habitus. Gradually, gender and sexuality are mixed with social class, especially when Eddy arrives at a more affluent high school:

> Here the boys kiss to say hello, they don't shake hands
> They carry leather bags
> They have delicate manners
> All of them would have been called *fags* in middle school
> The bourgeois don't use their bodies in the same way
> [...]
> (this will be much more visible at the École normale, those feminine bodies of the intellectual bourgeoisie)
> And I say to myself when I see them, at first
> I say to myself
> But what a bunch of faggots
>
> And also the relief
> *I may not be a fag, not like I thought,*
> *maybe I've always had a bourgeois body trapped in the world of my childhood.*[61]

The trajectory from one social group to another creates a dissonance, visible in the format of this final chapter: the italics and the line breaks register social mobility by turning trivial prose into noble poetry. The blanks allow the narrator to refine the causality from one sentence to the next. The last interpellation coming from Louis's classmates is ambiguous: "*So, Eddy, still a fag?*"[62] The remark makes Louis laugh, and can be a way to show that after having been bullied in middle school, the new high school will banalize the narrator's sexuality. But the joke can also be a question asked in earnest: is Eddy still homosexual now that he lives in an environment where straight men have effeminate bodies? Has he lost his sexual identity in favor of a social one? The narrator learns to flee his milieu, but he does not redo his body.[63] The form and wording of this first novel lead readers to think he was born bourgeois; that he had from birth what Bourdieu called a "connaissance par corps" or "bodily knowledge" of the bourgeoisie; that his body spontaneously developed the manners that society indexes as homosexual and upper class.[64] In this context, to change class amounts to putting the body—a remnant of determinism—in the right place.

With such a deterministic framework, Louis seems to be rewriting a popular 1988 comedy, Étienne Chatiliez's *La Vie est un long fleuve tranquille* (*Life Is a Long Quiet River*), especially since the film is set in the north of France, a one-hour drive west of Louis's hometown. The two large and stereotypical families—the precarious but joyous Groseille on welfare, and the bourgeois and practicing catholic Le Quesnoy—are told that two of their children were swapped at birth.[65] The exchange is visible on-screen even before the revelation: Maurice Groseille has the same shoulder tic as his father and siblings and is the smartest teenager in the family; conversely, Bernadette Le Quesnoy starts acting out by wearing conspicuous makeup and dressing like the Groseille women. Beyond the classist stereotype of lazy and lecherous poor versus the quiet and educated rich, the film essentializes class: the body can't avoid acting like its parents, even when separated at birth. Even more so than in Louis's novel, the bourgeois body is hereditary: Maurice has an unavoidable bodily tic, while Bernadette's heredity pertains to the surface, that is to say the accessories (pantyhose, eyeshadow) she puts on her body. Unlike Bernadette, Maurice becomes a parvenant, torn between families and loyalties. He is also remarkably quick at adapting his behavior to fit in his new social group. Like Rastignac, he is well born (the meaning of the first name "Eugène") but in the wrong family; "born in the wrong *class*," like Goethe's Wilhelm Meister.[66] Such an accelerated plotline reactivates the instantaneous upward mobility at play in nineteenth-century bildungsromane. In *L'Éducation sentimentale* (1869; *The Sentimental Education*) for instance, Frédéric Moreau is "Ruined, stripped, lost!" but then, less than ten pages later, "He was inheriting!" from his uncle.[67] Franco Moretti underlines a similar use of speed in *Illusions perdues* (1837–43; *Lost Illusions*): "The goals of a culture of social mobility may be vague, but one thing is not vague at all, they must be achieved quickly. An evening at the theater, an article, and Lucien *est parvenu*, he has 'made it.'"[68] Louis taps into these literary and cinematic archetypes through the body.

There is a striking difference between Louis's first two novels and his interviews, where the questions are often more political than literary. In public appearances, the writer confesses that the body of a social climber needs to change in order to fit into a different class. For instance, during a 2016 festival organized by the newspaper *Le Monde*, Édouard Louis stated, "What happened after *Eddy* was primarily a revolt through the body. When I left the place where I grew up, I spent days training myself to laugh in front of a mirror. Because I realized that I had the same laugh as my father, as my family, as my past."[69] Such an anecdote is at odds with *En finir avec Eddy Bellegueule*. The details of the bodily apprenticeship are left out in the writing of Louis's best-selling bildungsroman, as if the plot of upward mobility were tearing apart the novel: saying the body is innate inside, acquired outside. Louis's first novel ends before the narrator arrives in Paris, so we do not have access to the last stages of his physical and social transformation announced in the epilogue: "(this will be much more visible at the École normale, those feminine bodies of the intellectual bourgeoisie)."[70] This experience is expelled from the narrative and concealed between parentheses. We could read this absence and the tension between novel and interview the way Louis interprets his mother's discourses:

> It took me years to understand that her discourse was not incoherent or contradictory but that it was me, with a sort of *transfuge* arrogance, who was trying to impose a different coherence on her, one more compatible with my values [...]. That a multitude of dis-

courses ran through her, that these discourses spoke through her, that she was constantly torn between the shame at not having gone to school and the pride at nevertheless, as she used to say, *having gotten out and having had beautiful children*, that these two discourses only existed in relation to each other.[71]

Louis reproduces the contradiction not within a passionate speech (or *tirade*) but in two different forms of discourse: in interviews as well as in the first autobiographical narratives he insists on calling novels.

As readers of bildungsromane, we are trained to expect scenes and reflections on the social climber's clumsiness. We remember how Julien Sorel in *Le Rouge et le Noir* (1830; *The Red and the Black*) or Georges Duroy in *Bel-Ami* (1885) had difficulties with their bodies: "I still see provincial habits in you sometimes, you should get rid of them"; "He felt embarrassed once again, afraid of committing some error in the conventional handling of the fork, of the spoon or the glasses."[72] The tension between acquired and innate, between fiction and nonfiction, is the consequence of Édouard Louis telling his own story in the first person without having recourse to an omniscient narrator. His novels are as autobiographical as his interviews. For this reason, the story of this parvenant author is no longer contained within a single format. Especially when it comes to the body and its metamorphosis, readers can only get a full view of the writer's social and corporeal trajectory by reading his fiction and nonfiction. Sociologist Jules Naudet—who writes extensively on class migration—argues that social climbers use narratives to replace the "instability and discontinuity" of their trajectory with "coherence" and "resolution."[73] The transclass and transgeneric body (*and body of the text*) of Louis does not pertain to this strategy. Louis's first two novels contradict his interviews and are themselves interspersed with contradictions.[74] This is how an author formalizes the tensions at the core of an experience of class mobility.

In 2021 Louis published his fifth book, *Changer: Méthode* (*Change: Method*), the narrative of what he calls his social "odyssey."[75] The text recounts, point by point, the bodily metamorphoses he experienced in order to change classes and make it in Paris: "At just over twenty years old I had changed my surname in court, changed my first name, transformed my face, redesigned the structure of my hair growth pattern, undergone several operations, reinvented my way of moving, of walking, of speaking, eradicated the northern accent of my childhood."[76] Unlike *En finir avec Eddy Bellegueule*, this text is not subtitled "A Novel." It seems that Louis first had to publish novels that silenced his corporeal changes, then interviews in which he narrated them at length, before being able to couch his social molt in a nonfictional book. Franco Moretti observed a similar phenomenon—formulated as a question—in nineteenth-century fiction: "Neither Stendhal nor Pushkin therefore narrate the transition from youthful illusions to adult realism. Could it be that the theme of maturation has moved from the story to discourse?"[77] The displacement of Louis's body from fiction to nonfiction follows in these footsteps. His publication trajectory reinforces my argument that parvenants go through a generic and bodily transclass trance, that they need a tension between forms of discourses in and out of a published text to be able to fathom the contours of a classed body in transit.

The relationship between Ernaux's novels and essays is worth examining, too. I have already mentioned the episode in *La Place* where she detects the signs of her father's social condition by describing his body in a photograph. The setting of the picture reinforces the symbol: the father is building a ferry that will travel back and forth from one bank of the Seine River to another, as from one social class to another. Ernaux comes back to this image in an essay on Bourdieu: "In *La Place*, I talked about all that, without analyzing—an intentional writing choice—the turmoil that took over me. Brutally a reality that I knew, but only abstractly, *took shape* with the photo in the literal sense of the term: my father had for a long time, half of his life in fact, been a worker, subjected to hard labor, to the cold, to taking orders."[78] The body generates a "turmoil" here, and later "a kind of shock, a brutal coagulation of every experience."[79] Ernaux considers these feelings as the "preuve par corps" or "bodily proof" of the accuracy of Bourdieu's theory.[80]

Like Louis, her embodied reactions "take shape" outside of her literary prose; their relegation to the context of an essay is an "intentional writing choice." Ernaux even changes her mind about the nature of her writing in this text: "detached (rather than flat) writing," an adjective that involves the body more concretely. At the end of the article, she extends the metaphor to describe herself as a writer literally "stretched between two social worlds."[81] One format is not enough to render the corporeal reaction to social estrangement, to connect ascent and sensations. Genres can in turn affect the writer's body: Ernaux experienced "a feeling of disgust" when she started writing a novel about her father, which made her realize that nonfiction would be a more appropriate format.[82]

Parvenant writers are torn between birth and becoming, which explains why some of them rewrite as their own Simone de Beauvoir's landmark motto, *On ne naît pas femme, on le devient*, often translated into English as "One is not born, but rather becomes, a woman," although a more syntactically accurate translation would be "You are not born a woman, you become one." About forty years after the publication of *Le Deuxième Sexe* (1949; *The Second Sex*), Linhart rewrites the slogan in *L'Établi* as follows: *Personne ne naît O.S.; on le devient* (Nobody is born a skilled worker; you become one).[83] Linhart broke Beauvoir's parallelism: he did not write *On ne naît pas OS, on le devient* but substituted *personne* for the first *on* and added a semicolon between the two clauses. The birth and the becoming are uncoupled; they do not concern the same individual when it comes to working in a factory. Linhart finally succeeds, through rhetoric, in de-essentializing the social fate of laborers since anybody (*on*), that is to say the working class and the "établis" alike, have to adapt to the assembly line. Édouard Louis's rewrite is different: "I wasn't born different, I became different."[84] He restores Beauvoir's parallelism, but with the pronoun *I* and the context of an interview, he does not aim at stating a case in general but just his own. By changing the tenses and using two verbs in the past, he signals that the becoming is over. He has arrived. French writer, theorist, and activist Monique Wittig, who considered women as a social class, famously rewrote Beauvoir's statement, too, as the title of one of her essays, published in 1980: "On ne naît pas femme" ("One Is Not Born a Woman"). The motto is truncated because no one has to become a woman.[85]

Essentialism is key for feminist as for class identities.[86] In this chapter I have tracked the literary and social versions of this concept by examining the way upwardly and downwardly mobile authors narrate their corporeal journey, in an attempt at uncovering moments, flashes, when the parvenant does not fully make it but instead ends up living her life (and writing) on the ladder. The next chapter will expand on this liminality through the character of the maid, whose (interchangeable) body at work, wavering between social groups and between person and protagonist, embodies a peculiar form of class mobility. It is through the body—of parvenants, of maids—that we will transition from setting (chaps. 1–3) to movement (chaps. 4–6), before broaching the topic of social immobility in the final chapter (chap. 7).

# Self-Maid? 4

## THE SOCIAL MOBILITY OF LITERARY AND CINEMATIC SERVANTS

What do Leïla Slimani's novel *Chanson douce* and Bong Joon-Ho's film *Parasite* have in common? They were both released in the 2010s, won French awards, had record-breaking audiences in France, and a plot centered on domestic servants. Franco-Moroccan writer Leïla Slimani won the Goncourt prize in 2016 for *The Perfect Nanny* (also translated as *Lullaby* for the UK), a novel on class, care, and motherhood. On the first page, readers are told that the sitter will eventually kill the two children under her supervision, and the rest of the novel unpacks the tragedy. It contrasts a boho couple, Myriam and Paul, with a precarious nanny, Louise. It explores the tenuous frontier between paid caregiver and extended family member. And it tackles questions of race and labor, as the Franco-Moroccan mother refuses to hire a North African employee in order to avoid "immigrant solidarity."[1] *Chanson douce* sold more than one million copies, was translated into forty or so languages, was adapted into a film, and is considered one of the best-selling Goncourt prizes in recent years as well as one of the *New York Times* ten best books of 2018. Slimani has become an international public figure and commentator, especially after she published an essay on sexuality in Morocco, *Sexe et Mensonges* (2017; *Sex and Lies*). In 2017 she was hired by Emmanuel Macron to be his personal representative at the International Organization of La Francophonie.

South Korean filmmaker Bong Joon-Ho won the French Palme d'Or at Cannes in 2019. His feature *Parasite* brings two families together; the poor Kims, whose four members scheme to get hired by the affluent Parks—the two children as English and drawing tutors, then the mother as housekeeper and the father as chauffeur. After many plot twists, the film, like Slimani's novel, ends in a bloodbath. *Parasite* attracted almost two million spectators in France, a record for a Palme d'Or winner and for an Asian film, at first released only in a subtitled version. The last two Palmes d'Or to have had such success—that is to say more than one million spectators—also dealt with social disparities: Abdellatif Kechiche's *La Vie d'Adèle* (2013; *The Life of Adèle*) on a transclass romance in northern France, and Laurent Cantet's *Entre les murs* (2008; *Between the Walls*) on the everyday life of underprivileged middle schoolers and their teacher in Paris.

The keen interest of French readers and moviegoers for inequality and its representation through housework coincides with what economist Clément Carbonnier and sociologist Nathalie Morel have called "the return of domestic workers." In steep decline in the twentieth century, the pattern has shifted since the 1990s to a point where caretakers now account for about 5 percent of the active population. As *Le Retour des domestiques* (2018) argues, the government is increasingly subsidizing these jobs because they accommodate unskilled workers and cannot be offshored. In a country like France were inequalities are rising, the population aging, and women working, more and more citizens resort to domestic employees, especially seniors, families, and well-off households.[2] In a different field of humanities research, Bruce Robbins in *The Servant's Hand: English Fiction from Below* (1986) has documented the "surprising and (to one trained as a historical critic) annoying sameness of these formal manifestations of literary service."[3] While Robbins explores realist British fiction from the nineteenth century, Carbonnier and Morel focus on the contemporary French job market, only devoting one sentence to literature: "From Balzac to Proust by way of Flaubert, all of literature testifies to the centrality of 'household workers.'"[4] In *Service ou Servitude* (1979; *Service or Servitude*), philosopher Geneviève Fraisse broadens the literary corpus "from the valet of Beaumarchais to the maids of Jean Genet."[5] This chapter will test the "sameness" and "return" of domestic service in contemporary prose, plays, and films beyond Proust's 1920s (Carbonnier and Morel) or Genet's 1947 play (Fraisse).

The most recent headline about housekeeping is a case of class mobility. In 2019 Ivoirian-born French maid Rachel Keke and her colleagues—African women, for the most part—started protesting the working conditions, and their effects on the body, at a hotel in the northwest of Paris. After twenty-two months of struggle and an eight-month strike, the social movement achieved the majority of its objectives (especially the demand for a salary increase and a manageable pace of work).[6] In 2022 Keke became the first cleaner to be elected to France's National Assembly. In line with this event, my analysis here will not be centered on the character of the servant per se, as a representant of the people and of low-wage or unwaged workers, but in its relationship with social mobility.

## Maids and Parvenants

Maids are unequivocally precarious in contemporary France, but as I will show now, in literature as in previous centuries, the emphasis has been less on precarity than on their ambivalent status as socially disparate workers. Because they mix, at times very closely, with various classes, they can aptly incarnate parvenants even when they remain on the threshold of upward mobility.

Maids in the eighteenth century were socially ambiguous, especially because they lived with their employers. Historian Sarah Maza honed in on these "transient" and imitative maids, cooks, and lackeys who constituted "a class apart" in early modern France, alienated from the working and the ruling class alike.[7] They were literally and metaphorically "entrenched on the doorstep" between social groups, forever ringing the employer's doorbell without rising to the higher class.[8] Such mingling is everywhere in the nineteenth century too. In the first part of her 1832 novel *Indiana*, George Sand continuously intertwines the figures of the lady of the house and of the chambermaid until the latter commits suicide. In Edmond and Jules de Goncourt's *Germinie Lacerteux* (1865), the maid pronounces the first lines of the novel but ends up in an intermediary space: "Her undefined grave was this undefined terrain."[9] In Flaubert's *Un coeur simple* (1877; *A Simple Heart*), the proximity between Félicité and her employer can be declarative — "they embraced each other, soothing their sadness in a kiss that equalized them" — and spatial — despite the house's "different levels," the *huis-clos* draws the two women closer in a "narrow vestibule."[10] But the ambiguity is first and foremost expressed formally:

For half a century, the bourgeois women of Pont-l'Évêque had envied Madame Aubain her servant Félicité.

For a hundred francs a year, she did the cooking and the cleaning, sewed, washed, ironed, knew how to bridle a horse, fatten the poultry, churn the butter, and remained loyal to her mistress,—who however was not an agreeable person.

She had married a handsome young man, with no fortune, who died at the beginning of 1809, leaving her with two small children and a number of debts.[11]

Flaubert's syntax juxtaposes "Madame Aubain her servant Félicité." At the end of a lengthy sentence made of multiple verbs in different tenses, a dash separates "who" from its obvious reference "her mistress." The multiplication of "she" and "her" redoubles the grammatical indeterminacy, not to mention the use of free indirect discourse throughout *Un cœur simple*. Like Félicité and Germinie, Octave Mirbeau's Célestine in *Le Journal d'une femme de chambre* (1900; *The Diary of a Chambermaid*) is isolated, marginalized, and always in between two states: "something halfway between a dog and a parrot"; "between the ephemeral semi-luxury of places and the distress of jobless tomorrows."[12] One long tirade paints a full portrait of Mirbeau's maid:

> A domestic worker is not a normal being, a social being ... He is someone disparate, fabricated from pieces and scraps that cannot fit into one another, juxtapose one another ... He is something worse: a monstrous human hybrid ... He is no longer of the people, where he comes from; he is not, either, of the bourgeoisie where he lives and where he aims ... From the people he has renounced, he has lost the generous blood and the naive strength ... From the bourgeoisie, he has gained shameful vices, without having been able to acquire the means to satisfy them ... and vile sentiments, cowardly fears, criminal appetites, without the setting, and, consequently, without the excuse of riches ... His soul completely sullied, he traverses that honest bourgeois world and just having breathed the mortal odor that rises from these putrid cesspools, he loses, forever, the security of his spirit, down to the very form of his self ... At the bottom of all these memories, among this population of figures where he

wanders, a phantom of himself, he finds nothing to churn but filth, which is to say suffering...."[13]

In Mirbeau's description, servants lack harmony, bodily integrity, and agency. They are not "self-made" but fabricated; they are monsters, ghosts, chimeras. The author's word choice in this passage accentuates the in-betweenness of the domestic servant: "du peuple, d'où il sort [...]. De la bourgeoisie où il vit et *où* il tend [the bourgeoisie where he lives and *where* he aims]." Mirbeau did not write the more expected "*vers laquelle* il tend [*toward which* he aims]." The odd repetition of the adverb *où* (where) undermines the possibility of breaking *into* the ruling class, as if a chambermaid was forever arriving in a place. Célestine here "traverses that honest bourgeois world"; elsewhere she falters over "an untraversable space, an abyss."[14] To follow up on the mud and dirt of chapter 2, the social mobility of the maid, however thwarted, is also signaled in this passage by a "putrid" workplace that replaces memory with "filth."

In Marcel Proust's *À la recherche du temps perdu* (1913–27; *In Search of Lost Time*), too, "domestic servants [...] remain, alas, domestic servants and more cleanly demonstrate the limits (that we would like to efface) of their caste even as they come to believe that they are most penetrating ours."[15] One can read, in the same paragraph, that housekeeper "Françoise was in a sense less of a domestic servant than the others" and yet that she had their "monstruous strangeness."[16] Critics have shown how Françoise's French—half-classic, half-slangy—symbolizes this social duplicity by combining preciosity and patois.[17] Finally, in Jean Genet's *Les Bonnes* (1947; *The Maids*), the two housekeepers Claire and Solange imitate and cross-dress as their employer, Madame. Genet uses a pun that has become commonplace in literary texts on chambermaids, as he plays with the polysemy of *bonne*, meaning "maid" as a noun and "good" as an adjective: "C'est facile d'être bonne, et souriante, et douce. Quand on est belle et riche! Mais être bonne quand on est une bonne!"[18] (It's easy to be happy, and smiling, and sweet. When you are beautiful and rich! But to be happy when you are a hapless servant!). In *Saint Genet, comédien et martyr* (1952; *Saint Genet, Actor and Martyr*), Jean-Paul Sartre perceives Genet's maids as "the most extraordinary example of those revolving doors of being and appearance, of imagination and reality"; the fact that there are two maids reinforces the constant permutation of roles.[19] In these classics from Flaubert, the Goncourt brothers, Sand, Mirbeau, Proust, and up until Genet, maids are mobile and intermediary characters, socially and symbolically shunted back and forth.

A literary servant can be apprehended as the metonymy of social mobility. As Franco Moretti argues in his book on European bildungsromane, *The Way of the World* ([1985] 2000), adventurers, parvenus, and servants are "thousand-eyed" and "eavesdropping" characters who, according to an author he often quotes, Bakhtin, "fulfill analogous functions in the novel," "the role of one who has not yet found a definite or fixed place in life, but who seeks personal success."[20] For Daniel Shaviro in *Literature and Inequality*, Rastignac himself is a "flunky" because he basically works as a servant for the Baron de Nucingen: "Rastignac deems himself the architect of his own rise, but learns that he has actually been more of a useful cat's paw to a shadowy master of high finance than himself a prime mover."[21] In the last scene of *Le Père Goriot* (1835; *Old Man Goriot*), Rastignac attends Goriot's funeral with domestic workers: the "help" of Goriot's two daughters and Christophe, a housekeeper and "hired hand" who lives in an attic room (literally a "maid's room" in French, *une chambre de bonne*) at the Pension Vauquer.[22] The last pages repeatedly bring "Rastignac and Christophe" together as if Rastignac, before exclaiming "À nous deux maintenant!" ("It's down to you and me now!") and ratifying his upward mobility, had only been a servant thus far, halfway between a provincial and a parvenu.[23]

The nexus of service and mobility is even more striking because systematic in *Le Rouge et le Noir* (1830; *The Red and the Black*). Even if Julien Sorel curtly affirms, "I don't want to be a domestic worker" and refuses to marry the chambermaid Elisa, he soon realizes that his ambition will require this intermediary step, that he will be compared to a valet at every turn: house servants mock his manners; Monsieur de Rênal, who employs Sorel as a tutor, nonetheless calls him a "domestic worker"; Madame de Rênal, too, realizes that Julien thinks like a servant when he lets his guard down to discuss money and class; when he first envisions his upward mobility through the clergy, he learns that wealthy families think of priests as valets; Julien is a "valet-lover" when he feigns to court Mme de Fervaques; and when he (son of a peasant) and Mathilde (daughter of a marquis) fall in love, she becomes his "servant" and he the "master."[24] In a word, Stendhal has the entire cast of *Le Rouge et le Noir* measure Sorel's class and success at social climbing in light of his distance to house service. These upward trajectories reflect the word *domestique* itself, first and foremost an adjective in French, and a subordinate epithet attached to an invisible and implied noun only pretending to be independent. Departing from this canonical literary history, how do writers and filmmakers adapting novels today take up the precarious, liminal, and "aggressively vestigial" characters of domestics?[25]

## Intersectional Maids and Social Migrations

On May 14, 2011, the head of the International Monetary Fund and potential candidate in the French presidential election Dominique Strauss-Kahn was accused of sexually assaulting Nafissatou Diallo, a cleaner working at the New York Sofitel hotel who had emigrated from Guinea, a former French colony in West Africa. The criminal case *New York v. Strauss-Kahn*, known as "L'affaire DSK" in France, produced a series of outrageous reactions in the media. Jean-François Kahn, for instance, founder of the magazine *Marianne*, called it "un troussage de domestique [tumbling a chambermaid]."[26] While *trousser* designates the action of lifting clothes, *trousser un domestique* more bluntly means to rape a servant. This old expression refers to the alleged caste "right" of an employer to have sex with house employees with or without their consent, thus perpetuating their stereotypical sexualization. In English, for example, a "French maid" is an eroticized and flirtatious servant. Sociologist Christine Delphy subsequently edited *Un troussage de domestique* (2011), a volume that did not focus on Strauss-Kahn's culpability but on the media coverage of the case as a *"triggering fiction."*[27] Delphy underlined the "class arrogance" toward Diallo, as well as *"three kinds of solidarity*: that of gender, which unites men against women, that of class, which unites the rich against the poor, and that of race, which unites white people against darker skin people."[28] Contemporary maids are not only on the threshold between classes but at various intersections.[29]

In this section, I will look at maids and cleaners in the minor mode, lodged in unexpected places, instead of considering texts entirely devoted to these workers and their precarity.³⁰ Three contemporary French authors strikingly intertwine social mobility and the figure of the maid: Annie Ernaux, Marie NDiaye, and Maryse Condé. In *Mémoire de fille* (2016; *Girl's Memory*), Ernaux recounts her 1960 au pair experience in England. This trip—in a different country and a different household—is the turning point of her social trajectory. She left France after quitting the training school for elementary teachers, and when she came back several months later, she started a different training at a higher rank, this time to become a high school teacher of French literature. She received the *agrégation de lettres* in 1971 and started a dissertation on Marivaux (that remains unfinished). Yet, she also remembered how her father perceived her role as an au pair: "Basically, this immersion in a higher social milieu made me accept being what my father, upon my return to France, said that I had been: 'Really, you were a little maid in England!' A reflection that, even said with a laugh, mortified me profoundly, like a humiliating truth."³¹ *Pair* and *père* (father) sound exactly the same in French; and in nineteenth-century Parisian department stores such as Le Bon Marché—a model for Émile Zola's 1883 novel *Au Bonheur des dames*—an "au pair" was a salesclerk who "received no pay for the first several months."³² Trying to flee her social class through an experience abroad, Ernaux is brought back to her father's rank, he who entered the world of work at thirteen to serve as a farm boy and later became a storekeeper. As for many nonnational workers, a foreign experience is often associated with social demotion even when it eventually leads to upward mobility. And indeed, Ernaux's interlude in the UK is the first step of her literary career. She recalls the emergence of "the desire to write a novel" when she was "scrubbing the tiles" and "cleaning the bathroom."³³ Ernaux's mother also treated her as a maid right before her marriage: "Try to keep up with your housework [*ménage*], he must not send you back."³⁴ The verb *send back* (*renvoyer*) is surprising in this context because in French, it often means "lay off." And since the word *ménage* means both household and housework, the mother's recommendation turns Ernaux's marriage with a man from the upper class into a contract for domestic service.

Ernaux even called herself her husband's "favorite cleaning lady" in *La Femme gelée* (1981; *The Frozen Woman*), a scathing narrative on how an emancipated young girl raised to be independent ended up in a normative relationship.[35] Like Sorel, Ernaux entered a different class through service. Whether at work or in her marriage, her social origin confined her to the threshold of a new class, a limbo in which she was more likely to serve than to belong. While the metaphor of the maid is no news in feminist studies, it acquires a specific social meaning for Ernaux at the intersection of nationality (a French citizen in an affluent household in the suburbs of London) and gender (a working-class woman who married a bourgeois man).[36]

Ernaux's relationship to the function of the maid is not limited to waged and domestic labor. It is also part of her reading practice. When the author and teacher reflects on her favorite books, she often explains how she used to identify with the only representative of the people in canonical fiction, namely, the servants. It is the case with Françoise in Marcel Proust's *À la recherche du temps perdu*, Catherine Leroux in *Madame Bovary* (1856), and Rosalie in Guy de Maupassant's *Une vie* (1883; *A Life*). In *La Place*, Ernaux's narrator criticizes literary and linguistic class contempt as follows: "Thus Proust emphasized with delight the errors and the antiquated words of Françoise. Only aesthetics matter to him because Françoise is his maid and not his mother. Because he himself never felt these turns of phrase come to his lips spontaneously."[37] In this final sentence isolated from the rest of the paragraph by periods, the phrasing suggests, although implicitly, that Ernaux inherited her mother's language and that it could crop up in her body (*come to her lips*) against her will. Later in her writing career, in one of the sentences opening *Les Années* (2008; *The Years*), Ernaux loops back to this character as she compares her mother to both the duchess of Guermantes and Céleste Albaret, Proust's real-life servant and the model for Françoise, thus showing again how the figure of the maid stands on the threshold between person and personage, the way transclass authors like Louis move between fiction and nonfiction, the textual and the extratextual (see chap. 3).[38]

About *Une vie*, Ernaux explains the role it played in her own life in an interview that now prefaces the paperback edition of Maupassant's first novel: "Very quickly, the differences of time period and especially of social milieu, even if I was conscious of it—for I belonged, myself, to Rosalie's world—ceased to matter in my reading."[39] There is an interruption here between the formulation of social differences and the fact that they *cease to matter*. The sentence thereby mimics Ernaux's trajectory: it makes a detour by way of the maid to do away with social classes. Ernaux also remembers, using a similarly intermittent syntax, that she discovered Flaubert through the portrait of an old servant in an elementary school textbook: "It is difficult for me today to explain why this passage [...] troubled me, enticed me irresistibly, except perhaps by the discovery of the real—in the end, it could have been my grandmother or my great-aunts—through writing."[40] The literary maid connects, via dashes, Ernaux's life to literature. These interpolated clauses resonate with Alex Woloch's interpretation of the place of servants in Proust's prose: "The sentence's distention, I would argue, registers its problematic incorporation of two minor characters: the gardener, who extends the main ellipses in the sentence, and the maid, who adds on the final (and thus most disruptive) subordinate clause."[41] For the critic, the servant's "subordination" pertains to labor and grammar. But for Ernaux, Maupassant's maid and the dashes that isolate her ("—for I belonged, myself, to Rosalie's world—") rather function as the rungs of her social and literary ladder, a stylistical metaphor for her emancipation. Maupassant is the ideal "inter-text" for Ernaux's trajectory. On the one hand, he is Normand like her family and was read by her mother. On the other hand, Ernaux's identification with Rosalie not only compares her to an impoverished nineteenth-century maid from the provinces but to an aristocrat: Rosalie is the foster sister of the upper-class heroine Jeanne Le Perthuis des Vauds.[42] Unable to identify with idle duchesses, Ernaux uses the maid as an entryway, however vexed, into fiction: not a *voie royale* but an effective transit zone between classes; not (only) a way out of her condition, but a way of reconciling all her social classes. In return, maids also connect Ernaux to a diverse audience, as she remembers "a reader of Spanish descent, a cleaning lady, having borrowed my book from the library, and writing me a four-page letter, in which she transcribes passages of the text and accompanies them, by way of commentary, with events, situations, sentiments, belonging to her own life."[43]

In Marie NDiaye's *Ladivine* (2013)—an eerie portrayal of four generations of women through class, race, and trauma—Malinka's mother Ladivine is a housecleaner, but she becomes her own daughter's servant when Malinka begins her social ascent into the middle class: "In such a way that, one day when her mother had come to fetch her at school and a girl, speaking to her for the first time, asked her, with a startled and disgusted expression, who was that woman, Malinka answered: That's my servant, and it seemed to her that she was telling a great truth."[44] In NDiaye's scene, "my servant" stands halfway between kinship and labor, a strategy to hold heredity and reinvention together. As an upstart class, the bourgeoisie distinguishes itself from the proletariat by the capacity to afford domestic workers.[45] Thus, even if Malinka works in service (first as a nanny, then as a server), having a servant herself creates a class gap with her mother. While the transclass and the working class live under the same roof, envisioning motherhood as domestic labor allows Malinka to sever ties and begin her social journey. Édouard Louis describes a comparable situation in the biography of his mother, *Combats et métamorphoses d'une femme* (2021; *Battles and Metamorphoses of a Woman*), when she asks, "I would need a job. And I thought that I could clean your house. I would come when you're not there of course, I wouldn't disturb you. I clean, you leave the money on the table and I go."[46] This time, it is the mother who offers her service to her transclass son. While such arrangement strains kinship and reveals the economic underpinning of what a family is, deep down, it might also be a way for the mother to normalize the uneasy relationship with her son, to transfer the cause of the estrangement from social mobility to an employment contract. Across genres, the fiction of the signifier "maid" designates the moment when parvenants come to terms with their social mobility.

NDiaye also named a whole play after a housemaid: *Hilda* (1999). All the scenes unfold on thresholds, which means that although Hilda is barred from crossing the doorsteps of her workplace and of her household, she dwells, in discourses, on a dividing line.[47] The employer self-identifies as liberal and claims a desire to emancipate Hilda: "I want for Hilda to be my equal. I want to eat lunch with Hilda and chat with Hilda between two household chores."[48] Hilda will always refuse this artificial social mobility that amounts to being friendly only "between chores." The employer is awkwardly fascinated by Hilda's name, and wants to hire it more than the person herself: "I am bewildered, Franck, by the coming of this name of

Hilda tomorrow to my house."⁴⁹ In *The Servant's Hand*, Robbins underlines the connection between maid and linguistic signs: they are socially powerless but occupy strong "narrative functions"; they are not modeled on real workers but on early modern plays; and they represent their employers' wealth.⁵⁰ Similarly, in the words of Jean-Paul Sartre, the two maids of Genet's play can be seen as "pure emanations of their masters."⁵¹ Inspired by Genet's *Les Bonnes*, NDiaye radicalizes these observations.⁵² With such an emphasis on names, Hilda, who never speaks, becomes an empty signifier generated by the discussion between the employer and the husband, an effect of language at the intersection of two forms of "domestic" service: cleaning and marrying.

NDiaye's play slowly unpacks why Hilda's name matters: "The one we had up till now was named Monique. And we had Françoise, Consuelo, Brigitte, Yvette, Françoise, Brigitte. Never were any of our women named Hilda, never."⁵³ The list is not arbitrary. The first two names are those of Marcel Proust's housemaid Françoise and George Sand's socially mobile Consuelo. But the list jams and repeats two names twice, thus drawing the attention of the reader. The employer will later clarify: "The umpteenth Brigitte we had, she had to go back to Mali."⁵⁴ Readers could have imagined that Françoise and Yvette named French and white employees. The delay between these two sentences puts into question Hilda's own origin. Despite some ambiguous clues here and there, the Germano-Nordic name is meant to disorient the readers' expectations as to who performs service in contemporary France. Being a maid is thus a matter of "complexion." As the employer claims, "one acquires, once they become a domestic worker, a sort of complexion particular to that condition."⁵⁵ Philosopher Chantal Jaquet proposed to use Spinoza's concept of *ingenium* (*complexion* in French) instead of Bourdieu's *habitus* to account for the strategy of social climbers.⁵⁶ Jaquet, who describes the phenomenon of class-based passing in the works of Nella Larsen and Frantz Fanon, also notes that "complexion" means skin tone. NDiaye's strategic inserting of "complexion" in a sentence that does not mention skin color subtly underlines the intersectionality of housework, the interplay between race and class when it comes to representing domestic labor in literature.

When she retired from her professorship at Columbia University in 2002, Maryse Condé started writing about her grandmother. Condé's mother was one of the first black schoolteachers in Guadeloupe, but her grandmother Victoire Quidal was an illiterate cook born in the Caribbean island of Marie-Galante. In *Victoire: Les Saveurs et les mots* (2006; *Victoire: The Flavors and the Words*)—a novelistic and highly documented biography—Condé retraces the upward mobility of women in her family over three generations. At every turn, Victoire keeps her service job to offer a better future to Condé's mother, Jeanne: "Education, education, she swore, would be the tool of her emancipation. Her daughter would be educated. She would sacrifice herself for that."[57] Victoire works for a white family so Jeanne, "always dressed like a duchess," can benefit from the wealth of her mother's employers and is educated like their own children.[58] As in NDiaye's texts, social disparities are also racial. Jeanne is black but her mother is mixed-race. Victoire is thus caught between loyalties. On the one hand, she remains a friend of her white employer Anne-Marie after the end of her contract, but Jeanne, *noiriste*, prevents her mother from pursuing her affair with Anne-Marie's white husband.[59] On the other hand, Victoire is rejected by the black working-class community: "However, that class to which she belonged, had rejected her since childhood. Because of her color."[60] The isolated sentence on skin color enacts the distance between black and mixed-race Guadeloupeans. For Condé, to write about Victoire amounts to uncovering complex racial and social hierarchies from the standpoint of domestic work, at the intersection of gender, race, and class exploitation and unexcepted alliances.

For these three prominent French writers of the late twentieth and twenty-first centuries, the figure of the house worker is deeply connected to social mobility through language and literature. Ernaux identifies with novelistic portraits of housekeepers. For NDiaye, the word *servant* and the name Hilda either represent the complex status of maids or designate the first step of a social journey. Hilda's employer pretends, "We have housekeepers, like everyone, but we never forget to elevate them, through speech, to our level."[61] Social mobility amounts to a speech act. As for Condé, she traces back her creativity to her grandmother's manual work: "What I want is to claim the inheritance of that woman who apparently does not leave one. Establish the link that unites her creativity with mine. Shift from

the flavors, colors, smells of flesh or vegetables to those of words."⁶²
Writing is not a spontaneous talent but the final product of a transclass lineage. NDiaye perceived a similar connection between writing and housework. In *La Cheffe: Roman d'une cuisinière* (2016; *The Cheffe: A Cook's Novel*), the main character is a socially mobile cook whose story is narrated by an infatuated employee. Born in a family of agricultural laborers, the *cheffe* starts working as a housemaid then as a cook, and ends up owning a Michelin-starred restaurant in Bordeaux. The novel resonates with NDiaye's biography: her grandparents were farmers. *La Cheffe* fulfills the promise of its subtitle. It truly is "a cook's novel": although the character has difficulties writing because she quit school at fourteen, every sentence reads as an ars poetica on how to select ingredients like words, prepare dishes like works of art, and win a star in the Michelin guide like a Goncourt prize.⁶³ The novel's last meal summarizes the *cheffe*'s radical art of cooking: enjoying a glass of wine in a garden filled with roaming chickens, growing vegetables, and ripe cherries on the trees.⁶⁴ This final *tableau vivant* in which the ingredients of the dish have not yet been cooked bridges the creative work of the *cheffe* and the farm labor of her parents.⁶⁵

The three writers are also deeply connected to the school system: Ernaux taught French in high school; NDiaye's mother was a biology teacher; Condé taught in French and American universities, and her mother was an elementary school teacher.⁶⁶ Furthermore, NDiaye's very first novel was accepted when she was a junior in high school, turning her into a "student writer" for life.⁶⁷ For each author, service underwrites and inverts school as the connecting rod between childhood and creation, either at the scale of the family (Condé) or in one's own trajectory, fictive and biographical (Ernaux and NDiaye's *cheffe*). The servant allows Condé and NDiaye to reach the generation before their teaching mothers.

The intersection of school and service can be traced back to Albert Camus's *Le Premier Homme* (*The First Man*). In this autobiographical novel, unfinished and posthumously published in 1994, the school teacher is a catalyst of upward mobility as he allows young Jacques Cormery to get a scholarship. On his first day in secondary school, Cormery—whose mother, like Camus's, is an illiterate house cleaner—has to deal with his mother's profession:

In the forms that had been given to them, he did not know what to put for "parents' profession." He had first put "housekeeper," while Pierre had put "post office employee." But Pierre explained to him that housekeeper was not a profession but was said of a woman who kept the house and did her own cleaning. "No, said Jacques, she does the housework for other people and especially for the haberdasher across the street. —In that case, Pierre said, hesitating, I think you should put domestic." That idea had never occurred to Jacques for the simple reason that this word, all too rare, was never uttered in his home—for the reason also that no one in their house had the feeling that she worked for the others, she worked foremost for her children. Jacques started to write the word, stopped and all at once knew all at once the shame and the shame of having been ashamed.[68]

The passage is famous for its description of this *honte au carré*, the shame of being ashamed, redoubled by the contradictory repetition of "all at once" on each side of the verb "knew."[69] But to me, the scene performs something different than affects. First of all, it shows how class is a matter of word choice: the young pupil learns about his social rank by having to fill out a document, and *domestic* was not used at home because it belongs to a formal register. Camus plays on the double meaning of the phrase "working for someone"; "someone" can either be the employer who profits from the cleaner's work or the employee's son who benefits from the mother's wage. There is also more mother (*mère*) in *ménagère* (housekeeper) than in *domestique*. Second, Camus embeds the reference to service at school, when he has to do something his mother cannot: write.[70] Like Ernaux, NDiaye, and Condé, Camus's mother maid is the stitch between work and school, and between social determinism and emancipation.[71]

Via their paper maids, these four writers debunk the myth of the spontaneous and instant self-made person to uncover a more patient fabrication of the self in families across generations. They encase their protagonists' mobility within a genealogy of manual work that gathers various forms of labor. The liminal figure of the maid also testifies to the complex status of transclass workers who, once they integrate a new social sphere, seem to be working with and *for* their new colleagues. The maid thus stands as the metaphor for what a working-class person or family has to do before becoming an artist.

Writing about—or inventing—maids can be understood as an efficient literary device to describe a parvenant torn between her family heritage and the new set of rules imposed at work, between a homogeneous household and an alien workplace. We can read maids in narratives of class mobility as transitional archetypes, identifiable figures that facilitate the apprehension of what social mobility will entail. What are we looking at when we see people of drastically different classes housed under the same roof? A bourgeois household living with its servant, or a working-class family cohabiting with an aspiring parvenant.

Maids can also bring the French and francophone corpuses together so as to think social mobility in light of migration. France does not allow ethnic statistics, but economists agree that nannies and maids are often nonwhite and/or non-French.[72] As Franco-Senegalese writer Fatou Diome wrote in the short story "Le Visage de l'empoi" ("The Face of the Job"), "As for the sound of the vacuums, it nearly always signals the presence of an African, Portuguese, or Asian woman."[73] Born in Senegal, Diome immigrated to France to study literature but had to work six years as a cleaner to complete her master's degree. Racism prevented her from being tutor or cashier, so she cleaned for employers who always assumed her illiterate. The short stories of the collection *La Préférence nationale* (2001; *The National Preference*) circle around domestic work to a point where it is studying itself that becomes a side job: "I dedicated my days without cleaning to my studies."[74] Mother maids like Camus's are also crucial for the social mobility of second-generation children. Take Faïza Guène, for instance, who published her first novel *Kiffe kiffe demain* in 2004 when she was still a high school student. The title superimposes words imported from the Arabic: *kif-kif* could be translated as "same old, same old" and *kiffer* means "to love." "Kiffe kiffe tomorrow" thereby embodies the tension between social determination (the return of the same) and the possibility of a likable future. The heroine, Doria, born from immigrant Moroccan parents, lives in a project in the Parisian suburbs. Her illiterate mother, Yamina, works as a maid in a low-cost hotel in Bagnolet, a commune right on the eastern border of Paris. Guène writes about social mobility and migration in her novels, but as she sold more than four hundred thousand copies of the first one, the publication itself enacted her upward trajectory. This example mixes the intra- and extradiegetic, from a narrator writing a diary about her hopes (Doria) to an author who writes and publishes this diary and thereby changes social class (Faïza).[75] School is not far in these examples either: Guène is a "student writer"; Diome and her protagonists cleaned to finance their studies.

## Playing the Maid

Besides symbolic servants (Ernaux), mothers or grandmothers working as maids (Camus, Condé, NDiaye, Guène), and cleaning as a temporary position (Diome), does the maid break away from omniscient, ventriloquizing narrators to tell her own tale in the first person? And if not, who gets to pass on and perform the stories of domestic service in twenty-first-century France?[76]

The first example that comes to mind would be *Le Quai de Ouistreham* (2010). In 2009, journalist Florence Aubenas decided to investigate precarity and recession from within. She hid her diplomas, except the baccalaureate, and found a night job: cleaning the ferries that shuttle back and forth between Normandy and England on the Ouistreham wharf in Caen, hence the title. She quits on the day she is offered a permanent contract to avoid taking the place of someone else. The most striking element of her infiltration and narrative is how they show that cleaners are no longer looking for "a place" but for "hours," which does not generate social mobility but forces them to be physically mobile throughout the day, from place to place.[77] Today's market has maids trade one form of mobility for another. In Emmanuel Carrère's film adaptation of Aubenas's narrative (*Ouistreham*, 2022), the maid-journalist, now a writer, is played by professional actress Juliette Binoche, surrounded by a cast of nonprofessional actors.

About thirty years before Aubenas, Sophie Calle narrated a comparable experience in Venice, where she was hired as a hotel chambermaid for a three-week replacement. The name of the hotel, C., gives readers a hint that the work in question will be more focused on herself (C like Calle) than on the daily routine of cleaning. Calle could appropriate what Genet wrote in his foreword to *Les Bonnes*: "*This is not a plea regarding the fate of domestic workers. I imagine there exists a union for housekeepers—that does not concern us.*"[78] The photo journal *L'Hôtel* (1984; *The Hotel*) that resulted from Calle's limited and nonchalant experience is organized by date, hour, and room, like a diary or reservation logbook. The artist barely cleans. Her manual work is either minimal, summarized, or a task to be done as a break in between reading sessions: "The room done, I leave"; "I pause my reading to go do #43"; "Today, not much work. I sit down on their bed and flip through the datebook I glimpsed yesterday."[79] She spends her time skimming letters or organizers and photographing the clients' personal belongings. Calle does not experience precarity. In *L'Hôtel*, she identifies as a cleaner only when she expects instant social mobility: "For the first time, I imagine for a few seconds a client considering my lot as a cleaning lady and proposing that I drop everything, leave with him."[80] The writer (Sophie Calle), the journalist (Florence Aubenas), and the actress (Juliette Binoche) "play the maid." Calle and Aubenas temporarily switch comfortable jobs to become cleaners in real life. They socially demote so as to be able to tell a true story.[81]

In 2015, Octave Mirbeau's *Le Journal d'une femme de chambre* was adapted for the screen by Benoît Jacquot. I will linger on this case study because it raises an important set of questions about what it means to revive a Belle Epoque chambermaid in the twenty-first century, and about who gets to "play the maid" today, not as a temporary worker but as an actress.

Mirbeau's Célestine is highly mobile, and not only because as a maid she navigates various classes. Readers are told right off that she worked in twelve different houses in the past two years. The author constantly insists on her concrete spatial movements: "two floors that I will have to go down and up endlessly."[82] At the end of the novel, she becomes a shopkeeper, although the extent of this upward mobility is debatable since it amounts to marrying Joseph, an anti-Semite robber, possibly rapist, who wants her to remain immobile behind the café counter and flirt with customers. Célestine also acquires the status of a writer since Mirbeau pretends, in the dedication, that the novel is hers: "*This book that I publish under the title:* The Diary of a Chambermaid *was actually written by Mademoiselle Célestine R ..., chambermaid.*"[83] In the first sentence, Mirbeau gives his seat to Célestine: "I entered into my new place."[84] The sentence is a social threshold for the author and character alike. The new place is the maid's new house *and* the author's fake social and gendered identity. Like Florence Aubenas and Sophie Calle, although only through writing, Octave Mirbeau experiences social demotion. He passes as a late nineteenth-century chambermaid so as to be able to write his novel as an autobiography. The blurb of Jean Renoir's 1946 American adaptation of *Le Journal d'une femme de chambre* could thus caption Mirbeau's literary stratagem: "The very true confessions... of an untrue girl!" While he plays a maid, Mirbeau is also robbing Célestine of her upward mobility. The final chapter, which details her new social position as a shop owner, is the only one that does not look like a diary entry: there is no date at the top of the page. It is as if Mirbeau had wanted to regain authorship and control over the format of his novel at the very moment Célestine was being emancipated from her employer (and creator).

There is an interesting parallel between Mirbeau's fictional Célestine and Marcel Proust's real housekeeper, Céleste Albaret. In *Monsieur Proust* (1973) subtitled "Remembrances Collected by Georges Belmont," the journalist explains his role as a recorder of the servant's experience in italics and in these terms: "*Furthermore, the least we can say is that there are accents that are unmistakable. If, reading this book, we hear it as it was spoken and as I myself heard it, I am sure that we will only be able to recognize in it the most sincere of all voices: that of the heart* [of Céleste]."[85] Within Belmont's narration, Albaret's "accents" testify to the veracity of the anecdotes and give readers access to her voice. The foreword to Mirbeau's diary uses the same lexicon and typeface: "*In carrying out this work that she asked of me, which is to say in adding, here and there, a few accents to this book, I am quite afraid of having altered its slightly corrosive grace, of having diminished its sad force, and especially of having replaced with simple literature what there was in these pages of emotion and life...*"[86] The labor of the maid is replaced by the commissioned work of the author, what "she asked of me." Unlike the journalist who recorded Céleste's intonations, Mirbeau's literature amounts to playing the maid and faking Célestine's true "accent."[87]

In literature, a servant is a theatrical character.[88] As a playwright and theater critic, Mirbeau filled his novel with theatrical moments. Célestine performs her work like an actress: "The scenes change; the settings transform."[89] During the hiring of maids—described as "a social tragedy"—the antechamber resembles a backstage.[90] *Le Journal d'une femme de chambre* offers an original combination of theater and diary. On the one hand, Célestine is a credible diarist as she occupies all the narrative functions. On the other hand, Mirbeau's novel is full of what could be called "novelistic asides," especially when Célestine answers back to her employer: "I cry out, on the inside"; "You think if I mumble, if I rage, if I insult Madame deep down inside of me?..."; "I want to reply, because I am agitated, irritated, aggravated ... but, fortunately, I contain myself ... I limit myself to grumbling a bit:—What's that you say?... / I say nothing ...'"[91] Célestine refrains from talking, and her potential asides lose their theatricality since she says all the lines.

Jacquot's 2015 film adaptation of Mirbeau's 1900 novel does not imitate the format of the diary. Often located at nonhuman heights, the camera does not align with Célestine. The point of view is polycentric and the shots disorienting, multiangled. Célestine is also not the only voice-over reading diary entries. In the very first scene, the recruiter tells her, "You are unstable," like the camera itself, and like Jacquot's cinema, known as "impure," heterogeneous, multigeneric.[92] One cinematic detail stands apart: Mirbeau's novelistic asides recover their full theatrical function in Jacquot's film. Here is an example from Mirbeau's *Le Journal d'une femme de chambre*: "— My girl, you know that this lamp is very expensive, and that it can only be repaired in England. Be careful with it, as if it were the apple of your eye ... I wanted to respond:—Hey! Tell me, little mother, what about your chamber pot ... is it expensive?...'"[93] In the film, "I wanted to respond" is deleted, and Célestine mumbles her line for the audience. In this context, the maid is an intermediary not only between two classes but between the dominant characters and the passive audience.[94] What does it mean for the lead actress playing a maid to break the referential illusion in this way? Is it a simple case of Brecht's distancing effect?[95] According to Sartre, Genet had planned to break the fourth wall in *Les Bonnes* by casting male teenagers and putting a sign on stage that would have constantly reminded the audience of the distance between male actors and female characters.[96] In *The Servant's Hand*, Bruce Robbins analyzes how theatrical maids possess a "privileged immediacy to the audience," how they easily transition from dialogue to monologue and occupy a specific space since medieval theater: "At the edge of the dramatic illusion, the actors in the *platea* could recognize the time and space of the audience, and the audience in turn could recognize itself in those actors who gravitated to the *platea*. As the border zone where the symbols and hierarchies of official representation could be ignored or undercut, it tended to be occupied by figures of questionable moral stature and low social position, like fools and servants."[97] What is the function of Jacquot's *platea* in the film version of *Le Journal d'une femme de chambre*? To answer this question means to look more closely at the actress who incarnates Célestine.

The maid is played by Léa Seydoux, which is not anecdotal. Seydoux is what could be called a literary actress. She was first noticed as Junie, a high school student in Christophe Honoré's film *La Belle Personne* (2008; *The Beautiful Person*), freely adapted from Madame de Lafayette's 1678 novel *La Princesse de Clèves*.[98] Seydoux often features in literary adaptations and in films concerned with the portrayal of precarity and social classes: Abdellatif Kechiche's *La Vie d'Adèle* (2013, adapted from Jul Maroh's 2010 graphic novel *Le Bleu est une couleur chaude—Blue Is a Warm Color*—hence the English title of the film, *Blue Is the Warmest Color*); Christophe Gans's *La Belle et la Bête* (2014; *The Beauty and the Beast*, adapted from Madame Leprince de Beaumont's fairy tale); Xavier Dolan's *Juste la fin du monde* (2016; *Just the End of the World*, adapted from Jean-Luc Lagarce's play of the same name); Arnaud Desplechin's *Roubaix, une lumière* (2019; *Roubaix, A Light*). Seydoux can play working-class and wealthy characters alike; she incarnates the socially mobile actress. In interviews, she says she had focused on finding specific bodily postures to portray Célestine's pride and snobbery. Seydoux had already played a servant in another film by Jacquot, *Les Adieux à la reine* (2012; *Fairwells to the Queen*), adapted from Chantal Thomas's 2002 novel of the same name and written, like Mirbeau's novel, as a diary. Seydoux was Sidonie Laborde, one of Queen Marie-Antoinette's readers at Versailles. To summarize her role, Jacquot added a line that was not in Thomas's novel: "I am only her servant. What am I saying? The servant of the books in the library of her Majesty." At the end of the film, Sidonie dresses as Gabrielle de Polignac (herself dressed as a servant) so that Marie-Antoinette's mistress could safely flee France and avoid the guillotine (the film is set in July 1789). Thus Seydoux appears particularly apt to play a literary maid, a character who navigates social classes and can even, at times, switch roles with her employers.

Asked about her background by a journalist working for *Madame Figaro*, Seydoux answered that she attended "l'école de la vie," an expression that means "the university of life" or "the school of hard knocks."[99] Because she omitted to mention that she attended a private theater school, that many of her relatives were film producers, and that her family was included in a list of the wealthiest people in France, her interview was widely criticized in the media. Two politicians even published an opinion page in *Libération* to coin the "Léa Seydoux Syndrome:"

> The actress went to "the school of hard knocks." A nice expression to stage the marvelous story of a star who owes her success to her talent alone—and who, at the same time, wants to erase where she comes from. For, after all, what does it matter that Léa Seydoux is one of the heirs of the founders of Pathé and Gaumont? [...] Dressed in these new modern-day Cinderella clothes, who transcend social boundaries, Léa Seydoux is bringing back, with sequins and spotlights, the Republican myth of meritocracy that binds, as securely as the fingers of a hand, work, talent, and success. She whispers in our ear the lovely history of a France that offers opportunity to everyone, and whose School allows each person the possibility, on the condition that they work, to break through the screen of social success. We could have been content to laugh at the star's words, as those on the internet permit themselves to do—justifiably—if these were only isolated statements. Unfortunately, it's the crushing majority of our leaders who are in the grips of this "Léa Seydoux syndrome," which invisibilizes social discrimination to better valorize the success of the children of those who already have a great deal.[100]

Born Léa Hélène Seydoux-Fornier de Clausonne, the actress comes from an affluent background yet holds no diploma (no middle school or high school certificate), which might explain why she perceives her career as a talent-based success with no connection to her social origin. Seydoux is the symptom of a flawed or failed meritocracy monopolized by the upper class.

As a spokesmodel for Vuitton, Seydoux's social and cinematic status is reminiscent of another actress, Margaret Qualley. Rhonda Garelick writes, in an article for the *New York Times*, "The same woman who stars as the embodiment of poverty in Netflix's 'Maid' is a brand ambassador for one of the world's largest luxury companies. How very 2021."[101] Whether in Jacquot's film (*Diary of a Chambermaid*) or in Molly Smith Metzler's miniseries (*Maid*), actresses Seydoux and Qualley share, through the fictional figure of the maid, this "unique position representing simultaneously the extreme 'rags' and 'riches' poles of the classic princess story line" along with the "inevitable upward mobility" associated with the Cinderella myth. Indeed, Alex in *Maid* ends up in college thanks to her writing talent. Chanel further represents Qualley's dual social status: Garelick explains in her article that Coco Chanel was a social climber herself and that "her little black dress recalls the typical uniform worn by French housemaids at the time." In *Maid*, the social status of the actress pushes the working-class character upward; it foreshadows the series' dénouement. The wealthy actress temporarily demotes (from life to film) but quickly climbs the ladder again through fiction.

In Jacquot's *Journal d'une femme de chambre*, Seydoux plays opposite Vincent Lindon, who is Joseph, the house valet. Lindon has been scrutinized for the distance between who he is and who he plays. He is one of the highest-paid actors in France and was born into a wealthy and cultivated family of CEOs, politicians, and publishers. His uncle Jérôme Lindon, for instance, was the editor of Les Éditions de Minuit. He is also known for playing roles of precarious laborers and union leaders. In Stéphane Brizé's *La Loi du marché* (2015; *The Law of the Market*), for instance, he is Thierry, a long-term unemployed worker who finds a new job as a security guard in a supermarket.[102] Like Binoche in Carrère's adaptation of *Le Quai de Ouistreham*, Lindon was the only actor in a cast of nonprofessionals. At the beginning of the film, he reprimands Yves Ory, an unemployment advisor who plays his own role. In the view of *Les Cahiers du cinéma*, "Citizen Lindon" here looks like a wealthy man screaming at a real worker, performing his dominant social condition, breaking the fourth wall.[103] The camera pans from one man to the other but never holds them together in the same shot. This first sequence appears before the title of the film, giving it an ambiguous status between fiction and reality. The actors' lines read very differently when you know who Lindon and Ory are in real life, especially when Lindon asks, "How am I supposed to live on five hundred euros?" and tells the advisor from Pôle emploi (the French employment agency): "You're screwing with all of us. Not you personally." On the contrary, this discussion is actually very personal for the man working at the unemployment office and being accused of incompetence.

This form of social metacomment—which involves judging a performance with regard to an actor's wealth—could also apply to Seydoux because of her social background and of the so-called Seydoux syndrome. In an interview, she explained: "I am never inhabited by a character. I am inhabited by myself." Indeed, her asides in *Journal d'une femme de chambre* feel like the actress talking to the audience as Léa Seydoux answering back to the acting employer because she will not submit to her authority.[104] The main characters of *Journal d'une femme de chambre*, Seydoux and Lindon, "crèvent l'écran" in all senses of the term: they have a great screen presence and they appear on screen as themselves, torn between their real person and their characters, a tension that reveals and redoubles the socially ambiguous roles they play.

Such a distinct reception is not new when it comes to Mirbeau's *Le Journal d'une femme de chambre*. In the Mirbeau Papers I consulted at the Bibliothèque Universitaire d'Angers, I found reviews in which journalists addressed the social credibility of the lead actress in theatrical adaptations of the novel. About Marie-Line Lefebvre in a 1998 Belgian adaptation, for instance, journalists underlined her "rural and blue-collar roots" to explain why "she really embodies this role."[105] Asked "what explains the power of Marie-Line as Toinette-Dorine-Célestine?" the director of the play replied, "*The credibility of the origins, of the culture, of the knowledge, of the experiences.*"[106] The actress is brought back to her background and Célestine to the backdrop of literary history: the servants in Molière's *Le Malade imaginaire* (Toinette) and *Tartuffe* (Dorine). Mirbeau himself was passionate about this question of credibility, especially when it came to theatrical maids: "She's a maid [*soubrette*] and not one of Molière's servants."[107] The author had also anticipated the Lindon and Seydoux phenomena in an 1882 article for *Le Figaro* in which he described the figure of the actor: "not content to be king of the stage, he also wants to be king in real life."[108] In this discussion, I do not want to argue that a bourgeois actor should not be allowed in a working-class role or that Lindon and Seydoux are falling for some sort of "social appropriation." My interest lies in the representation of social mobility.

Jacquot, like Mirbeau, robs the character of the maid, Célestine, of her emancipation. The film ends when she departs with Joseph to become a shopkeeper in a nighttime scene that could well be a dream, especially as the film is full of such ambiguous moments. In Renoir's American adaptation of Mirbeau's diary, by contrast, social mobility was a given. Dressed like a duchess, chatting with a poor-looking maid hired with her, Célestine declares right away, "I am not going to be a chambermaid any longer, I am going to be a mistress and have a house of my own." From Mirbeau's ventriloquy to Seydoux's performance, the social mobility at play in *Journal d'une femme de chambre* then and now is only that of the authors and actors who play the servants. Maids thus point to an area of interference at the crossroads of social classes and genres (literature, theater, cinema), a zone that swaps the upward mobility of the maid for the temporary demotion of the actress playing her. Literary and cinematic maids blur the line between fact and fiction, between autobiography and character study, in a way that is reminiscent of how parvenant writers like Ernaux and Louis need multiple genres to capture a socially mobile body in transit (see chap. 3).

The Seydoux Syndrome is not an isolated case. Take French singer Chris, formerly Christine and the Queens and also known as Redcar. His father is a university English professor, and his mother is a middle school French teacher; he attended prep school and the École normale supérieure (ENS) but decided to quit. During a television interview, he identified as a class renegade and claimed a "muscle memory of the working class," "silent" and "not formulated or unconscious," because his grandparents were peasants and laborers.[109] Here, we find anew the elasticity of the Rastignac plot of social mobility that equally applies to bourgeois (Macron) and working-class (Louis) parvenus: the singer grew up in the provinces, and his parents were not musicians, two sufficient reasons to tie himself to a working-class upbringing. Chris was of course widely mocked for this remark, but commentators often omit another segment of the discussion. He also said, "I don't speak in the same way to servers, I look at the cleaning women."[110] In this broad understanding of mobility, playing the maid (Seydoux) or looking at one (Chris) can replace performing the job or seeing your mother do it.

There is one rare example of a contemporary first-person maid at the intersection of literature and cinema. In 2006 Fatima Elayoubi published a volume of poetry, *Prière à la lune* (*Prayer to the Moon*), in which she retraced her immigration from Rabat to Lyon, her work as a maid, and her difficulty speaking French. Following a work accident, she started writing about her experience. Every week, her doctor translated the pages from Arabic to French. Filmmaker Philippe Faucon adapted the text for the screen. His feature, *Fatima*, won the 2016 César for best film. The actress who plays the maid was not Fatima Elayoubi herself but a nonprofessional actress, a maid, too, and an immigrant from the Maghreb, Soria Zeroual. Although Elayoubi spoke for herself in the initial diary (unlike Célestine), her story went through layers of filtration: her poems were translated into French by someone else, and in Faucon's film, her role was played by an Algerian maid. As Elayoubi wrote in *Prière à la lune*'s dedication, "To all the Fatimas."[111] Yet neither of the two maids (Elayoubi and Zeroual) was concretely playing her own role. Unlike contemporary transclass writers, maids remain opaque and rarely tell their own stories. Instead, they are indicative of someone else's social trajectory, whether up or down.

## Marivaux's Maids On-screen

Marivaux lurks between the lines when one looks at social mobility and maids together: Ernaux had started a PhD dissertation on his work, and Jacquot, before *Journal d'une femme de chambre*, also adapted Marivaux in *La Fausse Suivante* (2000; *The False Servant*). The valets and the fake servant of the title use numerous asides, and the film, set in a theater, constantly blurs the line between fiction and reality because the actors perambulate from the seats to the stage and the backstage. Marivaux's plays are important pieces of the transclass canon because they are full of valets and maids cross-dressing as their masters, although critics have noted how temporary such social mobility often is.[112] Another filmmaker is famous for adapting Marivaux twice: Abdellatif Kechiche. In *La Vie d'Adèle*—whose title sounds like *La Vie de Marianne* (1741; *The Life of Marianne*)— Marivaux's unfinished novel is Adèle's favorite book, read and analyzed in class at the very beginning of the feature. But it is in *L'Esquive* (2003; *The Dodge*) that social mobility meets maids, as the plot centers on a group of high school students who rehearse Marivaux's play *Le Jeu de l'amour et du hasard* (1730; *The Game of Love and Chance*) in class for an end-of-year show.

The main protagonists, Lydia and Abdelkrim (Krimo), play Lisette and Arlequin, two servants themselves playing their masters, Silvia and Dorante. As critic Louisa Shea argues, "Kechiche erases the figure of the *maître*, and gives the scene over entirely to the *valets and soubrettes* of today, the young *banlieusards*. [...] By rejecting the logic of 'passing for' and erasing the masters from the story line, *L'Esquive* eschews the topos of the 'escape from the banlieue,' and with it a certain dream of successful integration."[113] I agree with this interpretation of Kechiche's sidelining of the masters, but it should not for all that put Lydia and Krimo on the same plane. They both play domestic servants, but they do not have the same relationship to acting. Unlike Lydia, Krimo has great difficulties getting into someone else's shoes, to the great displeasure of the teacher who repeatedly screams "Get out of yourself!" Krimo cannot, which is actually the very point of Marivaux's play: servants can never fully be in character when they play their masters. However disguised, they recognize themselves behind costumes and fall in love with each other. As the teacher explains about *Le Jeu de l'amour et du hasard*, "we cannot rid ourselves of a language, of a certain kind of conversation topic, of a way of expressing ourselves, of a way of standing, which signals where we come from." There are thus two levels in the film: the play, whose message is that one cannot change class beyond a temporary cross-dressing; and the rehearsal, during which the teacher paradoxically encourages a student to become someone else.

There is yet a third level if one takes into account the actors. Osman Elkharraz (the thirteen-year-old boy who played Krimo) published his memoir in 2016. In *Confessions d'un acteur déchu, de "L'Esquive" à la rue* (*Confessions of a Fallen Actor, from "The Dodge" to the Streets*), he recounts his precarious childhood: the death of his parents; the life with his siblings in a house without water or electricity; how he started burglarizing and selling drugs. Kechiche's film was only a parenthesis, thanks to a casting on the fly in a Parisian mall. After the shooting, Elkharraz became homeless. About the lead actress who played Lisette (the now famous Sara Forestier), Elkharraz wrote: "She played someone from the Parisian *banlieue* 24/7 but, in her voice, you could hear it sounded odd. It's like you asked me to play the petit bourgeois, you kind of see how I'm going to do it."[114] Indeed, Krimo had difficulties playing a servant (Arlequin) mimicking his own master (Dorante) while Elkharraz had altercations on the set with Kechiche. The social mobility at play in *L'Esquive*, as in *Le Jeu de l'amour et du hasard*, amounts to "playing" a domestic worker, which did not help Elkharraz get out of poverty. Unlike Léa Seydoux, Osman Elkharraz really attended "the school of hard knocks." But like her, when it came to playing a servant, he could not get out of his social condition, on screen and outside.

Once you know Elkharraz's story, the last scene of Kechiche's *L'Esquive* looks very different. Krimo drops the theater project and does not even attend the end-of-year representation as a spectator. Kechiche's unsteady shoulder camera seems to surreptitiously steal shots of him briefly peering at the show from outside the window, strolling the *platea*. It is as if Krimo had not only dropped the role of Arlequin but his own part in the movie. We don't know whether the character could not act in general or whether the problem came from playing a servant or from playing a servant playing a master. What we do know is that the challenge of becoming someone else (for Krimo as for Elkharraz), of getting out of one's social class, unfolds in a film that represents domestic labor through the canon (Marivaux) between the walls of a classroom.

Across genres and embodied subjectivities, the figure of the maid is a phantom rung of the social ladder, a transitional position that brings together writers and characters traveling to the upper class (Camus, Condé, Diome, Elayoubi, Ernaux, Guène, Mirbeau, NDiaye) on the one hand, and on the other hand authors and actors experiencing a lower class (Aubenas, Calle, Kechiche, Jacquot). No matter the direction of the trajectory, the liminal position of the domestic worker blurs the difference between author, actor, and character (Camus and Cormery; Seydoux and Célestine; Krimo and Elkharraz). To paraphrase Mirbeau, servants reveal socially mobile workers and writers to be "phantoms of themselves among a population of figures." The next chapter asks whether such liminality can also be positive and mitigate the estrangement of the parvenant.

# A Foot in the Door 5

PASSING ON SOCIAL MOBILITY

In May 2019 the French newspaper *Libération* published a petition in support of the Gilets jaunes social movement signed only by artists. Annie Ernaux and Édouard Louis—authors of landmark narratives on class inequality and social mobility—were part of a list of more than 1,400 signatories. The document criticized the ways in which the government and the media were inaccurately portraying the demonstrators, hence the title of the petition: "We Are Not Fooled," meaning *by the anti-Gilets jaunes rhetorics*.[1] The text ended on a collective appeal: "Let's use our power, the power of words, of speech, of music, of images, of thoughts, of art, to invent a new narrative and support those who have been fighting in the streets and at roundabouts for months."

Writers are often solicited to comment on the news, even more so in the case of pressing social topics. Like historians, politicians, or sociologists, Louis and Ernaux regularly intervene in the public sphere to discuss the links between inequality and voting, or the school system's false promise of meritocracy. And yet despite being able to formulate their arguments and defend their opinions publicly and at length, these writers feel that their unique perspective would be best expressed in what the petition calls "a new narrative." What are its features? What is the knowledge of literature when it comes to social questions? How can form contribute to our understanding of class mobility?

In contemporary prose, the trajectory of transclass writers and characters is at times so singular it becomes miraculous. A way to look at social mobility then is to question the closure or the exclusiveness of upward mobility. The keyword here is *reproduction*. If, according to philosopher Chantal Jaquet, a transclass is a person who is not condemned to reproduce her class, does she in turn become an agent of mobility, capable of emancipating others? Can we halt reproduction for ourselves as for our acquaintances, or is the infraction to social determinism only supposed to be an exception? The answer is at least twofold since we can read texts in which social climbers either return to their class or leave their relatives. Each trajectory leads to different narratives, topoi, and devices. In this section, I will play on the double meaning of the verb *transmettre* in French: how does an author *convey* a socially mobile voice and journey? And can a social climber *pass on* social mobility beyond her own miraculous exception?

This set of questions led me to focus on the representation of doors. We have already started exploring this liminal space in the previous chapter with the figure of the maid—a peculiar type of transfuge who is continually crossing doorways. As a transit zone or threshold (for departure, arrival, or return), the door has also acquired a social symbolism when it comes to the transmission of social mobility.[2] In Fatou Diome's *Le Ventre de l'Atlantique* (2003; *The Belly of the Atlantic*), for instance, when the immigrant narrator travels back to Senegal for the holidays and refuses to feed into the myth of a paradisical France, her brother exclaims: "Now that she's there, now that she's making her dough, she's closing the door."[3] Does a social migrant hold the door open or close it behind her?

To frame this discussion, I turn to Jacques Rancière and the opening chapter of his 2017 book *Les Bords de la fiction* (*The Edges of Fiction*), "Portes et fenêtres" ("Doors and Windows").[4] Taking his examples from Balzac, Flaubert, Stendhal, Proust, and Sebald, Rancière reads doors and windows literally and metaphorically. On the one hand, these openings generate descriptions and participate in the plot. It is the case for the jail windows in Stendhal's *La Chartreuse de Parme* (1839; *The Charterhouse of Parma*). On the other hand, an incipit is in itself an overture into fiction, what Rancière calls an "unsaid" door.[5] He also considers the chapters' ends in Victor Hugo's novels and the length of Guy de Maupassant's short stories as narratological entryways. Whether concrete of symbolic, the door has a role in the representation of social mobility. Rancière mentions, for instance, "the windows of bygone picaresque fictions that young people climbed up to on ladders of fortune."[6] He also comments on a book review of *Madame Bovary* (1856) published in Flaubert's time: "In democratic times, doors and windows can be too open, letting onto the blank pages, with the mud of the countryside, the triviality of common people and the embarrassment of petty things."[7] Here again, mud delineates the threshold between the lower and the upper classes, between the matter of the world and the materiality of the text.

I, too, will track tangible doors in the works of Édouard Louis, Annie Ernaux, Christine Angot, and Kaoutar Harchi, because they reveal each author's relationship to emancipation, reproduction, and transmission. I will also examine intangible doors, not in the sense of Rancière's entryways but in their connection to reported speech, as a pivot between the transclass narrator and the voices of those who remain behind the door. Critics have noted how Rancière "does not ventriloquize" but enables the "actual voices of workers to speak for themselves" in *La Nuit des prolétaires* (1981; *The Night of the Proletarians*), and how he "places the reader in direct contact with the words of the original ignorant schoolmaster" in his case study on the pedagogue Joseph Jacotot.[8] Via the door, this chapter will map out the formal mobility and social polyphony at play in today's prose.

### Strait Is the Gate (Édouard Louis)

After publishing a first novel on his class mobility—*En finir avec Eddy Bellegueule* (2014; *Ending Eddy Bellegueule*), Édouard Louis kept on exploring the intersection of emancipation and violence with his second book, *Histoire de la violence* (2016; *History of Violence*). The narrator, Édouard, recounts how on the eve of Christmas 2012, he met a man named Reda. They had sex, consensually, then Reda raped Édouard and tried to strangle him after Édouard accused him of stealing his electronic devices. Édouard (the narrator and the author) subsequently filed a complaint for sexual assault. Riadh B., who also goes by the name of Reda, was arrested and tried, identified as the perpetrator by the DNA that had been collected for another case. The affair caused vivid controversies on the relationship between truth and literature, especially because Riadh was arrested two days after the publication of the novel and because a magistrate,

Édouard's lawyer, and his friend the writer Didier Éribon all referred to the novel in court. For some, *Histoire de la violence*—presented as a true novel during its promotion—was corroborating Louis's complaint; for others, it constituted a literary breach of the presumption of innocence because of its will to blur the boundary between fact and fiction. Riadh B. was acquitted in November 2020 on the basis of what the magistrates' court's ruling described as "inconsistent" statements on the side of Louis.[9]

Instead of telling the story from his sole perspective, the parvenant narrator of *Histoire de la violence* hides behind a door and listens to his sister Clara (who did not flee her milieu) as she narrates Édouard's sexual assault to her husband: "Now I don't move anymore to continue listening to her, and I don't know if I manage to remain so still behind the door thanks to my concentration and my own strength or if it's what she's just said that shames me and wounds me to such a degree that I find myself paralyzed by it and as fixed and hard as the door opposite me."[10] The door is rigid and sealed; the sister won't cross its threshold to meet her brother. Because Louis tells us that the rooms of his childhood home had no doors, their presence can be read as a concrete sign of his upward mobility.[11] By the end of the novel, the social function of the door has changed: "he [Geoffroy] would leave slowly, on tiptoe without slamming the door, and he would come back the next day with Didier."[12] The door that separates the narrator from his family is firmly closed, but it remains open to the comings and goings of his friends, the sociologists Geoffroy de Lagasnerie and Didier Éribon, who belong to Louis's new social status and who bookend the novel's last sentence. In Louis's *Changer: Méthode* (2021; *Change: Method*), we learn that it was initially the well-off mother of his best friend who suddenly started calling him "Édouard" instead of "Eddy," on the threshold of her house.[13] His acculturation and career as a writer originate in entrances.

The door also stands as a metaphor for the rape in *Histoire de la violence*, especially because Louis quotes William Faulkner's *Sanctuary* (1931), a novel on the rape and abduction of Temple Drake: "Temple backed from the room. In the hall she whirled and ran. She ran right off the porch, into the weeds, and sped on. She ran to the road and down it for fifty yards in the darkness, then without a break she whirled and ran back to the house and sprang onto the porch and crouched against the door just as someone came up the hall."[14] In the first part of *Sanctuary*, the description of the bootleggers' house where Temple will be assaulted contains numerous references to doors. Louis uses Faulkner to explain how Temple and he share a similar "inability to flee."[15] Temple Drake is downwardly mobile: she, the wealthy daughter of a judge, is forced into prostitution in a Memphis brothel. In the excerpt selected by Louis, we can thus read Temple's trajectory socially, in comparison to Édouard's upward mobility: he ran and turned away from his family, then, with the same impulse, he came back to sit in front of a door that was not there at the beginning of the sentence. The door appears when the parvenant returns, as in *Histoire de la violence* in which Louis reconnects with his sister on a threshold.[16]

The door also symbolizes Reda's social status vis-à-vis Édouard's. Before the rape and after a first consensual intercourse, the two men hear a drunkard who tries to open the door of Édouard's apartment, probably because he is on the wrong floor:

> The two of us were under my thick red covers, lying down, naked; we heard someone come dangerously close to the doorway of my apartment, or rather, in fact not someone approaching but someone who had appeared, already and immediately close. [...] We heard all the little machinery of the lock resist, the lock stayed fixed in place, the person behind the door pushed it with their shoulder, removed the key and entered it again, removed it once more, entered it once more, did not manage to open it, applied force, insisted.[17]

Because of the sexual connotation of the verbs, we can read this passage as a prefiguration of the rape. But my hypothesis is that the door here also functions as a metaphor for social immobility. Reda, a second-generation Kabyle immigrant of humble origins, crossed the entrance of Édouard's apartment. Despite this seeming proximity, he is still on the threshold: the man "immediately close" yet "behind the door" is not a tipsy neighbor but Reda. This difference of status is visible in the use of the verb *parvenir* (to manage) planted twice in the French version. About Édouard: "I manage to remain still behind the door." But about Reda: "the person did not manage to open the door." Unlike the intruder, the narrator is a parvenu who has achieved his social goal.

*Histoire de la violence* displays other kinds of thresholds that underline the social class of and the social gap between characters. On the one hand, in addition to the narrator's monologue transcribed in standard font, the novel includes his reactions to the sister's narrative in italics, themselves enclosed in parentheses. There is thus a concrete *and* a typographical partition between Édouard and his sister, his past, his class. On the other hand, the door is not only a spatial metaphor for social distance but a literary device that underpins the montage of reported speech. It is the case when Reda leaves the apartment: "I came back, I closed the door. Reda returned. He pressed his face to the door, I heard him do it, and he said to me: 'You're sure you want me to leave? I'm sorry. Forgive me.' I answered: 'Leave.' It was over."[18] In this passage, the door, the quotation marks, and the punctuation have the same function. The colon's two dots even look like door hinges. The door also signals reported speech when Édouard listens to Clara: "I keep my eyes riveted to the door to maintain my concentration and to not be found. I study the bifurcations and the brown streaks that advance along the beige of the wood. I try to figure out how the streaks manage to escape the door, starting from the center to the extremities where they disappear. Clara tells her husband that Reda had asked me if I was going to speak to him eventually."[19] The door introduces indirect discourse; the streaks reflect the plurality of voices.

*Histoire de la violence* starts with a door and with reported speech:

> I'm hidden on the other side of the door, I listen to her, she says that a few hours after what the copy of the complaint that I keep folded in four in a drawer calls the *attempted homicide*, and that I continue to call as such, for lack of another word, because there is not another term more appropriate for what happened and because of that I carry the painful and unpleasant sensation that as soon as it's uttered, by me or anyone else, my story is falsified, I left my place and I went down the stairs.[20]

This long hypotactic sentence delays the junction between Clara's speech and Édouard's action. "She says that" is not immediately followed by the reported discourse in question. The author separates the two voices by inserting a digression, a run-on, by multiplying the subordinate clauses: "she says that a few hours after what the copy of the complaint that," and so forth. The junction is not even seamless. If we were to erase the digression, the sentence would call for the mandatory repetition of the relative pronoun in French, which is not the case ("she says that [...] I left my place and *that* [*que*] I went down the stairs). The novel opens with an attempt at polyphony through a literary device (the reported speech) and a symbolic object (the door), but the narrator immediately dissociates from his sister's discourse to formulate an autonomous "I." If Louis wanted to introduce another voice and another version of his story, in fact, the reported speech further isolates the transclass narrator. Surprisingly, this opening paragraph—present in the original edition of *Histoire de la violence* and in its English translation—has disappeared in the paperback, and this without any editorial indication of this important change. The new version (published in 2019) starts like its 2018 stage adaptation, whose script, *Au Cœur de la violence* (*In the Heart of Violence*), was published in 2019: "ÉDOUARD / and so, a few hours after what the copy of the complaint that I keep folded in four in a drawer calls the *attempted homicide*, I left my place and I went down the stairs."[21] The devices at the core of *Histoire de la violence*—that is to say the sister's discourse and the motif of the door—are no longer foregrounded. As a result, even if the door is "ajar" in the play, the rewrite further undermines the attempt at social polyphony by getting rid of the working-class sister's voice.[22]

The symbol of the door was already present in Louis's first novel, *En finir avec Eddy Bellegueule*. The penultimate section is called "La porte étroite" ("Strait Is the Gate"), less after the New Testament (Luke 13:24) than André Gide's 1909 novel of the same name. The chapter recounts how Eddy got a foot in the door of social emancipation by acting, an extracurricular activity that allowed him to attend a high school with a theater section in Amiens. He thus dodged the local high school, left his region to become a boarder, and started his social journey: "The acting I did in the middle school drama club had opened an unexpected door for me."[23] Louis captures this social swerve through the metaphor of the door. *En finir avec Eddy Bellegueule* also displays a specific montage of discourses. First, on a thematic level, Édouard and his parents do not communicate. About his mother: "She spoke to me a lot, long monologues; I could have put someone else in my place, she would have continued her story."[24]

And about his father: "He and I never had real conversations. Even simple things, *hello* or *happy birthday*, he had stopped saying them to me."²⁵ Second, on a typographic level, clauses in italics signal slang, dialect, and insult. They are often juxtaposed to their "translations": "they look after the children *I'm taking care of the kids*."²⁶ Édouard's and his parents' discourses are superposed, juxtaposed, but they do not meet. Italics are not only associated with poverty but also with any form of class disjunction. When the narrator's cousin Sylvain appears in court, the judge's sophisticated phrasing is transcribed in italics. At the end of *En finir avec Eddy Bellegueule*, when the narrator arrives in a more affluent high school, italics are used by the students and Eddy alike, as if the class difference had been reduced. Italics have the same function in Louis's third book, *Qui a tué mon père* (2018; *Who Killed My Father*). They appear in the prologue to explicitly formulate a discrepancy between Louis and his father: "*The fact that only the son speaks and only him is a violent thing for them both: the father is deprived of the possibility of recounting his own life and the son hopes for a response that he will never obtain.*"²⁷ Italics also signal the distance between the narrator and the father's discourse: "You said that I was going to become a professor, an important doctor, a minister, you didn't know yet, but that in any case I was going to study at the highest level and that I was nothing like the delinquents (*sic*)."²⁸ The Latin word *sic*, in italics and between parentheses, creates a complicity with the readers. It tells them that the narrator is transcribing the father's exact wording but that he does not support the argument. Such complicity supposes a certain cultural capital, that of knowing what *sic* means. The typeface matters in and of itself in *Histoire de la violence*: "it was the truth of the form that interested me and not the content."²⁹ Indeed, italics are often used when the narrator as a child tells stories or tries, as an adult, to transcribe sentences he would have pronounced in the past, all the while admitting that the stories are invented and the quotes inexact. Typography underlines the distance between Louis then and now. It allows the author to convey that the life of a social climber is a reinvention of all temporal strata, including the past, and that what matters in such literary endeavor is what the form reveals, not the accuracy of the content.³⁰

By comparison, quotation marks have a very different meaning in *En finir avec Eddy Bellegueule*. Their only occurrence signals two exact quotes, one from Simone de Beauvoir's *Une mort très douce* (1964; *A Very Gentle Death*), the other from Stefan Zweig's *Marie-Antoinette* (1932).[31] Although Louis had mentioned reading Zweig's biography of the queen sixty pages earlier, he does not introduce or source the citation here. Louis's doors and discursive thresholds thereby construct rigid barriers not only between his past and present classes, or between his friends and family, but also between reported speech and intertextuality, further isolating him from his background. The insertion of quotes is an important difference between *En finir avec Eddy Bellegueule* (dedicated to Didier Éribon, one of his professors at the Université de Picardie) and Éribon's own narrative of social mobility, *Retour à Reims* (2009; *Return to Reims*). Éribon's book is not a novel; it stands halfway between an autobiographical narrative and an essay and is filled with literary, philosophical, and sociological references, all sourced in footnotes.[32] With such a format, Éribon responds to his own mentor Pierre Bourdieu, whose narrative of social mobility, *Esquisse pour une auto-analyse* (2004; *Sketch for a Self-Analysis*), was not sufficiently sourced: "He doesn't mention any of the books that he was reading."[33] Unlike Éribon, Louis is not returning home but fleeing. His use of reported speech reinforces the distance between him and his original social class and may find its impetus in this upward trajectory.[34] Louis's narrator felt the need to increase the distance between the two sides of what Éribon coined as a "social closet"; a "class closet" in Michael Lucey's translation.[35] No matter the reason, the gate of social mobility is strait in the works of Édouard Louis. He leaves his family at the door in *Histoire de la violence*; he does not open the door of his library to the readers of *En finir avec Eddy Bellegueule*. Despite the insertion of multiple discourses, quotes, and typographical signs, the narrative fails to be formally and socially polyphonic.

I am under the impression that this one-sidedness caught the attention of contemporary writers who published responses to Édouard Louis. In *L'Effraction* (2016; *The Break-In*), Omar Benlaala rewrites *Histoire de la violence* with Reda as the main character: "Playing with all the possibilities literature offers, I reversed the apparatus chosen by Édouard Louis, the roles of the executioner and the victim, to evoke the voice of the person that I was: a young French man of Kabyle origin confronted by the difficulty of living his sexuality in a society torn apart by its colonial past."[36] Eddy Bellegueule is renamed Hédi ("the guide" in Arabic) in order to "shorten the distance" with the Kabyle narrator.[37] Reda's presence is overwhelming: he narrates the story, answers the questions of a sociologist, and transcribes his dialogues with Hédi in bold. The format reminds readers of Kamel Daoud's postcolonial rewrite of Albert Camus's *L'Étranger* (1942; *The Stranger*) from the point of view of an Arabic character, *Meursault, contre-enquête* (2013; *Meursault, Counter-Investigation*). Yet there is a notable difference: Louis and Benlaala are contemporary with each other. David Fortems for his part often mentions the influence of Édouard Louis in interviews. With *Louis veut partir* (2020; *Louis Wants to Leave*), he seems to offer a rewrite of *En finir avec Eddy Bellegueule* from the point of view of the father: the protagonist is the son of a factory worker; he is gay, loves books, and plans to attend Sciences Po; his first name is Louis, and the epilogue is entitled "En finir."[38] The father barely speaks, but this novel is polyphonic. After his son's suicide, he meets Louis's friends to better understand him. The author thus shows how one can tell the story of a parvenant teenager through the voices of others, although it entails violently erasing, through a suicide, the perspective of Louis's narrator. As we have seen, Louis's siblings (his sister Clara in *Histoire de la violence*) are not part of his social mobility. His books do not portray people that might reproduce Louis's trajectory (such as students, friends, or partners from different social classes). Yet there is an exception, his mother in *Combats et métamorphoses d'une femme* (2021; *Battles and Metamorphoses of a Woman*), who reinvents herself and moves to Paris under her son's impulse. This reproduction—although confined to the family—complicates our usual understanding of the habitus and the chronology of social influence.

### Flat Is the Prose (Annie Ernaux)

After losing her father, Annie Ernaux published *La Place* (*The Place*) in 1983, a narrative of social estrangement in which she retraces her father's biography and her own upward mobility in light of this recent death. The text—whose paragraphs are separated by blanks of various lengths—won the Renaudot prize and stands as Ernaux's most read, acclaimed, and commented work. Yet despite appearances, it does not tell the story of a unique and miraculous social climber. On the contrary, Ernaux realizes that her parents—successively peasants, factory workers, and shopkeepers—were *transfuges* too: "She was a woman who could go anywhere, in other words, break through social barriers"; "He borrowed to become the owner of the walls and the land. No one in the family had ever been such a thing."[39] There is also this sentence: "Half-shopkeeper, half-worker, on the two sides at the same time," whose wording conveys the ambivalent social status of the father.[40] Ernaux thus echoes *Esquisse pour une auto-analyse*, in which Pierre Bourdieu self-portrays as a "transfuge son of a transfuge," a second-generation parvenant.[41] In this context, Ernaux's trajectory loses its singularity: she repeated her parents' upward mobility, although more publicly and spectacularly, since she became not only a teacher but a writer. She even considered calling *La Place* "La Continuation."[42] The narrator describes this singular heredity only obliquely: "Once, I read that when Bécassine was an apprentice, having to embroider a bird on a bib, and *ditto* on the others, embroidered *ditto* with a bourdon stitch."[43] Bécassine does not reproduce the image but the word. This anecdote can be read as a comment on class mobility. Instead of repeating the same usage of the hands, instead of becoming a worker who embroiders birds on bibs or the shopkeeper who sells them, Ernaux is subject to a more abstract, tautological, and linguistic reproduction: she rewrites the word *ditto* (*idem* in French) on the fabric. She is the Bécassine who reproduced her parents' mobility by copying a word on an object (the bib) twice associated with reproduction: manufacturing and infancy. By referring to the archetypical maid in popular culture, Ernaux also points to her liminal social status in between classes. For this reason, writing that Ernaux is "an exemplary figure of non-reproduction in the absence of antecedents," as does Chantal Jaquet in *Les Transclasses ou la non-reproduction* (2014; *The Transclasses or Non-Reproduction*), is a misinterpretation because Ernaux clearly is an heir to her transclass parents.[44] Ernaux also formulated this unexpected familial legacy in *Une femme* (1987; *A Woman*), a book similar to *La Place* only focused on Ernaux's mother: "This knowledge, transmitted from mother to daughter for centuries, stops at me, who is no longer anything but the archivist."[45] This statement raises a question: can Ernaux (as a writer, teacher, and commentator) spread the mobility she had inherited from her parents? Is literary transmission restricted to gathering and conveying information like an archivist, or can it be a truly performative handover that has the tangible effect of emancipating readers and students?

To answer this question, we should compare Ernaux's descriptions of her ascendance (her parents), descendance (her two sons), and mentees (her students). There is a very distinct treatment of parents and children in *La Place*: the narrator underlines the kinship with her husband and uncle by calling them respectively "my husband" and "the brother of my father," but her son is repeatedly designated as "the child."[46] Legacy seems to stop with her.[47] In *La Femme gelée* (1981; *The Frozen Woman*), published right before *La Place*, we learn about Ernaux's status as an only child: "I am too, the only [...]. First and last, that's for sure."[48] Ernaux is an only child or literally a "unique" daughter in French—a socially loaded adjective in the context of her trajectory. The organization of *La Place* seems to contradict the very possibility of reproducing nonreproduction, of transmitting upward mobility outside of the family sphere. The narrative opens on the promise of an ascent since the narrator passes an exam to become a teacher. But by the end of the text, the emancipation announced at the beginning becomes an exception: the narrator realizes that the cashier at her local supermarket is a former student. Except for the first two paragraphs, *La Place* is a loop (a narrative epanadiplosis) from the parents' little grocery store to the suburban mall. Ernaux's professional status becomes an anomaly, apposed at the beginning of the text. She got out of determinism by reading, writing, and teaching words—or by stitching them like Bécassine— but she didn't succeed in sharing this experience in class.

Upward mobility is thus limited in *La Place*; it does not take Louis's "strait gate" but "path": "Straight path, in writing, between the rehabilitation of a way of life considered inferior, and the denunciation of the alienation that accompanies it. [...] Impression, rather, of swaying from one side to the other of this contradiction."[49] Ernaux's writing strategies have a double aim: acknowledging the in-between social environment in which she was raised and bridging the gap between her *petit commerçant* upbringing and bourgeois adulthood. Social thresholds are not strait gates but swaying and invisible frontiers: "J'ai fini de mettre au jour l'héritage que j'ai dû déposer au seuil du monde bourgeois et cultivé quand j'y suis entrée."⁵⁰ There are two ways to read this sentence in French. First reading: "cultivé" is an adjective coordinated with "bourgeois." "I finished uncovering the inheritance that I had to leave at the threshold of the bourgeois and cultivated world when I entered." Second reading, just as grammatically correct because the sentence has no punctuation until the final period: Ernaux conjugates the verb *cultiver*, which depends on the same auxiliary as the verbal group *devoir déposer*: "I finished uncovering the inheritance that I had to leave at the threshold of the bourgeois world and that I cultivated as I entered it." Either Ernaux frees herself from her modest background before integrating a lettered world or she files this legacy at the entrance of the bourgeoisie to capitalize on it afterward. The word *threshold* here functions as an ambiguous and unstable pivot.

Ernaux started depicting porous boundaries between social classes from her first novel *Les Armoires vides* (1974; *The Empty Cupboards*): "During that vacation, I find the juncture, the sneakiest way of getting myself out of it [...], of jumping head first into my studies, literature, especially literature, to float above everyone."⁵¹ Ernaux's way out paradoxically is a "joint": a seal *and* a joining device. The narrator wants to climb the social ladder but turns the scission with her original class into an oxymoronic waterproof junction point. Ernaux later extends this metaphor when she locates her writing style "at the joining of the familial and the social."⁵² After the death of her parents, Ernaux admits, in the last sentence of *Une femme*, "I lost the last link with the world that I come from."⁵³ The separation was implicitly announced in the first sentence: "For the first time the door of her room was closed."⁵⁴ Unlike Louis, Ernaux is not recounting her escape through a strait gate that can only accommodate one but a return to her native Normandy. Her writing style amounts to a homecoming that gives rise neither to miserabilism nor to populism: it is not meant to sever ties further but to mend a lost bond, to retrace the steps of the straight path that originates in the lower-class and yet socially ambiguous household of her transclass parents.

The image of the door or threshold is one possible entryway into what Annie Ernaux calls "flat writing" (*l'écriture plate*) an egalitarian style, a potential vector of social mobility that makes it possible to address the greatest number of readers by fusing the language registers of her original social class and of her class of arrival. Writing has the power to overcome social estrangement: "I write perhaps because we had nothing more to say to each other."⁵⁵ The phrase "écriture plate" reminds us of Roland Barthes's "blank writing" (*l'écriture blanche*). Both agree that "writing is thus essentially the morality of the form, it's the choice of the social zone within which the writer decides to situate the Nature of their language."⁵⁶ In *Le Degré zéro de l'écriture* (1953; *The Degree Zero of Writing*), Barthes traces a genealogy of the "*tearing of the bourgeois conscience*" from Flaubert to Camus, whose "non-style" is "the anticipation of an absolutely homogeneous state of society."⁵⁷ Ernaux's writing is not Barthes's degree zero: she does not deem society to be classless yet does not want to renounce being a "witness of the universal" either.⁵⁸ On the contrary, her goal is to reach the collectivity through individual trajectories, to "[wrest herself] from the trap of the individual" in order to transcend assigned positions.⁵⁹ Ernaux's *Une femme* and Barthes's paradigmatic example of "l'écriture blanche," Camus's *L'Étranger*, open on the same event, formulated in simple words: the death of a mother. But Ernaux could simply not use the adjective *blanche* like Barthes because Blanche is her mother's first name.⁶⁰ It could nonetheless have been a social juncture between her past and her present, as "la Blanche" is also the title of the Gallimard series in which Ernaux publishes her books. But when the adjective pops up in her prose, it is all but neutral or literary, as it brings back the souvenir of her mother: "A blank period [*période blanche*], without thoughts. Several times, walking through the streets, 'I am a grown up' (my mother, formerly, 'you are a big girl' because of my period)."⁶¹ Ernaux's writing is not neutral either: "Thus, I write in the most neutral manner possible, but certain expressions [...] cannot be neutral for me."⁶² Whiteness cannot be a synonym of blankness or neutrality. Only the adjective *flat* can create a dialogue between classes and generate a stylistical leveling that aims to do away with social ladders and hierarchies.

Ernaux's leveling strategy is particularly visible in her use of reported speech, especially in letters—an important genre throughout her work.⁶³ The epistolary genre is central to exemplify "l'écriture plate" in *La Place*: "Flat writing comes to me naturally, the same writing that I used formerly to write to my parents to give them essential news."⁶⁴ And here is how Ernaux puts this definition into practice: "My mother wrote me a report of the surrounding world. It's cold here we hope it won't last. We went Sunday to see our friends from Granville. Old lady X died at sixty that's not old. [...] My father signed it. I also answered them in the tone of an official statement. They would have perceived any attempt at style as a way of keeping them at a distance."⁶⁵ The style is flat in the sense of constative. Ernaux quotes her mother's letter without distinguishing between the two voices. The only infringement to the free indirect discourse is the phrase "old lady X." Ernaux taps into the familiar register by designating the lady as "la mère," which literally means "the mother," but the phrase also evokes the title of Balzac's novel, *Le Père Goriot* (1835), often translated into English as "Old Man Goriot" and mentioned on the very first page of *La Place*. While the letter *X* usually indicates anonymity, here it looks like a crossroads, a possible visualization of how a mother and daughter from different classes can interact through language and literature. Ernaux also wrote to her parents right after passing the teaching exam:

> "You really dragged them through, your students," the inspector reproached me later, in the principal's office. [...] The inspector extended his hand to me. Then, looking me right in the eyes: "Madame, congratulations." The others repeated "congratulations" and shook my hand, but the woman with a smile.
> [...] That very night, I wrote to my parents that I was a "tenured" professor. My mother answered that they were very happy for me.⁶⁶

Ernaux uses punctuation to signal reported speech. We immediately hear the professor's voice through direct discourse: "You really dragged them through, your students," the inspector reproached me. The narrator introduces the words only after the citation. At the very moment Ernaux passes the exam, when social mobility is enacted and becomes official, direct discourse is also abruptly juxtaposed to the narration without an introductory verb: Then, looking me right in the eyes: "Madame, congratulations." This use of reported speech represents the violent rupture of social mobility. The achievement is a social verdict that creates a clear distinction between before and after the colon. Ernaux had thought of another beginning for *La*

*Place*: a scene in which the narrator would hear, *behind a closed door*, a professor teaches her lesson—a door that would have reinforced the anticipated rupture of class mobility.[67] Conversely in the aforementioned quote, Ernaux uses indirect discourse to describe her letter: "I wrote ... that," "[she] answered that." It is as if she tried to soften the exam results, to convey them as flatly as possible to somehow undo the social estrangement they announce. Only one word in quotation marks, "tenured," stands as a transition between the assessors' direct style and the indirect discourse between Ernaux and her mother. Unlike Jean Genet, who writes in the language of the enemy (the upper class), Ernaux is thus writing in the language of her family.[68]

To better understand how, or whether, social mobility can be transmitted outside of the family sphere, beyond Ernaux's parents and Louis's mother, I would like to compare the use of reported discourses in Ernaux's letters to her mother to the last paragraph of *La Place* where she meets one of her former students:

> In October of last year, I recognized, behind the register where I was in line with my cart, a former student. Which is to say that I remembered she had been my student five or six years earlier. I didn't know her name anymore nor in what class I'd had her. To say something, when my turn arrived, I asked her: "You're doing well? You like it here?" She answered yes yes. Then after scanning the canned food and the drinks, with embarrassment: "The technical school, it didn't work out." She seemed to think that I still remembered her course choices. But I had forgotten why she'd been sent to the technical school, and in what branch. I said to her "goodbye." She was already grabbing the next groceries with her left hand and keying things in without looking with her right hand.[69]

The markers of reported speech and the montage of discourses are chaotic. The narrator first asks a question with all the features of the direct discourse: an introductory verb, a colon, a quotation mark, and a question mark: I asked her: "You're doing well? You like it here?" The student's answer is radically different: She replied yes yes. No quotation marks, no colon, no relative pronoun. Ernaux didn't write, *She replied yes* or *Elle a répondu que oui*. And when the cashier speaks again, the narrator does not introduce her words: after scanning the canned food and the drinks, with embarrassment: "The technical school, it didn't work out." Finally Ernaux says "goodbye" with quotation marks, but without an introductory colon.

There is a strong heterogeneity between the rendering of Ernaux's and her student's discourses as well as between this scene and Ernaux's use of free indirect discourse in the correspondence with her mother. The response of the nontransclass student-cashier abruptly crops up: she answered yes yes. This "yes yes" is at the edge of indirect and free indirect discourse. It is less autonomous than the free indirect speech of the mother (a transclass herself). Yet Ernaux does not insist on distance but uses a hybrid free indirect speech that levels the two women. I see it as way of bringing the cashier's speech into her prose, of not leaving her at the door, of not emphasizing the class gap with quotation marks, colons, relative pronouns, or italics. The questions turn out to be statements with quotation marks at the end: "You like it here?" instead of "Do you like it here?" We could say that such phrasing limits the possibility of a free conversation, yet at the same time, it merges the voice of the author and that of the student. Certainly, emancipation is not concretely transmitted in *La Place*, but stylistically, Ernaux, at the risk of a grammatical hiatus, blurs the difference between the student and herself by erasing the junction between narration and speech. She leaves the stylistical door of social mobility ajar. In the beginning as in the end of *La Place*, readers can find a similar insertion of direct discourse in between quotation marks, without an introductory verb, to signal a class gap. But in each case, through free indirect discourse, Ernaux tries to express social mobility in literary terms.

Frederic Jameson in *The Political Unconscious* (1981) considers Flaubert's free indirect discourse as one of the "strategic loci for the fully constituted or centered bourgeois subject."[70] He favors instead Balzac's "heterogeneous narrative registers" and his "rotation of character centers which deprives each of them in turn of any privileged status."[71] Two decades later in *La Parole muette* (1998; *The Mute Speech*), Jacques Rancière argues that Flaubert uses the free indirect style in order to "erase all trace of voice," while for Pierre Bourdieu in *Les Règles de l'art* (1992; *The Rules of Art*), Flaubert's play on the various forms of reported speech is a tool among others (citation, the phrase "as if," verb tenses, blanks, asyndeton) to "maintain a distance" between the narrator and the characters so as to offer an exhaustive representation of the social field.[72] Ernaux's free indirect discourse is neither classist nor classless; she plays with innovative free forms of reported speech to capture not the entire social field but the specific process of class mobility conveyed from the vantage of a first-person narrative.

Ernaux's most recent novel, *Mémoire de fille* (2016; *Girl's Memory*), raises this same set of questions, although this time, instead of interacting with her mother, student, or assessors, Ernaux confronts two versions of herself:

> In these conditions, must I merge the girl of '58 and the woman of 2014 into an "I"? Or, what seems to me, not the most just—a subjective evaluation—but the most adventurous, dissociate the former from the latter through the use of "her" and "I," to go as far as possible into the exposition of facts and acts. And as cruelly as possible, like when we hear people behind a door speaking about us by saying "she" or "he" and at that moment we feel as though we're dying.[73]

The door is a metaphorical airlock between the "she" of the past and the "I" of the present. The distance is eventually erased through the use of the subject pronoun *on*. Again, Ernaux refuses the rigidity of the door and creates instead a literary and grammatical juncture: "Must I alternate constantly between one and the other historical vision—1958/2014? I dream of a sentence that could contain them both, without friction, simply through the trick of a new syntax."[74] This enunciation and syntax are the latest iterations of the "écriture plate" described thirty years earlier in *La Place*.[75]

Critics such as Gerald Prince and Alex Woloch have shown how *Le Père Goriot* owes its polyphony to Rastignac, especially the "mimetic and citational italics" and the range of devices (omniscience, reported speech) used to represent "Eugène's consciousness."[76] But Rastignac doesn't speak much, while today, narratives of social mobilities are no longer told by an omniscient narrator but by the contemporary equivalent of Rastignac himself. As we have seen in the previous examples, the works of Édouard Louis and Annie Ernaux strive to be polyphonic too. To this end, they deploy devices to shed light on various forms of discourses: quotation marks, parentheses, italics, footnotes, and reported speech. Ernaux formulated this goal explicitly in her published writing diary, *L'Atelier noir* (2011; *The Dark Workshop*): "July 4, 2001. I finally see the difference between *Une femme* and *La Place*. *La Place* is much more polyphonic, a reconstitution through the language of the first world, which at the same time tells of the tear. I bring more into this world than into *Une femme*. Immersion, and the narrative—like Zola—merges the voices (mine and that of others)."[77] The diary entry itself multiplies the symbols, such as the parentheses, dashes, italics, and underlining, in order to break the narrator's univocality. As we have seen, reported speech can aptly capture social mobility by putting the voices of characters from different classes on the same level, upending the apparent tension between flatness and polyphony. In her prose, Ernaux also uses italics and quotation marks, but she is wary of typography and its social connotation. As she writes in *La Place*: "Naturally, no joy in writing, in that enterprise where I stand as closely as possible to heard words and phrases, sometimes highlighting them through italics. Not to indicate a double meaning to the reader and offer them the pleasure of complicity [...]. Simply because these words and these phrases tell of the limits and color of the world where my father lived, where I lived too. And we never mistook one word for another."[78] Indeed, her italics delimit the borders of a social condition: "My father entered in the category of *simple* or *modest* or *honest people*."[79] Ernaux also uses italics to describe school as the starting point of her class mobility but also as a space that is not easily accessible to all: "So I will never leave school, after that day when my father brought me *and we tried the wrong door*."[80] About quotations marks, she explains that "the text of *La Place* conveys the point of view of my father but also of an entire laborer and peasant social class through the words inserted into the framework of the story. There is also a 'pointing to' the hierarchizing role of language to which we don't generally pay any attention, through the use of quotation marks: 'simple people,' 'modest milieu,' etc."[81] Quotation marks underscore the distance between classes and the confinement to a class. The proof is that Ernaux titled the book on her mother's Alzheimer's disease by using one of her mysterious remarks: *"I Have Not Emerged from My Night."* In French, the mother's medical and social imprisonment appears in italics *and* between quotation marks. We have seen how quotation marks introduce the direct discourse of the assessors and of the student. They can also convey Ernaux's own social class: "All of a sudden, with shock, 'now, I'm really a bourgeoise' and 'it's too late.'"[82] The irruption of the punctuation tears the fiber of the text and demonstrates the radicality of the social rupture at stake. Here is what a first-person narrative provides in terms of class that nineteenth-century bildungsromane did not; Rastignac would never say this.

## Imperfect Is the Tense (Christine Angot)

Christine Angot writes novels and plays about parenthood, family, couples, and sexual violence; she also explores the figure of the author and the contemporary French literary scene.[83] Known as an uncensored writer of the self, she was obligated to pay damages to her partner's ex-wife who recognized herself in the unflattering portrait of the mother in the narrative *Les Petits* (2011; *The Little Ones*). From 2017 to 2019, Angot was a television commentator on the Saturday night talk show *On n'est pas couché*. Some, like me, found value in the way she asked artists and politicians to justify a word choice, to narrate an event, to describe a feeling. Many others hated her interventions and thought she was too polemical and self-centered. Angot's novels and narratives often address bluntly the sexual abuse her father inflicted on her. She was translated into English for the first time in 2017 with her controversial 1999 autofiction, *L'Inceste* (*The Incest*).[84] Her autobiographies have broader objectives than the self, as in *Quitter la ville* (2000; *Leave the City*): "I'm not airing out MY dirty laundry. But the social sheet."[85]

Angot's parents, Pierre Angot and Rachel Schwartz, did not come from the same social class: he was a translator on an American operating base in Chateauroux while she rose through the ranks from typist to executive secretary and chief of staff in the social security administration. At first, he refused to recognize Christine officially because he and his family considered the union with Rachel to be socially unsuitable (because she was poor and Jewish). He accepted paternity only after the beginning of the sexual abuse. In a long dialogue with her mother at the end of *Un amour impossible* (2015; *An Impossible Love*), the narrator interprets the incest in social terms. Pierre Angot symbolically annulled the official recognition of his mésalliance with Rachel by molesting their daughter, thereby undoing this socially inacceptable kinship: "Not recognizing a prohibition that applies to everyone, that's the highest distinction. You see! What class! And for him, it was the ultimate, irrefutable way to annul the recognition."[86] The incest was a sexual violence, a social revanche, a class punishment.

In a subsequent narrative, *Le Voyage dans l'Est* (2021; *The Journey to the East*), Angot uses the word *banishment* to describe the abuse as a family downgrading. Yet she also underlines how, from the point of view of the father, incest was not only a way to accentuate the social distance with his daughter but to move upward: he envisioned it as a "sign of distinction" found in aristocracy and Ancient Egypt.[87] Angot resorts to the metaphor of the door to express her father's gesture: "And what he did with me was the final way he found, in the end, to slam the door in your face, and on top of that to turn the key one more time in the lock."[88] Here as in the works of Annie Ernaux and Édouard Louis, the door reveals the rigidity of class borders, and in Angot's case the father's classism. This image crops up in a scene set next to a door: "All week we saw each other in that café. At the same table. Inside, not far from the door."[89] After years of a tumultuous relationship, Angot and her mother are finally able to come together next to a half-open door, a symbol of their estrangement and mixed social status. When Angot and her father are near a door, the social connotations are strikingly different. One afternoon, Pierre Angot steps outside the apartment while Christine, following him, closes the door. He then realizes he had left the keys inside and starts yelling and lecturing his daughter on her lack of good manners: "He told me that you don't close the door yourself, when you're not in your own home."[90] The scene takes place in the father's official, bourgeois family house in Strasbourg while his wife and children are abroad. The father's control of the door reinforces Christine's bastardy: only he can decide who belongs to his family and kinship, who can bear his name, who can cross the threshold of social mobility.

In *Le Marché des amants* (2008; *Lovers Market*), Angot addresses social mobility through romance. She recounts how she dated a rap singer of Guadeloupean descent born into disadvantage, Bruno Beausir, known by the stage name of "Doc Gynéco" in France. The text is filled with dialogues during which Bruno and Christine find common ground in their passion for words and musicality. And yet Christine's friends constantly try to convince her that she and he do not belong, thus reproducing the social verdict that fell on Rachel and Pierre in the 1950s. Bruno also puts Christine at a distance: he considers that despite her modest origin, she now belongs to "them," the Parisian, bourgeois, and intellectual elite. A train door becomes the symbol of their transclass affair:

> Going to the bathroom, I had been struck by the violent noise near the bellows. An image came to me and never left me again. Just after the compartments and the swinging door in the hallway, I had a flashback of Bruno and me lying on the ground in the same two square meters of a Corail train. Me, back to the swinging door that opened regularly, him, against the door of the car which let the cold in, his folded knees against my feet. He read *Rendez-vous*, we had just met, it was the day after our first night. He had his brown leather winter jacket, his sky-blue jeans with holes in the knees, his black skin showing through. After four hours, when we got off the train, we walked for the first time in the street the two of us hand in hand. He carried our two bags on his shoulder and gave me his hand in the pocket of my coat, I squeezed it through my glove, I took the glove off to better feel his skin, the breadth of his hand and its firm way of holding mine.[91]

Despite the racial and class disparities, Christine and Bruno meet in this passageway between wagons as between social worlds. The encounter is precarious: cold air rushes as the door keeps opening; the sound is deafening and the two bodies are uncomfortably seated. The door is a "porte battante" that can swing in both directions at any time and close automatically. The adjective *battant* also means combative in French: Christine and Bruno had to beat the odds to sit together in this carved out space, to hold hands tightly in the tiny pocket of her coat.

For Angot, texts have to be performative: "The important thing was for the texts to have a use value, to be active, to incite life, to have consequences."[92] What is the performativity at stake in *Le Marché des amants*? Or more precisely, how does Angot convey her transclass romance beyond the meaning of each sentence? If you were to look at the long excerpt in French, you would be struck by the unusual use of the imperfect tense. Take this sentence, for instance: "Au bout de quatre heures, quand on sortait du train, on marchait pour la première fois dans la rue tous les deux main dans la main." An English speaker should translate it as, "After four hours, when we got off the train, we walked for the first time in the street the two of us hand in hand." But the original French version does not respect the tense agreement. The expression "for the first time" is incompatible with the imperfect tense that can indicate either a habit or an ongoing action. A grammatically faulty but faithful translation would be: "After four hours, when we were getting off the train, we used to walk for the first time in the street together hand in hand." Take this other sentence: "Il lisait *Rendez-Vous*, on venait de se rencontrer, c'était le lendemain de notre première nuit." To clarify the meaning of each clause, the sentence could be translated as follows: "He was reading *Rendez-vous*, we had just met, it was the day after our first night." But the tenses are the same in French, hence the chosen translation in the block quote above: "He read *Rendez-vous*, we had just met, it was the day after our first night." Keeping the same tenses should make the English reader feel the imperfect's strangeness to a French ear.

These two sentences are not exceptions. Angot started implementing and systematizing the use of this verb tense in 2004 with *Les Désaxés (The Unbalanced Ones)*. French New Novelist Alain Robbe-Grillet would have disapproved such a stylistic choice, he who wrote that the imperfect was a "falsification" of reality.[93] On the contrary, Angot thinks the tense is not as uniform as one would think: it contains nuances and multiple layers; it gives her the possibility to delineate and capture different moments within the same temporal paste. The imperfect also creates tactile "delights," as she says, a sensual proximity between past and present well suited to portray her relationship with Bruno.[94] Critics have already commented on this tense, but as yet, no one has suggested a social interpretation. I would like to argue that the imperfect creates a social bond with Bruno, a space akin to the train's passageway, an airlock where social groups can connect. Throughout *Le Marché des amants*, Bruno and Christine dwell in the imperfect. They speak for hours "to stretch the moment before separating, to drag it out."[95] Angot compares their meeting and parting to an escalator, a cinematic fading, the cross-fading of songs: "It couldn't be spasmodic, stopped and resumed, but fluid. It had to continue, again and again, it could be slowed down."; "He kept the previous cadence until he found another one with me, the transition had to be gentle and progressive."[96] Even when Bruno and Christine are not together or when they quarrel, the imperfect is plastic enough to encase the vicissitudes of their transclass and transrace relationship.

Reading the twenty or so successive typescripts of *Un amour impossible* at the Institute for Contemporary Publishing Archives (IMEC) in France allowed me to see how Angot crafts her imperfect. On one folder, she had written and underlined four or five times with a green pencil, "shape time."[97] And she did it thoroughly. One sentence in particular caught my attention. It reads as follows in the published version: "The break was clean [La coupure était nette]."[98] This assessment comes from the narrator: on Christine's eighteenth birthday, the mother received a letter from her father saying he would no longer provide child support. Although the imperfect was there in the first place, Angot hesitated. Here is a selection from the various versions:

> ~~But~~ apart from that, the break *had been* ~~was~~ clean [~~Mais~~ à part ça, la coupure *a été* ~~était~~ nette]
>
> ~~Apart from that,~~ *The break had been clean* [~~À part ça,~~ La coupure a été nette]
>
> There is a separation *that happens*, it was surely inevitable [Il y a une séparation *qui se fait*, c'était sûrement inévitable].[99]

Oscillating between long and short, simple and complex, the sentence slowly meandered its way to the final version, which captures the definitiveness of the split by its shortness. The imperfect imposed itself through the passive voice and the additional clause (*there is*; *that happens*; *it was*). The sentence circled back to the imperfect by way of two other tenses. Angot tried the present perfect (which indicates a onetime action that ended in the past) and the present that can be used to narrate, describe, or simply record an event. Please note that "a été" and "était" would both be translated as "was" in this context; but the past perfect "had been" makes it possible to distinguish between the two tenses and to use a compound verb.

The imperfect fits neither with the expression "for the first time" (*Le Marché des amants*) nor with a definitive separation (*Un amour impossible*), but it can contain different temporal layers and signal the repercussion of a single event. The meeting and parting of Rachel and Pierre had a lasting influence on Angot's life and prose, an influence that the imperfect's plasticity is able to capture. Here again, although differently than in *Le Marché des amants*, the imperfect takes on a social meaning. The sentence describes the separation between her mother and father, motivated by social reasons. It can also attest to the separation between the father and the law: he had volunteered to send a small unofficial child support, but when he decided to stop, Rachel had no legal recourse because Christine was now over the age of majority. As with the incest, Pierre unties from Christine and Rachel; he undoes the social mobility. We could also argue that the split in question concerns Angot and her mother, who grew apart when Christine reconnected with her father and wished to acquire his cultural capital. Christine is a parvenant child who lives in the imperfect: tangled between classes because of her parents, between the law (the official recognition of a mixed-class union) and the offense (the molestation). The imperfect's elasticity allows Angot to formally depict her social mobility. More broadly, the imperfect could be the parvenant's tense, a way for the narrator to turn a single event into a habit, to pass in a different class, to fake ease when confronted with the codes of a new social sphere.

On the unpublished short version of *Un amour impossible*, someone—the author herself, the editor, a friend reading—wrote by hand in the margins: "it's getting a little A. Ernaux."[100] The reader could be mentioning Ernaux in order to underline the social thread of *Un amour impossible* or to compare Rachel's and Pierre's encounter to Ernaux's vexed relationship with her parents-in-law in *La Femme gelée*. Like Angot, Ernaux strategically selects her verb tenses and lives in the imperfect. As she explains in one of her diaries, "The things that happen to me, at the moment I am living them, are always already writing themselves in the imperfect."[101] Life—considered here as a literary form—unfolds in the imperfect for those who change milieus. In her writing, Ernaux refuses to use the artificial and literary preterit (*passé simple*) and imperfect subjunctive (*imparfait du subjonctif*) because they create too much distance with the reader. Such tenses, she says, are artificial, intellectual, and make any narrative look unreal. Conversely, the perfect tense (*passé composé*) "communicates that things are not finished, that they still persist in the present."[102] She thereby diverges from Jean-Paul Sartre's analysis of Albert Camus's perfect tense as a means to isolate sentences so that they become "islands."[103] Even if the perfect tense is severed from the past, its compound of an auxiliary and a past participle can aptly represent Ernaux's life, always in tangle between worlds and tenses. The very name of the tense, "composé," supposes a blending as in the expression "famille recomposée" (blended family). *Composer* also means to make compromises and to arrange (an essay or work of art), which underlines the necessity to craft stylistical devices to put social mobility into words. Like Angot, although through a different use of temporality, Ernaux favors a tense that can show the lasting effect of the past in the present, as if a parven*ant* (present participle) could only capture her trajectory through an unusual timeframe. Verb tenses encapsulate the strategy of each author: despite her bourgeois father and her status as a writer and public figure, Angot sees herself as underclass and uses the imperfect to be on par with her underprivileged lover; by contrast, Ernaux's compound tense acknowledges a social estrangement (with her family as with her husband) while attempting to attenuate or repair it.

Angot and Ernaux share another characteristic: while Ernaux mentions *Le Père Goriot* in the first scene of *La Place*, Christine lectures Bruno on Balzac in *Le Marché des amants*. Additionally, the typescript of *Un amour impossible* contains two references to Balzac that did not make it to the final version: "cf. Illusions perdues" on a post-it and "Illusions perdues (accent)" on a folder.[104] Here, as in the works of Ernaux, Balzac is a code name: it signals an upcoming discussion on social mobility; it binds together the volumes of the parvenant's library.

## Present Is the Participle (Kaoutar Harchi)

Dorothea Tanning's 1942 *Birthday* (fig. 4) had a great influence on Annie Ernaux's writing. She refers to this image several times in her

**Figure 4.** Dorothea Tanning, *Birthday* (1942). Oil on canvas. © 2022 Artists Rights Society, New York / ADAGP, Paris. Photograph: The Philadelphia Museum of Art / Art Resource, New York (purchased with funds contributed by C. K. Williams, II, 1999).

prose. In her writing diary *L'Atelier noir*, she writes, in 1989, "A question I asked myself before, what structure corresponds to D. Tanning's painting, *Birthday*?"[105] This self-portrait of an American painter deeply influenced by Surrealism could aptly caption Ernaux's writing and education, she who completed a master's thesis on women and love in Surrealism. The French title "Anniversaire" also contains the author's birth name, Annie, a sonorous detail that can partly explain Ernaux's fascination with this object. She returned to this painting about twenty years later, in *Les Années* (2008; *The Years*): "She thinks that this painting represents her life and that she is inside it as she was formerly in *Gone with the Wind*, in *Jane Eyre*, later in *The Nausea*."[106] The author of *L'Atelier noir* seems to ask, in the first person, a question that the narrator of *Les Années* answers in the third. These two successive excerpts point to a superimposition of life and form: the "structure" of the first quote is the "life" of the second. Ernaux lives in the painting in the same way as she inhabits a world crafted by novels. *Birthday* multiplies symbols of in-betweenness: a clothed but naked woman; natural and manufactured features; myth and reality; flora and fauna. This self-portrait—like Ernaux's autobiographical writings—is not a testimony but a structure left to our interpretation: do the doors look out onto her home or inner thoughts? Is Tanning showing us her past or the future? More importantly, although Ernaux does not underline this possible analogy when she refers to *Birthday*, the painting shows the concrete and symbolic "doors" I have analyzed in this chapter as the representations of a parvenant's life, entrenched on the doorstep, a hand on the doorknob, even more so in Tanning's painting as one threshold only leads to another.[107]

After Louis and Angot, I have encountered another literary version of this painting in *Comme nous existons* (*As We Exist*), a 2021 narrative of class mobility written by the novelist and sociologist Kaoutar Harchi. Many parallels could be made between Ernaux and Harchi: they refer to sociologists in their texts (Pierre Bourdieu and one of his former assistants, Abdelmalek Sayad); they attended private, catholic schools outside of their social catchments; they experienced various types of discrimination—classism, racism, misogyny; they are both writing to "avenge [their] race," although the phrase takes on a different meaning in each example, since Harchi was born to a family of Moroccan immigrants.[108] In the vein of Abdellah Taïa's and Marie

NDiaye's works, Harchi compellingly merges social mobility and migration. Referring to her parents and to herself, she uses literature to record their "postcolonial and proletarian existences."[109] The end of *Comme nous existons* could be read as a sociological ekphrasis of Tanning's *Birthday* painting:

> That day, a photograph should have been taken, which would have expressed, on its own, more than everything I'm writing here, in all sincerity. You would see me standing on the doorstep of the parental apartment, a bag on my back, a new suitcase in my hand. And you would see Hania, standing on the threshold of her kitchen, leaning slightly forward, hands plunged into her apron, and Mohamed, on the threshold of his living room, hands behind his back, very straight, head high. I'll say it again: a photograph should have been taken to freeze, never to lose that scene of our existence. That tableau.[110]

Harchi's transclass narrator stands on the threshold of her book, as these words are the last. This excerpt starts with a "photograph" but ends with a "tableau," a picture or painting, a primordial "scene" of mobility. While the parents remain on the threshold (*seuil*), Harchi sets forth from the doorstep (*pas-de-porte*). The three of them inhabit two different acoustic worlds underlined by opposite consonances: "sur le seuil de son salon" (on the threshold of his living room) for the father; "sur le pas-de-porte de l'appartement parental" (on the doorstep of the parental apartment) for the daughter. The French hyphens are reminiscent of Abdelmalek Sayad's own punctuation when he describes immigrant "transfuges" as "émigrés-immigrés" "— the between-two-places, between-two-times, between-two-societies, etc.—."[111] It seems to me that Harchi makes an intentional mistake when she uses hyphens here: in French, doorstep is not "pas-de-porte" (which is a legal term that refers to a commercial form of security deposit in France) but "le pas *de la* porte." Literally in French, Harchi's compound "pas-de-porte" could be understood as "not-a-door." The author thus anticipates a social voyage at the same time as she reduces the distance through the use of hyphens that unite these three words and persons as well as through the literal meaning of the compound: no door, no separation, no journey without a return.

In *Comme nous existons*, Kaoutar Harchi also emphasizes the social in-betweenness of places and trajectories: "I who knew I had never left but felt in spite of it all the feeling of being back."; "At that time, I was standing tall, foot on the starting line, without conceiving or trying to conceive of any form of arrival. Never had the arrival mattered to me."[112] Harchi uses the present participle—that of the parvenant—to formally render the singularity of her social trajectory: "I had—to face the fact of leaving, to be able to say *I'm leaving*, to really leave—to inscribe my departure in a plan that was more vast, bigger than me, that could also be Hania and Mohamed's plan, as if, with me leaving, they were leaving with me."[113] The phrase "with me leaving" (*moi partant*) is isolated between commas, and the verb *parvenir* (to be able) does not indicate a destination but the very possibility of a departure. Harchi continues the same literary strategy a couple of pages later: "I'm a daughter who goes already thinking of returning. A daughter who is always *there*."[114] Social mobility is captured by the gerund *en pensant* (thinking) inserted between the two-way trajectory of the verbs "goes" and "returning" (in the infinitive in French). The *there* that the narrator inhabits stands for the multiple thresholds of Tanning's painting but also for the elusive staircase of Kertész's photograph, discussed in the introduction. Because of italics, this *there* is first and foremost the place of the text, its form, its materiality. Another aspect of Harchi's carefully crafted style is the constant interruption of her sentences after verbs, the postponement of the object, as in this section from the aforementioned excerpt: "I had—to face the fact of leaving, to be able to say *I'm leaving*, to really leave—to inscribe my departure in a plan that was more vast." This style ressembles Abdelmalek Sayad's, characterized by the author of *Comme nous existons* as "labyrinthine" in a sentence that mimics what it describes: "I keep in my memory, because they were dazzling, those sentences with their complex structure."[115] I also read this postponement as a formal depiction of what Harchi calls the "social verdict that surpassed me, preceded me."[116] Sentences are interrupted to challenge such class determinism and preordained chronology. Through the syntax, the gerund, the present participle, and the imagery of the door, *Comme nous existons*—like so many novels and narratives of social mobility—allow us to see, through the details of a text, the flashing figure of the parvenant.

Concrete and metaphorical doors can represent violent events: rape in Louis's *Histoire de la violence*; incest in Angot's *Un amour impossible*. Coupled with the use of reported speech and typographical signs, they can realize, materialize social mobility of various scales: a strait gate (Louis), a straight path (Ernaux), a swinging door (Angot), a capacious threshold (Harchi). Doorways can reinforce class distance (Clara and Édouard; Angot and her father; Annie Ernaux and her student) or mitigate it (Angot and her mother; Ernaux and her readers; Kaoutar Harchi and her parents). In her Nobel lecture, Ernaux underlines the uniqueness of each door by referring to Franz Kafka: "I couldn't read 'Before the Law' in *The Trial*, without seeing in it the portrayal of my destiny: to die without having walked through the door that was made only for me, the book that only I could write."[117] In this scene of reading, passing through a door and writing a book have become comparable activities. As in Kafka's parable, doorways (and paths toward social mobility) are not prefabricated, portable, one-size-fits-all structures or devices but idiosyncratic thresholds. The writers discussed in this chapter have shown what getting a foot in the door means.

# Travel Class   6

FROM THE LADDER
TO THE TRAIN

Literature and social sciences rely massively on spatial metaphors to describe class and mobility: women function as step ladders for the social climbers portrayed in Flaubert's *L'Éducation sentimentale* (1869; *The Sentimental Education*) and Balzac's *La Maison Nucingen* (1838; *The Nucingen House*), while class division is envisioned as a sliced "bamboo" in Stendhal's *Souvenirs d'égotisme* (1892; *Memories of Egotism*). More recently, philosopher Chantal Jaquet used the image of the leg up to discuss Jules Michelet's social mobility, sociologists Sam Friedman and Daniel Laurison defined the notion of a "class ceiling," and feminist sociologist Rose-Marie Lagrave located her own mobility on the "service staircase."[1] The more traditional imagery and coined phrases have to do with tools and technologies: the French "social elevator" (*l'ascenseur social*), on the one hand, and on the other hand, the American "social ladder." According to sociologists, American society is not divided into classes but is "stratified" so that social mobility is not a question of groups but of individuals.[2] And indeed a ladder—in contrast to an elevator—can only accommodate one parvenant at a time (or at least per rung) and dispatches climbers to more strata and places; there are more rungs than floors, and the structure could a priori lean against any wall. The American ladder also requires physical effort, while the elevator is mechanized, as if upward mobility was guaranteed by the French government but only between certain preprogrammed floors. As philosopher Edmond Goblot wrote in his 1925 landmark essay, *La Barrière et le Niveau: Étude sociologique sur la bourgeoisie française moderne* (*The Barrier and the Level: Sociological Study of Modern French Bourgeoi-*

*sie*), "For a society to divide into classes, something artificial and false must replace the continuous ramps with steps, leaving behind or visible only a few rungs spaced far apart, which is to say creating one or many obstacles that are difficult to overcome, and those who overcome them must be placed on the same plane."[3] Strata turn into classes when the continuous ramp is replaced by more distinct demarcations. The "few rungs spaced far apart" deemed "artificial and false," possibly technological, would make a staircase impracticable but invoke the image of the elevator or the train (stations are more spaced out than floors). If combined, the keywords of Goblot's title even point to the railway: a gate (*barrière*) and a level (*niveau*) are the main features of a railroad crossing (*la barrière du passage à niveau*).[4]

In 2020 Jeannine Cummins's migration novel *American Dirt* strikingly merged a ladder and a railway car: "You must match your speed to the train's speed, she sees, adjusting as you go. You must find the ideal point of access, a protrusion, a ladder, a spot with plenty of grip and some way to quickly get to the roof of the car."[5] Here, she is describing the "beast" or "La Bestia," a network of freight trains carrying migrants from Central America to the Mexico-US border on top of its cars, leading to death and mutilations (fig. 5). I am not suggesting a parallel between American and French migrations; instead, I want to foreground a striking superimposition: Cummins telescopes the tenor with the vehicle, the metaphor with reality, namely, the symbol of the American Dream of upward mobility (the ladder) with its concrete vehicle (the train). Cummins and Goblot describe two different evolutions: the ladder can either be replaced by or merged with a train. This chapter will show how the train has supplanted other forms of social visualization.

Scholars on both sides of the Atlantic are more and more critical of vertical spatializations that pit upward against downward. Chantal Jaquet in *Les Transclasses* (2014; *The Transclasses*) dislikes the "moral" connotation of these metaphors.[6] Similarly, Bruce Robbins in *Upward Mobility and the Common Good* (2007) is "Suspicious of ladders and of stories that involve climbing," and he rejects the "crude social topography of 'up' and 'down'" in his analysis of H. G. Wells's 1905 bildungsroman, *Kipps: The Story of a Simple Soul*.[7] Robbins also uses the expression of a "lateral mobility" to characterize the merging of migration and social mobility in Julia Alvarez's novel, *How the Garcia*

**Figure 5.** Eduardo Verdugo, *Ixtepec, Mexico* (July 12, 2014). © Associated Press. Photograph: AP Photo/Eduardo Verdugo.

*Girls Lost Their Accents* (1991).[8] This "lateral" trajectory could aptly subtitle Cummins's *American Dirt*: the Mexican mother travels, horizontally, by train, and she is not a precarious menial worker looking for social mobility up north but a bookstore owner fleeing persecution. It is quite tempting to superimpose all these examples in order to read the train as the emblem of lateral mobility and as a vehicle that could date the transformation of spectacular rags to riches narratives into more modest bourgeois short stops. The two images (lateral social mobility and horizontal train tracks) can overlap at times, but in this chapter I will rather focus on the railway car as a setting or a shuttle that captures not only an upward trajectory but the transit zone between two social groups.

By bringing together a curated corpus of nineteenth- to twenty-first-century narratives and films, mostly French with a few American counterpoints, we will see how the train has become the leading metaphor for upward trajectories. Such a shift, I argue, registers the transformation of social mobility from one-way success stories of arrival to an ongoing process of pendular movements. On the train, travel times and distances lengthen; voyagers cannot control the machine except by pulling the emergency break. Contrary to ladders and elevators, trains do not travel upward and often assume a return ticket: social passengers are thus under the threat of a round trip, while commuters go through different neighborhoods without settling for good in a new place. At the same time, the railroad offers social climbers a buffer and a way home, a means to reconnect with their past class and relatives so as to mitigate the social estrangement.

### The Train as Social Setting

A train car is a place of social negotiation where classes are either separated, suspended, or mixed. Many authors have described how public transportation can generate a concrete social mobility for daily commuters: vehicles transport all kinds of passengers and go through different neighborhoods, thus forcing a temporary cohabitation between classes. In *Engine of Modernity* (2019), Masha Belenky describes how this was already the case with the omnibus in the first half of the nineteenth century: "more than any other aspect of the omnibus, it was the *potential* for class inclusiveness that captured the imagination of contemporary commentators. Despite historical evidence to the contrary, textual and visual representations of the omnibus interior consistently place travelers of widely diverse social classes within the confined space of the vehicle."[9] The two rows of benches facing each other led to physical contact and prolonged gazing *in literature*, where the evocative fantasized space of the omnibus replaced the accuracy of the experience.

Opened in the 1970s to connect Paris to the suburbs, the commuter rail (Réseau Express Régional [RER]) brings about a similar social mixing in literary representations, although the social mobility in question could be seen as passive, uncertain, or simply spectatorial. In *Les Passagers du Roissy-Express* (1990; *The Passengers of the Roissy-Express*), François Maspero and Anaïk Frantz become commuter rail tourists on the RER B line, traveling from housing projects in the northeast greater Paris to affluent suburbs in the southwest. For Franco-Algerian writer Leïla Sebbar in *Métro: Instantanés* (2007; *Metro: Snapshots*), the subway is a "Babel" of languages, cultures, and classes that transports the former French empire.[10] In her diaries *Journal du dehors* (1993; *Diary of the Outside*) and *La Vie extérieure* (2000; *The External Life*), Annie Ernaux observes that social inequality is strikingly more visible in public spaces, such as rapid transit trains. Emmanuel Macron is the author of a comparable, although classist, observation. In 2017, while inaugurating the start-up incubator Station F, housed in a former railroad building of the Austerlitz rail terminal, he stated, "a train station is a place where we encounter people who succeed and people who are nothing." The train station reveals his political views on those who are neither wealthy entrepreneurs nor — to use the president's talking points and mountaineering metaphor — "lead climbers."[11]

On the train — the vehicle invented between the omnibus and the subway car — social cohabitation is more relative. As in other modes of transit, train seats are sold by travel classes and therefore reproduce social divisions. As anthropologist Julie Kleinman shows in *Adventure Capital: Migration and the Making of an African Hub in Paris* (2019), the Gare du Nord, for instance, was initially designed to assimilate non-Parisians but then switched gears to contain the so-called dangerous classes (from poor rural travelers to foreigners) via corridors and separate waiting rooms.[12] We can trace the history of railway compartmentalization through literature. In Émile Zola's landmark railroad novel *La Bête humaine* (1890; *The Human Beast*), a snowstorm forces the passengers to exit the vehicle in order to find shelter in the humble house of the crossing keeper:

> And there, in the snow, a train arrived at their door: the natural order was perverted, they were staring at this unknown world that an accident had thrown on the rails, they were gazing upon it with the wide eyes of savages who had come running to a shore where Europeans have shipwrecked. Those open doors revealing women wrapped in furs, those men who step out in thick coats, all that comfortable luxury, washed up among that sea of ice, froze them in awe.[13]

These cross-class interactions do not occur on the train, reserved for rich French, English, and American families and merchants. Zola reinforces the class gap by comparing the event to a New World encounter, as he already did by choosing the Gare Saint-Lazare, an affluent

Parisian station that did not cater to the majority of nineteenth-century train travelers: third-class passengers (mostly workers and immigrants from the provinces).[14] Zola also uses the train to underline the social difference between France and the US. As one character exclaims, "In America, Monsieur, everybody gets out and grabs a shovel."[15] Conversely, the French railroad employees become the passengers' servants: they clear out the tracks, offer hospitality and food, and even carry some of the passengers in their arms. A century later, the elements of this scene (train, snow, accident, social class) are rearranged in Jacques Lob's and Jean-Marc Rochette's graphic novel *Le Transperceneige* (1984), also adapted for the screen in 2013 by the South Korean director of *Parasite*, Bong Joon-Ho. The comic book and the movie (*Snowpiercer*) are set on a gigantic train rushing through postapocalyptic icy landscapes, carrying all social classes in separate cars. In this context, class struggle and the social ladder are spatialized as a horizontal journey from railcar to railcar, especially during a revolt led by a character aptly named Proloff (*prolo* is short for proletarian in French). At the end of the nineteenth century, Zola had to describe two train stations and an entire railway line—its employees, its passengers—to paint a full picture of French society. He also had to invent a catastrophe (a monstrous snowstorm) to create interactions across classes. In the twentieth century, a single train can transport all social groups. From *La Bête humaine* to *Le Transperceneige*, trains and railroad journeys have become more accessible, although class demarcations continue to be rigid aboard.

### The Train as Framing Device

To be a social setting or a metaphor for upward mobility, the train does not need to be front and center. In Maupassant's *Bel-Ami* (1885), Georges Duroy works in the railway industry. The trains are discreet witnesses to his daily life and attempt at social climbing. Duroy's first Parisian apartment is indeed located near the Batignolles train station and oversees the tracks: "And he often dreamed at night, watching the trains pass from his window, of the strategies he could employ [to acquire wealth]."[16] In a very different book, a 2005 memoir titled *L'Ascenseur est en panne, j'ai pris l'escalier!* (*The Elevator Was Broken, I Took the Stairs*), entrepreneur Aziz Senni recounts his upward mobility, from growing up in a large and poor family of Moroccan immigrants living in the Parisian suburbs to creating a successful company of collective cabs. This climber mobilizes three different kinds of vehicles to narrate his social journey: the cars of his business, the elevator in his title, and the train, since Senni's father worked for the SNCF (Société nationale des chemins de fer français, the National society of French railroads). In Maupassant as in Senni, the railroad can be a metonymic detail of the parvenant's biography.

The railway can also bookend novels and narratives of social mobility. The opening of Émile Zola's *Au bonheur des dames* (1883) introduces readers to Denise Baudu as follows: "Denise had come on foot from the Gare Saint-Lazare, where a train from Cherbourg had dropped her and her two brothers off, after a night spent on the hard bench of a third-class car."[17] Denise will rise, from working in a little shop to clerking in a megastore and, through marriage, from employee to director. Zola uses the train's travel class (third) to socially characterize Denise. This first sentence also anticipates her upcoming social mobility via three different forms of movement: walking, riding a train, and landing. More than a century later, two writers adopt a similar device. Journalist Nesrine Slaoui starts her narrative of class mobility, *Illégitimes* (2021; *Illegitimate*), with this observation: "It's a city where the trains no longer run."[18] Now stationary, trains signal a social landscape of arrested mobility. In *Educated* (2018), Tara Westover tells the story of her social mobility, from growing up in Idaho without going to school until she was seventeen to getting a graduate degree in history at Cambridge. As in Zola, the prologue launches her transclass trajectory by way of the railroad: "I'm standing on the red railway car that sits abandoned next to the barn. [...] Behind me a gentle hill slopes upward and stitches itself to the mountain base."[19] The author repeats a similar scene in the first chapter: "I climbed the railway car and looked over the valley. It was easy to pretend the car was moving, speeding away, that any moment the valley might disappear behind me. I'd spent hours playing that fantasy through in my head."[20] Tara's desire to flee originates in this game of starting up an immobile vehicle. The landscape atop the wagon announces her trajectory through numerous prepositions of place, verbs, and adverbs: "next to;" "behind;" "climbed;" "upward;" "speeding away." It also anticipates how torn she will be between her family (the mountain "base") and her education (the "upward" hill). In Zola as in Slaoui and Westover, the train functions as an entryway into the plot of social mobility.

Conversely, Didier Éribon's autobiographical bildungsroman *Retour à Reims* (2009; *Return to Reims*) ends with his reading of a railroad novel: "But I had promised myself that only once I had finished writing my last chapter would I read Raymond Williams's novel, *Border Country*. I sensed that it would imprint itself on me too intensely. So I waited. I close the book today, as I conclude my own."[21] In *Border Country*, Williams—the founder of cultural studies in the UK—tells the story of a London academic visiting his father, a railway signalman. But the train is more than just an occupation: "As he walked downstairs to the kitchen, he felt the past moving with him: this life, this house, the trains through the valley."[22] The trains and the fictional station in South Wales allow the social climber to reflect on the distance generated by upward mobility: "'[. . .] And Glynmawr station is closing, but I remember when I first left there, and watched the valley from the train. In a way, I've only just finished that journey.' 'It was bound to be a difficult journey.' 'Yes, certainly. Only now it seems like the end of exile. Not going back, but the feeling of exile ending. For the distance is measured, and that is what matters. By measuring the distance, we come home.'"[23] The book cover features Charles Burton's 1950 oil painting, *Coal Train in the Rhondda*. In *Retour à Reims*, Éribon does not underline the railroad thread in *Border Country*, as it might seem anecdotal in the context of his intellectual trajectory.[24] Yet the train not only captures a parvenant's constant coming and going but unites a corpus of social mobility narratives.

Laurent Cantet's 1999 film *Ressources humaines* (*Human Resources*) combines these two framings: the beginning (as in Zola's and Westover's books) and the end (like Éribon who, in the last chapter of his memoir, refers to Williams's railroad novel). As Lauren Berlant writes in the chapter on Cantet's cinema in *Cruel Optimism* (2011), "The filmic action begins and ends on a train, but what's in transit is what's at home."[25] After graduating from a business school, the son of a laborer, Franck, comes back to Normandy by train to do an internship in the human resources department of his father's factory. He is torn between loyalties: his family, the CEO, the employees, and the trade unionist who, strangely enough, is named "Madame Arnoux"—a name familiar to all French readers of Flaubert—and calls Franck a "little arriviste," as if Cantet wanted to suggest that *Ressources humaines* was an updated version of *L'Éducation sentimentale*. Indeed, the film could be seen as a factory remake of Flaubert's novel in which Franck (the late twentieth-century version of Frédéric) falls for Madame Arnoux, not as a potential love interest but as an ally across class differences. By organizing a strike with her, Franck gets away from his model, the ambitious but indolent Frédéric, who keeps his distance from the 1848 Revolution. The plot unfolds between two train trips to symbolize the protagonist's transclass journey. The film does not exactly end on a train but rather on a close-up of Franck announcing his return to Paris. Filming the railway was only necessary as a framing device, a way to characterize Franck in the first scene as a young man on the move, contemplating an industrial landscape in decline; Franck stands as the archetype of the "jeune cadre dynamique" (young and dynamic executive, or yuppie) looking through the "cadre dynamique" (the dynamic frame or frame in motion) of the train window.

The train also plays an important role in Mirbeau's *Le Journal d'une femme de chambre* (1900; *The Diary of a Chambermaid*) and its two film adaptations, previously discussed in chapter 4. Toward the end of Mirbeau's novel, the train announces Célestine's upcoming mobility from chambermaid to shopkeeper: "And I hear, in the distance, coming from the invisible valley, the very soft sound of a locomotive whistle. It's the train carrying Joseph and my destiny."[26] The first scenes of Jean Renoir's and Luis Buñuel's films both take place on a train. In Buñuel's 1964 version, the opening credits roll against a countryside landscape seen from a train. Then Célestine, alias Jeanne Moreau, filmed from the back, exits the railway car as if she were going through a cinema screen, entering both the film and her new chambermaid position. The train is used as a cinematic tool to introduce the narrative as well as the character, always on the move between places and classes. In Renoir's 1946 adaptation, first we see Célestine's diary, then Célestine writing an entry while the train whistles to announce the next station. At the end, she is sitting in the same corner of a different railcar, next to the wealthy man she is going to marry, writing down vows in her diary. In this American version from Renoir, the train encircles the film, as if the maid were destined to move and climb. The shrill sound of the vehicle announces a social rise for Mirbeau and Renoir; as for Buñuel, it represents the physical and social mobility of the maid through the nature of her work.

In addition to being a framing device, the train can be located in the paratext to signal the topic of a work of art, to underline its central metaphor. There is a train, for instance, on the poster of Anne Fontaine's 2017 adaptation of Édouard Louis's 2014 *En finir avec Eddy Bellegueule* (*Ending Eddy Bellegueule*), titled *Marvin, ou la belle éducation* (*Marvin, or The Beautiful Education*)—like Eddy Bellegueule, who became Édouard Louis, the lead character transitions from Marvin Bijou to Martin Clément. The train is crucial yet minimal in Louis's novel: "I took the train to Amiens."[27] The narrator's father drives him to the station so that he can audition for the drama section of a distant high school, the first step of his upward mobility. We also learn in a subsequent book, *Changer: Méthode* (2021; *Change: Method*), that when Louis met his mentor Didier Éribon, they always chatted while walking to and from the university and the Amiens train station.[28] While Louis's novel ends when the narrator arrives in high school, Fontaine's film shows a full transclass trajectory up to the protagonist's arrival in Paris, career as an actor, and struggle to adapt to his new social status. She creates a jump cut between Marvin's first theater lesson in school and a train trip that leads to his arrival on the stairs of the Saint-Michel subway station. On the French poster, the melancholic gaze and reflection suggest that the train shuttles the character between his past and present selves: the train window does not reflect the person on the train (the adult actor playing Marvin) but the youngest one. In the end, Marvin reconnects with his father and inscribes the first page of his memoir for him while aboard the train. The English poster for *Reinventing Marvin* also relies on a split, but with different implications. On the left side of the visibly torn paper, we see train tracks behind the cut-in-half head of young Marvin—a way to represent his childhood on the wrong side of the tracks. The background of adult Marvin is solid and the character naked, so as to signal his full reinvention. Only in the French context does the train (not the tracks) become the repository of Marvin's internal social split.

I have noticed a similar editorial strategy in two of Christine Angot's narratives. *Une semaine de vacances* (2012; *A Week's Vacation*) is a clinical description of how Angot's father sexually abused her. The text comes to an end when he drops her off in the southern train station of Carcassonne. The 2013 paperback's book cover takes us inside the railcar that transports Christine from one (upper-class) parent to the other (modest) one. The word "train" itself partakes in Angot's poetics—namely the utilization of the imperfect verb tense to represent social tensions and alliances (see chap. 5). Indeed, *Une Semaine de vacances* is filled with numerous occurrences of *en train*, which literally means "by train" but also "doing" (*en train de*), an adverbial phrase that is used, like the imperfect tense, to describe an ongoing situation. *Un amour impossible* (2015; *An Impossible Love*) is a larger narrative focused on the transclass affair of Angot's parents. The illustrated band of paper wrapped around the cover (a tried and true commercial strategy in French publishing) seems to represent Christine and her mother waiting for the arrival of the father's train. The machine is important in *Un amour impossible*: Angot's father and mother separate on a station platform when he refuses to make the union official, and when Christine, now a teenager, comes back home after a school trip to Venice, she announces, also on a platform, that she wants to leave her hometown. Filmmaker Catherine Corsini understood the metaphorical power of the railway. In her film adaptation of *Un amour impossible* (2017), both train scenes are present, as if the father and the daughter were leaving and coming back via the same machine. Thus, the train appears as the vehicle of social emancipation; only the well-off father and his parvenant daughter are mobile. The two book covers are dissimilar: one person versus two; a teenager versus a child; color versus black and white; a full page versus a half; inside versus outside the train. Unlike other book covers, though, Angot's face is not visible but always mediated or replaced by a train: we see the reflection of a face in the train's window (*Une Semaine de vacances*); the child is pictured from the back while the train is full face (*Un amour impossible*). In both cases, despite differences, the train is such a powerful metaphor of what the parvenant's trajectory entails that it can stand in for the book's author.

Finally, the covers of J. D. Vance's bildungsroman *Hillbilly Elegy* (2016), its American cinematic adaptation, and its French translation, show significant variations. The focus on a decrepit house on the original cover signals a homecoming, a narrative of social origins, a memoir. Similarly, the film poster is centered on a car and a road, the concrete vehicles of Vance's mobility. The serpentine path possibly points to his tortuous childhood and to the difficulties of getting out and coming back. The direction of the car is not entirely obvious: it seems to be moving downward, that is to say back home, as on the original book cover. But the car could also be on its way up, near the frame. Vance's book is filled with remarks on the multidirectionality required to flee social determinism: "the best way up for the hillbilly was out"; "To move up was to move on."[29] But there is no train. The melodramatic Netflix adaptation features many machines (a bike, a car, a calculator) but no train either. This is why the train on the cover of the French translation seems incongruous at first glance. Vance's mobility is clearly upward, from a poor family to a Yale law degree, so there is no reason for wanting to represent lateral mobility, as in *American Dirt*. Since French is written and read from left to right, a train traveling right to left indicates a backward, homebound movement, a return. Given the other examples I have collected thus far, I would argue that the French book cover is part of the translation. Translating *Hillbilly Elegy* means replacing the idiomatic American car, road, or barn by a train. This French or European element is compensated by the American flag, fall foliage, and untranslated English title. The French version is not subtitled *A Memoir*, which explains the choice of the train as a collective means of transportation supposed to portray not an individual but a group: the hillbillies. Yet we only see the locomotive, that is, the driving force that represents the whole group. Conversely, the individual American car or house symbolizes Vance's unique social trajectory. In the same way that we do not expect a character to use a ladder or an elevator in books that mobilize such social imagery, the train does not need to be present in a text to be its master key, the shapeshifting signifier of class mobility.

### The Train as Formal Device

A commuter is a reader, a semiologist, whether the signs in question are social or literary. Some critics have underlined the proximity between reading and riding a train or a subway. In the essay *Flaubert à* la Motte-Picquet (2015; *Flaubert at the Motte-Picquet Station*), Laure Murat describes two subway commuters reading books about close reading: Fisher and Frey's *Pathways to Close and Critical Reading* in Los Angeles and Barry Brummett's *Techniques of Close Reading* in Paris. These two scenes of reading lead Murat to reflect on the features of what she calls a *metroreading*, that is, "an inevitably bumpy and chopped-up reading because train rides in Paris never take very long, [...] a vagabond reading, associated with the displacement from one world to another."[30] The epigraph to her essay comes from Georges Perec's *Penser/Classer* (1985; *Thinking/Classifying*): "The place where one reads, it's the metro. That could almost be a definition."[31] Murat also quotes Walter Benjamin, who argues, in a text on detective novels, that "Reading is as related to rail travel as stopping at train stations is."[32] The train is not only a topos; it does not only carry passengers versed in close reading; it can team up with literary forms to represent class mobility and instability. The more the train blends with style, the more this social setting becomes the vehicle of a parvenant's individual trajectory.

Marcel Proust's protagonists often read on public transportation. Two references to Balzac are set on a train in *À la recherche du temps perdu* (1913–27; *In Search of Lost Time*), thus turning the machine into a vehicle of intertextuality. First example: aboard the Balbec train in *Sodome et Gomorrhe* (*Sodom and Gomorrah*), the narrator asks Charlus what he likes the most in Balzac's *La Comédie humaine* (1829–48; *The Human Comedy*). Charlus replies by referring to Eugène de Rastignac's castle and Lucien de Rubempré's death: "What do you mean you haven't read *Lost Illusions*? It's so beautiful, the moment when Carlos Herrera asks the name of the château his carriage passes: it's Rastignac, the residence of the young man he once loved."[33] Inserted like this in the sentence, Rastignac becomes the name of a locality, a landscape in front of which the Balbec trains passes by.[34] Second example: in *Albertine disparue* (*Albertine Gone*), while traveling from Venice to Paris, the narrator and his mother read letters announcing two transclass marriages: Gilberte Swann with Robert de Saint-Loup on the one hand, and on the other hand Léonor de Cambremer and Marie-Antoinette d'Oloron.[35] To comment on this surprising news, the narrator's mother quotes Madame de Sévigné and considers the marriage to be as virtuous as the end of a George Sand novel. The narrator disagrees, but only replies to himself: "'That's the price of vice, it's a marriage at the end of a Balzac novel,' I thought."³⁶ Proust stages, on a train, the tension between virtue (Sand) and vice (Balzac), which will be at the core of Margaret Cohen's literary and cultural history of the 1830s: namely the competition between women's "sentimental social novels" and men's bildungsromane. *La Recherche* overflows with spatial representations of class (staircases, ladders), especially in Balbec (the hotel lift, the omnibus). Critic Yolande Jansen, for instance, hones in on the carriage ride in the fog and the "revolving doors" of a café where the narrator and Saint-Loup meet as a metaphor for flitting between classes: "I think Proustian metaphors function in the double-edged representation of both the heritage of aristocratic hierarchy, and a democratic ideal of equality."³⁷ The particularity of the train is that it situates Proust's novel within literary history (Sévigné, Sand, Balzac) while becoming an engine of social mobility: Rastignac is a social climber, and the union between Robert and Gilberte is mixed.³⁸

In the volume *Approaches to Teaching Balzac's Old Goriot* (2000), Sharon Marcus and Vanessa Schwartz contrast Balzac's character of Goriot, who "embodies the postrevolutionary achievements associated with the upward social mobility of a ladder," with the novel itself, *Le Père Goriot* (1835; *Old Man Goriot*), which "signals the victory of the map over the ladder."³⁹ Rastignac's social mobility supposes a geographical knowledge of and circulation between Parisian neighborhoods. Similarly, Pierre Bourdieu and Dominique Memmi included annotated maps of Paris in their books to visualize the upward mobility of Flaubert's character Frédéric in *L'Éducation sentimentale* and of French writer Jules Romains. By referring to Balzac and Rastignac aboard a train, Proust continues this process of horizontalization: the train replaces the map as the vehicle of class mobility. Years later, in Maryam Madjidi's 2021 narrative of class mobility, *Pour que je m'aime encore* (*So That I Still Love Myself*), the transclass narrator feels like "an impatient Rastignac lacking in ambition" when she takes the RER from Paris to her house in the suburbs.⁴⁰ There is no train in *Le Père Goriot*, but Peter Brooks found a formal sign that, in my view, announces this transition from the ladder to the train: "the tailor whom Rastignac convokes after remarking how poorly his suits compare to Maxime de Trailles', a tailor who considers himself 'a hyphen between young men's present and their future.' A hyphen is the beginning of a relationship, of a juxtaposition and a passage; it is related to metaphor, to the construction of a ladder out of the mudhole."[41] The hyphen is a rung of the social ladder. But its grammatical role (to compound two words) designates a horizontal, train-like movement.

Balzac is not the only thing to be "read" aboard Proust's train cars. In *Sodome et Gomorrhe*, the Balbec local slow train is a place of "social enigmas" for the author, of "social apartheid" for a critic, in which ranks are hard to guess.[42] In a twofold scene of reading, the narrator mistakes Princess Sherbatoff for a brothel owner. He misreads her socially while she is herself reading *La Revue des deux mondes*. The title of the journal points to a social cohabitation between "two worlds," in the vein of Robert Linhart's "2CV" in *L'Établi* (chap. 3). Roland Barthes reads this passage as a symbol of the novel's reversals, its "incessant permutation" and "grammar of advancement, of class mobility."[43] The literary critic is particularly interested in the "effect of time: [...] it's not, to the letter, the same Narrator who reads the brothel madam and the Russian grande dame: two trains separate them."[44] Although Barthes uses words like *junction* and *voyage*, the train is only a prop or a backdrop for this temporal effect, not its central feature.

Proust's syntax is, according to Barthes, "concomitant" and "metaphorical, because the metaphor, unlike what rhetoric thought for so long, is a work of language deprived of all vectorization: it goes from one term to another only circuitously and infinitely."[45] Yet Barthes does not underline the etymological proximity between a train and a metaphor, as Michel de Certeau does in *L'Invention du quotidien* (1980; *The Invention of Everyday Life*): "In today's Athens, modes of public transport are called *metaphorai*. To go to work or return home, one takes a 'metaphor'—a bus or a train."[46]

There are two main commonalities between train and prose in *À la Recherche du temps perdu*: creativity and social mobility. Consider this scene aboard a train, when Marcel is en route to visit Balbec's church: "I spent my time running from one window to another to bring closer, to reline the intermittent and opposing fragments of my fine scarlet and changeable morning so that I could have a complete view and a continuous tableau."[47] The train meanders; it does not travel on an unyielding road. The Balbec train, too, is a slow, local train; a *tortillard* in French, from the verb *tortiller* (to wiggle). The very movements of Proust's trains allow the narrator to pitch so as to hold together (in one canvas *and* in a single sentence) two different moments observed through two different windows. For Gilles Deleuze, this excerpt from *La Recherche* turns the railcar into an agent of "transversality that permits us, in the train, not to unify the viewpoints of a landscape, but to bring them into communication."[48] A couple of lines later, Deleuze formulates this transversality in social terms: "This dimension causes the viewpoints to interpenetrate and brings into the communication the sealed vessels that nonetheless remain closed: Odette with Swann, the mother with the narrator, Albertine with the narrator, and then, as a last 'brushstroke,' the old Odette with the Duc de Guermantes—each one is a captive, and yet all communicate transversally."[49] To summarize, from Proust to Barthes to Deleuze, the wiggling train around Balbec leads the narrator—a budding writer—to create a work of art *and* to bring different social classes together. If according to Barthes, Proust invented a new syntax aboard the Balbec train, the next examples will consolidate the idea that the railcar is no longer solely a setting but a formal device used to artistically represent the trajectory of socially mobile persons. In modern and contemporary literature, especially since Proust, the train is the metaphor par excellence—in the sense of rhetorical device and mode of transportation—of class mobility.

In the previous chapters, three of my case studies were related to the railway. Malinka's transclass malaise in Marie NDiaye's *Ladivine* (2013) is set aboard a train: her trembling and the ternary repetition of her name in tortuous sentences mimic the sound and rhythm of a railroad trip (chap. 3). In Christine Angot's *Le Marché des amants* (2008; *Lovers Market*), the train door stands as a metaphor for Christine and Bruno's transclass romance coupled with a rather idiosyncratic use of the imperfect tense. Even the name of the machine points to class cohabitation: "Corail" (the brand name given to the passenger cars that started operating in the 1970s) combines "comfort" and "rail."[50] It literally means coral—the doors of this model were initially orange. But we can also hear "co-rail," that is to say a form of cotraveling by rail (chap. 5).

Finally, in Annie Ernaux's *La Place* (1983; *The Place*), the train is coupled with her use of reported speech and quotation marks as a way to measure the social distance (chap. 5). In the following passage, for instance, she travels from her hometown to Paris after the death of her father. The train car becomes the place of a sudden social realization that triggers her creativity:

> On the return train, on Sunday, I was trying to keep my son entertained so that he would stay calm, first-class travelers don't like noise or children who move. All of a sudden, with shock, "now, I'm really a bourgeoise" and "it's too late."
>
> Later on, during the summer, waiting for my first job, "I will have to write all of this." I meant, write about my father, his life, and that distance that emerged in adolescence between him and me. A class distance, but a particular kind, that has no name. Like separated love.[51]

It is hard to tell here whether Ernaux includes herself or not in this first-class group because of the impersonal formulation, "travelers." Does she amuse her son because *they* "don't like noise," or because *she* is the one who no longer does? There is no "I" in the rest of the sentence when there is one within the quotation marks, so as to distinguish between two voices. The first two sentences are separated by a period, not a comma, a detail that reinforces the indeterminacy of the narrator's travel class. The abrupt, juxtaposed, unintroduced direct discourse is meant to make us readers feel formally, typographically, materially, the sudden realization of class distance. It is this distance that led Ernaux to craft a specific style in *La Place*.

Marie-Hélène Lafon has a lot in common with Ernaux. She, too, made it in Paris through reading, teaching, and writing, although not from a family of Normand shopkeepers but of farmers from the mountainous and depopulated Cantal region. In her 2012 bildungsroman *Les Pays* (*The Countries*), train doors and juxtaposition alloy to materialize the space of class mobility: "In the train and on the metro, at the edge of people and in the screech of more or less docile machines, locomotive cars crossbars barriers sliding doors [locomotives wagons portiques portillons portes coulissantes], Claire lets unfurl the junction between the two countries, the two times, the two bodies."[52] This passage confuses bodies, spaces, and technologies: the narrator is "at the edge of people" the way you would be near a ravine, and the railcar screeches or chirps like an insect. Parts of the machine are juxtaposed in a list that rhymes, in French as in English, so as to imitate the train's din. Although the list starts with the driving force, the locomotive, it moves on to the sliding door, a more passive space where the two classes join together. Like Ernaux and Angot, Lafon represents her social mobility through form and train.

This emphasis on forms can even be the detail that catches the attention of quotidian readers. Critic Lyn Thomas has studied the many letters received by Ernaux, and she cites the following one, from a person who read *La Place* on a train traveling between Bordeaux and Bayonne: "I got off the train feeling drunk with that specific inebriation born of what I can find no other word to describe, the ecstasy [*jouissance*] of language. I was in love with your italics (F.)."[53] As in Laure Murat's examples, the train is not only a place to skim airport novels leisurely—called "train station novels" in French—but to close read them.

An entryway into the bourgeoisie, the train is also a way for Ernaux to reconnect with her childhood: "It's thus outside, in the passengers on the metro or the R.E.R., the people who take the escalator in Galeries Lafayette and Auchan, that my former existence is deposited."[54] The memory of her social trajectory is stored on public transportation. In the 1980s Pierre Bourdieu also used the metaphor of the subway to argue that explaining the life trajectory of someone without the network was "about as absurd as trying to make sense of a journey in the metro without taking into account the structure of the network, which is to say the matrix of the objective relationships between the different stations."[55] Such a description that pits a single trajectory against a broader mapping of the social field particularly applies to Ernaux's transclass journey and successive books. In her first novel, *Les Armoires vides* (1974; *The Empty Cupboards*), the train already was the locus of a two-way movement. A young and fictional version of the author lies in bed in her parents' house when "the snorting [*renâclante*] locomotive sets off and gallops like mad toward Rouen, Paris, the big cities."[56] The verb *renâcler* (to snort) designates a movement forward—the train on its way from Yvetot to Rouen and Paris—as well as the sniffling associated with animals, especially (iron) horses straining with all their might; but the verb could also be translated as "to balk" and thus express reluctancy. Although the engine transports the narrator's dream of going away, the direction is all but clear cut: jointly forward and backward. In *Les Années* (2008; *The Years*), a young version of the narrator espies her "future" in Chaïm Soutine's painting *L'Escalier rouge à Cagnes* (ca. 1923).[57] Yet the bright and skewed, almost undulating "red staircase" of the title looks less like steps and more like tracks cutting through a hilly landscape.

The train also played an unexpectedly crucial role in a telling anecdote of her literary life. In a book on literary prizes, sociologist Nathalie Heinich interviewed Ernaux about the Renaudot prize she won for *La Place* in 1984. After the reception, at one in the morning, the author insisted on taking a train home to Cergy in the suburbs of Paris instead of a cab, whose fare would have been covered by Gallimard: "No no, I want to go back by train."[58] At the Saint-Lazare station, while reading a newspaper, a young man accosted Ernaux and asked, "Oh so you know how to read?"[59] Taking a train home was a way for Ernaux to continue inhabiting not the ladder, but the railroad space between classes, between childhood and adulthood, especially because her parents' shop in Yvetot was located near the station. Although she had just been awarded a prize for her prose and for a narrative on upward mobility, the young commuter reminded Ernaux—whose grandfather was illiterate—that class affiliations remain ambiguous in train stations.

Moroccan writer Abdellah Taïa stages his social mobility aboard trains too. In his novel *La Vie lente* (2019; *The Slow Life*), the author draws a parallel between two sexual and social events on public transportation. Aboard a bus from Rabat to Salé in Morocco, the narrator Mounir has a sexual encounter with a stranger, Soufiane: "I didn't guess who he really was."[60] Once the latter exits the bus, he turns out to be a state employee, a bourgeois commuter in striking contrast with the poor narrator. The sexual encounter was classless, but only on the bus. Years after his immigration to France, Mounir starts strolling commuter rail stations in order to reconnect with his class of origin: "To get out of my comfort and discomfort zone, I had finally decided, with much shame I admit, to go explore the suburbs, to go looking for Arab and African French people, born here but whom France still saw as immigrants."[61]

The narrator's transclass trajectory unfolds between two stations on the opposite sides of the social spectrum: Palais-Royal and Nanterre-Préfecture. Mounir meets Antoine at the station La Défense-Grande Arche, one of the "gates" between Paris and the suburbs.[62] He reenacts, on the RER, the silent sexual encounter he had had with Soufiane on a Moroccan bus. But the roles are reversed this time: Mounir now represents the bourgeois commuter who lives on the fancy Rue de Turenne in the center of the capital and Antoine, a precarious and uncultivated white policeman who, unlike Mounir, never set foot in Le Louvre. The move from a slow suburban bus to a rapid transit train underscores the narrator's upward trajectory. At the same time, the commuter rail allows him to connect with other classes and to reconnect with his former self so as to measure the distance he has come.[63] Researching contemporary migration as well, Kleinman shows in *Adventure Capital* that West African migrants, who envision themselves as "adventurers," "are not seeking settlement, citizenship, and dependence." Rather, they repurpose the Gare du Nord as "a space for dwelling in motion. From that place, departure need not entail rupture."[64] Taïa's depiction of commuter rail stations resemble the usage of railroad infrastructures by the African migrants interviewed by Kleinman.

Like Angot, Ernaux, and NDiaye, Taïa couples the train with a formal device: punctuation. His bildungsroman *L'Armée du salut* (2006; *The Salvation Army*) recounts how the narrator's elder brother Abdelkébir played a crucial role in Abdellah's social mobility and migration from Morocco to Switzerland: "As we waited for the departure of the train Abdelkébir brought us, my little brother Mustapha and me, to a café."[65] The absence of comma between "train" and "Abdelkébir" is so unsettling it looks like a typo: punctuation is expected to clarify the fact that Abdelkébir is the subject of the verb *to bring*. The mistake is present in both the first edition and the paperback, so either it went unnoticed or it was fully intentional. A French reader would think the train is named after the narrator's brother. And indeed, Abdelkébir is Abdellah's social-mobility vehicle: "He helped me to form sentences, to write letters. I cried with his words, thinking of him. He bought me a plane ticket, a sugar doughnut one night in the Rabat medina, a blue toothbrush, white swimming trunks and a green winter coat that I still wear today."[66] Abdelkébir's role is so central it must be represented by an eclectic list of gifts. The plane ticket—that is to say the concrete vehicle of Abdellah's mobility—opens and organizes the list up to the coat that makes the connection between Abdellah then and Abdellah now. Abdelkébir had studied political sciences at the university and introduced his brother to cinema and literature in French, especially Mohamed Choukri's 1973 *Le Pain nu* (*The Naked Bread*), at the end of which the illiterate narrator goes to school to learn how to read.[67]

The trip from Rabat to Tangiers aboard the "Abdelkébir train" is particularly important in *L'Armée du salut*. In this coastal city at the western tip of the African continent, strollers can see Spanish lights across the channel. The chapter on Tangiers comes at the very end of the second part, right before an ellipsis: the narrator turns up at the Geneva airport at the beginning of part three. Although an aircraft transported the narrator from Morocco to Switzerland, in terms of the narrative, the train to Tangiers brings him to Geneva. Later in the novel, the train comes to represent the European continent: Abdellah has sex with Matthias (a German) and Rafaël (a Pole) on a Spanish train traveling from Algeciras to Madrid.[68] The initial trip to Tangiers also gives young Abdellah the impulse first to draw, then to write: "On the train, on a sudden impulse, I decided to assign this notebook to another role, that of a personal diary. Truly personal."[69] It is through a graduate degree in literature, and then through publishing books and directing a film, that Abdellah Taïa changes the direction of his life. As critic Denis Provencher argues, "Taïa's storytelling does not exemplify a once-and-for-all abandonment of the homeland followed by a 'coming out' or 'arrival' in the postcolonial capital; instead, his male protagonist Abdellah exemplifies a series of 'comings and goings' over time between France and the Maghreb, and illustrates a flexible accumulation of language and cultural legacies."[70] This two-way trajectory (of the train, of the author) is captured by the title of his spring 2019 Yale lecture, "Bouche du Métro [Subway Entrance, literally "The Mouth of the Metro"]: Where Sex & Culture Meet & Break Apart."[71] In *La Vie lente*, as in *L'Armée du salut*, the train forms the narrator's social launching pad. It also provides him with a tickler, a vehicle to return and remember.

As we have seen at the beginning of this section, the train runs through Proust's *Recherche*, stages discussions and observations, bringing together ways and characters as micro and macro "sealed social vessels." Critic Sara Danius wrote that "The very first sense impression recorded in Proust's novel is thus auditory and issues from the iron horse."[72] A hundred years later, the machine continues to be a social sensor and easel. Writers such as NDiaye, Angot, Ernaux, Lafon, and Taïa ride it again to capture their now multidirectional social trajectories of departure, arrival, and return; they use it as a formal tool of observation, introspection, and self-fashioning.

**Unyielding Routes**

The train is not necessarily the metaphor of a desired upward mobility. Take French writer Paul Nizan, for instance, the son of a railway engineer. In his 1933 bildungsroman *Antoine Bloyé*, he narrates a fictional version of his family's trajectory from agriculture to engineering. More precisely, he tells the story of his father, an "uprooted peasant" and "poor scholarship student," whose job assignments in railway compagnies made him move up the ladder from station to station, alongside new lines.[73] Mobility was less the result of his will than of the fast industrialization of France. His entry into the bourgeoisie thus felt solitary and boring:

> Since the age of fifteen, he has been set on an unyielding route where there is no place for the rest of body or mind, where there are no crossroads, no wanderings, only brief stops. In the countryside, there are still today small railway lines serving the local population where time is not costly: between Brest and Ploudalmézeau, the engineer stops to gather bouquets, to pick up on the tracks the women farmers headed to the Saint-Renan market, to play a game of manille with a friend at the station. But Antoine's life already resembles the high-speed trains he will drive tomorrow and that carry a force full of certitude and suffocation.[74]

Antoine Bloyé rises into the managerial class, from train driver to head of the repair shop with 1,500 workers under his command. But like nineteenth-century transclass writer Jules Vallès, who was forced into higher education by his parents, he will always miss physical labor, the solidarity among manual workers, and the relaxed everyday life spent along countryside railway lines. This trajectory led Susan Suleiman to read Nizan's novel as "an elegy, a negative bildungsroman mourning a wasted life."[75] Antoine Bloyé is passive, "set," and "carried" by the speed of modernization and of fast trains let loose on "unyielding routes."

Georges Perec was greatly influenced by Nizan. His 1965 bestseller *Les Choses: Une histoire des années soixante* (*Things: A Story of the Sixties*) ends on a train. While the book starts in the conditional, the railroad epilogue is written in the future: this tense authorizes the protagonists Jérôme and Sylvie—always referred to as *they* or as a couple—to dream of their putative upward mobility, from being marketing pollsters in Paris to possibly managing an advertising branch in Bordeaux. But the speculative railway car is "deserted," and the food on board is "insipid."[76] As in Nizan, the upward mobility that leads to bourgeoisie, management, and the financial resources to buy the "things" of the title only brings boredom.

In *Fast Cars, Clean Bodies* (1995), Kristin Ross comments on the protagonists' dangling social class:

> Childless and possessing no visible parents or extended family, the characters Sylvie and Jérôme are reduced to their pure function of embodying the desires of a new, streamlined, middle-class couple, a couple disencumbered of both the anxieties and the privileges of lineage, inheritance, and transmission characteristic of an older, nineteenth-century bourgeoisie. Gone is the thick web of interfamilial intrigue, the violent struggles over patrimony that filled the pages of Balzac's *Comédie humaine*.[77]

The moving train symbolizes this new, uprooted milieu: Jérôme and Sylvie inhabit a transitional class symbolized by a railcar on the move toward a hypothetical future. Even before this final episode, Perec portrays the couple's ambition as a rectilinear train ride:

> From station to station, antique dealers, bookstores, record sellers, restaurant menus, travel agencies, haberdashers, tailors, cheesemongers, cobblers, confectioners, high-end delicatessens, stationers, their routes made up their true universe: there lay their ambitions, their hopes. There was real life, the life that they wanted to know,

that they wanted to lead: it was for these salmon, for these rugs, for these crystals that, twenty-five years prior, an employee and a hairdresser had brought them into the world.[78]

In this excerpt, Perec superimposes mercantile and social trajectories "from station to station" by noting in passing the modest occupations of Jérôme's and Sylvie's mothers. Perec's own mother was also a hairdresser. After his parents died during World War II (his father on the front, his mother in Auschwitz), he was adopted by his paternal uncle and aunt. Perec was torn between two childhoods: one before the war, in the working-class neighborhood of Belleville, with Polish immigrant parents struggling to speak French, and one after the war in a new, wealthy, and lettered family.[79] Like Nizan, although for different reasons, Perec could not portray social climbing in a positive light. Besides, the traumatic origin of his upward mobility is connected to the role of the railroad during World War II: the death train that carried his mother to Auschwitz; the Red Cross train that spared him a similar fate by transporting him to the *zone libre* in the south.

As we have seen in the previous section, there is a train at the beginning and end of Laurent Cantet's *Ressources humaines*. A train also appears in the first sequence of his subsequent film, *L'Emploi du temps* (literally "The Employment of Time," released as *Time Out*, 2001). When he loses his job, the main protagonist Vincent does not tell his family and fakes being employed while he spends his days driving on French and Swiss highways. Practically, he is upwardly mobile, from a real executive job in a consulting firm to pretending he's in charge of development projects in Africa at the Geneva headquarters of the United Nations. This film is one of Berlant's case studies in *Cruel Optimism*, a book on "the new affective languages of the contemporary global economy in Europe and the United States—languages of anxiety, contingency, and precarity—that take up the space that sacrifice, upward mobility, and meritocracy used to occupy."[80]

One experiences "cruel optimism" when the attempt at having a better life is precisely what makes you unhappy, including yearning for upward mobility. Within this framework, Berlant reads Vincent's trajectory in *L'Emploi du temps* as an "affective shift toward valuing lateral freedoms and creative ambitions over strict upward mobility."[81] The lead character transitions from "good life" to "impasse," from upward mobility to "lateral or sideways mobility" that consists in "simulated, improvised, scavenged enjoyment in a present beyond which there is nothing."[82] Vincent admits that what he liked the most about his real job was the commute by car, which is why he decides to keep only this pleasurable aspect of work. At the very beginning of the film, after he wakes up in his car on an interstate rest area, he starts driving alongside a train. He races against it while examining the commuters. Then he has to stop when the train crosses the road he is driving on. Alone in his car and going nowhere in particular, Vincent seems to contemplate the train as he would his past, or the possibility to work again with others toward a specific task, goal, and professional destination. The train that overtakes him represents a concrete, possible upward mobility and the collective routine he refuses to participate in any longer. Incidentally, the French idioms for the daily grind involve the railway: "métro-boulot-dodo" (subway, job, sleep), and the everyday "train-train" or drudge.

These three examples update Zola's portrait of the train as a vehicle of heredity, the so-called beast of the title, carried on from generation to generation in *La Bête humaine*. Through metaphors, Zola has turned his driver's flaw into a thermodynamic machine made of "fissures, holes through which his self was escaping him, amid a sort of great smoke that deformed everything."[83] Even if the railway now functions as a social ladder, its rigid tracks can continue to represent what falls onto someone, whether it is interwar meritocracy (Nizan), war trauma and postwar consumerism (Perec), or management in the late-capitalist era (Cantet). Unlike Zola's realist novel, the successful stories of class mobility I have gathered here were published as memoirs. The next and final chapter will show that when it comes to fiction, the railroad immobilizes. Contemporary social novels are the demoted heirs to nineteenth-century bildungsromane. They depict trains to nowhere, trains who break down, as in *La Bête humaine*'s snowstorm, arrested trains that tell us of demotion, precarity, and the rigidity of classes.

# From Rastignac to Subutex 7

THE IMMOBILIZATION OF THE
FICTIONAL CHARACTER

Many say that Balzac is back because the Romanesque is back.[1] In my view, such a statement does not work if, instead of focusing on Balzac, we hone in on Rastignac. There is a clear, dividing line in literature today: successful and lettered Rastignacs tell their own story in autobiography, autofiction, and nonfiction, in first-person *Künstlerromane* and tales of educational success. But upward trajectories have ceased to be the staple of the realist novel. In fiction, Rastignac comes back as an outcast; he cannot, or refuses to climb any farther. In *Degenerative Realism: Novel and Nation in Twenty-First-Century France* (2020), Christy Wampole surveys the literary genres of the twenty-first century (new journalism, ideological novels) to show how, especially in the works of Michel Houellebecq, "realism degenerates in a variety of ways throughout the course of the narrative, with sudden departures into the mode of science fiction or dystopian horror, or with an abrupt introduction of implausible or hyperbolic elements into the story."[2] When it comes to plots of social mobility, realism degenerates, too, insofar as realist novels transfer successful tales of upward mobility to nonfiction and autobiographies.

Within this landscape, I would say that Marie NDiaye inhabits the dividing line between these two groups of texts—narratives of social mobility and novels of social immobility. Although I have discussed NDiaye's novels alongside autobiographical narratives in the previous chapters, her fictional parvenus are questionable social climbers in the long term. Her 2021 book *La Vengeance m'appartient* (*The Vengeance is Mine*) states this thwarted upward mobility plainly. The character of Me Susane—who grew up in a working-class family—starts a law firm in the harbor city of Bordeaux. Yet a legal practice does not guarantee her success: "she had failed in every respect."[3] Readers are not even sure whether "Me" refers to the protagonist's first name or to the abbreviated professional title of a lawyer, $M^e$ (even though the superscript is more common in French). Moreover, NDiaye writes neither autobiographies nor realist fictions. She publishes fantastical novels in which socially mobile characters, even if they manage to climb the ladder, end up in tragic or magic settings. They die or disappear; they morph into ghosts and animals. The character of the maid is left ambiguously lifeless at the end of the play *Hilda* (discussed in chap. 4); Malinka/Clarisse in *Ladivine* has difficulties inhabiting her new position and experiences bodily discomfort when she travels between two different social spheres (discussed in chap. 3). In the end, she is murdered by her partner and reincarnates as a dog. In Wampole's words, we could thus say that NDiaye's parvenants "degenerate" twice: their class mobility dwindles, and the novel gets unrealistic. In this chapter, I move away from NDiaye's magic to examine the leading voices of realism who also cast downgraded Rastignacs: Julia Deck, Michel Houellebecq, and Virgine Despentes.

## The Precarity of Characters after the New Novel

The paths from the provinces to Paris and from another country to France have generated distinct topoi and discourses. Although Paris remains the epitomic locus of attempts at social climbing, harbor cities have become crucial sites to reinvent the bildungsroman and to think migration, labor, and classes together. Many writers and filmmakers have relocated their narratives to the coasts of France.[4] Think, for instance, of the importance of the coastal city Tangiers in Abdellah Taïa's *L'Armée du salut* (2006; *The Salvation Army*), discussed in the previous chapter. In the conclusion of *Upward Mobility and the Common Good* (2007), Bruce Robbins follows in the footsteps of Gayatri Spivak: he opens his corpus of American, British, and French bildungsromane to literary works that are not confined to the "scale of the nation-state" but are concerned with the "international division of labor."[5] He discusses two twenty-first-century anglophone refugee novels connected by their titles and places: Lorraine Adams's *Harbor* (2004) and Caryl Phillips's *A Distant Shore*

(2003). The refugee characters in these texts (from Algeria and from an unnamed African country) arrive at their destinations by boat: in Boston's harbor for the former, on the English coast for the latter. And to take a cinematic example, in Aki Kaurismäki's film *Le Havre* (2011), a young Gabonese refugee en route to London, Idrissa Saleh, meets an old shoe shiner, Marcel Marx. In the process of recounting the effort to reunite Idrissa with his family across the channel, the film shows the solidarity between immigrants and the working class, that is to say between Idrissa, Marcel's wife (who has a Finnish accent), and his fellow shoe shiner who immigrated from China on the one hand, and on the other hand, workers from the neighborhood: the fisher, the grocer, the baker, and the barmaid. In art as in research, the port thus appears as a literal and metaphorical, literary and critical foreshore or interface where international migration and domestic class mobility converge.

French writer Julia Deck locates her 2014 frustrated bildungsromane in coastal cities. *Le Triangle d'hiver* (*The Winter Triangle*) is an exploration of space, class, and the memory of World War II. Unable to keep her various jobs (sales assistant, cashier), and after an umpteenth conversation with her employment counselor, the main protagonist decides to become a writer. Her pen name, Bérénice Beaurivage, is a toponym: *beau rivage* means "beautiful shore" in French. In search of inspiration, she wanders the streets of three harbor cities destroyed during World War II: Le Havre, Saint-Nazaire, and Marseille. The epigraph to *Le Triangle d'hiver* is from Auguste Perret, the architect of aesthetic concrete who rebuilt Le Havre (now a UNESCO World Heritage Site) with a grid street plan. This detail is reminiscent of Deck's first novel, *Viviane Elisabeth Fauville* (2012). The last name of the title points to an artificial topography: Fauville, or *faux ville* in French, means "false city," and the protagonist works in the cement industry. In *Le Triangle d'hiver*, Deck draws a parallel between the amnesic topography of cities destroyed during World War II and the protagonist's memory disorder, writer's block, and financial precarity. Aerial bombardment can indeed be read within the framework of class: as historians of the northern coastal city of Le Havre have shown, for instance, the maps of razed neighborhoods and of poor, insalubrious areas often match.[6] Deck portrays not a *flâneuse* but the countermodel of the harbor city wanderer whose perambulation and perception of space is not connected to leisure, dandyism, or consumerism but rather to war, precarity, and labor.[7] Coastal etymologies underscore the social vulnerability of the lead character. Bérénice Beaurivage is *radiée*, that is to say struck off a list (of unemployment benefits, for instance).[8] Planted in a novel set in port cities, the word deploys its polysemy. A *rade* in French is a "harbor," and to be *en rade* is "to be broken down" or "in dire straits," literally in a "desperate" strait. Bérénice is stranded, in all senses of the term. She is also "en grève," that is to say, "on strike" and "on the shore."[9]

With the exception of her translation of Maggie Nelson's *The Red Parts*, all of Deck's writings are published by Les Éditions de Minuit, a French publishing house known for its engagement in the resistance: their first opus in 1942 was an anti-Occupation novella, Vercors's *Le Silence de la mer* (*The Silence of the Sea*). Minuit is also the designated publishing house of the postwar literary avant-garde, the New Novel. Like most of Minuit's twenty-first-century publications, *Le Triangle d'hiver* bursts with references to "new novels" and films from the New Wave.[10] Deck's reflections on memory in a harbor city bombarded during World War II are reminiscent of Alain Resnais's *Hiroshima, mon amour* (1959; *Hiroshima, My Love*) and, in the context of the Algerian War, *Muriel, ou le temps d'un retour* (1963; *Muriel, or The Time of a Return*). The incipit evokes the geometrical beginning of Alain Robbe-Grillet's *La Jalousie* (1957; *The Jealousy*), a novel, like *Le Triangle d'hiver*, on the triangulation of desire (Deck's title also refers to an equilateral triangle of stars).[11] The wanderings and the "internal shipwreck" of Deck's protagonist echo Marguerite Duras's *Le Ravissement de Lol V. Stein* (1964; *The Ravishing of Lol V. Stein*), in which the destroyed seaside topography of S. Thala symbolizes the mental state of Lola.[12] Finally, like the self-conscious characters of a formal and reflexive novel or play, Bérénice Beaurivage does not know how she ended up "here" (in an apartment, in the novel).[13] The originality of *Le Triangle d'hiver* lies in the intertwining of formalist devices, intertextual references, and remarks on social class. Two examples among many: unable to afford a book, Bérénice steals a paperback edition of Jean Racine's play in the kiosk of a train station; the director of the unemployment office, Mr. Geulincx, is named after the Flemish philosopher who had a decisive influence on Samuel Beckett.

New Novelists would have recognized Deck's literary devices and concrete, seaside topographies. Alain Robbe-Grillet himself used this construction material to praise the renewal of literary forms and the creation of "new beauties": "We are always decadent in comparison to things of the past: reinforced concrete in comparison to stone [...], Proust in comparison to Balzac."[14] On the other hand, Robbe-Grillet would have frowned on the detailed, realist social portrait of Deck's precarious protagonist: "The fate of the world has stopped, for us, being associated with the ascent or the fall or a few men, of a few families," he tersely wrote in *Pour un Nouveau Roman* (1963; *For a New Novel*).[15] And yet, upon closer inspection, the so-called death or destruction of the nineteenth-century realist and naturalist character, extolled by Minuit writers, is actually theorized as social demotion in another manifesto by the doyenne of the New Novelists, Nathalie Sarraute's *L'Ère du Soupçon* (1956; *The Era of Suspicion*):

> Since the happy times of *Eugénie Grandet* when, at the peak of his power, he presided between the reader and the novelist, the object of their shared fervor [...], he kept losing all his attributes and privileges in succession.
>
> He was very richly endowed, provided with all sorts of goods, surrounded by meticulous care; he lacked nothing, from the silver buckles of his breeches to the veiny growth at the end of his nose. Little by little, he lost everything: his ancestors, his carefully constructed house, packed from the cellar to the attic with all kinds of objects, down to the smallest knick-knacks, his properties and his annuities, his clothing, his body, his face, and, above all, that most precious asset, his character, which belonged only to him, and often even his name.[16]

Characterization here is described as an "endowment," as Sarraute mixes things that can and cannot be bought: a clothing item and a body; a house and a personality; a piece of furniture and a family tree; a trinket and a name. The original French also contains the word *parvenu* to underline the *Bildung* of the character's fortune. Critic Hannah Freed-Thall, who reads New Novelists alongside Bourdieu, identifies the deterioration of transmission in Sarraute's *Vous les entendez?* (1972; *Do You Hear Them?*): "Later in the novel, the father bequests (or imagines bequesting) the statuette to his children. When he visits (or imagines visiting) their room, he discovers that they have—intentionally or absent-mindedly, we cannot know which—turned their precious inheritance into an ashtray."[17] The family heirlooms of New Novel characters have fallen in value. By referring to *Eugénie Grandet*, Sarraute is, like Deck, decentering the plot of social mobility not only from Paris to the provinces but also from a single, uprooted, and successful man (Eugène de Rastignac) to a woman (Eugénie), whose father refuses to pass on his recently acquired fortune. Sarraute needed an entire family to convey the demotion of Balzacian characters.[18]

Today, having lost its possessions and identity, the novelistic character is not dead but downgraded and amnesiac. Sixty years after these manifestos, Deck's protagonist wanders through the open-air museum of postwar reconstruction. She strolls along the topography of New Novels written during the bygone era of full employment and economic prosperity known as "Les Trente Glorieuses" (1945–75; "The Glorious Thirty"). As a character shaped by postwar literature, she also carries the memory of what the New Novel did to fiction and its protagonists. The social, topographical, and literary landscape of twentieth-century France was erased by what the author calls "modern means," which could refer to technological warfare, postwar reconstruction, *and* literary techniques.[19]

The protagonists of today's reflexive novels are captives of literary history. Incidentally, there are a lot of concrete and metaphorical museums in the *Le Triangle d'hiver*; on many occasions, Bérénice visits naval and coastal museums to gaze at replicas of ships and at impressionist and pointillist seascapes. Stranded, penniless, and amnesiac, she is, I would argue, trapped in the museum of the twentieth century, condemned to roam in postwar novels and films. *Le Triangle d'hiver* is a novel in which strolling a port and its maritime museums becomes a metaphor for being a literary character.

Bérénice is a made-up parvenu who fakes her social status by pretending to be a writer. The end of *Le Triangle d'hiver* is particularly undecided: does she marry the wealthy "inspector" to achieve upward mobility off-screen? Or does she change her hair color and go back to square one at the unemployment agency? This undecidability is a narratological tool meant to represent the precarious status of twenty-first-century workers and characters, their imposed flexibility and interchangeability. Upward mobility in this context can only be the literary trick of a (fake) writer.

One name keeps coming back in the New Novel manifestos: Balzac, the author of the book discussed by Sarraute, *Eugénie Grandet*. Robbe-Grillet mocked his fellow, mainstream writers for plagiarizing him: "The majority of our traditional contemporary novelists— which is to say those who actually receive the approval of consumers— could copy long passages of *The Princess of Clèves* or *Old Man Goriot* without raising the suspicion of the vast audience that devours their content."[20] According to Robbe-Grillet, a Balzacian novel is not a work of art but a commodity, and those interested in such texts are not readers but voracious consumers. In the first pages of *Fast Cars, Clean Bodies* (1995), Kristin Ross gathers examples from Alain Robbe-Grillet, but also from Claude Chabrol and Françoise Giroud, to underline this (vexed) passion for Balzac:

> The Balzac of his day, the Rastignac of her day, the Lucien de Rubempré of the present. In the late 1950s and early 1960s—the roughly ten-year period I examine in this book, the years after electricity but before electronics—Balzac provides a way for people to establish the particular hopes, anxiety, fears, and aspirations of their own era; he is a recurrent figure in an allegory by way of which the present appears as both a repetition and a difference, a means of continuity and a mark of rupture.[21]

In Chabrol's 1959 film *Les Cousins* (*The Cousins*), Charles is a postwar Rastignac coming from the provinces to study law in Paris. When he first visits a bookstore to buy a novel by Balzac, the seller expresses bitterness at the literary proclivities of his generation, namely detective novels and porn: "I wanted to give *Old Man Goriot* to one of them. He practically flung it in my face." Charles (a customer, in Robbe-Grillet's eyes) leaves the store with a free copy of Balzac's *Illusions perdues* (1837–43; *Lost Illusions*). Charles's cousin Paul studies law, too, but spends his time partying instead of working. Yet he is the one who passes the exam while Charles works hard and fails. At the end of the film, Paul accidentally kills Charles.

Unlike Chabrol, Deck does not kill Rastignac. Her novel partakes in the twofold movement of "continuity" and "rupture" described by Ross, and that I extend, especially in chapter 1, from the postwar period through "the Rastignac of her day," Annie Ernaux. *Le Triangle d'hiver* does not revive Balzacian characters but their degraded selves, their "mommies," as Robbe-Grillet once called them.[22] Deck reassigns social characteristics to the flimsy silhouettes of New Novel characters, hence their precarity. While writing à la Balzac was considered "bourgeois" by Robbe-Grillet, Georges Perec deemed the absence of time, change, and history in New Novels to be "bourgeois" and "reactionary."[23] Deck bypasses all these anathemas: her novel is experimental and historicized, metadiscursive and socially situated. The triangulation at play in the title of her book operates between the realist novel (and its social climbers), the New Novel (and its dehistoricized characters), and the precarious workers of today.

Deck's novels are bathed in a light fog of references to Balzac. The protagonist of *Le Triangle d'hiver* reads the diary of the former mayor of Le Havre, Pierre Courant who, in order to praise the population's bravery during World War II, invoked Balzac's novel *Modeste Mignon*, set in Le Havre, and published a hundred years before the 1944 siege. Reading Deck's twenty-first-century novel alongside one from the nineteenth century creates a spatial and temporal telescoping: architect Perret rebuilt Le Havre according to the 1840–50s renovations, which means that its current orthogonal plan is not that different from the way it looked in Balzac's realist novel.[24] Bérénice Beaurivage thus walks in three different centuries at the same time: that of Balzac in the nineteenth century, Sarraute in the twentieth century, and today in the twenty-first. Deck's first novel *Viviane Elisabeth Fauville* refers more directly to Balzac to mock a dated choice of vocabulary: "And they have these words, I swear, no one speaks like that anymore. Fickle, passion, inheritance—we are right in the middle of a scene of provincial life."[25] One can easily be trapped in a novelistic setting, that of Balzac or Robbe-Grillet, with no way up and no way out.

## *Medium-Light* Balzac

Alain Robbe-Grillet and Michel Houellebecq are both trained agronomist engineers from the same *grande école*, but the comparison stops here. They hated each other's literature when the former was still alive. As Houellebecq indicates, "A silent and coded battle ensued between us for several years. Was he declaring again, against all evidence, that Balzac represented a sterile, static period in French literature? I would immediately praise Balzac, asserting that he was the second father of every novelist, and that anyone who didn't declare his allegiance and love to him could not pretend to understand the first thing about the art of the novel."[26] While Robbe-Grillet had wanted to erase nineteenth-century realist characters à la Balzac, Houellebecq conversely considers his main skill to be "the creation of *characters*."[27] His novel on sexual tourism, for instance, *Plateforme* (2001; *Platform*), starts with an epigraph from Balzac's *Splendeurs et misères des courtisanes*, although the title is omitted, so as to showcase even more deliberately the name of the realist author. Houellebecq claims he had not read Balzac before writing his first novel. But once he did, he had the impression that nothing had changed since the nineteenth century, especially the social and sexual competition between human beings as well as the power of determinism, even in cases of social mobility.[28] References to Balzac are not limited to the paratext. The narrator of *La Possibilité d'une île* (2005; *The Possibility of an Island*) considers that his "perspective was that of an *acerbic observer of social realities*, that of a *medium-light* Balzacian."[29] In the original version, too, *medium-light* is in italics and in English. The phrase could simply designate the distinctive feature of a commodity, such as a *medium-light* cigarette—a staple of Houellebecq's persona. But as I will argue here, there is a strong connection throughout the works of Houellebecq between "medium" or the middle, Balzac, and the representation of social classes.

Houellebecq, who is both a best-selling and a controversial author, is known for what critic Ruth Cruickshank calls the "drama of middle-class, middle-aged middle managers" in despair, but the importance of the "middle" is even broader.[30] Wherever you lay your eyes in Houellebecq's novels, things are moderate, mediocre, medium, mixed, monotone, or midway. For example, a chapter of *Les Particules élémentaires* (1998; *The Elementary Particles*) is titled "Standard Fare," and the epigraph to the novella *Lanzarote* (2000) is "The world is medium-sized." In *Plateforme*, life is "monotonous and romantic," the future of humanity is "intermixing, [a] widespread lack of differentiation," and the narrator "behaved like an exemplary client, average" by "dipp[ing] with moderation" in the sea. The narrator's "track record [was] mixed" and the present an "unlimited, unending stasis" in *La Possibilité d'une île*. The "uniform tepidness" of the car's cockpit in *La Carte et le Territoire* (2010; *The Map and the Territory*) makes the narrator feel "definitively neutral" as he dreams of driving "on the highway at a constant speed." The carpeting of a hotel room is "medium-gray" in *Soumission* (2015; *Submission*). Finally, the narrator of *Sérotonine* (2019; *Serotonin*) faces a "stagnant burn-out" and lives in a chalet "lost halfway up the hill in the middle of the woods."[31] The emphasis on middleness, often redoubled as in the previous sentence (half- *and* middle), is testament to Houellebecq's perception of humans as banal and average beings.

Such an apprehending of the world—namely the absence of singularities—poses a literary problem for the narrator of Houellebecq's first novel, *Extension du domaine de la lutte* (1994; *Extension of the Domain of Struggle*): "This entire accumulation of realistic details, meant to delineate cleanly differentiated characters, has always seemed to me, I am sorry to say, utter nonsense."[32] The artist Jed Martin in *La Carte et le Territoire* comes to the same conclusion: "I know that human beings are the subject of the novel, of the *great occidental novel*, one of the great subjects of painting, too, but I cannot help but think that people are much less different than they usually think."[33] Houellebecq's writers and painters wave goodbye to the necessity of creating extraordinary characters. The *"great occidental novel"* (in italics and in English in the original version too) has morphed into the poetics of "a *medium-light* Balzacian." For Houellebecq, it is precisely a "crushing monotony" that gives novels (especially detective novels) "a unique scent of authenticity, of realism."[34] During an interview, he defined the genre of his texts as a *"middle road"* between testimonial and imaginative literature.[35] His fellow writer Aurélien Bellanger—who wrote a monograph titled *Houellebecq, écrivain romantique* (2010; *Houellebecq, Romantic Writer*)—comments on the subtitle of *Plateforme*, "In the Middle of the World," as follows: "Is this the name of a new *Human Comedy*, now global, with *Platform* as its first chapter?"[36] The emphasis on the middle is what connects Houellebecq to Balzac but also what signals the return, and the updating, of nineteenth-century literature in the twenty-first century.

In *Degenerative Realism*, Christy Wampole describes "a *collective worsening of life in the contemporary moment*," notably in Houellebecq's and Bellanger's realist novels.³⁷ By degeneration, she means "decay, decline, decadence, disintegration, *déchéance*," to which I would add "demotion."³⁸ My interest here lies in the decoupling between novel and *Bildung*. Against this backdrop, Houellebecq's emphasis on middleness points out precisely how contemporary realist novels display a subdued or demoted form of *Bildung*. If you shift the focus from nation to class, what Wampole calls a "nineteenth-century ectoplasm" becomes a downgraded Rastignac plot of upward mobility.³⁹

Houellebecq's characters, however Balzacian, are stuck in the middle. They are no longer socially mobile but immobile, confined to a platform, even when they do climb the social ladder. Consider this passage from *La Possibilité d'une île*:

> When I made my first million euros (I mean when I really had it, taxes deducted, and placed in a secure investment), I understood that I was not a Balzacian character. A Balzacian character who has just made his first million euros would in the majority of cases start thinking of ways to approach the second—with the exception of those rare few who would be dreaming of the moment when they could count their money in the tens of millions. As for me, I was mainly wondering whether I could quit my job—before concluding that I could not. [...]
>
> When I met Isabelle, I must have had about six million euros. A Balzacian character, at this stage, would buy a sumptuous apartment, fill it with pieces of art, and ruin himself for a dancer. I was living in a banal two-bedroom, in the 14th arrondissement, and I had never slept with a *top model*—I had never even felt the desire. It just seemed to me that I had copulated, one time, with a midrange model; it didn't leave a lasting memory.⁴⁰

In the first sentence of this excerpt, the reference to Balzac is caught between piles of money: "When I made my first million euros [...], I understood that I was not a Balzacian character. A Balzacian character who has just made his first million euros." This chiasmus points to the immobilization of the novel character. He no longer wants to continue climbing at all costs but prefers to linger in the middle of his social and financial ascent, in a "banal" apartment; even the "top" model he once slept with is "midrange," literally "intermediary" in the original version. Earlier in the same novel, Houellebecq's narrator explicitly argues that "the *social elevator*" has been replaced today by "a few flimsy footbridges" between the rich and the poor, or rather, between the "medium-poor" and the "medium-high classes in the middle of their life."[41] While the "middle" class expands its contours, upward mobility is being replaced by minimal and lateral movements (not a bridge, but a footbridge). The main character of *La Carte et le Territoire*, who used to read nineteenth-century novels on social climbers, is not a Rastignac but "a middling Bill Gates."[42] And at one point in *Plateforme*, the narrator contemplates a billionaire's yacht "halfway from the horizon."[43] In *Narrative Middles* (2011), Caroline Levine and Mario Ortiz-Robles argue that "nineteenth-century novelists, dwelling lengthily and lovingly on the middle, were absorbed in the experience of middleness *per se*. Spending hundreds of pages *in medias res*, absorbed in complex processes of *Bildung* and characterization."[44] For Houellebecq, the middle no longer functions as a step in the *Bildung*'s process, but as a point of arrival.

Two other spatializations are particularly telling in this regard: the middle of a staircase, and a raised platform. Let's start with the staircase in *Les Particules élémentaires*:

> Bruno woke up with a start around three in the morning, exited his tent; he was sweating. The campsite was calm, there was a full moon; you could hear the monotone song of the tree frogs. At the edge of the pond, he waited for breakfast time. Just before dawn, he felt a bit cold. The morning workshops began at ten. Around ten fifteen, he headed toward the pyramid. He hesitated in front of the writing workshop door; then he went down a floor. For about twenty seconds he tried to make sense of the watercolor workshop's program, then he climbed back up a few stairs. The stairwell was composed of straight ramps, separated halfway up by short curved sections. On the inside of each segment the width of the stairs increased, then diminished again. At the cusp of the curve, there was a stair wider than all the others. On that stair he sat down. He leaned his back against the wall. He started to feel good.

> The rare moments of happiness during his high school years Bruno had spent them thus, seated on a stair between two floors, just after the beginning of classes. Calmly leaning against the wall, equidistant from the two floors, his eyes sometimes half-closed sometimes wide-open, he would wait. Of course, someone might come; he would then have to stand up, grab his schoolbag, walk quickly to the room where class had already begun. But, often, no one came; everything was so peaceful; then, gently and almost furtively, in small brief surges, on the tiled gray stairs (he was no longer in history class, he was not yet in physics class), his mind would climb toward joy.[45]

Bruno wakes up in the middle of the night (3 a.m.) and waits for the first activities of the day, scheduled to take place midmorning (10 a.m.). The narrative hesitates at first between the preterit—which indicates a single event—and the imperfect, used for description, repetition, and monotony. Once the narrator recalls his teenage years, the text fully transitions to the imperfect. Paragraphs are interspersed with semicolons that keep on interrupting sentences in the middle. Many phrases also point to the middleness of the setting: "the monotone song," "halfway up," "between two floors," "equidistant," "eyes sometimes half-closed," "(he was no longer in history class, he was not yet in physics class)." The narrator stands in the middle of the staircase, between two floors and two courses. In *Les Particules élémentaires*, we could certainly fold such a spatialization onto an earlier description of the middle class: "On the professional level, his sole objective was—quite reasonably—to blend into that 'vast middle class with its blurry contours' as later described by President Giscard d'Estaing."[46] But because they are at times compared to Bill Gates, Houellebecq's characters cannot be considered middle class, even if, as in the previous sentence, the contours of this social group are blurry and keep on expanding. Only the poetics of Michel Houellebecq's novels, and the aspirations of his characters, are truly middle class. The dissonance between a character's mindset and his effective financial resources undermines social mobility; it masks the influence of class on lifestyle.

To distinguish between the middle in general and the middle class in particular, let's consider this other spatial metaphor in *Plate-*

*forme*: "One day, when I was twelve years old, I had climbed to the highest point of an electric pylon in the high mountains. Throughout the entire ascent, I hadn't looked at my feet. Once at the top, on the platform, it had seemed tricky and dangerous to go back down. The mountain chains stretched as far as the eye could see, crowned with eternal snow. It would have been much simpler to stay in place, or to jump."[47] First of all, the passage is evocative of Houellebecq's biography. His father came from an underprivileged background but rose up to become a mountain guide.[48] The platform here stands as a metaphor for Houellebecq's inherited social mobility and access to the middle class. Second, the vocabulary here is different from the excerpt about the staircase: top, high, ascent. Word choice helps us understand that the use of average metaphors in Houellebecq is a ploy: a platform, however immobile and intermediary, is a raised space. Likewise, Houellebecq's characters belong to the upper middle class when they are not straight out millionaires. *Sérotonine* even gives us an indication of the expected social class of the readers. After the phrase "master suite," inserted between quotation marks, the narrator adds, scathingly: "([…] like a bedroom, but with a walk-in closet and a bathroom, I point this out for my working-class readers)."[49] Such a clarification indicates that the working class and the lower middle class are not Houellebecq's usual or targeted readership. His most recent novel *Anéantir* (2022; *Annihilate*) represents a significant transition in Houellebecq's writing: "There were now only […] two automobile markets, the low cost and the high end, just as there were now only […] two social classes, the rich and the poor, the middle class had evaporated."[50] Although these are the words of the Minister of Economics and Finance for whom the main protagonist works, they show that the middle class can no longer be the horizon of Houellebecq's characters. In *Sérotonine* as in *Anéantir*, the gap between writer and readers, rich and poor, widens.

### Supermarket Milieus

Economist Bernard Maris—killed during the 2015 *Charlie Hebdo* terrorist attacks while he and his colleagues were discussing Houellebecq's *Soumission*—compared the works of his friend to canonical novels on money: "Of course, there was *The Lost Illusions*, or *The*

*Money*, or *The Mad Rush*, or *Bel-Ami*, even *The First Man* (which begins with a 'monetary' murder) and, we could say, all the great novels. As soon as it comes to ambition, to cruelty, to egotism, passion, money, dough, success or failure mingle with crimes and cooing. But no one [meaning until Houellebecq] caught that faint economic music, that supermarket background noise which, with its haunting and dull notes, pollutes our existences."[51] Similarly, French writer Dominique Noguez calls his writer friend a "Baudelaire of supermarkets."[52] The store is thus what connects Houellebecq to, and distinguishes him from, the nineteenth- and twentieth-century classics written by Balzac, Baudelaire, Maupassant, Zola, and Camus. Finally, David Coward in the *Times Literary Supplement* describes the English translation of *La Possibilité d'une île* as "a charging bull in the china shop of modern fiction."[53] I would like to pick up more literally on these references to a "supermarket background noise" in order to continue fleshing out social classes in the works of Houellebecq and to compare him to Ernaux's writing on class and consumerism.

Houellebecq's novels are full of references to everyday life, especially brands and supermarkets. In *La Carte et le Territoire*, the narrator awaits "the fusing of different chain stores in a total superstore, which would cover every human need."[54] The most frequent (and telling) supermarket in Houellebecq's works is the "Monoprix." One paperback edition of *Les Particules élémentaires* even features Houellebecq holding a cigarette in one hand and a Monoprix bag in the other. Initially created as a cheap variety store in the 1930s—hence a name that suggests a fixed and low price—Monoprix is now, like Whole Foods, an emblem of urban, fancy consumerism, a sign of gentrification, as well as the most expensive supermarket in France. This brand partakes in Houellebecq's strategy of hiding the upper class behind references to middleness. In *Les Particules élémentaires*, the narrator "ate sea bass with chervil from the *Monoprix Gourmet* prepared foods section, which he paired with a mediocre Valdepeñas."[55] Planting "*Monoprix Gourmet*" between a mediocre wine and a ready-to-eat, microwavable dish gives readers a socially misleading impression about the social status of Monoprix customers. Monoprix's slogan, "vivement aujourd'hui" (looking forward to today), points to a monotonous and never-ending day; it addresses a group of people who rejoice in the present, in what they already have, in the repetition of the same. As Houellebecq said in an interview, "In the end, this is really what the twentieth century has been most successful at, distribution. You can babble on forever about whether it was better living in the old days, but shopping is indisputably better now than it ever has been. It's really well organized. The last time I went to Paris, I listened to Radio Monop' and I was happy straight away, I love their line of products, I feel great when I'm in a Monoprix."[56] One of Houellebecq's photographs, displayed at the Palais de Tokyo in Paris in 2017, portrays not a Monoprix but a hard-discount store chain selling only one low-cost brand, *Leader Price* (fig. 6). The big-box store—trapped between a countryside landscape and a traditional village of hexagonal France—is seen from a hill, from a platform, as if the photographer (a Monoprix client?) was a social tourist who did not belong to the setting. The ordinary is observed from above. The photographer is located at the same place and height as Houellebecq's protagonists, as in one of his poems: "In the midst of

**Figure 6.** Michel Houellebecq, *France #002* (2016). © Michel Houellebecq. All rights reserved. Pigment print on Baryta paper mounted on Dibond. 49.5 × 73 × 3.3 cm. Photograph: Courtesy of the artist and Air de Paris, Romainville.

this landscape / Of medium-high mountains."[57] The middleness is redoubled: "in the midst" and "medium-high." The first line points to a speaker on a par with the reader and the landscape, but then, after the caesura, the standpoint turns out to be a high-angle shot.

Michel Houellebecq and Annie Ernaux share a literary and sociological interest in supermarkets. Ernaux grew up in a grocery store on the outskirts of a small city, far from the "downtown venders" associated with "middle-class people."[58] Later in her life, she bought a house in a "new city" near Paris, built in the 1970s (Cergy-Pontoise), developed around a sprawling mall: "Here, there are no traditional streets, we meet for the most part in shopping centers, in stations."[59] The "city center" became a "shopping center" in which "the majority of the clientele belong to the middle and working classes."[60] Spatially, Ernaux belonged neither to the center nor to the middle class: she grew up on its modest margins and now lives in an upper-class residential neighborhood at a distance from the mall.

Her first encounter with a supermarket is connected to an important step of her social trajectory, her au pair trip: "I remembered the first time I entered a supermarket. It was in 1960 in the London suburbs and it was simply called *Supermarket*."[61] The suburban store introduces an element of difference in Ernaux's text; its tautological name in English clashes with the French narrative. In Cergy, the mall allows Ernaux to spatialize her social mobility: "Other times, I recognized my mother's gestures and sentences in a woman waiting at the supermarket checkout. It's thus outside, in the passengers on the metro or the R.E.R., the people who take the escalator in Galeries Lafayette and Auchan, that my former existence is deposited."[62] The supermarket is a place of transclass memory. Ernaux here wants to tell us how memory lives outside of our bodies, yet she clearly distinguishes between her mother and herself. While she finds traces of her mother in a client waiting in line, her own "existence" is marked by mobility, since it lies in rapid transit trains and on the escalator of a mall. Ernaux relies on a comparable form of in-betweenness when she discusses literature bought in supermarkets: "After all, placing a book on the conveyor belt always embarrasses me, as if it were sacrilege. Though I would be happy to see one of mine there, pulled out of a cart, slid between a packet of butter and a pair of tights."[63] Her books alone, as reflections of her social mobility, belong in the supermarket, in between other commodities.

The names of stores are as important for Houellebecq as they are for Ernaux. In her first novel, *Les Armoires vides* (1974; *The Empty Cupboards*), the family grocery store is simply called "café-épicerie Lesur."[64] Although fictitious, naming a supermarket after one's last name creates a confusion between body and store for the young protagonist: "When I wake up too early, I slide into their bed, [...]. The grocery-café shrank, became a house with a roof made of covers, with walls of warm flesh that pressed into me and protected me."[65] The grocery store replaces the contours of Ernaux's own body. In English, to say that people receive equal treatment, you say they are "in the same boat"; in French, the idiom is *être logé à la même enseigne*, literally, "to be lodged under the same sign." Ernaux, her parents, and her fictional avatar Denise Lesur are "housed by the same brand." As I have mentioned in chapter 1, Annie renames herself Denise in her first novel, most probably after Émile Zola's sales assistant character Denise Baudu in *Au Bonheur des dames* (1883). Unlike Denise, Ernaux's upward mobility veers off from commerce. But because the French use the same words for "sign" and "to teach," *enseigne* and *enseigner*, there remains a sonorous link between Ernaux's supermarket childhood and her later function as a teacher.

By contrast in Cergy, the supermarket is called Auchan, a hegemonic name that subsidizes the brands it sells, removing their labels: "At the entrance, an enormous display of ornate bottles: **champagne for 6.31 euros per bottle with the Auchan card 20% off**—whose brand is not revealed."[66] Auchan's slogan is important too: "La vie. La vraie. Auchan" (The Life. The Real One. Auchan.) Each term of this consumerist maxim is separated by a dot, and the prosody of the three phrases can lead you to see Auchan as two words. Because Ernaux grew up in the provinces, I find it hard not to hear "field" (*champs*) in this brand, especially because the author repeatedly compares the supermarket to a garden in *La Vie extérieure* (2000; *The External Life*): "In deserted Auchan, this morning, sensation of pure happiness. I roam in the middle of abundance [...], gathering food here and there, like in a garden"; "Nine in the morning, Auchan, at opening, nearly empty. As far as the eye can see, hills of tomatoes, peaches, grapes [...]. Strange sensation of beauty. I am on the edge of Eden"; "From the baby carriage to the tomb, life increasingly plays out between the shopping mall and the television. Neither more strange nor more stupid than life of former times, between the fields and the evening gatherings or the bar."⁶⁷ The words "shopping mall" and "fields" occupy the exact same place in the last excerpt, thus reinforcing the parallel between the two settings. Throughout these examples, location phrases remind us of Houellebecq: "in the middle of abundance," "between the shopping mall and the television." But Ernaux's standpoint is not elevated.

Ernaux's maiden name is not Lesur, as in *Les Armoires vides*, but Duchesne. These two names point to a rooting (a *chêne* is an oak tree) and to certainty (*Lesur* literally means "the certain"). The author went from Duchesne to Lesur to Ernaux, her married name. No longer married, Annie Duchesne is the person who goes to Auchan, "du chêne aux champs" (Duchesne Auchan), from social determinism and heredity to the open field of social mobility. Brands mark her reinvention, so that the "field" in question could well be the social field of Bourdieu, who greatly influenced Ernaux.

It is also mischievously tempting to compare Auchan's slogan ("La vie. La vraie. Auchan") to Marcel Proust, quoted by Ernaux: "Real life, life finally discovered and illuminated, the only life in consequence really lived, it's literature."⁶⁸ Proust and Ernaux agree that writing is "the real place," the title of her 2014 book-length interview with Michelle Porte. Her presence in a supermarket is indeed coterminous with her work as a writer: "Something like a surge of pleasure just now at the idea of going to Trois-Fontaines and doing some necessary shopping at Auchan. Like a rupture in the work of writing, an effortless distraction in a familiar place."⁶⁹ I see this break, this separation between writing and consumerist leisure, in the jolt of the prepositions, in the hiatus *à Auchan*, which in French literally reads as "to to-field," or "to out in the fields." Other French supermarket brands could resonate with Ernaux's writing style: "Leclerc" indicates brightness and "Franprix" frankness. Ernaux's "écriture plate" (a "flattened" or surface style that allows her to be faithful to her modest background) resonates with supermarkets. In *Les Armoires vides*, the narrator describes her shopkeeper mother as "flattened" when she serves the clientele.⁷⁰ Ernaux herself feels like a "smooth surface" when she shops in a superstore that, in French, we call a "grande surface."⁷¹ Being in a supermarket also "flattens" time: "Curious impression that time does not pass here, that it is a present repeated many many times."⁷² The deep connection between supermarket and surface is accessible through the "slow pace, receptiveness, and fixed attention" of Stephen Best and Sharon Marcus's "surface" reading, that is to say through an attention to sonority, polysemy, and prosody.[73]

Let's go back for a moment to the contrapuntal example of Houellebecq. What has been considered his absence of style could well be a "flat" writing style too. As the narrator of his first novel *Extension du domaine de la lutte* says, "we would need to invent a flatter, more concise and bleaker form of expression" for one to become the painter of contemporary life.[74] The narrator rejoices in his own flattening: "No doubt today I lead a vague existence in a doctoral dissertation, in the midst of other real-life cases. The thought of having become a part of a dossier soothes me. I imagine the volume, its glued binding, its slightly sad cover; gently, I flatten myself between the pages; I crush myself."[75] This is also how we could read the title of Houellebecq's 2001 novel *Plateforme*: flat form. But there are two major differences between Houellebecq's and Ernaux's flatness. First of all, while Houellebecq writes poetry and novels, Ernaux explains that today's consumerism and her own social trajectory cannot lead to novels, "no description, no story either" but to "the ethnotext."[76] Second, contrary to Ernaux, who mixes social classes in her flat prose as we have seen in chapter 5, Houellebecq aims at describing neither transclass characters nor interclass encounters but clones, that is to say standard, average people devoid of singularity (although in practice, they are often upper middle-class middle-aged white occidental men). Ernaux's "surface" is thus closer to the space described by French writer Maylis de Kerangal in *Corniche Kennedy* (2008): "La Plate," a rocky coastal platform in Marseille from which teenagers plunge into the sea and on which social classes mix. Houellebecq's "flat form" is a raised "platform" distinct from Kerangal's and Ernaux's social inclusiveness. Ernaux's "flat writing" does not point to the amorphous middle class but to an upwardly mobile trajectory and to an attempt at reconnecting, in stores, with the class she left. Thus, Ernaux's and Houellebecq's comparable keywords, *flatness* and *middleness*, do not portray the same genres, spaces, or social groups.

In his 1989 "Literary Manifesto for the New Social Novel," Tom Wolfe exclaims that to depict the power and vastness of the United States, especially New York City, "we need a battalion, a brigade, of Zolas."[77] He opposes this ambition to the minuscule style of Kmart

Realism: a literary movement from the long 1980s characterized by working-class protagonists developing in uneventful plots and prose surrounded by the brands of the consumer society.[78] To what extent are Ernaux and Houellebecq practicing the French equivalent of Kmart Realism? Houellebecq, we could say, has a novelistic (Balzacian or Zolian) ambition to depict France. As the narrator of *Soumission* observes while contemplating a nineteenth-century painting: "Maupassant, Zola, even Huysmans, were much more immediately accessible."[79] Yet Monoprix Realism is limited in its scope because it only aims to capture the averageness of the population. As for Ernaux, her works refer to Zola: in the narrative *Regarde les lumières, mon amour* (2014; *Look at the Lights, My Love*), for instance, the narrator notices that "nothing had changed since *Le Bonheur des dames*" regarding women and consumerism.[80] But after writing three books, Ernaux abandons the genre of the novel, a form that could not render her social trajectory and the marginal life of her parents. In this context, Zola is no longer a model to emulate but an intertextual reference: planted in autobiographies, it signals Ernaux's social emancipation through books. Annie Ernaux left her parents' store; a twentieth-century Denise Baudu exited Zola's megastore and is now writing the story of her own emancipation in the first person.

### From the Bildungsroman to the Picaresque Novel

Michel Houellebecq and Virginie Despentes come from different generations: the former from the Giscard d'Estaing era (1974–81), the latter from the Mitterrand years (1981–95).[81] The two writers, often compared to each other, are anthropologists of today's society with trenchant, however radically different, views on politics.[82] And they both emulate Balzac. We have previously seen how this works in the case of Houellebecq. As for Despentes, the first volume of *Vernon Subutex* announces a Balzacian "inhuman comedy" on its back cover.[83] In this trilogy (2015–17), Despentes captures twenty-first-century France through characters of all types, trades, backgrounds, and genders. According to Antoine Compagnon, characterization is what makes Despentes more Balzacian than Houellebecq. He contrasts Houellebecq's single-use protagonists to the recurring characters of Despentes's trilogy, Balzac's multivolume collection, Eugène

Sue's serial literature, and television series.[84] *Vernon Subutex* 2 and 3 even start with a character index.

The first line of *Vernon Subutex* immediately puts readers in the twenty-first-century world of work: "The windows of the building opposite are already lit up. The silhouettes of cleaning women bustle in the vast open space of what must be a communication agency."[85] The place (an open space), the firm (a communication agency), the job (cleaning), and the ghostly presence of the workers (silhouettes) all point to a degraded social landscape. The protagonist of the title, Vernon Subutex, is named after a brand of heroin substitute (*Subutex*) and after one of the pseudonyms of a jazzy, provocative French writer from the middle of the twentieth century, Boris Vian, a.k.a. *Vernon* Sullivan. When the music industry transitions from audio CDs and vinyl discs to digital platforms, Subutex closes his record shop and slowly becomes homeless. Despentes's lead character emerges as the living archive of how social mobility was brought to a standstill at the turn of the twenty-first century:

> It was not only for him that things had deteriorated rapidly. Until the beginning of the 2000s, loads of people had been faring rather well. We still saw gofers become label managers, freelancers land jobs as heads of TV columns, even the slackers ended up in charge of a record shelf at Fnac ... At the bottom of the pack, the least motivated for success sorted themselves out with a part-time work at a festival, a job of tour roadie, putting up posters on the streets ... [...]
>
> His store was called Revolver. Vernon had started there as a salesclerk at twenty years old and had taken over the place when the boss had decided to take off for Australia, where he became a restaurant owner.[86]

This passage brims with various kinds of upward trajectories. But the name of the shop—Revolver—points to the deterioration of the job market, to the violent revolving or reversal of social mobility from upward to downward. Subutex's first name also reads as a *vers non* in French, literally "toward no," which is an appropriate last name for a character who is going nowhere, immobilized by the precarity of late capitalism.[87] He will not open a megastore like Octave Mouret in Émile Zola's *Au Bonheur des dames*, nor will he urge his hypothetical children (he is childless) to become teachers and writers, like Annie Ernaux's (storekeepers) parents.[88]

Despentes narrates the transition from social climbing to inequality, showing how Paris is no longer accessible to nonheirs: "Over forty, Paris only tolerated within its ranks the children of property owners, the rest of the population could carry on elsewhere."[89] At the end of the first volume of the trilogy, Subutex, running out of state allowance and of friends with an extra bed, homeless and in a state a mental haze, climbs to the top of a Parisian hillock, the Butte Bergeyre. The narrator then recites a litany: "I am a single man, I'm fifty years old, […]. I am Diana […]. I am Marc […]. I am Eléonore […]. I am the tree with bare branches beaten by the rain, the child screaming in their stroller, the dog pulling on her leash, the prison guard jealous of her carefree women prisoners, I am a black cloud, a fountain, the abandoned fiancé going through photos of his life from before, I am a bum perched on a hillock, in Paris."[90] Vernon becomes each and every inhabitant of the capital; he merges with his environment. In the second volume, Despentes calls him a "mini-guru of the XIXth."[91] The "nineteenth" designates the Parisian arrondissement, home to the Butte Bergeyre of the first volume and to the Buttes-Chaumont of the second. Because of the numerous nods to Balzac and of the use of roman numerals, we could also read the "XIXth" as a reference to the *century*, and the final scene of *Vernon Subutex 1* as a rewrite of *Le Père Goriot*'s ending. But the hillock (not even a hill) does not represent the character's upward mobility. Contrary to Rastignac, Subutex does not defy Paris in a duel ("You and me!"). Paradoxically stuck *up above town* on a Parisian *Butte*, he channels the voices of the novel's struggling characters. Climbing no longer metaphorizes social mobility as an attainable or desirable goal (*un but* in French) but the social immobility of a downgraded ghost of the bildungsroman stumbling over (*buter*) precarity. Rastignac turns into Subutex who is, as the book cover enumerates, "An urban legend. A fallen angel. A missing person who keeps resurfacing. The keeper of a secret. The last witness of a bygone world. The final face of our inhuman comedy. The ghost of us all." If Subutex is a heroin substitute, he also replaces the hero of the realist novel.

In the third volume, Subutex lives in a community in the south of France that regularly organizes rave parties. To his great surprise, he learns he is supposed to inherit half a million euros from a dead friend, who never told him he had won the lottery:

> Then there was the news of the inheritance. At least, of a possible inheritance—pledged. Because there's still no money on the table.
>
> It should have been Vernon, the inheritor. It's logical, he's the leader. Even if he doesn't look the part.[92]

The inheritance breaks the harmony of the group, but the money never materializes. The blank space between the paragraphs represents this absence. At the end of the trilogy, after a shooting, Subutex's friends are decimated: "There were no survivors."[93] A couple of pages later, readers realize that Vernon alone, "almost absent, already" survived the attack.[94] *Vernon Subutex* 3 is full of references to resurrection: an epigraph from David Bowie's *Lazarus*; explicit comparisons between Vernon and Jesus; one character named Orphea and another obsessed with the *Walking Dead* series. Vernon even lives the rest of his life on the Greek island of "Hydra," the monster whose severed heads always grow back. Vernon Subutex goes from legend to hobo, and from guru to ghost. He haunts, half dead, the twenty-first-century social novel.

As a writer, Despentes transitioned from the bildungsroman to what could be called a contemporary picaresque. Her publisher Olivier Nora called the Subutex trilogy a "postmodern picaresque novel."[95] As critic Joshua Armstrong argues, "This novel of Balzacian scope would take the concept of *Bildungsroman* and apply it to society at large: that is, not the initiation of a single protagonist, but a more collective awakening," especially through the use of free indirect discourse.[96] The narrator and the reader are mobile, transported from one perspective to another. Subutex is mobile, too: he goes places; he encounters people from all backgrounds. But he no longer climbs the ladder. Like a picaro, Subutex is the central character organizing the novel's polyphony, embarked in "a fall eternally begun again."[97] There are two major echoes between Vernon Subutex's and Virginie Despentes's trajectories. Her last name, Despentes, is a pseudonym meant to evoke the slopes of a hill in Lyon, La Croix Rousse, where she grew up in a family of leftist post office workers.

Setting her trilogy's climax up a hillock therefore takes on an autobiographical meaning. As I mentioned in chapter 1, critics called Despentes—and the heroines of her 1998 novel *Les Jolies Choses* (*Pretty Things*)—"Rastignacs in underskirts." The success of this book helped Despentes financially, and the novel itself depicts a social mobility of sorts. After the suicide of her twin Claudine, Pauline moves to the capital, impersonates her deceased sister, and achieves social mobility in the music industry under a false identity. The novel points to the cost of upward mobility, to the necessity to fake it or to kill a part of ourselves. From Pauline to Vernon, Despentes pursues the same social line, but the main character transitions from a social climber to a homeless person. While Houellebecq holds fast to the middle class despite his protagonists' increase in wealth from book to book, Despentes transitions from the bildungsroman to the picaresque, from individual social mobility to a mosaic of struggles and vulnerabilities.

As a result of the transition from bildungsromane to picaresque novels, the trains that transport fictional characters are no longer vehicles of social mobility. In Deck's *Le Triangle d'hiver*, each ride functions as a reset button: "memory resets to zero."[98] The protagonist is unable to build something up. In the works of Houellebecq, and especially in his poetry, the train has left but does not arrive. It becomes an intermediary, stagnant space: "And the train has just reached its cruising speed." The static verse is surrounded by many instances of middleness: "Amidst hills," "semi-social," "in the middle of the Earth," "in the middle of the journey."[99] In a different poem, the TGV has "medium-gray plastic partitions" with "moderate lighting."[100] And in the novel *Sérotonine*, the railcar is caught "in the middle of two abstract immensities."[101] The railway accompanies Houellebecq's poetics of middleness.

In Despentes's trilogy, the train symbolizes the social class of the novel's character. After the episode on the hillock, Subutex goes to the Parc des Buttes-Chaumont and finds shelter in the abandoned tracks of the so-called small belt railway, the "Petite Ceinture." Opened as a freight line, it also transported passengers from the second half of the nineteenth century up to the 1930s, especially during World Fairs. It was then supplanted by the subway. The tracks continued to transport goods until the 1990s and have been turned progressively into greenways—a Parisian version of New York City's High Line. By living in a former section of this circular railway line, Subutex inhabits the ruins of the nineteenth century and of industrial France. *Vernon Subutex 3* opens in the Bordeaux train station, and after the mass murder, Vernon resurrects in the Châtelet hub: "From train stations to airports, he travels with his ghosts."[102] Conversely in *Les Jolies Choses*, the train underscores Claudine's desire to make it in Paris: "Line at the ticket counter, first-class ticket even though she barely had a dime, for the symbolism; she wasn't going to arrive there like a fucking piece of trash."[103] The train—like the music industry, the geography of Paris, and French literary history itself—archives the transition from prosperity to precarity and stagnation.

# A Demoted Canon   Conclusion

I started this book with an epigraph from Annie Ernaux's *Journal du dehors* (1993; *Diary of the Outside*): "(I realize that I am always searching for the signs of literature in reality)."[1] This miniature ars poetica guided my critical inquiry throughout, from perusing a corpus of modern and contemporary literature to tracking the evolution of social tropes, crafting a reading method attentive to forms, and forging a new conceptual character that can bring out the tensions of class mobility. Ultimately, *On Both Sides of the Tracks* demonstrates that when it comes to class mobility, the "signs of literature" come first. Socially mobile authors and characters dwell in books. In *Cultural Capital: The Problem of Literary Canon Formation* (1993), John Guillory argues that the value of literature has declined because the educational needs of the "professional-managerial class" are no longer aligned with the parsing of great works: "the category of 'literature' names the cultural capital of the old bourgeoisie, a form of capital increasingly marginal to the social function of the present educational system."[2] The figure of the parvenant tilts this observation, as literature remains, more than ever, a vital site of class mobility in twenty-first-century France: a site of identification through reading; a source of cultural capital through which working-class students reappropriate what used to be reserved for a few; a place, like school, that still permits cross-class conversations. Guillory argues that the canon is marginalized because it has diminished in value on the job market and at school, its antechamber. On the contrary, since contemporary French authors climb the (book) ladder through education and literature, they revitalize the classics in and out of school. If the canon suffers a certain depreciation today, it would only be *within* the very realm of literature.

What is demoted is not the value of classics but the novel form itself, in the sense that is no longer portrays successful social climbers but stagnant and demoted protagonists. It is the case in the works of Marie NDiaye, Julia Deck, Michel Houellebecq, and Virginie Despentes discussed in the previous chapter. But the list of demoted characters roaming the contemporary novel and the job market grows longer: Nicolas Mathieu's *Leurs enfants après eux* (2018; *Their Children after Them*) follows a group of three teenagers in a postindustrial eastern region of France. By the end of the text, Anthony—now a temporary worker—has not managed to get out but contemplates the social mobility of Steph, who already comes from a privileged background. Sociologist Paul Pasquali opens his 2021 book with an excerpt from this novel in order to illustrate how meritocracy should now be apprehended as "heritocracy" (as in heir and inheritance).[3] Mathieu's subsequent novel *Connemara* (2022) also depicts a parvenant, Hélène, who returns home in the provinces after making it in Paris and, like the other characters, is part of "an average epic," not a bildungsroman.[4] Likewise, David Lopez's noteworthy 2017 novel *Fief* narrates the stagnation of a variegated group of young adults stuck between precarity and the middle class, between urban and rural settings. Many more French novelists—younger, less known, not translated as often—decouple the genre of the novel from the plot of social mobility. They increasingly do so through the canon: these authors rewrite nineteenth-century classics but reverse the typical direction of the protagonist's social movement from upward to downward.

In *Le Grand Paris* (2017), one of Houellebecq's emulators, Aurélien Bellanger, portrays Alexandre Belgrand, a Rastignac with a doctorate in urbanism who becomes the advisor of a fictional version of Nicolas Sarkozy. His role is to build "Le Grand Paris," to decenter the capital by connecting it to the suburbs, thus relegating the provinces to a distant background. By the end of the novel, the urbanist has fallen into disfavor. He leaves Paris and his prestigious position: "I've become an anonymous inhabitant of Greater Paris."[5] Belgrand comes from the suburbs (the affluent Hauts-de-Seine department in the west) and returns to the suburbs (the poor but dynamic northeastern Seine-Saint-Denis). He does not survey Paris from the heights of the Père Lachaise Cemetery but contemplates a panoramic photograph of the banlieue taken from the Sacré-Coeur, located right in front of the border between the Seine-Saint-Denis and the Hauts-de-Seine.[6] As the author explains in an interview, "My narrator begins as a sort of Rastignac, except that Rastignac arrives in his ministry and stays in Paris, while mine will change. He realizes that he is a suburbanite, an inhabitant of Greater Paris and, in the end, he accepts his fate. Starting out as a demiurge urban planner, he proceeds to the level of a small ant who will humbly repair the city. He does not fulfill his bourgeois destiny."[7] Bellanger alters the Rastignac trope of upward mobility: he does not come from the provinces, does not keep on climbing, and gives up living in Paris.[8]

To express social shame through literature, Emmanuelle Richard says she has been inspired by Annie Ernaux. She titled her 2018 social mobility novel—about a young woman from the middle class who becomes a writer—*Désintégration* (*Disintegration*). The narrator (a fictionalized version of the author) received "an inheritance of frustration" and works strenuous, precarious jobs to finance her studies.[9] She describes a generation of "social half-bloods, indefinable hybrids who have already passed through dozens of positions, hardworking and worn out before their time. We didn't expect anything anymore from the professional or corporate world but already we no longer had the strength to reinvent ourselves elsewhere."[10] In such a situation, success no longer feels like integration: "When I had an article in that trendy monthly magazine, the double-page spread ended with 'welcome.' I couldn't help but interpret it as 'Welcome among us.' I didn't know what to make of it, unable to determine whether it pleased me or not. [...] But I was at their service before I was in their ranks. I don't forget a thing."[11] Once the narrator finally publishes a book and gets positive reviews, she is too tired and angry to enjoy her social mobility.

In Claire Baglin debut novel *En salle* (*In the Dining Room*), published by Minuit in 2022, the student narrator works in a fast-food restaurant during the summer. Through manual work, she connects with her father, a factory worker. The parents (Jérôme and Sylvie) are named after the characters of Georges Perec's novel *Les Choses*, and they, too, hoard "the things" of the title. While the daughter formulates the project to break determinism by not accumulating any object, her social future is nonetheless uncertain, as the story—about what is supposed to be a temporary job—ends, unresolved, in the locker room. Readers don't know whether she will accept the offer of a permanent job or go to college.

Thomas Flahaut's 2020 *Les Nuits d'été* (*The Summer Nights*) can be read as a postindustrial version of *Le Rouge et le Noir* (1830; *The Red and the Black*). Thomas travels from Besançon to Verrières, the same topography but the opposite trajectory of Julien Sorel. Enrolled at the university, he "fails all his exams assembly-line style," comes back home, and starts working in a factory like his father, to the great displeasure of his parents who sacrificed themselves to emancipate their son from working-class determinism. His body becomes the receptacle of this demoted trajectory: "And although the student's hump remains like a relic, it now cohabitates with the horned tip of his thumb and of his factory worker's index finger."[12]

Likewise with *La Tannerie* (2020; *The Tannery*), Célia Levi offers a compelling twenty-first-century rewrite of *L'Éducation sentimentale* (1869; *The Sentimental Education*) in which the revolution of 1848 has been replaced by Nuit Debout, a social protest movement launched in 2016.[13] The characters are named after landmark literary social climbers: Julien, Emma, Marianne. The contemporary version of Frédéric Moreau, Jeanne, who briefly works in a provincial library, becomes a low-wage receptionist in the outskirts of Paris in a decommissioned tannery turned into a cultural center. Like Jeanne, most of the employees are "demoted, paid peanuts, holding jobs that don't correspond to their level of education, nor to their competence."[14] Jeanne struggles to get a permanent position and does not become a "petty bourgeois" like Frédéric. She goes back to the provinces, and the narrator does not even specify her new job. But this obvious rewrite of *L'Éducation sentimentale* also ends like *Le Père Goriot*: Jeanne reconnects with a former Parisian friend with whom she visits the Père Lachaise Cemetery only to contemplate the precarious beginning of their professional lives.

Sophie Divry's 2014 *La Condition pavillonnaire* (*The Suburban Condition*), too, is a clear rewrite of Flaubert. The novel was even translated into English as *Madame Bovary of the Suburbs*. Emma, renamed M.A., grows up in the working class, moves to Lyon to study economics, starts a family, finds a job as an import-export manager, and has a disappointing affair with a coworker. She is obsessed with commodities, but she does not commit suicide like Emma, nor is her daughter forced to work on a spinning mill. Instead, the novel carefully describes the slow steps of M.A.'s demotion, her "weakened social status": she is fired from her first job, unemployed for a short period of time, then hired in a subaltern position and forced to accept a voluntary resignation two years before retirement.[15] In Maria Pourchet's 2021 own rewrite of *Madame Bovary* (1856), *Feu* (*Fire*), the enamored transclass character teaches at Cergy-University (a nod to Ernaux's beloved city). Despite her ascending trajectory, she says to herself: "You went to great lengths to remain in the same place."[16] The plot of social mobility no longer guarantees the improvement of social positions.

It is not surprising to see contemporary writers using Flaubert to downgrade the figure of the parvenu. Franco Moretti in *The Way of the World* (2000) writes that "Flaubert's novel [*L'Éducation sentimentale*] also marks the end of the great European *Bildungsroman*."[17] Similarly, for Marc Redfield in *Phantom Formations*, "Flaubert's novel will participate in this generic conundrum only as 'an *Unbildungsroman* of genius.'"[18] By rewriting Flaubert, sometimes by way of Balzac, Divry, Levi, and Pourchet transpose the death of the bildungsroman in the twenty-first century.

As important figures of contemporary life, aspiring, successful, or demoted parvenants pinpoint a shift in literature. *Le Père Goriot*, the archetypal bildungsroman or novel of education, has undergone two generic modifications in our age of social mobility narratives: to read a plot of upward mobility today, we no longer turn to fiction but to stories of "real lives" (whether they are the autobiographies of successful businessmen or the narratives of professional writers like Annie Ernaux). A second modification in the social mobility plot involves the turn away from the bildungsroman to the *Künstlerroman*: Rastignac would no longer be a banker but a writer. He would also no longer be a fictional character but the narrator of a nonfiction. In an article titled "Künstlermania," writer Erin Somers explains that "The hottest book trend in 2022 is this 200-year-old German word."[19] In France a growing number of coming-of-age stories turn out to be autobiographical narratives on up-and-coming authors. To come of age today is to become a writer. Unlike Balzac and Rastignac, the alignment of trade between transclass authors and their narrators forefronts literature as a mover of class. Art gives parvenants a leg up, and it provides readers with an access to socially mobile voices. This growing trend of nonfiction combines two literary tracks: the self and the metacommentary; the social and the textual. Although social science and formalism often do not go hand in hand, for parvenants, talking about themselves is talking about literature, and vice versa. They publish self-oriented narratives with broader social meaning.

If you study class mobility in the realm of literature, you will of course encounter a variety of authors. But I do not mean to say that all socially mobile people in France are readers, writers, and teachers. Other routes exist: think of Patrick Roméo, CEO of Shell France at the time, born into the working class. Think also of entrepreneur and television host Hapsatou Sy, who built a chain of beauty parlors from scratch. But we also have access to these self-made stories through books: Sy released *Partie de rien* (*Starting from Nothing*) in 2017; Roméo's career history was recounted in Jules Naudet's narrative, *Grand patron, fils d'ouvrier* (2014; *Big Boss, Son of a Worker*). Parvenants couch their ascension in books because social mobility is already a plot. Whether professional or amateur, the leading voices who comment on social mobility in the public sphere have published a book.

In *Egalitarian Strangeness: On Class Disturbance and Levelling in Modern and Contemporary French Narrative* (2021), Edward Hughes studies moments of "intersections around class boundaries" not in portraits of writers but of manual workers (Marie NDiaye's cheffe; Paul Nizan's railroad engineer).[20] However, to describe Nizan's social mobility, Hughes borrows a comment made by Jacques Rancière about transclass historian Jules Michelet: the only way for social climbers to "return" to the working class is not to become laborers again but to use the "detour of the book."[21] One departs and returns, claims a different class heritage, through literature.

The place to encounter successful social climbers today is in the nonfiction of budding writers. Conversely, what happens to fiction is what happens to *Martin Eden*, as the title of Jack London's 1909 novel and as the name of his sailor turned writer. The social novel dies along with its socially mobile character. Eden succeeds by writing and publishing but never fits in the upper class, and he commits suicide by jumping from a ship en route to Tahiti. *Martin Eden* is not the story of a joyful *Bildung* from rags to riches but of a constant struggle.

London documents the patient bodily transformation of his character who has to modify his gait and gestures to court a bourgeois woman. Martin is isolated and out of place. He is left with "no port to make" in the harbor city of San Francisco.[22] He is poor and hungry when creative; deprived of inspiration once he finally makes money. London's novel is all about the gap between the moment when writing is "performed" and the moment it is recognized. The final ship spatializes this social trap: "Up above nobody had wanted Martin Eden for his own sake, and he could not go back to those of his own class who had wanted him in the past."[23] The suicide—when Martin lets himself out through a porthole—is pictured as social demotion: "it seemed to him that he was falling down a vast and interminable stairway."[24] Like Rastignac, although more modestly, the main character of London's *Martin Eden* is recirculating today. In a recent article about reading practices, Annie Ernaux praises literature as a role-playing game through which one can get inside the head of characters, including "class *transfuge* Martin Eden."[25] French writer of Vietnamese descent Linda Lê wrote a preface to the reedition of *Martin Eden*, and Leïla Slimani, a Franco-Moroccan author concerned with social class, singled out this novel as her favorite: "Jack London is the one who made me want to be a writer myself. Martin Eden was a shock."[26] Eden succeeds through reading and writing, but he dies; conversely, today's writers—parvenants from the French provinces and immigrants from former French colonies alike—signal social issues by referring to London's novel. Martin Eden, tails; Eugène de Rastignac, heads—these protagonists embody the two sides of the class coin; their return allows us to map out the new tracks of social mobility in contemporary French literature.

# Acknowledgments

I would like to thank warmly Alan Thomas, Nan Da, and Randolph Petilos at the University of Chicago Press for their interest in the project and thoughtful support throughout the preparation of the text. I am also very grateful to Steve LaRue for his careful editing, to Theresa Wolner for her meticulous indexing, as well as to Beth Ina and Meredith Nini for their attentiveness in overseeing the production and promotion of this work. It has been a great pleasure and honor to work with them on my first book in English.

Throughout the years leading to the completion of my manuscript, colleagues and organizations have supported my research and significantly contributed to this book. I am happy to have the opportunity to acknowledge them here.

I would like to extend a very warm thank-you to my mentor and colleague at Yale University, Alice Kaplan, for her generous guidance. She went out of her way to read multiple versions of the manuscript and provided perceptive and tremendously helpful comments, from the detail of a close reading and of an English turn of phrase to suggestions on how to broaden the scope of my project. I am very fortunate to work in the collegial and intellectually dynamic environment of Yale's French department, a place that fostered the interdisciplinarity of my work and helped me develop new methodological skills. I am especially grateful to Maurice Samuels, Pierre Saint-Amand, and Jill Jarvis for fruitful conversations, their ongoing support, and for providing me with advice and references that have expanded the stakes of my claims. Many thanks as well to Christopher Miller and Edwin Duval, who offered discerning remarks at the earliest stages of this research. I have learned a lot as a Whitney Humanities Center Fellow from 2018 to 2020 and would like to thank Gary Tomlinson, for his invitation and for organizing productive conversations every week, as well as Molly Brunson and Peter Brooks for sharing useful references. I also had the chance to discuss social mobility in seminars, starting with the very first course I taught at Yale in the fall of 2014, created with the support of Christopher Semk. I would like to thank the undergraduate and graduate students and advisees who parsed this corpus with me and contributed to the understanding of my approach of social issues in literature.

The Yale Faculty of Arts and Sciences gave me the crucial opportunity to share the chapters of my manuscript with colleagues at other universities: Margaret Cohen, Bruce Robbins, and Thangam Ravindranathan, to whom I am indebted for excellent and detailed feedback. Their critical eyes and thoughtful remarks gave me confidence in the chapters I had drafted, and they were instrumental in helping me formulate a poetics of class mobility in the introduction. I would also like to thank the two anonymous readers at the University of Chicago Press for engaging so closely with my work and providing extensive suggestions on how to sharpen my claims.

A sincere thank-you to Emma Ramadan, who translated the French quotes of this book into English by remaining as close as possible to the original version, thus making my microanalyses accessible to a broader audience. Her hard work, patience, and willingness to discuss her choices taught me invaluable lessons on translation. The decision to always favor the literal over the idiomatic is mine, and I would like to thank Emma Ramadan for letting me do it.

I was lucky to receive invitations to discuss sections of my book at several institutions, where questions and rich conversations with students and faculty helped me develop this research. My gratitude goes to Pauline Carbonnel, Hanna Laruelle, and Andrea Goulet for inviting me in 2018 to talk about "Social Swerves" in the French Seminar Series at the University of Pennsylvania; Stéphane Gerson for his invitation to discuss "Mobility and Migration" with Minayo Nasiali as part of the 2018 "Future of French" series at New York University in a panel moderated by Hannah Freed-Thall and Tony Haouam; Marina Van Zuylen and Éric Trudel for their support of my research and for their invitation to partake in the engrossing 2019 conference on

"Snobbery, Class, and Exclusion in French Literature" at Bard College; Tyler Blakeney and Kaur Rupinder for inviting me to present the 2019 Rex Lecture on the return of Rastignac in contemporary France (this book's first chapter) in the Department of French at the University of California, Berkeley, where I also received important feedback from Michael Lucey, Debarati Sanyal, and Églantine Colon; Christy Wampole for inviting me to brainstorm my book's introduction at Princeton University in 2021 and for the constructive discussion that ensued; Lawrence Kritzman for inviting me to present the chapter 6 of this book, "Travel Class," at the 2022 Dartmouth Summer Institute of French Cultural Studies, where he fostered engaging conversations between all the participants, and my copanelist Martin Crowley for his astute remarks.

I am very grateful I had the opportunity to coedit the volume "Beaches and Ports" for *Comparative Literature* in 2021 with Hannah Freed-Thall. Her giving and insightful comments on my afterword were very useful to develop my section on harbor cities in chapter 7.

The conferences I have attended these past years provided themes to approach my corpus anew from different angles: the 20th and 21st-Century French and Francophone Studies International Colloquium; the Nineteenth-Century French Studies Colloquium; the American Comparative Literature Association Annual Meeting; and the Modern Language Association Convention. Many thanks to the organizers for creating conducive settings and to colleagues for their precious comments on papers related to this book: Michael Allan, David Bell, Aimée Boutin, Anne Brancky, Yasser Elhariry, Martine Gantrel, Lucas Hollister, Julien Lefort-Favreau, Warren Motte, Gerald Prince, and Christophe Wall-Romana, among others. I am also sincerely grateful to Anne Garréta, Laure Murat, and Annabel Kim for their continuous, supportive, and knowledgeable comments on various sections of this book presented at in-person and online conferences.

My research has been generously supported at Yale by the Department of French, the Whitney and Betty MacMillan Center for International and Area Studies, and the Frederick W. Hilles Publication Fund. I am also very grateful to have received Whitney Griswold Faculty Research Funds awards by the Whitney Humanities Center to help me conduct archival research at the Institut Mémoire de l'Édition Contemporaine in Caen, the Bibliothèque nationale de France in Paris, and the Bibliothèque Universitaire d'Angers, as well as urban and museal research in the harbor cities of Le Havre, Marseille, and Saint-Nazaire. My gratitude goes to the committees who carefully read my applications, to the administrators who facilitated the process (Agnès Bolton, Sayaka Hoak, Inessa Laskova), and to the staff of archival funds in France who helped me locate documents and organize my visits, especially Laurence Le Gal in Angers.

I would also like to thank Francesco Spandri for letting me reproduce in an expanded version my article "The Muddy Parvenu" in chapter 2, initially published in 2020 in the *Balzac Review*, a journal where readers offered thorough reviews of this text. Many thanks to the institutions that gave me the permission to use illustrations: the Yale University Art Gallery, the Air de Paris Gallery, the Estates of André Kertész and of Alexander Rodchenko, the Stephen Bulger Gallery, the Philadelphia Museum of Art, the Artists Rights Society and Art Resource in New York, the Belknap Press of Harvard University Press, and Associated Press.

Finally, a heartfelt thanks to Géraldine, Jérôme, and Hermann Cadieu for their kind and unflinching support throughout the years, and to Léo Tertrain for his daily contribution to the form and content of this book.

# Notes

## Introduction

1. Hoggart, *The Uses of Literacy*, 239.
2. See, among other examples, Valentine Faure, "Les Transfuges de classe, phénomène de la rentrée littéraire," *Le Monde*, September 24, 2021; Séverin Graveleau and Marine Miller, "Le Paradoxe des 'transclasses,' héros malgré eux," *Le Monde*, October 19, 2021; Thibaut Sardier and Cécile Bourgneuf, "Méritocratie: Les Transclasses sans strass," *Libération*, October 20, 2021; Leprince, "Un fils de cordonnier à l'Académie française."
3. Todd, *Les Luttes de classes en France au XXIe siècle*, 29, 20. On inequality and immigration, see Ravi Kanbur, "Inequality," in *Words and Worlds: A Lexicon for Dark Times*, ed. Veen Das and Didier Fassin (Durham, NC: Duke University Press, 2021), 243–60.
4. Also theorized as a return of Georges Orwell's "ordinary people." Guilluy, *Le Temps des gens ordinaires*, 17, 10.
5. On precarity, for instance, see Nicolas Léger, "The Literature of Inequality," *Eurozine*, October 10, 2018.
6. See Cuin, *Les Sociologues et la mobilité sociale*, 44, 206.
7. Adorno, *Minima Moralia*, 28. For a similar argument, see also Bourdieu et Passeron, *La Reproduction*, 206.
8. See Pasquali, *Passer les frontières sociales*, 12. Scholars often mention the following book as the first study on social mobility: Pitirim Sorokin, *Social Mobility* (New York: Harper & Brothers, 1927).
9. See Cuin, *Les Sociologues et la mobilité sociale*, 151–53. On the willingness to emancipate a whole social group, see also Jaquet, *Les Transclasses*, 199.
10. On the decline of social mobility, see Guilluy, *Le Temps des gens ordinaires*, 168–72; and Jaquet and Bras, *La Fabrique des transclasses*, 11. On social mobility and the welfare state, see Smith, *France in Crisis*, 139–41.
11. Foucault, "Pour une morale de l'inconfort," in *Dits et Écrits*, 786.
12. Leprince, "Un fils de cordonnier à l'Académie française."
13. Morton, *Moving Up without Losing Your Way*, 70.

14. Ernaux, *Une femme*, 65.
15. Ernaux, "Photojournal," in *Écrire la vie*, 20.
16. See Buckley, *Season of Youth*, 13; and Robbins, *Upward Mobility and the Common Good*, 128.
17. Vance, *Hillbilly Elegy*, 237.
18. Ernaux, *La Place*, 23.
19. Marivaux, *Le Paysan parvenu*, in *Romans*, 574, 634, 706.
20. Ernaux, "Preface," in *Écrire la vie*, 7.
21. Robbins, *Upward Mobility and the Common Good*, xvi.
22. Balzac, *Splendeurs et misères des courtisanes*, in *La Comédie humaine*, 6:552.
23. Maupassant, *Bel-Ami*, 216–17.
24. Jameson, *The Political Unconscious*, 20.
25. Jameson, 20.
26. Jameson, 76.
27. Jameson, 84, 56.
28. Jameson, 82.
29. Collomb, introduction to *L'Empreinte du social dans le roman depuis 1980*, 7–12; Dugast-Portes, *Annie Ernaux*, 13–15; Hunkeler and Soulet, introduction to *Annie Ernaux*, 12; Meizoz, *L'Œil sociologue et la littérature*, 15–16.
30. Vanessa Schneider, "Du Goncourt à Instagram, les réseaux très sociaux de l'écrivain Nicolas Mathieu," *Le Monde*, September 25, 2020.
31. Morson and Schapiro, *Cents and Sensibility*, xiii.
32. Shaviro, *Literature and Inequality*, 3.
33. Shiller, *Narratives Economics*, xxi, xviii.
34. Morson and Schapiro, *Cents and Sensibility*, 214; Shiller, *Narratives Economics*, 271.
35. Shiller, *Narrative Economics*, 279.
36. Some even express a barely concealed disdain toward noncanonical, contemporary texts with phrases such as "recent texts (hopefully good ones)." Morson and Schapiro, *Cents and Sensibility*, 235.
37. On money and the novel, see Piketty, *Le Capital au XXIe siècle*, 174–76. On novels and data, see Branko Milanović, "Was the Novel Born and Died with Bourgeois Society?," *Brave New Europe*, September 23, 2020, https://braveneweurope.com/branko-milanovic-was-the-novel-born-and-did-it-die-with-bourgeois-society: "I have not followed contemporary literature (contemporary meaning, written in the past 30 years) partly for that very reason, so I relied more on the judgment of others. But they too seemed at a loss of finding novels from which one could glean social inequality, or even more generally social issues linked with inheritance, position in society, class distinctions, and even money. So we ended with a very meagre yield."
38. Mecke, "Le social dans tous ses états: le cas Houellebecq," in Collomb, *L'Empreinte du social dans le roman depuis 1980*, 54.

39. Sapiro, *Dictionnaire international Bourdieu*, 302–3. Annie Ernaux is quoted across fields. She can appear in books written by literary critics, historians, sociologists, psychologists, and psychoanalysts alike. See, among other examples, Gaulejac, *La Névrose de classe*; Noiriel, *Penser avec, penser contre*, 256; the epigraph to Senni and Pitte, *L'Ascenseur social est en panne, j'ai pris l'escalier!*; Bantigny, *La France à l'heure du monde*, 380–81; and Naudet, *Grand patron, fils d'ouvrier*, 39–40.

40. Schwartz, "To Exist in the Eyes of Others." See also Ane Farsethås, "The State of the Political Novel: An Interview with Édouard Louis," *Paris Review*, May 3, 2016.

41. On Ernaux and Bourdieu, see Franz Schultheis, "Engagement et distinction: Pierre Bourdieu et Annie Ernaux," in Hunkeler and Soulet, *Annie Ernaux*, 119–30. On Ernaux and Steedman, see Lyn Thomas, "La 'Mémoire humiliée' et sa narration: Annie Ernaux et la 'communauté' internationale des transfuges de classe," in Best, Blanckeman, and Dugast-Portes, *Annie Ernaux*, 210–28.

42. Bourdieu, *Esquisse pour une auto-analyse*, 79. The following article mentions a "Bourdieu, come back!" sign held during a demonstration of professors on strike: Bergounioux, "Bourdieu, retour gagnant."

43. Goldmann, *Pour une sociologie du roman*, 15. See also Goldmann, *Structures mentales et création culturelle*, 300–301.

44. Lucey, *Misfit of the Family*, xxi. See also his article on Proust and Bourdieu, "'La Recherche que l'on peut dire formelle': Proust with Bourdieu," in Crowley and Jordan, *What Forms Can Do*, 233.

45. Hunkeler and Soulet, introduction to *Annie Ernaux*, 19.

46. Laacher, "Annie Ernaux ou l'inaccessible quiétude," 73.

47. Ernaux, "Épilogue: Raisons d'écrire," in Dubois, Durand, and Winkin, *Le Symbolique et le Social*, 345; Ernaux, *La Honte*, 38.

48. Ernaux, *L'Atelier noir*, 96.

49. Jérôme Meizoz, "Annie Ernaux: posture de l'auteure en sociologue," in Hunkeler and Soulet, *Annie Ernaux*, 27.

50. Fassin, *Le Sexe politique*, 252.

51. Fassin, 269.

52. Fassin, 270.

53. Leibovici, "Le verstehen narratif du transfuge," 94. See also Leibovici, *Autobiographies de transfuges*, 11–33; 325–35.

54. Fassin, *Le Sexe politique*, 291.

55. Lahire, introduction to *Ce qu'ils vivent, ce qu'ils écrivent*, 14–15.

56. Passeron, introduction to Hoggart, *La Culture du pauvre*, 24, 13.

57. Pasquali, *Passer les frontières sociales*, 13, 178, 405.

58. Jameson, *The Political Unconscious*, 42.

59. Jameson, 40, 99. On forms and ideology, see Sprinker, *History and Ideology in Proust*, 4.

60. Bourdieu, *Les Règles de l'art*, 20.

61. Bourdieu, 50. On sociology versus textuality in Flaubert's correspondence, see also Bourdieu, "Le critique ou le point de vue de l'auteur," in Zink, *L'Œuvre et son ombre*, 129–34. On Bourdieu and forms, see Jérôme Meizoz, "Pierre Bourdieu et la question de la forme," in Dubois, Durand, and Winkin, *Le Symbolique et le Social*, 185–94. On sociology and textuality, see also Meizoz, *L'Œil sociologue et la littérature*, 49.

62. Goldmann, *Pour une sociologie du roman*, 36, 35.

63. Viala, "Stylistique et sociologie," 623.

64. Merllié, *Les Enquêtes de mobilité sociale*, 161.

65. Naudet, "L'expérience de la mobilité sociale," 45. See also Naudet, "Mobilité sociale et explications de la réussite," 39–59.

66. Bergounioux and Bergounioux, *L'Héritage*, 189.

67. Jablonka, *L'Histoire est une littérature contemporaine*, 19, 225.

68. Jablonka, 226.

69. Rosanvallon, *Le Peuple introuvable*, 15.

70. On this collection, see Thérenty, "'Débusquer la part la plus nocturne et la plus quotidienne de l'existence,'" 179–95.

71. Jablonka, *L'Histoire est une littérature contemporaine*, 241.

72. Jablonka, 105.

73. Barthes, *Mythologies*, 218.

74. On the return of the self in literature, see Annabel L. Kim, "Autofiction Infiltrated: Anne Garréta's *Pas un jour*," *PMLA* 133, no. 3 (2018): 559–74.

75. Hollister, *Beyond Return*, 9.

76. Kornbluh, *Realizing Capital*, 14, 15.

77. Kornbluh, 13.

78. See Meizoz, "Annie Ernaux, une politique de la forme," in Durrer and Meizoz, "La Littérature se fait dans la bouche," 45–62; and Meizoz, "Annie Ernaux," in Hunkeler and Soulet, *Annie Ernaux*, 27–44.

79. Barthes, "Les deux sociologies du roman," in *Œuvres complètes*, 2:250.

80. Bensmaïa, *Experimental Nations*, 6.

81. Bensmaïa, 7.

82. Ernaux, *Journal du dehors*, 46.

83. Éribon, *Retour à Reims*, 108.

84. Ernaux, *L'Atelier noir*, 101.

85. Eyers, *Speculative Formalism*, 10.

86. Ernaux, *L'Écriture comme un couteau*, 83. On literature as a user's manual, see Ernaux, *Retour à Yvetot*, 26.

87. Ernaux, *Les Armoires vides*, 160. See also Ernaux, "Prix Formentor," in Fort, *Annie Ernaux*, 301–5.

88. Ernaux, *La Femme gelée*, 108.

89. Ernaux, *L'Écriture comme un couteau*, 22.

90. Ernaux, *Une femme*, 25. On Ernaux's attention to word choice, see Fau, "Le Problème du langage chez Annie Ernaux," *The French Review* 68:3 (February 1995): 501–12.

91. On metacommentaries in Ernaux, see Hugueny-Léger, *Annie Ernaux*, 132–40.

92. Ernaux, *Une femme*, 73.

93. Ernaux, *La Place*, 108. On how Ernaux first sees a historical image then a private image when she looks at a picture of her father, see Stéphane Chaudier, "Rhétoriques du social," in Collomb, *L'Empreinte du social dans le roman depuis 1980*, 140.

94. Ernaux and Lejeune, "Un singulier journal au féminin," in Thumerel, *Annie Ernaux*, 258.

95. Ernaux, "Vers un *je* transpersonnel," in Doubrovsky, Lecarme, and Lejeune, *Autofictions et cie*, 220.

96. Ernaux, "Vers un *je* transpersonnel," 221.

97. Same intuition in a different critical context in Bacholle-Bošković, "L'intersémiotique chez Annie Ernaux," in Kahn, Macé, and Simonet-Tenant, *Annie Ernaux*, 129.

98. Bourdieu, *Les Règles de l'art*, 9.

99. See Ernaux, "Reading, Memories and Notes;" "To read is to be momentarily separated from oneself."

100. Levine, *Forms*, 2. On social class and mobility, see her chapter on Dickens.

101. Macé, "Ways of Reading, Modes of Being," 223.

102. Macé, *Styles*, 31, 88–89.

103. Freed-Thall, *Spoiled Distinctions*, 79.

104. Macé, "Ways of Reading, Modes of Being," 224.

105. Freed-Thall, *Spoiled Distinctions*, 69, 74.

106. Freed-Thall, 80.

107. Ernaux, *L'Atelier noir*, 69; *L'Écriture comme un couteau*, 95.

108. See Ernaux, *L'Écriture comme un couteau*, 95–96. See also Ernaux, "Mise à distance," 103.

109. Ernaux, *La Honte*, 18; Freed-Thall, *Spoiled Distinctions*, 44.

110. Freed-Thall, *Spoiled Distinctions*, 59.

111. Ernaux, *La Honte*, 48–49.

112. Ernaux, 30.

113. Freed-Thall, *Spoiled Distinctions*, 140; Ernaux, *L'Écriture comme un couteau*, 75–76. On Ernaux and the New Novel, see Hunkeler, "Annie Ernaux et le Nouveau Roman: Une histoire d'amour ratée?," in Kahn, Macé, and Simonet-Tenant, *Annie Ernaux*, 69–80.

114. Bourdieu, *Esquisse pour une auto-analyse*, 15.

115. Redfield, *Theory at Yale*, 3.

116. Casey Gerald, *There Will Be No Miracles Here* (New York: Riverhead Books,

2018); Jeff Hobbs, *The Short and Tragic Life of Robert Peace: A Brilliant Young Man Who Left Newark for the Ivy League* (New York: Scribner, 2014).

117. Dunn, "Yale Recognized for Fast Growth." Although nonliterary, Yale Law graduate and professor Daniel Markovits's 2019 book belongs to this list: *The Meritocracy Trap: How America's Foundational Myth Feeds Inequality, Dismantles the Middle Class, and Devours the Elite* (New York: Penguin Press, 2019).

118. Éribon, "The Dissenting Child: A Political Theory of the Subject," lecture given on the occasion of his James Robert Brudner Memorial Prize, awarded by Yale Lesbian, Gay, Bisexual, and Transgender Studies on April 9, 2008, discussed in *Retour à Reims*, 240–46.

119. Ernaux, *L'Écriture comme un couteau*, 80–81.

120. Bourdieu, *Esquisse pour une auto-analyse*, 131.

121. See Jameson, *The Political Unconscious*, 59.

122. Senior, "'The End of Eddy.'"

123. Guilluy, *Le Temps des gens ordinaires*, 28, 32–33.

124. Guilluy, 28.

125. Ernaux, *L'Atelier noir*, 106; Ernaux, *Les Armoires vides*, 76; Ane Farsethås, "The State of the Political Novel: An Interview with Édouard Louis," *Paris Review*, May 3, 2016.

126. Bhabha, *The Location of Culture*, xiii.

127. Lagrave, *Se ressaisir*, 375.

128. Westover, *Educated*, 87; Louis, *En finir avec Eddy Bellegueule*, 205.

129. Vance, *Hillbilly Elegy*, 9.

130. Westover, *Educated*, 331.

131. See David Caviglioli, "Qui est vraiment Eddy Bellegueule?," *Bibliobs*, March 11, 2014; Édouard Louis, "À propos d'un article du *Nouvel Observateur* et d'un problème plus général," Édouard Louis's personal website (no longer posted), accessed March 6, 2014; David Caviglioli, "Eddy Bellegueule, le mépris de classe et le 'fact-checking' littéraire," *Bibliobs*, March 12, 2014.

132. Diallo, *Ne reste pas à ta place!*, 11.

133. Kaplan, "Resisting Autobiography," in Smith and Watson, *De/colonizing the Subject*, 115–38.

134. Charpentier, "'La littérature est une arme de combat...,'" in Mauger, *Rencontres avec Pierre Bourdieu*, 161.

135. See Deleuze and Guattari, "Les personnages conceptuels," in *Qu'est-ce que la philosophie?*, 60–81.

136. Dryef, "Édouard Louis."

137. Le Clerc, *Un homme sans titre*, 109.

138. See Jake Ryan and Charles Sackrey, *Strangers in Paradise: Academics from the Working Class* (Boston: South End Press, 1984); Bourdieu, *Esquisse pour une auto-analyse*, 16; Bernard Lahire, *L'Homme pluriel: les ressorts de l'action* (Paris: Nathan, 1998), 46–52; Morton, *Moving Up without Losing Your Way*, 4–8; Helen

Lucey, June Melody, and Valerie Walkerdine, "Uneasy Hybrids: Psychosocial Aspects of Becoming Educationally Successful for Working-Class Young Women," in *Feminist Critique of Education: Fifteen Years of Gender Education*, ed. Christine Skelton and Becky Francis (London: Routledge, 2005), 322–37; Hoggart, *The Uses of Literacy*, 238–49; Goldmann, *Pour une sociologie du roman*, 23; Jean-Paul Delahaye, *Exception consolante: Un grain de pauvre dans la machine* (Amiens: Librairie du labyrinthe, 2021); David Pollock and Ruth Van Reken, *Third Culture Kids: The Experience of Growing Up among Worlds* (Yarmouth: Intercultural Press, 1999). On naming social climbers, see also Naudet, "L'expérience de la mobilité sociale," 44, 49–50, 58; Paul Pasquali, "Déplacements ou déracinement?," in Jaquet and Bras, *La Fabrique des transclasses*, 112–16; and Lagrave, *Se ressaisir*, 21. On Ernaux and sociological characters, see Danilo Martuccelli, "Le personnage social à l'épreuve," in Hunkeler and Soulet, *Annie Ernaux*, 65–82.

139. On reading Bourdieu and Ernaux affectively, see also Christian Baudelot, "'Briser des solitudes...,'" in Thumerel, *Annie Ernaux*, 167. On trauma and shame in the works of Ernaux, see Willging, *Telling Anxiety*, 73–113.

140. On the origins of the word *transclasse*, see Jaquet, *Les Transclasses*, 13–14, 119, 122; Jaquet and Bras, *La Fabrique des transclasses*, 13–14.

141. Jaquet, *Les Transclasses*, 11–12.

142. "The prefix 'trans' here does not signify a surpassing or an elevation, but the movement of transition, of passing to the other side"; Jaquet, *Les Transclasses*, 13. "The notion of social mobility is a source of confusion because it asks us to consider above all the result of a trajectory, by positioning ourselves in relationship to its points of departure and arrival, without pausing at the mediations, the stopovers, the bridges and the barriers, or even the setbacks." Bras and Jaquet, *La Fabrique des transclasses*, 16.

143. Lucey, *Someone*, 2.

144. Wittig, "One Is Not Born a Woman," in *The Straight Mind, and Other Essays*, 20. On Ernaux and Wittig, see Merete Stistrup Jensen, "Écrire dans la langue de tous: Le Point de vue particulier de Monique Wittig et d'Annie Ernaux," in *Lire Monique Wittig aujourd'hui*, ed. Benoît Auclerc and Yannick Chevalier (Presses Universitaires de Lyon, 2012), 95–109.

145. Hoggart, *The Uses of Literacy*, 245.

146. Slaoui, *Illégitimes*, 192, 188–89. The whole section reads as follows: "They lied to me, they lied to us; there is nothing that can erase what we are. We can't reinvent ourselves. No diploma, no reward, no prestigious school [*grande école*] can truly rib out our origins. Having fought against my Southeastern accent to the point of suppressing it does not make me a Parisian. Sciences Po did not make me into a bourgeoise. [...] Forever distanced from my people whom I ended up watching through sociological glasses and at the same time forever apart from that new social class that claimed to open its doors to me."

147. Kim, *Unbecoming Language*, 6.

148. Beaubatie, *Les Transfuges de sexe*, 15.
149. Beaubatie, 99.
150. Preciado, *Je suis un monstre qui vous parle*, 19.
151. Saint-Gelais, *Fictions transfuges*, 7–8.
152. Ernaux, *L'Écriture comme un couteau*, 65–77.
153. Bourdieu, *Questions de sociologie*, 76; Ernaux, *L'Écriture comme un couteau*, 35.
154. On this topic, see Bras, "Monter et rester peuple. Les leçons de Michelet," in Jaquet and Bras, *La Fabrique des transclasses*, 35–58.
155. Éribon, *Retour à Reims*, 209.
156. Ernaux, *Une femme*, 106. See also Elsa Gautier, "Refuser de parvenir," *Socialter* 46, no. 4 (June/July 2021): 40–43.
157. Ernaux, *La Vie extérieure*, 78.
158. Ernaux, 44.
159. See Ernaux, "Épilogue: Raisons d'écrire," in Dubois, Durand, and Winkin, *Le Symbolique et le Social*, 345; and Ernaux, *L'Atelier noir*, 24.
160. Jaquet, *Les Transclasses*, 110.
161. Éribon uses the word in his sequel to *Retour à Reims*: Éribon, *La Société comme verdict*, 97.
162. Freud, *The Uncanny*, 162.
163. Schor, *Reading in Detail*, 129.
164. For a description of reading as decoding, see Louis, *Changer: Méthode*, 230.
165. Ernaux, "Photojournal," in *Écrire la vie*, 73.
166. Danasségarane, "Immigration et transclasse," in Jaquet and Bras, *La Fabrique des transclasses*, 224.
167. On returning to Haiti and Congo, see for instance, Dany Laferrière, *L'Énigme du retour* (Montreal: Boréal, 2009); and Alain Mabanckou, *Lumières de Pointe-Noire* (Paris: Seuil, 2013).
168. See also Clerc, "Pour un nouveau Bildungsroman: le roman 'beur,'" in Collomb, *L'Empreinte du social dans le roman depuis 1980*, 271–85.
169. Rushdie, *Imaginary Homelands*, 277.
170. Ernaux, *Écrire la vie*, 24.
171. Guibert, "Rétrospective du photographe André Kertész, Le mouvement de la vie," in *La Photo*, 29.

**Chapter One**

1. *Oxford English Dictionary*, 2nd ed., s.v. "antonomasia."
2. The online dictionary WordReference lists "Rastignac" as the second translation of "social climber" into French, but this usage is not listed in the *Trésor*, *Larousse*, or *Robert* dictionaries. See the entry "Rastignac" in Bordas, Glaudes, and Mozet, *Dictionnaire Balzac*, 1096.

3. See Guichardet, *Le Père Goriot d'Honoré de Balzac*, 15.
4. Bordas, Glaudes, and Mozet, *Dictionnaire Balzac*, 12.
5. Assouline, "Balzac," in *Autodictionnaire Simenon*, 56.
6. Chevillard, *L'Autofictif père et fils*, 160.
7. Baecque, *La Nouvelle Vague*, 98. See also Heathcote and Watts, *Cambridge Companion to Balzac*; Massol, *Balzac contemporain*; Mura-Brunel, *Silences du roman*. On how the twentieth and twenty-first centuries can misread the nineteenth, see Prince and Sanyal, "Incipit," 207, 219.
8. See, among other examples, Woloch, *The One vs. The Many*; Alan Palmer, *Fictional Minds* (Lincoln: University of Nebraska Press, 2004); Jens Eder, Fotis Jannidis, and Ralf Schneider, eds., *Characters in Fictional Worlds: Understanding Imaginary Beings in Literature, Film, and Other Media* (New York: De Gruyter, 2010); Blakey Vermeule, *Why Do We Care about Literary Characters?* (Baltimore: Johns Hopkins University Press, 2010); Figlerowicz, *Flat Protagonists*; Eric Naiman, "Kalganov," *Slavic and East European Journal* 58, no. 3 (2014): 394–418; Ibrāhīm Ṭāhā, *Heroizability: An Anthroposemiotic Theory of Literary Characters* (Boston: De Gruyter, 2015); Gary Hagberg, ed., *Fictional Characters, Real Problems: The Search for Ethical Content in Literature* (Oxford: Oxford University Press, 2016); Amanda Anderson, Toril Moi, and Rita Felski, *Character: Three Inquiries in Literary Studies* (Chicago: University of Chicago Press, 2020); Claire Messud, "How Can We Read Edith Wharton Today?," *New York Times*, January 20, 2021; and S. Pearl Brilmyer, *The Science of Character: Human Objecthood and the Ends of Victorian Realism* (Chicago: University of Chicago Press, 2022).
9. Gérard Genette, *Bardadrac* (Paris: Seuil, 2006). On the "bric-à-brac" so dear to Balzac's Cousin Pons, see Lyon-Caen, "Bric-à-brac," in Bordas, Glaudes, and Mozet, *Dictionnaire Balzac*, 193–94.
10. Delestré and Desanti, *Dictionnaire des personnages populaires*, 11.
11. See Figlerowicz, *Flat Protagonists*, 2–8. See also Delestré and Desanti, *Dictionnaire des personnages populaires*, 571; and Marceau, *Balzac et son monde*, 58: Marceau underlines the multiplicity of "Rastignac" when he argues that "Rastignac is not exactly Rastignac" in *La Peau de chagrin* and *Étude de femme*.
12. Balzac, *La Muse du département*, in *La Comédie humaine*, 4:696–97. On literary characters and their capacity to break the fourth wall, see Émilie Pézard, ed., "Le personnage, un modèle à vivre," Colloques fabula, 2018, https://www.fabula.org/colloques/sommaire5074.php. On contemporary French literary characters, see also René Audet and Nicolas Xanthos, "Le roman contemporain au détriment du personnage," *L'Esprit Créateur* 54, no. 1 (Spring 2014): 1–7.
13. Valance, *Thiers*, 12.
14. Proust, *Correspondance*, 19:224.
15. Maupassant, *Bel-Ami*, 222.
16. Balzac, *Splendeurs et misères des courtisanes*, in *La Comédie humaine* 6:490; Stendhal, *Le Rouge et le Noir*, in *Œuvres romanesques complètes*, 1:749. On how

"Julien Sorel is much more a 'hero' than the characters of Balzac, to say nothing of Flaubert," see also Auerbach, *Mimesis*, 466.

17. Cohen, *Sentimental Education of the Novel*, 112.
18. Woloch, *The One vs. The Many*, 257.
19. See Rohmer, "Lignées balzaciennes," preface to Balzac, *La Rabouilleuse*, ii.
20. Flaubert, *L'Éducation sentimentale*, in *Œuvres complètes*, 4:166.
21. See Sagnes, "Tentations balzaciennes," 54–55.
22. Barthes, "Proust et les noms," in Robert Abernathy et al., *To Honor Roman Jakobson*, 153.
23. Balzac, *Le Père Goriot*, in *La Comédie humaine*, 3:181–82.
24. Duteurtre, *À nous deux, Paris!*, 101.
25. Véronique Bui, "Balzac ou le 'Phénix du Ciel,'" in Massol, *Balzac contemporain*, 168.
26. On the power of authors' names in upward mobility (esp. Beauvoir and Sartre), see Éribon, *La Société comme verdict*, 109–34.
27. Cerdan, "'Rastignac est une caillera.'"
28. Méra, *La Méthode Rastignac*, 99, 57.
29. Molière, *Monsieur de Pourceaugnac*, in *Œuvres complètes*, 2:416.
30. Voltaire, "Dixième lettre. Sur le commerce," in *Lettres philosophiques*, 67.
31. Zola, *La Curée*, in *Les Rougon-Macquart*, 1:334, 364.
32. Hamon, *Le Personnel du roman*, 116.
33. Balzac, *Le Père Goriot*, in *La Comédie humaine*, 3:272.
34. Fischler, "Rastignac-Télémaque," 842.
35. Rancière, *Le Maître ignorant*, 66.
36. Fischler, "Rastignac-Télémaque," 845.
37. Balzac, *Le Père Goriot*, in *La Comédie humaine*, 3:52.
38. See, for instance, Daniel Mendelsohn, *An Odyssey: A Father, A Son, and An Epic* (New York: Knopf, 2017). For another reference to Telemachus in the context of social mobility, see Dan-el Padilla Peralta, *Undocumented: A Dominican Boy's Odyssey from a Homeless Shelter to the Ivy League* (New York: Penguin Press, 2015), 93–94.
39. Balzac, *Le Père Goriot*, in *La Comédie humaine*, 3:54.
40. See Jacques Le Brun's preface to Fénelon, *Les Aventures de Télémaque*, 7.
41. Brooks, *Balzac's Lives*, 11.
42. Lucey, *Misfit of the Family*, 285.
43. Butor, "Les Parents pauvres," in *Répertoire II*, 194.
44. Piketty, *Le Capital au XXIe siècle*, 654.
45. Piketty, 655.
46. Piketty, 377.
47. Auerbach, *Mimesis*, 473, 471. Bourdieu, *Raisons*, 23. On Balzac and Bourdieu, see Ebguy, "Représenter l'être social," in Del Lungo and Glaudes, *Balzac, l'invention de la sociologie*, 279–84.

48. Auerbach, *Mimesis*, 472.
49. Woloch, *The One vs. The Many*, 36.
50. Pommier, "Naissance d'un héros," 209.
51. Pommier, 192, 196.
52. Guichardet, *Le Père Goriot d'Honoré de Balzac*, 99.
53. Py, *Les Parisiens*, 82.
54. Jordan, *Contemporary French Women's Writing*, 150. She quotes Olivier Le Naire, "Despentes abrupte," *L'Express*, October 1, 1998; and Philippe Cusin, "Virginie Despentes: Deux sœurs arrivistes," *Le Figaro*, November 13, 1998.
55. Hadni, "Abdellah Taïa."
56. Idier, "'Sortir de la peur,'" 201.
57. Tasma, *Rastignac ou les ambitieux*.
58. See Camille Jourdan, "Pourquoi cherche-t-on toujours le 'nouveau Balzac'?," *Slate*, January 23, 2016: "Who hasn't glimpsed, in any ambitious person, a modern-day Rastignac?"
59. Beauvoir, *Les Mandarins*, 117.
60. Naselli, *Et tes parents, ils font quoi?*, 12.
61. Fabrice Pliskin, "Le père Goriot et le père Le Pen," *Bibliobs*, May 9, 2015; Mathieu Dejean, "Quand le jeune Jean-Luc Mélenchon était un 'agitateur politique,'" *Les Inrockuptibles*, September 10, 2016; Muriel Frat, "Une Rastignac en jupon," *Le Figaro*, March 3, 2009; Raphaëlle Bacqué, "Rachida Dati, Rastignac des temps modernes," *Le Monde*, September 25, 2015.
62. Michel Onfray, "Le 7/9," *France Inter*, September 12, 2014.
63. "From the sacred mountain of Republican elitism, Emmanuel Macron's French surveying transforms into a literary field. [...] Stendhal for Fabrice, Rastignac and his Balzacian model Adolphe Thiers." Gilles Fumey, "Macron, un jeune président issu du vieux pays," *Libération*, May 8, 2017; Irina de Chikoff, "Emmanuel Macron, le Rastignac social-libéral," *Figaro Vox*, October 16, 2014; Laurence Cossé, "Emmanuel Macron," *La Croix*, April 6, 2017; and Michel Pinçon and Monique Pinçon-Charlot, "Itinéraire d'un apprenti Rastignac," in *Le Président des ultra-riches: Chronique d'un mépris de classe dans la politique d'Emmanuel Macron* (Paris: Zones, 2019), 43–52. See also Laurent Sagalovitsch, "Emmanuel Macron sera-t-il comparable à un héros de Fitzgerald?," *Slate*, March 26, 2017.
64. Gallo, "Rastignac est parmi nous." In 2008, following the republication of *La Comédie humaine* by Garnier, the book section of *Le Monde* published multiple articles on Balzac. They focused on various characters, such as Lucien de Rubempré and Eugénie Grandet. Although Vautrin was portrayed as the son of Jean Genet and Jacques Mesrine by Françoise Chanderargor, Rastignac was the only character to be considered alive in contemporary France.
65. Davet and Lhomme, *Le Traître et le Néant*, 606.
66. Besson, *Un personnage de roman*, 19.
67. Besson, 190.

68. Crépu, Duval-Stalla, and Macron, "L'Histoire redevient tragique," 79, 83, 80–81.
69. Macron, *Révolution*, 24.
70. Rambaud, *Emmanuel Le Magnifique*, 13.
71. Riché, "Alexandre Benalla."
72. "Décès de Bernard Tapie," *Élysée*, October 3, 2021, https://www.elysee.fr/emmanuel-macron/2021/10/03/deces-de-bernard-tapie.
73. David Caviglioli, "Qui est vraiment Eddy Bellegueule?," *Bibliobs*, March 11, 2014.
74. Dryef, "Édouard Louis."
75. Leyris, "'Changer: méthode,' d'Édouard Louis."
76. Algalarrondo, *Deux jeunesses françaises*, back cover.
77. Louis, *Qui a tué mon père*, 83.
78. See Édouard Louis's June 6, 2018, tweet (https://twitter.com/edouard_louis/status/1004337044976558082?lang=en), and Nathalie Segaunes, "'Qui a tué mon père.'" See also Ernaux's own letter to Macron: *Monsieur le Président*.
79. "My family history is that of a republican ascent in provincial France, between the Hautes-Pyrénées and Picardy. That ascent was made possible through knowledge." Macron, *Révolution*, 17–18.
80. Balzac, *La Peau de chagrin*, in *La Comédie humaine*, 10:166.
81. Déon, *Lettre à un jeune Rastignac*, 75.
82. See Éribon, *Retour à Reims*, 235–36.
83. Éribon, *La Société comme verdict*, 29–32, 152. Éribon refers to the inscrutable sentences in Kafka's *The Trial*.
84. Lucey, *Misfit of the Family*, 180.
85. Lucey, 180, 203, 204.
86. Lucey, 25.
87. "One can easily imagine the concern expressed by conservative or moralizing critics on finding that such a figure as Lucien was achieving popularity with readers, and even attracting imitators." Lucey, 180.
88. La Rédaction, "Qui est Mathieu Gallet?"
89. See, for instance, Nicole Vulser, "Micmac éditorial autour du nouveau pamphlet d'Éric Zemmour," *Le Monde*, September 15, 2021.
90. Paraschas, *Reappearing Characters*, 56.
91. Paraschas, 42, 46.
92. On Balzac and economic criticism, see also "Balzac: Narrative as Business," in Paine, *Selling the Story*, 41–97.
93. Piketty, *Le Capital au XXIe siècle*, 179.
94. Piketty, 384.
95. Piketty, 645–50.
96. Piketty, 382.
97. Piketty, *Capital et Idéologie*, 167.

98. Piketty, *Le Capital au XXIe siècle*, 378.
99. Piketty, 377–78.
100. Piketty, *Capital et Idéologie*, 164.
101. Lyon-Caen, *La Lecture et la Vie*, 21, 42, 183.
102. Piketty, *Le Capital au XXIe siècle*, 185.
103. Krueger, "Rise and Consequences of Inequality in the United States."
104. Fitzgerald, *The Great Gatsby*, 60.
105. Fitzgerald, 65.
106. Fitzgerald, 64–65.
107. Robbins, *Upward Mobility and the Common Good*, xvi.
108. Fitzgerald, *The Great Gatsby*, 51.
109. Engels, Letter to Margaret Harkness, April 1888, in Marx and Engels, *Collected Works*, 48:168.
110. Charentenay and Goudmand, "Fiction et Idéologie."
111. Piketty, *Le Capital au XXIe siècle*, 648. On how money does not disappear from literature after the nineteenth century but goes from "a grand estate" to "a nickel drop," see Ted Underwood, Hoyt Long, and Richard Jean So, "Cents and Sensibility: Trust Thomas Piketty on Economic Inequality. Ignore What He Says about Literature," *Slate*, December 10, 2014.
112. Ernaux, *Une femme*, 106.
113. Piketty, *Capital et Idéologie*, 32; Ernaux, *Les Armoires vides*, 105.
114. Ernaux, *Ce qu'ils disent ou rien*, 144.
115. Ernaux, *La Place*, 11.
116. See Gerald Prince, "A Narratological Approach," in Ginsburg, *Approaches to Teaching Balzac's "Old Goriot,"* 92.
117. Ernaux wrote the incipit of a text called "Paris" on the arrival of a character named Madeleine in the Latin Quarter. See Ernaux, "Vocation?," in Fort, *Annie Ernaux*, 21. On the importance of books in coming-of-age stories, see Mouloud Feraoun, *Le Fils du pauvre* (Paris: Seuil, 1954); Azouz Begag, *Le Gone du Chaâba* (Paris: Seuil, 1986); Condé, *Le Cœur à rire et à pleurer*; Marie-Hélène Lafon, *Liturgie* (Paris: Buchet-Chastel, 2002) and *Les Pays*; Assia Djebar, *Nulle part dans la maison de mon père* (Paris: Fayard, 2007); Abd Al Malik, *Camus, l'art de la révolte* (Paris: Fayard, 2016); Scholastique Mukasonga, *Un si beau diplôme!* (Paris: Gallimard, 2018); Ocean Vuong, *On Earth We're Briefly Gorgeous* (New York: Penguin Press, 2019), a novel often listed alongside works by Louis and Taïa; and Abdelilah Laloui, *Les Baskets et le Costume* (Paris: Lattès, 2020). See also Jean-Luc Seigle, *En vieillissant les hommes pleurent* (Paris: Flammarion, 2012); the narrator's upward mobility is accompanied by the reading of Balzac's *Eugénie Grandet*.
118. Prendergast, *Paris and the Nineteenth Century*, 1.
119. On education programs, see Lichtlé, "Balzac, une référence pour le XXe siècle?," 42. See also Gleize, "L'institution et le modèle," in *Honoré de Balzac*, 48–56; "the novel has acquired a special status, partially perhaps through being

repeatedly taught" (Ginsburg, "Preface," *Approaches to Teaching Balzac's Old Goriot*, x). On social mobility and school, see Paul Pasquali, "Déplacements ou déracinement?" and Annie Tardits, "Transclasse dans un lieu transclasse," in Jaquet and Bras, *La Fabrique des transclasses*, 89–116, 199–222.

120. Ernaux, *Une femme*, 41, 45, 56.

121. On *Passion simple*: "The victorious Emmas are back: they are little sexual time bombs that speak in first person and are as relatable as in a true story live on television." Pierre-Marc de Biasi, "Les petites Emma de 1992," *Le Magazine littéraire* 301 (July/August 1992): 90.

122. Ernaux, *La Femme gelée*, 84, 26.

123. See "Une 'place' à part," in Fort, *Annie Ernaux*, 34.

124. Moudileno, "Marie NDiaye's Discombobulated Subject," 92. See also Lydie Moudileno, "L'excellent français de Marie NDiaye," in "Marie NDiaye, l'étrangeté à l'œuvre," ed. Andrew Asibong and Shirley Jordan, special issue, *Revue des Sciences Humaines* 293 (January–March 2009): 33.

125. Ernaux, *L'Écriture comme un couteau*, 84.

126. Balzac, *Le Père Goriot* (Paris: Hatier, 1965), 34, 51, 66, 85.

127. Cohen, *Sentimental Education of the Novel*, 3.

128. Cohen, 6.

129. Ernaux, *La Place*, 79.

130. Ernaux, 54.

131. Nord, *Paris Shopkeepers*, 79.

132. See Ernaux, *Regarde les lumières, mon amour* on the supermarket Auchan, discussed in chapter 7. On intertextuality in Ernaux's first novel, *Les Armoires vides*, and especially on popular literature, see Lyn Thomas, "'Le texte-monde de mon enfance,'" in Bajomée and Dor, *Annie Ernaux*, 15–32.

133. Barrès, "La Contagion des Rastignacs."

134. "In pointing to universal primary education as the agent responsible for the rise of the anarchist, Barrès takes up the anxious discourse on *déclassement* that accompanied pedagogical reforms in the 1880s and 90s (Ringer 127–40)—making an implicit nod to Jules Vallès's *Le Bachelier*, and therefore to the trauma of the Commune recounted in Vallès's subsequent novel *L'Insurgé* (1882–1886). The bomber of the Café Terminus, Émile Henry—the son of a Communard—had been a state-sponsored *boursier* at a prestigious boarding school; he himself described the failed promises of the meritocratic educational system as the root of his anarchist convictions when he stood trial (Henry 162)." Proulx, "'À nous deux,' Balzac," 238.

135. Sartre, "Nizan," in *Situations*, 4:144.

136. Cuin, *Les Sociologues et la mobilité sociale*, 177.

137. Dominique Viart, "Les héritages de Mai 68," in Adely et al., *Écrire Mai 68*, 11. Leslie Kaplan made this parallel during the Q&A that followed her Yale lecture in October 2018, "Mai 68, le monde et son contraire."

138. Véronique Bui, "Balzac ou le 'Phénix du Ciel,'" in Massol, *Balzac contemporain*, 167.

139. Sprinker, *History and Ideology in Proust*, 5.

140. When Ernaux's *La Place* received the Renaudot prize, one commentator called it "a scholarship student's textbook." Heinich, *L'Épreuve de la grandeur*, 79.

141. Drieu La Rochelle, *Rêveuse Bourgeoisie*, 191.

142. For a comparison between Napoleon, Macron, and Rastignac, see Roger Cohen, "France Battles over Whether to Cancel or Celebrate Napoleon," *New York Times*, May 5, 2021.

143. Jaquet, *Les Transclasses*, 66–67, 78–79.

144. Examples mentioned by Camille Robcis during her lecture at Yale in March 2019, "The Gender Question."

145. Jourdan, "Living Balzac," in Heathcote and Watts, *Cambridge Companion to Balzac*, 193.

146. Gracq, *Un beau ténébreux*, in *Œuvres complètes*, 1:226.

147. Louis, *Histoire de la violence*, 91.

148. Bourdieu, *Les Héritiers*, 41.

149. Bourdieu, *Esquisse pour une auto-analyse*, 87. Franz Schultheis briefly compares Pierre Bourdieu and Annie Ernaux to Rastignac in "Engagement et distanciation," in Hunkeler and Soulet, *Annie Ernaux*, 125.

## Chapter Two

1. Ross, *Fast Cars, Clean Bodies*, 113.

2. Ross, 183.

3. Ross, 106.

4. See Merriman, *French Cities in the Nineteenth Century*, 17–25.

5. For more on Paris before Haussmann, see Loyer, *Paris XIXe siècle*, 108–13; and Jordan, *Transforming Paris*, 93–97.

6. Mercier, *Tableau de Paris 1*, 1238.

7. Hugo, *Les Misérables*, 1326.

8. Prendergast, *Paris and the Nineteenth Century*, 87.

9. Bellos, *Honoré de Balzac*, 65.

10. Corbin, *Le Miasme et la Jonquille*, 28.

11. On the connotation of mud and dirt, see also Stephanie Newell, *Histories of Dirt: Media and Urban Life in Colonial and Postcolonial Lagos* (Durham, NC: Duke University Press, 2020), 3: "dirt is far more than an empirical substance: it is also an interpretive category that facilitates moral, sanitary, economic, and aesthetic evaluations of other cultures under the rubric of uncleanliness."

12. Bachelard, *La Terre*, 116.

13. Compagnon, *Les Chiffonniers de Paris*, 69. His book is primarily focused on Baudelaire. For a discussion on cleanliness, hygiene, and mud in Baudelaire's

poetry, see Emily Cohen, "Mud into Gold: Baudelaire and the Alchemy of Public Hygiene," *Romanic Review* 87, no. 2 (1996): 239–55. For a comparison of Baudelaire's and Flaubert's mud, see Elisabeth Ladenson, *Dirt for Art's Sake: Books on Trial from Madame Bovary to Lolita* (Ithaca, NY: Cornell University Press, 2007), 51.

14. Sasson, *Longing to Belong*, 82.
15. Brooks, *Reading for the Plot*, 11.
16. Brooks, 12.
17. Brooks, 39, 84–85.
18. Stendhal, *Le Rouge et le Noir*, in *Œuvres romanesques complètes*, 1:671.
19. Stendhal, 1:573.
20. This lexical field would merit further investigation in poetry. In the poem "Perte d'auréole," for instance, Baudelaire seems to put "la boue" of the boulevard on the same level as "la fange du macadam." See Charles Baudelaire, *Le Spleen de Paris: Petits poèmes en prose* (Paris: Gallimard, 2000), 159. For a comparison between *Le Rouge et le Noir* and contemporary literature on the topic of class mobility, see Jaquet, *Les Transclasses*, 18.
21. Lascar, "De la boue balzacienne," 123. On the -rama suffix, see Balzac, *Le Père Goriot*, in *La Comédie humaine*, 3:91.
22. Lascar, 107.
23. Balzac, *Les Paysans*, in *La Comédie humaine*, 9:148.
24. Lascar, "De la boue balzacienne," 105.
25. Matzat, "L'image de la ville," 315.
26. Balzac, *Le Père Goriot*, in *La Comédie humaine*, 3:262.
27. Balzac, 70.
28. Balzac, *La Fille aux yeux d'or*, in *La Comédie humaine*, 5:1050.
29. Balzac, *Histoire de la grandeur et de la décadence de César Birotteau*, in *La Comédie humaine*, 6:257. Quoted in Lascar, "De la boue balzacienne," 117.
30. Balzac, *Illusions perdues*, in *La Comédie humaine*, 5:291.
31. Balzac, *Le Père Goriot*, in *La Comédie humaine*, 3:150.
32. Balzac, 49–50.
33. Balzac, 50.
34. Balzac, 74, 290.
35. Balzac, 51, 52.
36. Bell, "Balzac and the Modern City," in Ginsburg, *Approaches to Teaching Balzac's "Old Goriot*," 82.
37. In *Illusions perdues*, Balzac lists the dandies "qui tenaient le haut du pavé," including Rastignac. Balzac, *Illusions perdues*, in *La Comédie humaine*, 5:479.
38. Balzac, *Illusions perdues*, 5:357.
39. Balzac, *Le Père Goriot*, in *La Comédie humaine*, 3:115.
40. Balzac, 117.
41. Balzac, 91.

Notes to Chapter 2    265

42. Balzac, 126.
43. Balzac, 120.
44. Balzac, 176, 215, 268.
45. Balzac, 94.
46. Bell, "Balzac and the Modern City," in Ginsburg, *Approaches to Teaching Balzac's "Old Goriot,"* 85.
47. Balzac, *Le Père Goriot*, in *La Comédie humaine*, 3:106.
48. Woloch, *The One vs. The Many*, 273, 82.
49. Balzac, *Splendeurs et misères des courtisanes*, in *La Comédie humaine*, 6:481.
50. Zola, *Nana*, in *Les Rougon-Macquart*, 2:1485.
51. Zola, 2:1346.
52. Moretti, *Way of the World*, 246.
53. Flaubert, *Madame Bovary*, in *Œuvres complètes*, 3:316.
54. Zola, *Au Bonheur des dames*, in *Les Rougon-Macquart*, 3:413.
55. Balzac, *Illusions perdues*, in *La Comédie humaine*, 5:643.
56. Balzac, 5:552.
57. Balzac, 5:342.
58. Balzac, *Gobseck*, in *La Comédie humaine*, 2:971. Quoted in Lascar, "De la boue balzacienne," 121.
59. See Jean-Jacques Goblot, "Jules Vallès et Balzac," *Europe* 144 (1957): 23–28.
60. Vallès, *L'Enfant*, in *Œuvres*, 2:175.
61. Vallès, 2:257. On earth versus mud, see Vallès, *Le Bachelier*, in *Oeuvres*, 2:473–74.
62. Balzac, *Illusions perdues*, in *La Comédie humaine*, 5:346; Vallès, *L'Enfant*, in *Œuvres*, 2:365. On the "newly parvenu Bricolins" and their "huge heaps of manure" in Georges Sand's *Le Meunier d'Angibault*, see Cohen, *Sentimental Education of the Novel*, 150–53.
63. Balzac, *Illusions perdues*, in *La Comédie humaine*, 5:341.
64. Vallès, *Le Bachelier*, in *Oeuvres*, 2:672.
65. Vallès, 2:586, 598.
66. Vallès, *L'Enfant*, in *Œuvres*, 2:269, 319.
67. Balzac, *Le Père Goriot*, in *La Comédie humaine*, 3:116.
68. Vallès, *Le Bachelier*, in *Oeuvres*, 2:552–53.
69. Vallès, *Le Bachelier*, autograph manuscript, NAF 28124 (1), Bibliothèque nationale de France Richelieu.
70. See Vallès, "Notes et variantes," in *Œuvres*, 2:1683.
71. Vallès, *L'Insurgé*, in *Œuvres*, 2:895–96.
72. Vallès, 896.
73. Corbin, *Le Miasme et la Jonquille*, 61–62. See also the section "Décrotter le misérable," 184–88.
74. Compagnon, *Les Chiffoniers de Paris*, 62.
75. Moretti, *Way of the World*, 7.

76. For a comparison between Ernaux's novels and literary realism, see Siobhán McIlvanney, "Annie Ernaux: Un écrivain dans la tradition du réalisme," *Revue d'histoire littéraire de la France* 98, no. 2 (1998): 247–66.
77. Ernaux, *L'Écriture comme un couteau*, 51.
78. Ernaux, *Les Armoires vides*, 71.
79. Cagnati, *Le Jour de congé*, 16.
80. Zola, *Thérèse Raquin*, 41, 61.
81. Mirbeau, *Le Journal d'une femme de chambre*, 350.
82. Louis, *En finir avec Eddy Bellegueule*, 114.
83. Louis, *Histoire de la violence*, 51–52.
84. See Loyer, *Paris XIXe siècle*, 36.
85. Louis, *Histoire de la violence*, 44.
86. Louis, 134–35.
87. See Hagan, "The Poor Labyrinth," 169–78. On mess, waste, and stains in Dickens, see David Trotter, *Cooking with Mud: The Idea of Mess in Nineteenth-Century Art and Fiction* (Oxford: Oxford University Press, 2000), 161–75. "Raskolnikov is the Rastignac of the second half of the nineteenth century. Dostoevsky admired Balzac, had translated *Eugénie Grandet*, and surely quite consciously resumed the theme of his predecessor." Lukács, *Marxism and Human Liberation*, 181. On the American context—America as "a vacuous muck" for the proponents of settler colonialism, and laborers as "mudsills" according to proslavery advocate James Hammond, for instance—see Isenberg, *White Trash*, 3, 157.
88. See "The Real Dirt" in E. J. Wagner, *The Science of Sherlock Holmes: From Baskerville Hall to the Valley of Fear, The Real Forensics behind the Great Detective's Greatest Cases* (Hoboken, NJ: Wiley, 2006), 146–56.
89. Ross, "Polar Chaos," 222. Ross and Quintane's articles are part of the special issue of *Nineteenth-Century French Studies* edited by Robert St. Clair and Seth Whidden, "La Commune n'est pas morte ...," commemorating its 150-year anniversary.
90. Quintane, "Partage de l'insolence," 416.
91. See Disegni, "Vallès, écrivain de frontière," in Triaire, Bertrand, and Denis, *Sociologie de la littérature*.
92. Vallès, *L'Insurgé*, in *Œuvres*, 2:1060.
93. Vallès, 1087.
94. On the power of the novel over theater, see also Jules Vallès, "Les romans nouveaux," *Le Progrès de Lyon*, February 14, 1864, in Vallès, *Œuvres*, 1:323–30.
95. Vallès, *L'Insurgé*, in *Œuvres*, 2:898.
96. Vallès, 906.
97. Vallès, *Les Réfractaires*, in *Œuvres*, 1:244.
98. Vallès, *Le Cri du peuple*, April 10, 1884, in *Œuvres*, 2:1339.
99. Vallès, *L'Insurgé*, in *Œuvres*, 2:1077–78.
100. Louis, *Changer: Méthode*, 110–11.

101. Michèle Bacholle-Bošković, "Sophie Divry, militante pour une littérature française forte: interview," 126.
102. Louis, *Combats et métamorphoses d'une femme*, 20. See also Oriane Jeancourt Galignani, "Non Édouard Louis, le roman n'est pas mort," *Transfuge*, September 24, 2020.
103. Diatkine,"Édouard Louis."

## Chapter Three

1. Sallenave, *Jojo, le Gilet jaune*, 6.
2. Sallenave, *Jojo, le Gilet jaune*, 8. See also "Emmanuel Macron promet de 'faire très attention' à ses 'petites phrases,'" *Le Monde* and AFP, January 31, 2019.
3. "Gilets jaunes, verts, rouges, roses, convergeons!"
4. Annie Ernaux: "Le mouvement MeToo."
5. Édouard Louis, "Chaque personne qui insultait un gilet jaune insultait mon père," *Les Inrockuptibles*, December 4, 2018. Translated as Louis, "Can the Yellow Vests Speak?"
6. Schwartz, "To Exist in the Eyes of Others." See also François Bégaudeau, "De l'amitié," in *Gilets jaunes: Pour un nouvel horizon social* (Vauvert: Au Diable Vauvert, 2019), 66–67: "The reality of their bodies suddenly visible, audible, liberated from shame, uninhibited, reinvigorated, refreshed, rectified, reactivated, empowered." For novels more or less explicitly on the Gilets jaunes, see also Leslie Kaplan, *Désordre* (Paris: POL, 2019) and Aude Lancelin's *La Fièvre* (Paris: Les Liens qui libèrent, 2020).
7. "'Gilets jaunes:' l'ONU demande à la France d'enquêter sur 'l'usage excessif de la force,'" *Le Monde* and AFP, March 6, 2019.
8. Divry, *Cinq mains coupées*, 113.
9. Delsaux, Divry, and Michelis, "Pour dire notre époque monstrueuse."
10. Les gilets noirs en lutte, La Chapelle debout, and Droit devant!!, "Gilets noirs cherchent Premier ministre."
11. See Anna Mutelet, "Marche pour Adama Traoré: Avec les gilets jaunes, 'l'union fait la force,'" *Libération*, July 21, 2019.
12. Bellanger, "Édouard Louis est possédé par son destin."
13. Vance, *Hillbilly Elegy*, 264.
14. "In the colonial world, the colonized's affectivity is kept on edge like a running sore flinching from a caustic agent. And the psyche retracts, is obliterated, and finds an outlet through muscular spasms." Fanon, *Wretched of the Earth*, 19.
15. Linhart, *L'Établi*, 22.
16. Linhart, 25.
17. Linhart, 39.
18. Linhart, 19.
19. Kaplan, *L'Excès-l'usine*, 11.

20. Etcherelli, *Elise, ou la vraie vie*, 130.
21. Etcherelli, 35.
22. Éribon, *Retour à Reims*, 100.
23. Vincent, "Édouard Louis."
24. Ernaux, *La Place*, 47.
25. Ernaux, 100.
26. Ernaux, 19.
27. Angot, "Sentiment huit."
28. Éribon, *Retour à Reims*, 27, 14.
29. Éribon, 170–72.
30. Bourdieu, *Esquisse pour une auto-analyse*, 139.
31. Bergounioux, "Bourdieu, retour gagnant."
32. Ravindranathan, *Behold an Animal*, 238.
33. NDiaye, *Ladivine*, 10–11.
34. NDiaye, 15–16.
35. NDiaye, 31.
36. Ernaux, *Les Armoires vides*, 119–20.
37. On Ernaux and the body, see Elise Hugueny-Léger, "Annie Ernaux: une écriture palimpseste?," in Best, Blanckeman, and Dugast-Portes, *Annie Ernaux*, 58–59. The critic argues that Ernaux pays attention to the embodiment of social class, but the supporting excerpts describe Ernaux's relatives and her abortion.
38. Ernaux, *Les Armoires vides*, 11.
39. Ernaux, 73.
40. Ernaux, *L'Événement*, 29–30.
41. Ernaux, 46.
42. Ernaux, *Les Armoires vides*, 26.
43. NDiaye, *Mon cœur à l'étroit*, 289–90.
44. NDiaye, 295.
45. Ernaux, "La Distinction, œuvre totale et révolutionnaire," in Louis, *Pierre Bourdieu*, 31.
46. Bourdieu, *La Distinction*, 190–92. On Bourdieu, Ernaux, and the body in general, see also Christian Baudelot, "'Briser des solitudes...,'" in Thumerel, *Annie Ernaux*, 173–75.
47. Bourdieu, *Méditations pascaliennes*, 187.
48. Bourdieu, *Esquisse pour une auto-analyse*, 127. *Oxford English Dictionary*, 3rd ed., s.v. "malaise," 1.
49. Ernaux, *Mémoire de fille*, 97–99.
50. Ernaux, 98.
51. Ernaux, 99.
52. Ernaux, 16.
53. Ernaux, *L'Atelier noir*, 49.
54. Louis, *En finir avec Eddy Bellegueule*, 18.

55. Boltanski, "Les usages sociaux du corps," 218; Louis, *En finir avec Eddy Bellegueule*, 40.
56. Louis, *En finir avec Eddy Bellegueule*, 153.
57. Louis, 172–73.
58. Louis, 180.
59. Pierre Bourdieu, "Remarques provisoires," 51. See also the parvenus' "discordance" in Bourdieu, *La Distinction*, 122, 124. And more broadly on the body in Bourdieu, see the entrees "corps" and "hexis" in Sapiro, *Dictionnaire international Bourdieu*, 203–5, 404–7; and Dominique Memmi, "Le Corps fait social," in Mauger, *Rencontres avec Bourdieu*, 575–90. On the evolution of Bourdieu's discourse on the body, see Memmi, Guillo, and Martin, *La Tentation du corps*, 78, 84–85.
60. Louis, *En finir avec Eddy Bellegueule*, 27–28.
61. Louis, 217–18.
62. Louis, 220.
63. Louis, 197.
64. Bourdieu, *Méditations pascaliennes*, 153–93.
65. On a related topic—the importance and implications of orphanhood in narratives of social mobility—see Robbins, *Upward Mobility and the Common Good*, 57.
66. Moretti, *Way of the World*, 80.
67. Flaubert, *L'Éducation sentimentale*, in *Œuvres complètes*, 4:235, 242.
68. Moretti, *Way of the World*, 132.
69. Birnbaum, "Édouard Louis."
70. Louis, *En finir avec Eddy Bellegueule*, 218. It is the main difference between Louis's novel and Anne Fontaine's 2017 film adaptation, *Marvin ou la belle éducation*.
71. Louis, *En finir avec Eddy Bellegueule*, 75.
72. Stendhal, *Le Rouge et le Noir*, in *Œuvres romanesques complètes*, 1:594; Maupassant, *Bel-Ami*, 214. On the body in *Le Rouge et le Noir*, see Muriel Darmon, "Le corps de l'anatomiste," in Lahire, *Ce qu'ils vivent, ce qu'ils écrivent*, 184.
73. "The tendency of people to recount themselves is thus the manifestation of an effort to resolve tension; by placing themselves within a narrative, they are attempting to access a coherent self. When mobility produces instability and discontinuity, the narrative of mobility produces stability and continuity." Naudet, "L'expérience de la mobilité sociale," 54.
74. On contradictions, see also Vance, *Hillbilly Elegy*, 142: "Depending on her mood, Mamaw was a radical conservative or a European-style social Democrat. Because of this, I initially assumed that Mamaw was an unreformed simpleton and that as soon as she opened her mouth about policy or politics, I might as well close my ears. Yet I quickly realized that in Mamaw's contradictions lay great wisdom."

75. Louis, *Changer: Méthode*, 18.
76. Louis, 16. See also the following passage: "I had decided to learn a new laugh, through force of will. I would stand in front of a mirror and every day I would train myself to laugh differently, less loud, with my mouth less wide open, less expressive" (89).
77. Moretti, *Way of the World*, 93.
78. Ernaux, "La preuve par corps," in Martin, *Bourdieu et la littérature*, 23.
79. Ernaux, in Martin, 24.
80. Ernaux, in Martin, 24. Ernaux here plays on the idiom "to learn by heart," and in French, heart (*cœur*) and body (*corps*) rhyme.
81. Ernaux, in Martin, 27.
82. Ernaux, *La Place*, 23.
83. Linhart, *L'Établi*, 81.
84. Zerofsky, "'I Always Write with a Sense of Shame.'"
85. Wittig, "One Is Not Born a Woman," in Wittig, *The Straight Mind*, 9–20.
86. For an analysis of Ernaux through "feminist hermeneutics," see Siobhán McIlvanney, *Annie Ernaux: The Return to Origins* (Liverpool: Liverpool University Press, 2001).

**Chapter Four**

1. Slimani, *Chanson douce*, 28.
2. Carbonnier and Morel, *Le Retour des domestiques*, 13–17.
3. Robbins, *The Servant's Hand*, x.
4. Carbonnier and Morel, *Le Retour des domestiques*, 11.
5. Fraisse, *Service ou Servitude*, 7.
6. See, among other articles, Francine Aizicovici, "Fin de grève victorieuse pour les salariés du nettoyage de l'hôtel Ibis Batignolles," *Le Monde*, May 24, 2021.
7. Maza, *Servants and Masters*, 126, 122.
8. Maza, 135.
9. Goncourt, *Germinie Lacerteux*, 262. According to Zola, *Germinie Lacerteux* is "the book [that] brings the people into the novel" (Satiat, introduction to Goncourt, *Germinie Lacerteux*, 14). In their preface, the Goncourt brothers claim all classes have a "right to the Novel" (Goncourt, *Germinie Lacerteux*, 55). Yet, they did not simply portray any worker but one in their service. For this reason, critics such as Auerbach have argued that *Germinie Lacerteux* was first and foremost a literary object, not a social manifesto. See Auerbach, *Mimesis*, 505.
10. Flaubert, "Un Cœur simple," in *Trois Contes*, *Œuvres*, 2:611, 593.
11. Flaubert, 2:593.
12. Mirbeau, *Le Journal d'une femme de chambre*, 145, 270. For a comparative study of Mirbeau, Lamartine, and Goncourt, see Martine Gantrel, "Homeless Women: Maidservants in Fiction," in Suzanne Nash, ed., *Home and Its Disloca-*

*tions in Nineteenth-Century France* (Albany: State University of New York Press, 1993), 247–64.

13. Mirbeau, *Le Journal d'une femme de chambre*, 176–77.
14. Mirbeau, 271.
15. Proust, *Le Temps retrouvé*, in *À la recherche du temps perdu*, 2172. On the co-presence of "sadistic dismissal" and "approving images of a dutiful Françoise," see also Hughes, *Proust, Class, and Nation*, 264.
16. Proust, *À la recherche du temps perdu*, 795.
17. See Pierron, "La 'langue Françoise' dans *À la recherche du temps perdu* de Marcel Proust," 47–58.
18. Genet, *Les Bonnes*, in *Théâtre complet*, 138. Same play on words in two other texts discussed in this chapter: "Madame est très bonne pour moi," Mirbeau, *Le Journal d'une femme de chambre*, 131; "je serai bonne avec elle," NDiaye, *Hilda*, 18.
19. Sartre, *Saint Genet, comédien et martyr*, 561.
20. Moretti, *Way of the World*, 135, 136. Bakhtin, *The Dialogic Imagination*, 125. The founding bildungsroman, Goethe's *Wilhelm Meister's Apprenticeship*, also starts with the character of a maid, Barbara.
21. Shaviro, *Literature and Inequality*, 66–67, 12.
22. Balzac, *Le Père Goriot*, in *La Comédie humaine*, 3:290, 56.
23. Balzac, 3:289.
24. Stendhal, *Le Rouge et le Noir*, in *Œuvres romanesques complètes*, 1:366, 384–85, 724, 674. See also Duroy in Maupassant's *Bel-Ami*: "He removed one by one, adroitly and quickly, all the pieces of her costume, with the light fingers of a chambermaid." Maupassant, *Bel-Ami*, 405.
25. Robbins, *The Servant's Hand*, 42.
26. Marc Voinchet, "La Matinale," *France Culture*, May 16, 2011.
27. Delphy, "Avant-propos," in Delphy, *Un troussage de domestique*, 7.
28. Christine Delphy, "C'est le plus grand des voleurs, oui mais c'est un Gentleman" and "Avant-propos," in Delphy, *Un troussage de domestique*, 12, 8.
29. On the intersection of class and race in the figure of the maid in works by Flaubert and Zola, see Yee, *The Colonial Comedy*, 166: "And yet we have seen that in Flaubert's hands the black servant is not so very distant from the proletarian factory worker or the subaltern migrant."
30. See for instance Cécile Kovacshazy, "Épousseter la précarité: Narrer les femmes de ménage (littérature et cinéma)," in *Précarité: Littérature et cinéma de la crise au XXIe siècle*, ed. Roswitha Böhm and Cécile Kovacshazy (Tübingen: Gunter Narr, 2015), 39–49.
31. Ernaux, *Mémoire de fille*, 129.
32. Miller, *Bon Marché*, 92.
33. Ernaux, "Vocation?," in Fort, *Annie Ernaux*, 22.
34. Ernaux, *Une femme*, 71.
35. Ernaux, *La Femme gelée*, 184.

36. On how a journalist of *L'Action française Hebdo* called Ernaux a "skivvy" (*bonniche*) when discussing the writing style of her 1991 book *Passion simple*, see Isabelle Charpentier, "Anamorphoses des réceptions critiques d'Annie Ernaux," in Thumerel, *Annie Ernaux*, 225–42. On Ernaux, Woolf, and servants, see Lyn Thomas, "Ennemies de classe ou âmes-sœurs," in Kahn, Macé, and Simonet-Tenant, *Annie Ernaux*, 53–55.

37. Ernaux, *La Place*, 62.

38. For more on Ernaux, Proust, and *Les Années*, see Maya Lavault, "Annie Ernaux, l'usage de Proust," in Kahn, Macé, and Simonet-Tenant, *Annie Ernaux*, 44.

39. Ernaux, "Pourquoi aimez-vous *Une vie*?," interview, in Maupassant, *Une vie*, iii.

40. Ernaux, "Entretien sur Flaubert avec Françoise Simonet-Tenant," in Kahn, Macé, and Simonet-Tenant, *Annie Ernaux*, 24.

41. Woloch is commenting here on this sentence from *À la recherche du temps perdu*: "She would say, 'At last one can breathe!' and would run up and down the soaking paths—too straight and symmetrical for her liking, owing to the want of any feeling for nature in the new gardener, whom my father had been asking all morning if the weather was going to improve—with her keen jerky little steps regulated by the various effects wrought upon her soul by the intoxication of the storm, the force of hygiene, the stupidity of my education and the symmetry of gardens, rather than by any anxiety (for that was quite unknown to her) to save her plum-coloured skirt from the spots of mud under which it would gradually disappear to a depth which always provided her maid with a problem and filled her with despair." Woloch, *The One vs. The Many*, 28.

42. On social mobility and *Une vie*, see also Magyd Cherfi, *Ma Part de Gaulois* (Arles: Actes Sud, 2016), 31.

43. Laacher, "Annie Ernaux ou l'inaccessible quiétude," 78.

44. NDiaye, *Ladivine*, 26–27.

45. See Robbins, *The Servant's Hand*, 82, 15.

46. Louis, *Combats et métamorphoses d'une femme*, 65. Louis also experienced solidarity with a servant during a party with the upper class. Louis, *Changer: Méthode*, 298–99.

47. On thresholds in NDiaye, see Shirley Jordan, "La quête familiale dans les écrits de Marie NDiaye: Nomadisme, (in)hospitalité, différence," in *Nomadismes des romancières contemporaines de langue française*, ed. Audrey Lasserre and Anne Simon (Paris: Presses de la Sorbonne Nouvelle, 2008), 147–57.

48. NDiaye, *Hilda*, 31.

49. NDiaye, 27.

50. Robbins, *The Servant's Hand*, 92, 41, 15. On naming maids in literature, see Sonja Stojanovic, "Should the Subaltern Clean?," *Mosaic* 53, no. 1 (March 2020): 39–54.

51. Sartre, *Saint Genet, comédien et martyr*, 566.

52. On Genet and NDiaye, see Pauline Sales's interview of the writer, https://www.theatre-contemporain.net/spectacles/Hilda/ensavoirplus/idcontent/6484.

53. NDiaye, *Hilda*, 8.

54. NDiaye, 10.

55. NDiaye, 18.

56. Jaquet, *Les Transclasses*, 102.

57. Condé, *Victoire*, 70.

58. Condé, 89.

59. Noirisme: "Term generally used to describe a racialist view of culture and politics among intellectuals in Haiti. [...] In the 1930s, it could be called the Haitian brand of *négritude*, with its emphasis on the African past, the Vodoo religion, and the need for authentic black leadership." France, *New Oxford Companion to Literature in French*, 569. Noiristes were in opposition to the mixed-race elites.

60. Condé, *Victoire*, 94.

61. NDiaye, *Hilda*, 17.

62. Condé, *Victoire*, 85.

63. NDiaye won the Goncourt in 2009 with *Trois Femmes puissantes* (*Three Strong Women*) (Paris: Gallimard, 2009).

64. NDiaye, *La Cheffe: Roman d'une cuisinière*, 276.

65. For a comparison between servant and writer, see Nathalie Piégay-Gros, "Domesticité et subalternes," in Martin Mégevand and Nathalie Piégay-Gros, *Robert Pinget: Matériau, marges, écriture* (Paris: Presses Universitaires de Vincennes, 2011), 129–43.

66. On this topic, see Condé, "Lutte des classes," in *Le Cœur à rire et à pleurer*, 27–32.

67. See also Michael Sheringham, "La figure de l'enseignant chez Marie NDiaye," *L'Esprit créateur* 53, no. 2 (2013): 97–110.

68. Camus, *Le Premier Homme*, 187.

69. Chantal Jaquet reads this passage through the lens of affects. Jaquet, *Les Transclasses*, 165–67. Didier Éribon wrote a scene comparable to Camus's in Éribon, *Retour à Reims*, 56: "I who, so many years later, would still blush with shame when I was required, to obtain such or such an administrative document, to provide a birth certificate that displayed my father's first profession (unskilled worker) as well as my mother's (cleaning lady)."

70. See also the link between cleaning and word choice in Saphia Azzeddine's novel *Mon père est femme de ménage* (Paris: Scheer, 2009). The father is "une femme de ménage" (literally a cleaning lady) for lack of a better word in French, except when his son has to describe his father's job at school in an English course and can use the ungendered noun "cleaner" (96).

71. On Ernaux and Camus, see Linda Rasoamanana, "Annie Ernaux et Albert Camus," in Kahn, Macé, and Simonet-Tenant, *Annie Ernaux*, 57–68.

72. Carbonnier and Morel write that 96 percent of home helpers are women and 29 percent of them are of a foreign origin; Carbonnier and Morel, *Le Retour des domestiques*, 53–54. On the importance of giving visibility to the race of workers in the care and cleaning sectors, see the last section of Françoise Vergès, *Un féminisme décolonial* (Paris: La Fabrique, 2019).

73. Diome, *La Préférence nationale*, 70.

74. Diome, 108. Same trajectory in Diome's *Le Ventre de l'Atlantique*, 50.

75. See also Sedira, *L'Odeur des planches*, 113. Sedira narrates how she had to work as a house cleaner when her career as a theater actress abruptly stopped. The narrative intertwines her trajectory and that of her immigrant mother, a housemaid from Algeria. The writer connects acting to serving: "In theater, 'la servante' [ghost light] is the name given to the little light that remains illuminated on the set after everyone has left."

76. There is also a corpus of novels on maids written from the point of view of the employer. See Christian Oster, *Une femme de ménage* (Paris: Minuit, 2001) and Nathalie Kuperman, *J'ai renvoyé Marta* (Paris: Gallimard, 2005).

77. Aubenas, *Le Quai de Ouistreham*, 94–95.

78. Genet, "Comment jouer 'Les Bonnes,'" in *Théâtre complet*, 127.

79. Calle, *L'Hôtel*, 17, 56, 66.

80. Calle, 68.

81. See also Isaure and Bertrand Ferrier, *Mémoires d'une femme de ménage* (Paris: Grasset, 2012). It tells the story of Isaure, the pseudonym of a master's student of history and literature who renounces a PhD to become a cleaner.

82. Mirbeau, *Le Journal d'une femme de chambre*, 44.

83. Mirbeau, 29.

84. Mirbeau, 33.

85. Albaret, *Monsieur Proust*, 10.

86. Mirbeau, *Le Journal d'une femme de chambre*, 29.

87. This book-length interview also indicates that Proust and Albaret were imitating and quoting each other. See Albaret, *Monsieur Proust*, 151, 261.

88. As Robbins puts it, "Scott and Dickens were still borrowing their servants from Elizabethan drama." Robbins, *The Servant's Hand*, 48.

89. Mirbeau, *Le Journal d'une femme de chambre*, 269.

90. Mirbeau, 318.

91. Mirbeau, 88, 92. Lauren Berlant lists the aside as one of the genres "describing the activity of being reflexive about a contemporary historicity as one lives it" in Berlant, *Cruel Optimism*, 5.

92. See Cléder and Picard, *Détours et métissages*, 7, 75.

93. Mirbeau, *Le Journal d'une femme de chambre*, 44.

94. See Blanc, Freundlich, Perchellet, and Petiet, *Maîtres et valets*, 9. They explain how theatrical domestic workers allow the masters to address the audience without having to do it directly themselves.

95. See Jacques Rancière's description of the effect in *Le Spectateur émancipé* (Paris: La Fabrique, 2008), 14.

96. Sartre, *Saint Genet, comédien et martyr*, 562.

97. Robbins, *The Servant's Hand*, 57, 55.

98. Honoré is considered a literary filmmaker. He adapted Ovide, Georges Bataille, and la comtesse de Ségur for the screen; the New Novel and Proust in plays; and his characters often read books (in *Les Chansons d'amour*, for instance). See Honoré's interview with Florence Noiville, "'La littérature est partout dans le cinéma,'" *Le Monde*, May 14, 2009.

99. Lacourt, "Xavier Dolan et Léa Seydoux."

100. Belliard and Michel, "Finissons-en avec le syndrome Léa Seydoux!"

101. Garelick, "Cinderella Myth."

102. On security guards as socially intermediary figures, see Gauz, *Debout-payé* (Paris: Le Nouvel Attila, 2014).

103. Tessé, "Chiens battus," 16. During the coronavirus pandemic, Lindon suggested a "Jean Valjean tax" on patrimony to help struggling households. See Fabrice Arfi, "Un appel de Vincent Lindon: 'Comment ce pays si riche ...,'" *Mediapart*, May 6, 2020.

104. Mirbeau's *Le Journal d'une femme de chambre* comes to a similar, deterministic conclusion. When Célestine describes a former maid, now an employment agent, she underlines how her initial social class is still visible in her manners, thus hindering any attempt at a successful social change. Mirbeau, *Le Journal d'une femme de chambre*, 298.

105. Bellefroid, "Une femme de chambre et son diable au corps." R 500 280, box 38, Fonds Mirbeau, Bibliothèque Universitaire d'Angers.

106. Dauvister, "Spectacle Octave Mirbeau, au théâtre Blocry." Fond Mirbeau, Bibliothèque Universitaire d'Angers, R 500 280, box 38.

107. Mirbeau, "Revue des théâtres" (on *Tartuffe*).

108. Mirbeau, "Le Comédien."

109. Chris, interview by Mouloud Achour, *Clique*, Canal Plus, September 9, 2018.

110. On Chris's interview, see Laélia Véron, "Pourquoi se revendiquer 'transfuge de classe' alors qu'on ne l'est pas?," *Slate*, November 14, 2018; and Faure, "'On allait voir les films en VF.'"

111. Elayoubi, *Prière à la lune*, 9.

112. "True, several of his plays do raise the specter of social mobility, but only, as in *Le Jeu de l'amour et du hasard*, to reaffirm, in the end, the social order." Shea, "Exit Voltaire, Enter Marivaux," 1140.

113. Shea, 1146. See also Ari Blatt, "The Play's the Thing: Marivaux and the 'Banlieue' in Abdellatif Kechiche's 'L'Esquive,'" *French Review* 81, no. 3 (February 2008): 516–27.

114. Elkharraz with Dikoumé, *Confessions d'un acteur déchu*, 65.

## Chapter Five

1. "Gilets jaunes: nous ne sommes pas dupes!"
2. On doors and liminal social statuses, see "The *Portière* and the Personification of Urban Observation," in Marcus, *Apartment Stories*, 42–43: "the *portière* came from the working classes but lived among the bourgeoisie; worked as a servant but had the power to choose tenants and demand rents."
3. Diome, *Le Ventre de l'Atlantique*, 201.
4. In his *Méditations pascaliennes*, Pierre Bourdieu repeatedly uses the expression "porte-à-faux" to describe the singular position of parvenus. It was tempting to associate this sociological concept to the door as a literary object, but in "porte-à-faux," *porte* does not mean "door" but "to support" or "to carry."
5. Rancière, *Les Bords de la fiction*, 23. On how the space behind the door is the space inhabited by secondary characters in Franz Kafka's novels, see Tiphaine Samoyault, "Les trois lingères de Kafka: l'espace du personnage secondaire," *Études françaises* 41:1 (2005): 43–54.
6. Rancière, *Les Bords de la fiction*, 22–23.
7. Rancière, 21.
8. Bettina Lerner, "Rancière's Nineteenth Century" and Leon Sachs, "*The Ignorant Schoolmaster*," in Bray, *Understanding Rancière*, 35, 56.
9. See, among other articles: Cécile Bouanchaud, "Au procès de Riadh B., accusé d'agression sexuelle par Édouard Louis, l'œuvre littéraire omniprésente," *Le Monde*, October 24, 2020; and Chloé Pilorget-Rezzouk, "Affaire Édouard Louis: Après le récit littéraire, la relaxe de Riadh B. pour 'agression sexuelle,'" *Libération*, December 20, 2020.
10. Louis, *Histoire de la violence*, 48.
11. Louis, *Changer: Méthode*, 95.
12. Louis, *Histoire de la violence*, 230.
13. Louis, *Changer: Méthode*, 104.
14. Louis, *History of Violence*, 135. The translator uses the original excerpt from Faulkner here instead of retranslating the French version into English.
15. Louis, *Histoire de la violence*, 147.
16. Faulkner's quotation appears in a chapter titled "Intermission," a detail that foreshadows the adaptation of *Histoire de la violence* into a play by Louis and German theater director Thomas Ostermeier.
17. Louis, *Histoire de la violence*, 201–2.
18. Louis, 160.
19. Louis, 57.
20. Louis, 9.
21. Louis and Ostermeier, *Au Cœur de la violence*, 9.
22. Louis and Ostermeier, 21.
23. Louis, *En finir avec Eddy Bellegueule*, 201.

24. Louis, 72.
25. Louis, 111–12.
26. Louis, 63.
27. Louis, *Qui a tué mon père*, 10.
28. Louis, 67.
29. Louis, *Histoire de la violence*, 63–64.
30. See, for instance, Louis, *En finir avec Eddy Bellegueule*, 79, 82, 96.
31. Louis, *En finir avec Eddy Bellegueule*, 98, 124. The two other quotations marks are not related to reported speech but signal the name of a television show and the title of community centers' parties. Louis, 15, 118.
32. On "forms of digression and detour, be they theoretical, textual or bibliographical" in *Retour à Reims*, see Edward J. Hughes, "Circuits of Reappropriation," in Crowley and Jordan, *What Forms Can Do*, 180.
33. Éribon, *Retour à Reims*, 166.
34. Louis expresses the desire to "come back" in *Changer: Méthode*, 330.
35. Éribon, *Retour à Reims*, 22.
36. Benlaala, *L'Effraction*, 8.
37. Benlaala, 18.
38. Fortems, *Louis veut partir*, 185–86. See also Guillaume Perilhou, "David Fortems, l'écrivain queer et cinéphile qui va secouer la littérature," *Têtu*, November 10, 2020; and Tewfiq Hakem, "Fuir le monde de peur qu'il ne s'effondre, deux premiers romans anti-initiatiques signés par Lou Darsan et David Fortems," in "Le Réveil cultuel" on *France Culture*, October 19, 2020.
39. Ernaux, *La Place*, 43, 57.
40. Ernaux, 42.
41. Bourdieu, *Esquisse pour une auto-analyse*, 109.
42. Facsimile of *La Place*'s manuscript in Fort, *Annie Ernaux*, 42.
43. Ernaux, *La Place*, 60. The real story is a bit different. Bécassine was asked to embroider "bébé déjeune" on bibs. But after another employee told her she was using the word *idem* on the order book to avoid repetitions, Bécassine took the initiative to embroider "bébé déjeune" only once. Caumery and J.-P. Pinchon, *Bécassine en apprentissage* (Paris: Gautier-Languereau, 1992), 13.
44. Jaquet, *Les Transclasses*, 39.
45. Ernaux, *Une femme*, 26.
46. Ernaux, *La Place*, 19, 21.
47. On how Ernaux thinks her children will unjustly inherit something they did not work for, see Heinich, *L'Épreuve de la grandeur*, 102.
48. Ernaux, *La Femme gelée*, 13.
49. Ernaux, *La Place*, 54–55. See also Fabrice Thumerel, "Passage(s)," in Pierre-Louis Fort and Violaine Houdart-Merot, *Annie Ernaux: Un engagement d'écriture* (Paris: Presses Sorbonne nouvelle, 2015), 111–21.
50. Ernaux, *La Place*, 111.

51. Ernaux, *Les Armoires vides*, 148.
52. Ernaux, *Une femme*, 23.
53. Ernaux, 106.
54. Ernaux, 11.
55. Ernaux, *La Place*, 84.
56. Barthes, *Le Degré zéro de l'écriture*, 26. Ernaux often refers to this quote. See, for instance, Ernaux, "Prix Formentor," in Fort, *Annie Ernaux*, 303. On blank and flat writing, see also Ernaux, "Ne pas prendre d'abord le parti de l'art," in Dugast-Portes, *Annie Ernaux*, 175–80.
57. Barthes, *Le Degré zéro de l'écriture*, 13, 125.
58. Barthes, 9.
59. Ernaux, *La Place*, 45.
60. Ernaux, *"Je ne suis pas sortie de ma nuit,"* 41. See also Bourdieu's *Esquisse* in which he writes, about his inaugural address at the Collège de France, "They told me that I had a blank [*blanche*] voice." Bourdieu, *Esquisse pour une auto-analyse*, 139.
61. Ernaux, *La Place*, 21–22.
62. Ernaux, *Une femme*, 62.
63. To write about her sister (who died before Ernaux was even born), the author chose the epistolary format in *L'Autre Fille*. On letters in Ernaux, see also Barbara Havercroft, "(Auto)citation et initiation sexuelle dans *Mémoire de fille* d'Annie Ernaux," and Maya Lavault, "Lettres de fille: les usages de la lettre chez Annie Ernaux," in *Annie Ernaux, les écritures à l'œuvre*, Colloques Fabula, 2020, https://www.fabula.org/colloques/sommaire6613.php. In the last reprint of the truncated *Le Père Goriot* Ernaux read at fifteen, one of the essay prompts reads as follows: "Imagine a letter from Balzac to his mother during his stay at the Collège Vendôme (1807–13): his isolation, his punishments, his readings, his dreams of the future." Balzac, *Le Père Goriot* (Paris: Hatier, 1965), 9.
64. Ernaux, *La Place*, 24.
65. Ernaux, 89–90.
66. Ernaux, 12.
67. Ernaux, "La classe de français," in Fort, *Annie Ernaux*, 265.
68. See Genet, "Entretien avec Bertrand Poirot-Delpech," in *L'Ennemi déclaré*, 229.
69. Ernaux, *La Place*, 113–14.
70. Jameson, *The Political Unconscious*, 154.
71. Jameson, 179, 161.
72. Rancière, *La Parole muette*, 114; Bourdieu, *Les Règles de l'art*, 58–59.
73. Ernaux, *Mémoire de fille*, 22.
74. Ernaux, 57–58.
75. On in-betweenness in Ernaux, see "Avant-propos," in Thumerel, *Annie Ernaux*, 11–36.
76. "The very look of the French version of the text, which is sprinkled with

mimetic and citational italics, reflects the diversity of languages making up the narrator's language [...], and, early in the novel, he suggests that the latter owes much of its authentic quality to Rastignac and that the narrator himself often functions simply as a transcriber." Gerald Prince, "A Narratological Approach," in Ginsburg, *Approaches to Teaching Balzac's "Old Goriot,"* 92; "What a striking difference between Eugène's inconsequential place in the story and the attention that the narrative lavishes on him! In this short passage, the narrator attempts to fully represent one of Eugène's 'shocks' by spanning a range of different voices, from omniscient description of Eugène's consciousness ('Eugène watched him, not without envy') to direct quotation ('"So there,' he said to himself, 'is the man with the brougham!'") to free indirect discourse ('[h]e had one hundred and thirty francs for his trimester')." Woloch, *The One vs. The Many*, 271. See also Marceau, *Balzac et son monde*, 55.

77. Ernaux, *L'Atelier noir*, 134. Critic Jérôme Meizoz refers to Bakhtin's "hybrid construction" of voices to study the polyphony at play in Ernaux's *Ce qu'ils disent ou rien* in the article "Annie Ernaux, une politique de la forme," in Durrer and Meizoz, "La Littérature se fait dans la bouche," 45–62.

78. Ernaux, *La Place*, 46.
79. Ernaux, 80.
80. Ernaux, "Photojournal," in *Écrire la vie*, 28.
81. Ernaux, *L'Écriture comme un couteau*, 79.
82. Annie Ernaux, *La Place*, 23.
83. She also coauthored the scenario of Claire Denis's 2017 film *Un beau soleil intérieur*—translated as *Let the Sunshine In* (New York: Criterion Collection, 2019)—adapted from her book *Le Marché des amants* and starring Juliette Binoche and Gérard Depardieu.
84. Christine Angot, *Incest*, translated by Tess Lewis (Brooklyn: Archipelago Books, 2017).
85. Angot, *Quitter la ville*, 172.
86. Angot, *Un amour impossible*, 210.
87. Angot, *Le Voyage dans l'Est*, 190, 58–59.
88. Angot, *Un amour impossible*, 212.
89. Angot, 201.
90. Angot, 149.
91. Angot, *Le Marché des amants*, 11–12.
92. Angot, 82.
93. Robbe-Grillet, *Le Miroir qui revient*, 17. See also Annick Bouillaguet, "Nouveauté de l'imparfait," in *Proust lecteur de Balzac et de Flaubert: L'Imitation cryptée* (Paris: Champion, 2000), 109–17.
94. Devarrieux, "Tout d'Angot." See also Claire Devarrieux, "Un amour d'Angot," *Libération*, August 21, 2008. On incest and the imperfect, see Cruickshank, "Christine Angot," in *Fin de millénaire French Fiction*, 184.

95. Angot, *Le Marché des amants*, 75.
96. Angot, 64, 123.
97. Angot, *Un amour impossible* (typescript), IMEC, 291ANG/, box 84.
98. Angot, *Un amour impossible*, 158.
99. Angot, *Un amour impossible* (typescript), IMEC, 291ANG/, box 84.
100. Angot, *Cerisiers en fleurs*, IMEC, 291ANG/, box 28. On shame in Ernaux and Angot, see Natalie Edwards, "'Écrire pour ne plus avoir honte:' Christine Angot's and Annie Ernaux's Shameless Bodies," in *The Female Face of Shame*, ed. Erica L. Johnson and Patricia Moran (Bloomington: Indiana University Press, 2013), 61–73.
101. Ernaux, "Photojournal," in *Écrire la vie*, 101.
102. Ernaux, *L'Écriture comme un couteau*, 129–30.
103. Sartre, "Explication de *L'Étranger*," in *Situations*, 1:109.
104. Angot, *Un amour impossible* (typescript), IMEC, 291ANG/, box 84.
105. Ernaux, *L'Atelier noir*, 1.
106. Ernaux, *Les Années*, in *Écrire la vie*, 988.
107. On Ernaux and Tanning, see Isabelle Roussel-Gillet, "De *Birthday* au photojournal," in Best, Blanckeman, and Dugast-Portes, *Annie Ernaux*, 422–41.
108. Ernaux, "Littérature et politique," in *Écrire la vie*, 550; Harchi, *Comme nous existons*, 128.
109. Harchi, *Comme nous existons*, 91–92.
110. Harchi, 139–40.
111. Sayad, *L'immigration*, 1:156, 160, 158.
112. Harchi, *Comme nous existons*, 104, 124.
113. Harchi, 125.
114. Harchi, 138.
115. Harchi, 90.
116. Harchi, 94.
117. Ernaux, "'J'écrirai pour venger ma race.'" Reference also mentioned in "Prix Formentor," in Fort, *Annie Ernaux*, 303.

## Chapter Six

1. Flaubert, *L'Éducation sentimentale*, in *Œuvres complètes*, 4:503; Balzac, *La Maison Nucingen*, in *La Comédie humaine*, 6:333; Stendhal, *Souvenirs d'égotisme*, in *Œuvres intimes*, 1441; Jaquet, *Les Transclasses*, 204; Sam Friedman and Daniel Laurison, *The Class Ceiling: Why It Pays to Be Privileged* (Bristol: Policy Press, 2019), 1–27; Sonya Faure and Anastasia Vécrin, "Rose-Marie Lagrave: 'Il n'y a pas d'ascenseur social. Les transfuges de classe prennent l'escalier de service!,'" *Libération*, March 5, 2021. On "social frontiers," see also Pasquali, *Passer les frontières sociales*.
2. Cuin, *Les Sociologues et la mobilité sociale*, 41.

3. Goblot, *La Barrière et le Niveau*, 87. According to Goblot, the baccalaureate is the "gate" between classes.

4. The character of Flore is in charge of the "gate at the level crossing" in Zola, *La Bête humaine*, in *Les Rougon-Macquart*, 4:1028.

5. Cummins, *American Dirt*, 107. On the controversy surrounding this novel, see, for instance, Rachelle Hampton, "Why Everyone's Talking about *American Dirt*," *Slate*, January 21, 2020.

6. Jaquet, *Les Transclasses*, 11.

7. Robbins, *Upward Mobility and the Common Good*, 128, 127.

8. Robbins, 236.

9. Belenky, *Engine of Modernity*, 104.

10. "The metro in Paris, it's Babel, faces, gestures, and posed bodies with no voice, but the eyes say, in the language of the lost, left, abandoned country, what sisters, brothers might understand. The country, it's the suburb, the neighborhoods, the projects, on the periphery always, along with the native land, and the ancestors, in the backcountry." Sebbar, *Métro: Instantanés*, 11.

11. See, among other examples, Solenn de Royer and Bastien Bonnefous, "Derrière le discours d'Emmanuel Macron au Congrès, le spectre de l'omniprésidence," *Le Monde*, July 3, 2017. Left-wing politician Aurélie Filippetti wrote a novel on a transclass romance, she the daughter of a miner who became a minister of culture. In *Les Idéaux*, the train represents social mobility and is contrasted to Macron's vertical imagery of "lead climbers." Aurélie Filippetti, *Les Idéaux* (Paris: Fayard, 2018), 41, 298–99.

12. Kleinman, *Adventure Capital*, 38.

13. Zola, *La Bête humaine*, in *Les Rougon-Macquart*, 4:1176.

14. Kleinman, *Adventure Capital*, 34–36.

15. Zola, *La Bête humaine*, in *Les Rougon-Macquart*, 4:1171.

16. Maupassant, *Bel-Ami*, 250. See also this passage: "The young man's room, on the fifth floor, looked out, as though onto a deep abyss, onto the immense cutting of the Ouest railway, just above the exit of the tunnel, near the Batignolles station" (222).

17. Zola, *Au Bonheur des dames*, in *Les Rougon-Macquart*, 3:389.

18. Slaoui, *Illégitimes*, 11.

19. Westover, *Educated*, xi.

20. Westover, 11.

21. Éribon, *Retour à Reims*, 246.

22. Williams, *Border Country*, 20.

23. Williams, 341. On Éribon, Bourdieu, and Williams, see Sapiro, "Williams, Raymond," in *Dictionnaire international Bourdieu*, 888–90.

24. Didier Éribon briefly mentions *Border Country*'s train in one sentence of *La Société comme verdict*, 235.

25. Berlant, *Cruel Optimism*, 204.

26. Mirbeau, *Le Journal d'une femme de chambre*, 289.
27. Louis, *En finir avec Eddy Bellegueule*, 208.
28. Louis, *Changer: Méthode*, 214.
29. Vance, *Hillbilly Elegy*, 29, 56.
30. Murat, *Flaubert à la Motte-Picquet*, 56.
31. Murat, 7.
32. Benjamin, "Review: Detective Novels, On Tour," 111. See also Marielle Macé, "Lire dans le train," in *Façons de lire, manières d'être* (Paris: Gallimard, 2011), 61–66.
33. Proust, *À la recherche du temps perdu*, 1545.
34. On Proust's "implausible train route," see Conroy, *Literary Geographies in Balzac and Proust*, 55–58, 69.
35. On this passage, Edward Hughes argues that "the marriage arrangements are the by-product of another cross-class association (Charlus's homosexual relationship with Jupien)." Hughes, *Proust, Class, and Nation*, 62.
36. Proust, *À la recherche du temps perdu*, 2101.
37. Jansen, "Stuck in a Revolving Door," 82.
38. On Gilberte as a transclass character, see "Devenir duchesse," in Dubois, *Le Roman de Gilberte Swann*, 129–53.
39. Sharon Marcus and Vanessa Schwartz, "Teaching *Old Goriot* across the Disciplines," in Ginsburg, *Approaches to Teaching Balzac's "Old Goriot,"* 186, 185.
40. Madjidi, *Pour que je m'aime encore*, 170–71.
41. Brooks, "Balzac: Melodrama and Metaphor," 218–19.
42. Hughes, *Proust, Class, and Nation*, 188, 51.
43. Roland Barthes, "Une Idée de recherche," in Barthes, Genette, and Todorov, *Recherche de Proust*, 37.
44. Barthes, 36.
45. Barthes, 38.
46. Certeau, *L'Invention du quotidien*, 1:205.
47. Proust, *À la recherche du temps perdu*, 521.
48. Deleuze, *Proust and Signs*, 168.
49. Deleuze, 169.
50. Angot, *Le Marché des amants*, 11.
51. Ernaux, *La Place*, 23.
52. Lafon, *Les Pays*, 156.
53. Thomas, *Annie Ernaux*, 126.
54. Ernaux, *Journal du dehors*, 106–7. The subway escalator mixes ladder, elevator, and train, and would deserve a separate analysis. In the opening scene of Négar Djavadi's migration novel *Désorientale*, for instance, the narrator's father is an Iranian refugee who chooses the stairs over the escalator so as to underline his separation from the French population. Négar Djavadi, *Désorientale* (Paris: Liana Levi, 2016), 9–11.

55. Bourdieu, "L'illusion biographique," 71.
56. Ernaux, Les Armoires vides, 25.
57. Ernaux, Les Années, in Écrire la vie, 980.
58. Heinich, L'Épreuve de la grandeur, 83.
59. Heinich, 83.
60. Taïa, La Vie lente, 62.
61. Taïa, 70.
62. "The RER is a transit border, a vacuum neither in nor out of the city during the actual transit moment." Daniel N. Maroun, "Marginal Masculinities," in Bouamer and Provencher, Abdellah Taïa's Queer Migrations, 101.
63. For Ernaux, the bus is the opposite of the train. It severs instead of uniting. See, for instance, this dream recounted in an interview: "A dream, near the Gare St Lazare, I can't remember whether my mother is on the bus ... in any case, we're waiting for a bus. The bus arrives and my mother is there, I want to speak to her and she's not speaking to me, she vanishes, she signals to me that she can't speak to me and she disappears. I lose her. I see her and I lose her. Like Orpheus, Eurydice." Annie Ernaux and Pierre-Louis Fort, "Entretien," French Review 76, no. 5 (April 2003): 992.
64. Kleinman, Adventure Capital, 14, 157.
65. Taïa, L'Armée du salut, 39.
66. Taïa, 37.
67. Taïa, 33, 34, 36.
68. "The train transcends the nation because it is moving and represents neither Spain nor Morocco but a neutral space in which the characters can implement their own definition of sexuality and in which private and public spheres intertwine." Olivier Le Blond, "Sexual Fluidity and Movements in Abdellah Taïa's L'Armée du salut," in Bouamer and Provencher, Abdellah Taïa's Queer Migrations, 80.
69. Taïa, L'Armée du salut, 41.
70. Provencher, Queer Maghrebi French, 34.
71. https://french.yale.edu/event/encounter-moroccan-writer-abdellah-taia.
72. "The Education of the Senses," in Danius, The Senses of Modernism, 91. The train's distant "hoot" comes back in Proust, Le Temps retrouvé.
73. Nizan, Antoine Bloyé, 42, 48.
74. Nizan, 72. See also Annie Ernaux's article on Nizan, "Tout livre est un acte," Europe 784/785 (August/September 1994): 18–24.
75. Susan Suleiman, "Paul Nizan," in Kritzman, Columbia History of Twentieth-Century French Thought, 628.
76. Perec, Les Choses, in Œuvres, 1:90. On Perec and Ernaux, see Danielle Bajomée, "Penser la mélancolie: mémoire et blessures du temps chez Georges Perec et Annie Ernaux," in Bajomée and Dor, Annie Ernaux, 103-15.
77. Ross, Fast Cars, Clean Bodies, 126–27.

78. Perec, *Les Choses*, in *Œuvres*, 1:54.
79. Burgelin, *Album Georges Perec*, 37–38.
80. Berlant, *Cruel Optimism*, 19.
81. Berlant, 193.
82. Berlant, 221–22.
83. Zola, *La Bête humaine*, in *Les Rougon-Macquart*, 4:1043.

## Chapter Seven

1. See Massol, *Balzac contemporain*, and Mura-Brunel, *Silences du roman*, 21.
2. Wampole, *Degenerative Realism*, 4.
3. NDiaye, *La Vengeance m'appartient*, 197.
4. See, among other examples, Luc Lang, *Liverpool, marée haute* (Paris: Gallimard, 1991) in a British dock; Jean Rolin's *Terminal Frigo* (Paris: POL, 2005) from Calais to Marseille; Georges Perec's *Les Choses* (Paris: Julliard, 1965) in Sfax, Tunisia; Ousmane Sembène's *La Noire de…*, in *Voltaïque* (Paris: Présence Africaine, 1962) in Antibes, and *Le Docker noir* (Paris: Nouvelles Éditions Debresse, 1956) in Marseille; and Abdellatif Kechiche, *La Graine et le Mulet*, translated as *The Secret of the Grain* (New York: Criterion, 2010), and Agnès Varda, *La Pointe courte* (1955; Irvington: Criterion Collection, 2007) in the southern harbor city of Sète.
5. Robbins, *Upward Mobility and the Common Good*, 232–33.
6. On postwar reconstruction, see Denis Couchaux, Claire Etienne-Steiner, Christophe Kollmann, and Yvon Miossec, *Le Havre: Auguste Perret et la reconstruction* (Rouen: Inventaire général, 1999); Pierre Courant, *Au Havre pendant le siège: Souvenirs du 1er au 12 septembre 1944* (Paris: Fayard, 1946); and André Caudron, Michel Delebarre, G. Gachignard, Jean-Henri Gardy, and Jean-Luc Porhel, *Ports libérés, villes reconstruites: 1945–1955* (Dunkirk: Archives municipales and Musée des beaux-arts, 1995). See also Jean Rolin's book *Terminal Frigo*, a source of inspiration for Deck's second novel.
7. Deck, *Le Triangle d'hiver*, 134: "The lack of means limits my movements."
8. Deck, 174.
9. Deck, *Le Triangle d'hiver*, 158. On the history and etymology of *grève*, see Hannah Freed-Thall, "Introduction," in "Beaches and Ports," ed. Hannah Freed-Thall and Morgane Cadieu, special issue, *Comparative Literature* 73, no. 2 (2021): 131–49. On French fictions and precarity, see Ève Charrin, "Chômage fictif," *Esprit* 11 (2014): 73–78.
10. Deck's protagonist is named after Éric Rohmer's character in *L'Arbre, le maire et la médiathèque* (1993), translated as *The Tree, The Mayor, and The Mediatheque* (Paris: Pathé, 1997). Many consider Agnès Varda's *La Pointe courte* (1955), set in the southern harbor city of Sète, to be the first film of the New Wave.
11. On this topic, see Warren Motte, "Julia Deck's Geometries," *French Forum* 45, no. 1 (Spring 2020): 95–109. In a novel about French coastal cities, readers

could expect the "triangle" to refer to the "triangular" slave trade. The triangulation of Deck's novel is confined to the borders of metropolitan France. Her protagonist does not walk in the three major slave-trading ports of the French Atlantic coast: Nantes, Bordeaux, and La Rochelle. See Christopher L. Miller, *The French Atlantic Triangle: Literature and Culture of the Slave Trade* (Durham, NC: Duke University Press, 2008), 40. Deck named the central boat of her novel "Sirius." In the first novel of Senegalese writer Ousmane Sembène, *Le Docker noir* (Paris: Nouvelles Éditions Debresse, 1956), the main protagonist writes a book called *Le Dernier Voyage du négrier Sirius*. Yet Deck's reference to the slave ship does not seem intentional.

12. Marguerite Duras, *Le Ravissement de Lol V. Stein* (Paris: Gallimard, 1964). The perambulations and visions of big white boats are also very similar to those described by Marguerite Duras in *Le Marin de Gibraltar* (Paris: Gallimard, 1952), and *Moderato Cantabile* (Paris: Minuit, 1958). The seaside has a formalist tradition outside the New Novel. To take only two examples: Jean-Christophe Bailly's *Description d'Olonne* (Paris: Bourgois, 1992), is a detailed description of a coastal city that does not exist, meant to prove that language is able to generate a topography; in Perec's *La Vie mode d'emploi*, in *Œuvres*, vol. 2, Bartlebooth adopts the protocol of painting and destroying five hundred watercolors of ports. See, in this regard, Deck's third novel, *Sigma* (Paris: Minuit, 2017), in which the character of painter transitions from figurative harbors to monochromes after the war. For another novel on the abandoned industrial harbor (of Trieste) as a site of creativity, see Pauline Delabroy-Allard's first novel, also published by Minuit, *Ça raconte Sarah* (Paris: Minuit, 2018). Finally, the malaise of Deck's character echoes Roquentin's in Jean-Paul Sartre's *La Nausée* (Paris: Gallimard, 1938), his novel set in "Bouville," which literally means "mud city" in French and is a code name for Le Havre.

13. "I possess very few things—jeans, a T-shirt, sneakers. To be honest, I think I was stripped of my personal effects upon my arrival in the apartment, so impossible does it seem that I appeared thus on the doorstep, with no past or plan. I seek no explanation for my presence here." Deck, *Le Triangle d'hiver*, 132–33.

14. Robbe-Grillet, *Pour un nouveau roman*, 143.

15. Robbe-Grillet, 28.

16. Sarraute, *L'Ère du soupçon*, 57. Robbe-Grillet drew up a similar portrait of the nineteenth-century realist character who needs attributes to bequeath: names, parents, goods. See Robbe-Grillet, *Pour un nouveau roman*, 27.

17. Freed-Thall, *Spoiled Distinctions*, 132.

18. Sarraute's focus on *Eugénie Grandet* also stems from her interest in Dostoevsky, who translated Balzac's novel into Russian.

19. Deck, *Le Triangle d'hiver*, 162.

20. Robbe-Grillet, *Pour un nouveau roman*, 15–16.

21. Ross, *Fast Cars, Clean Bodies*, 2.

22. Robbe-Grillet, *Pour un nouveau roman*, 26.

23. Robbe-Grillet, 25. Perec, "Le Nouveau Roman et le refus du réel," in Perec, L.G., 35, 42.
24. See *Le Havre, la ville reconstruite par Auguste Perret*, Dossier Unesco (Le Havre, 2005).
25. Deck, *Viviane Elisabeth Fauville*, 79.
26. Houellebecq, "Alain Robbe-Grillet."
27. Houellebecq and Lévy, *Ennemis publics*, 266.
28. Novak-Lechevalier, "Michel Houellebecq," 11. See also Bruno Viard, "Houellebecq et Balzac," in *Les Tiroirs de Michel Houellebecq* (Paris: Presses Universitaires de France, 2013), 137–41.
29. Houellebecq, *La Possibilité d'une île*, 151.
30. Cruickshank, *Fin de millénaire French Fiction*, 155.
31. Houellebecq, *Plateforme*, 99, 244, 111–12; *La Possibilité d'une île*, 159, 426; *La Carte et le Territoire*, 253, 269; *Soumission*, 214; *Sérotonine*, 320, 294.
32. Houellebecq, *Extension du domaine de la lutte*, 20.
33. Houellebecq, *La Carte et le Territoire*, 176.
34. Houellebecq, 304.
35. Houellebecq and Lévy, *Ennemis publics*, 33.
36. Bellanger, *Houellebecq*, 109.
37. Wampole, *Degenerative Realism*, 2.
38. Wampole, 3.
39. Wampole, 2.
40. Houellebecq, *La Possibilité d'une île*, 30–31.
41. Houellebecq, 21; *Les Particules élémentaires*, 9; *La Carte et le Territoire*, 98.
42. Houellebecq, *La Carte et le Territoire*, 190.
43. Houellebecq, *Plateforme*, 99.
44. Levine and Ortiz-Robles, *Narrative Middles*, 7.
45. Houellebecq, *Les Particules élémentaires*, 162–63.
46. Houellebecq, 82.
47. Houellebecq, *Plateforme*, 331.
48. See Houellebecq and Lévy, *Ennemis publics*, 62–65.
49. Houellebecq, *Sérotonine*, 47–48.
50. Houellebecq, *Anéantir*, 44.
51. Maris, *Houellebecq économiste*, 21.
52. Noguez, *Houellebecq, en fait*, 30.
53. Coward, "The Newest Barbarism."
54. Houellebecq, *La Carte et le Territoire*, 196.
55. Houellebecq, *Les Particules élémentaires*, 20. See also Marc Weitzmann, "Monoprix pour un maxi livre," *Les Inrockuptibles* 161 (August 1998): 12–16.
56. Houellebecq, "The Joy of Supermarkets."
57. "17–23," in Houellebecq, *Non réconcilié*, 117.
58. Ernaux, *La Place*, 70.

Notes to Chapter 7  **287**

59. Ernaux, *Le Vrai lieu*, 18.
60. Ernaux, *Regarde les lumières, mon amour*, 14.
61. Ernaux, 9.
62. Ernaux, *Journal du dehors*, 106–7. On memory and supermarkets, see Fort, "Pulsations de la ville nouvelle," in Best, Blanckeman, and Dugast-Portes, *Annie Ernaux*, 121–36. On Ernaux, Vallès, and supermarkets, see also Violaine Sauty, "Annie Ernaux sur le terrain du quotidien: Ethnographie urbaine de l'hypermarché," *Autour de Vallès* 48 (2018): 197–99.
63. Ernaux, *Regarde les lumières, mon amour*, 62.
64. Ernaux, *Les Armoires vides*, 135.
65. Ernaux, 25.
66. Ernaux, *Regarde les lumières, mon amour*, 17–18.
67. Ernaux, *La Vie extérieure*, 102, 27, 82.
68. Ernaux, *Le Vrai lieu*, 84.
69. Ernaux, *Regarde les lumières, mon amour*, 17.
70. Ernaux, *Les Armoires vides*, 92.
71. Ernaux, *Regarde les lumières, mon amour*, 40.
72. Ernaux, 42.
73. Best and Marcus, "Surface Reading," 18.
74. Houellebecq, *Extension du domaine de la lutte*, 49.
75. Houellebecq, 174.
76. Ernaux, *Journal du dehors*, 65.
77. Wolfe, "Stalking the Billion-footed Beast," 55.
78. On Kmart Realism, see notably John Aldridge, *Talents and Technicians: Literary Chic and the New Assembly-Line Fiction* (New York: Scribner's, 1991); Robert Clark, *American Literary Minimalism* (Tuscaloosa: University of Alabama Press, 2015); James McDermott, *Austere Style in Twentieth-Century Literature* (New York: Edwin Mellen Press, 2006); Madison Smartt Bell, "Less Is Less: The Dwindling American Short Story," *Harper's Magazine* 272 (April 1986): 64–69; and Bill Buford, "Dirty Realism: New Writing from America," *Granta* 8 (June 1983). On Kmart Realism, Bildungsromane, and MFA programs, see Christopher Findeisen, "Injuries of Class: Mass Education and the American Campus Novel," *PMLA* 130, no. 2 (March 2015): 284–98.
79. Houellebecq, *Soumission*, 67.
80. Ernaux, *Regarde les lumières, mon amour*, 63.
81. See Schaal, "Whatever Became of 'Génération Mitterrand'?," 87–99.
82. See Sylvain Bourmeau, "Virginie Despentes: 'Je sens bien que je viens d'ailleurs,'" *Grazia*, June 11, 2015.
83. For a broader comparison between Balzac and Despentes, see Maxime Goergen, "*Vernon Subutex* et le roman 'balzacien,'" *Rocky Mountain Review* 72, no. 1 (Spring 2018): 165–82; and Christèle Couleau, "Modélisation 3D: Balzac, Houellebecq, Despentes," *L'Année balzacienne* 21, no. 1 (2020): 271–88. See also

Guy Duplat, "Virginie Despentes, la Balzac d'aujourd'hui," *La Libre*, June 6, 2017. Despite nods to Balzac, Despentes does not envision her characters as Balzacian. See Jean-Christophe Laurence, "La métamorphose de Virginie Despentes," *La Presse*, June 20, 2017.

84. Compagnon, "La langue plate et instrumentale de Houellebecq."
85. Despentes, *Vernon Subutex 1*, 9.
86. Despentes, 12.
87. Subutex travels under the name of Nicolas Nil: *nil* as in *nihilism*, and the repetition of *ni* as *neither, nor*.
88. "Some have succeeded yet at the cost of their aspirations, some have fallen down the social ladder, some have never risen or cannot rise above their dire conditions, some still try to cling on to youthful ideas, some have benefited from class privileges, and some have never known anything but the neoliberal system." Schaal, "Whatever Became of 'Génération Mitterrand'?," 95.
89. Despentes, *Vernon Subutex 1*, 18–19.
90. Despentes, 395–97.
91. Despentes, *Vernon Subutex 2*, 324.
92. Despentes, *Vernon Subutex 3*, 146.
93. Despentes, 373.
94. Despentes, 385.
95. Drouard, "Comment Virginie Despentes a rendu toute une génération accro à son 'Vernon Subutex.'"
96. Armstrong, *Maps and Territories*, 132.
97. Pinçonnat, Serrier, and Tettamanzi, *Échos picaresques dans le roman du XXe siècle*, 19.
98. Deck, *Le Triangle d'hiver*, 43.
99. "Nous roulons protégés dans l'égale lumière," in Houellebecq, *Non réconcilié*, 163. See also Christy Wampole, "Conceptual Botany: Michel Houellebecq and a Burgeoning Vegetal Interest," *French Forum* 44, no. 2 (2019): 210. Some of the poems she discusses point to a botanical middle: "We were in the midst of a vegetal chaos" and "In the middle of a garden."
100. "Le TGV Atlantique glissait dans la nuit," in Houellebecq, *Non réconcilié*, 178–79.
101. Houellebecq, *Sérotonine*, 98.
102. Despentes, *Vernon Subutex 3*, 191.
103. Despentes, *Pretty Things*, 6.

## Conclusion

1. Ernaux, *Journal du dehors*, 46.
2. Guillory, *Cultural Capital*, x.
3. Pasquali, *Héritocratie*, 7–9.

4. Mathieu, *Connemara*, 381.
5. Bellanger, *Le Grand Paris*, 476.
6. Bellanger, 312.
7. Kapriélian, "Aurélien Bellanger."
8. The transclass character of Bellanger's 2021 novel *Téléréalité* is also called, mockingly, "my dear Rastignac." See Bellanger, *Téléréalité*, 86.
9. Richard, *Désintégration*, 181.
10. Richard, 165.
11. Richard, 197.
12. Flahaut, *Les Nuits d'été*, 104.
13. See, for instance, Ulysse Baratin, "Un roman d'apprentissage intersectionnel," *En attendant Nadeau*, November 14, 2020.
14. Levi, *La Tannerie*, 233.
15. Divry, *La Condition pavillonnaire*, 190. See also Sophie Divry, *Madame Bovary of the Suburbs*, trans. Alison Anderson (London: Maclehose Press, 2017).
16. Pourchet, *Feu*, 49.
17. Moretti, *Way of the World*, viii.
18. Redfield, *Phantom Formations*, 172.
19. Somers, "Künstlermania."
20. Hughes, *Egalitarian Strangeness*, 3.
21. Hughes, 117.
22. London, *Martin Eden*, 412.
23. London, 477.
24. London, 482.
25. Ernaux, "LIRE, souvenirs et notes."
26. "Leila Slimani: By the Book."

# Works Cited

Abernathy, Robert, V. Adrianova-Peretc, Emilio Alarcos-Llorach, R. M. Aliev, W. Sydney Allen, Nikolaj Andreev, Howard I. Aronson, et al. *To Honor Roman Jakobson: Essays on the Occasion of His Seventieth Birthday*. Vol. 1. Paris: Mouton, 1967.
Adams, Lorraine. *Harbor*. New York: Knopf, 2004.
Adely, Emmanuel, Pierre Bergounioux, Julien Blaine, Pierre Bourgeade, Michel Butor, Florence Delay, Henri Deluy, et al. *Écrire Mai 68*. Paris: Argol, 2008.
Adorno, Theodor. *Minima Moralia: Reflections from Damaged Life*. Translated by E. F. N. Jephcott. London: Verso, 1978.
Albaret, Céleste. *Monsieur Proust: Souvenirs recueillis par Georges Belmont*. Paris: Laffont, 1973.
Algalarrondo, Hervé. *Deux jeunesses françaises*. Paris: Grasset, 2021.
Angot, Christine. *Le Marché des amants*. Paris: Seuil, 2008.
———. *Le Voyage dans l'Est*. Paris: Flammarion, 2021.
———. *Quitter la ville*. Paris: Stock, 2000.
———. "Sentiment huit." *Libération*, April 4, 2018.
——— *Un amour impossible*. Paris: Flammarion, 2015.
———. *Une semaine de vacances*. Paris: J'ai lu, 2013.
Armstrong, Joshua. *Maps and Territories: Global Positioning in the Contemporary French Novel*. Liverpool: Liverpool University Press, 2019.
Assouline, Pierre. *Autodictionnaire Simenon*. Paris: Omnibus, 2009.
Aubenas, Florence. *Le Quai de Ouistreham*. Paris: Éditions de l'Olivier, 2010.
Auerbach, Erich. *Mimesis: The Representation of Reality in Western Literature*. Translated by Willard R. Trask. Princeton, NJ: Princeton University Press, 2003.
Bachelard, Gaston. *La Terre et les rêveries de la volonté*. Paris: Corti, 1948.
Bacholle-Bošković, Michèle. "Sophie Divry, militante pour une littérature française forte: interview." *Fixxion: Revue critique de fixxion française contemporaine* 20 (2020): 122–29. http://www.revue-critique-de-fixxion -francaise contemporaine.org/rcffc/article/view/fx20.11/1433.

## Works Cited

Baecque, Antoine de. *La Nouvelle Vague: Portrait d'une jeunesse.* Paris: Flammarion, 1998.
Baglin, Claire. *En salle.* Paris: Minuit, 2022.
Bajomée, Danielle, and Juliette Dor, eds. *Annie Ernaux: Se perdre dans l'écriture de soi.* Paris: Klincksieck, 2011.
Bakhtin, Mikhail. *The Dialogic Imagination: Four Essays.* Translated by Caryl Emerson and Michael Holquist. Austin: University of Texas Press, 1981.
Balzac, Honoré de. *La Comédie humaine.* 12 vols. Paris: Gallimard, 1976–81.
———. *La Rabouilleuse.* Paris: POL, 1992.
———. *Le Père Goriot.* Paris: Hatier, 1965.
Bantigny, Ludivine. *La France à l'heure du monde: De 1981 à nos jours.* Paris: Seuil, 2013.
Barrès, Maurice. "La Contagion des Rastignacs." *Le Voltaire,* June 28, 1887.
———. *Les Déracinés.* Paris: Plon, 1947.
Barthes, Roland. *Le Degré zéro de l'écriture.* Paris: Seuil, 1953.
———. *Mythologies.* Paris: Seuil, 1957.
———. *Œuvres complètes.* Vol. 2, *1962–1967.* Paris: Seuil, 2002.
Barthes, Roland, Gérard Genette, and Tzvetan Todorov. *Recherche de Proust.* Paris: Seuil, 1980.
Beaubatie, Emmanuel. *Les Transfuges de sexe: Passer les frontières du genre.* Paris: La Découverte, 2021.
Beauvoir, Simone de. *Les Mandarins.* Paris: Gallimard, 1954.
Belenky, Masha. *Engine of Modernity: The Omnibus and Urban Culture in Nineteenth-Century Paris.* Manchester: Manchester University Press, 2019.
Bellanger, Aurélien. "Édouard Louis est possédé par son destin." *France Culture,* December 20, 2018.
———. *Houellebecq, écrivain romantique.* Paris: Scheer, 2010.
———. *Le Grand Paris.* Paris: Gallimard, 2017.
———. *Téléréalité.* Paris: Gallimard, 2021.
Bellefroid, Éric de. "Une femme de chambre et son diable au corps." *La Libre Belgique,* April 3, 1998. R 500 280, box 38, Fonds Mirbeau, Bibliothèque Universitaire d'Angers.
Belliard, David, and Agnès Michel. "Finissons-en avec le syndrome Léa Seydoux!" *Libération,* May 27, 2016.
Bellos, David. *Honoré de Balzac: Old Goriot.* Cambridge: Cambridge University Press, 1987.
Benjamin, Walter. "Review: Detective Novels, On Tour." In *The Storyteller: Tales Out of Loneliness.* Translated by Sam Dolbear, Esther Leslie, and Sebastian Truskolaski. New York: Verso, 2016.
Benlaala, Omar. *L'Effraction.* La Tour-d'Aigue: Éditions de l'Aube, 2016.
Bensmaïa, Réda. *Experimental Nations, or, The Invention of the Maghreb.* Translated by Alyson Waters. Princeton, NJ: Princeton University Press, 2003.

Bergounioux, Pierre. "Bourdieu, retour gagnant." *Libération*, November 23, 2016.
Bergounioux, Pierre, and Gabriel Bergounioux. *L'Héritage: rencontres*. Paris: Flohic, 2002.
Berlant, Lauren. *Cruel Optimism*. Durham, NC: Duke University Press, 2011.
Bernanos, Georges. *Monsieur Ouine*. Rio de Janeiro: Atlantic Editora, 1943.
———. *Un mauvais rêve*. Paris: Plon, 1951.
Besson, Philippe. *Un personnage de roman*. Paris: Julliard, 2017.
Best, Francine, Bruno Blanckeman, and Francine Dugast-Portes, eds. *Annie Ernaux: Le temps et la mémoire*. Paris: Stock, 2014.
Best, Stephen, and Sharon Marcus. "Surface Reading: An Introduction." *Representations* 108, no. 1 (Fall 2009): 1–21. https://doi.org/10.1525/rep.2009.108.1.1.
Bhabha, Homi. *The Location of Culture*. New York: Routledge, 2004.
Birnbaum, Jean. "Édouard Louis: 'Mon apprentissage de la politique a été un apprentissage du corps.'" *Le Monde*, September 22, 2016.
Blanc, André, Francis Freundlich, Jean-Pierre Perchellet, and Philippe Petiet. *Maîtres et valets dans la comédie française du XVIIIe siècle*. Paris: Ellipses, 1999.
Boltanski, Luc. "Les usages sociaux du corps." *Annales: Économies, sociétés, civilisations* 26, no. 1 (1971): 205–33. https://doi.org/10.3406/ahess.1971.422470.
Bordas, Éric, Pierre Glaudes, and Nicole Mozet, eds. *Dictionnaire Balzac*. Paris: Classiques Garnier, 2021.
Bouamer, Siham, and Denis Provencher, eds. *Abdellah Taïa's Queer Migrations: Non-Places, Affect, and Temporalities*. Lanham, MD: Lexington Books, 2021.
Bourdieu, Pierre. *Esquisse pour une auto-analyse*. Paris: Raisons d'agir, 2004.
———. *La Distinction: Critique sociale du jugement de goût*. Paris: Minuit, 1979.
———. *Les Héritiers*. Paris: Minuit, 1985.
———. *Les Règles de l'art: Genèse et structure du champ littéraire*. Paris: Seuil, 1992.
———."L'illusion biographique." *Actes de la recherche en sciences sociales* 62–63 (June 1986): 69–72. https://doi.org/10.3406/arss.1986.2317.
———. *Méditations pascaliennes*. Paris: Seuil, 1997.
———. *Questions de sociologie*. Paris: Minuit, 1984.
———. *Raisons pratiques sur la théorie de l'action*. Paris: Seuil, 1994.
———. "Remarques provisoires sur la perception sociale du corps." *Actes de la recherche en sciences sociales* 14 (April 1977): 51–54. https://doi.org/10.3406/arss.1977.2554.
Bourdieu, Pierre, and Jean-Claude Passeron. *La Reproduction: Éléments pour une théorie du système d'enseignement*. Paris: Minuit, 1970.
Bray, Patrick, ed. *Understanding Rancière, Understanding Modernism*. New York: Bloomsbury, 2017.
Brizé, Stéphane, dir. *La Loi du marché*. Translated as *The Measure of a Man*. 2015; New York: Kino Lorber, 2016.

Brooks, Peter. "Balzac: Melodrama and Metaphor." *Hudson Review* 22, no. 2 (Summer 1969): 213–28. https://doi.org/10.2307/3849403.

———. *Balzac's Lives*. New York: New York Review Books, 2020.

———. *Reading for the Plot: Design and Intention in Narrative*. New York: Vintage Books, 1985.

Buckley, Jerome Hamilton. *Season of Youth: The Bildungsroman from Dickens to Golding*. Cambridge, MA: Harvard University Press, 1974.

Buñuel, Luis, dir. *Le Journal d'une femme de chambre*. Translated as *The Diary of a Chambermaid*. 1964; Chicago: Home Vision Entertainment, 2001.

Burgelin, Claude. *Album Georges Perec*. Paris: Gallimard, 2017.

Butor, Michel. *Répertoire II: Études et conférences, 1959–1963*. Paris: Minuit, 1964.

Cagnati, Inès. *Le Jour de congé*. Paris: Denoël, 1973.

Calle, Sophie. *L'Hôtel*. Paris: Éditions de l'Étoile, 1984.

Camus, Albert. *Le Premier Homme*. Paris: Gallimard, 1994.

Cantet, Laurent. *L'Emploi du temps*. Translated as *Time Out*. 2001; Burbank, CA: Buena Vista Home Entertainment, 2003.

———. *Ressources humaines*. Translated as *Human Resources*. 1999; Brooklyn, NY: Kino International, 2008.

Carbonnier, Clément, and Nathalie Morel. *Le Retour des domestiques*. Paris: Seuil, 2018.

Cerdan, Audrey. "'Rastignac est une caillera': Yassine Belattar raconte le livre qui a changé sa vie." *L'Obs*. July 27, 2018.

Certeau, Michel de. *L'Invention du quotidien*. Vol. 1, *Arts de faire*. Paris: Union Générale d'Éditions, 1980.

Chabrol, Claude, dir. *Les Cousins*. 1959; New York: Criterion Collection, 2011.

Charentenay, Alice de, and Anaïs Goudmand. "Fiction et Idéologie: Marx lecteur des *Mystères de Paris*." *COnTEXTES* (November 2014). https://doi.org/10.4000/contextes.5991.

Chatiliez, Étienne, dir. *La Vie est un long fleuve tranquille*. Translated as *Life Is a Long Quiet River*. 1988; London: Artificial Eye, 2009.

Chevillard, Éric. *L'Autofictif père et fils*. Talence: L'Arbre vengeur, 2011.

Chris. Interview by Mouloud Achour, *Clique*, Canal Plus, September 9, 2018.

Cléder, Jean, and Timothée Picard, eds. *Détours et métissages: Le Cinéma de Benoît Jacquot*. Latresne: Bord de l'eau, 2008.

Cohen, Margaret. *The Sentimental Education of the Novel*. Princeton, NJ: Princeton University Press, 1999.

Collomb, Michel, ed. *L'Empreinte du social dans le roman depuis 1980*. Montpellier: Université Paul-Valéry-Montpellier III, 2005.

Compagnon, Antoine. "La langue plate et instrumentale de Houellebecq." *Le Monde*, January 3, 2019.

———. *Les Chiffonniers de Paris*. Paris: Gallimard, 2017.

Condé, Maryse. *Le Cœur à rire et à pleurer: Contes vrais de mon enfance.* Paris: Laffont, 1999.

———. *Victoire: Les Saveurs et les mots.* Paris: Mercure de France, 2006.

Conroy, Melanie. *Literary Geographies in Balzac and Proust.* Cambridge: Cambridge University Press, 2021.

Corbin, Alain. *Le Miasme et la Jonquille: L'Odorat et l'imaginaire social, xviiie–xixe siècles.* Paris: Aubier Montaigne, 1982.

Coward, David. "The Newest Barbarism." *Times Literary Supplement,* September 16, 2005.

Crépu, Michel, Alexandre Duval-Stalla, and Emmanuel Macron. "L'Histoire redevient tragique (une rencontre)." *Nouvelle Revue Française* 630 (May 2018): 77–86.

Crowley, Patrick, and Shirley Jordan, eds. *What Forms Can Do: The Work of Form in 20th- and 21st-Century French Literature and Thought.* Liverpool: Liverpool University Press, 2020.

Cruickshank, Ruth. *Fin de millénaire French Fiction: The Aesthetics of Crisis.* Oxford: Oxford University Press, 2009.

Cuin, Charles-Henry. *Les Sociologues et la mobilité sociale.* Paris: Presses Universitaires de France, 1993.

Cummins, Jeannine. *American Dirt.* New York: Flatiron Books, 2020.

Danius, Sara. *The Senses of Modernism: Technology, Perception, and Aesthetics.* Ithaca, NY: Cornell University Press, 2002.

Dauvister, Christine. "Spectacle Octave Mirbeau, au théâtre Blocry." *Vlan,* January 21, 1998.

Davet, Gérard, and Fabrice Lhomme. *Le Traître et le Néant.* Paris: Fayard, 2021.

Deck, Julia. *Le Triangle d'hiver.* Paris: Minuit, 2014.

———. *Viviane Elisabeth Fauville.* Paris: Minuit, 2012.

Delestré, Stéfanie, and Hagar Desanti, eds. *Dictionnaire des personnages populaires de la littérature: XIXe et XXe siècles.* Paris: Seuil, 2010.

Deleuze, Gilles. *Proust and Signs.* Translated by Richard Howard. Minneapolis: University of Minnesota Press, 2000.

Deleuze, Gilles, and Félix Guattari. *Qu'est-ce que la philosophie?* Paris: Minuit, 1991.

Del Lungo, Andrea, and Pierre Glaudes. *Balzac, l'invention de la sociologie.* Paris: Classiques Garnier, 2019.

Delphy, Christine, ed. *Un troussage de domestique.* Paris: Syllepse, 2011.

Delsaux, Aurélien, Sophie Divry, and Denis Michelis. "Pour dire notre époque monstrueuse, il faut des romans monstrueux." *Le Monde,* November 3, 2018.

Déon, Michel. *Lettre à un jeune Rastignac.* Paris: Fasquelle, 1956.

Despentes, Virginie. *Pretty Things.* Translated by Emma Ramadan. New York: Feminist Press, 2018.

———. *Vernon Subutex 1.* Paris: Grasset, 2015.

———. *Vernon Subutex 2.* Paris: Grasset, 2015.

———. *Vernon Subutex 3*. Paris: Grasset, 2017.
Devarrieux, Claire. "Tout d'Angot." *Libération*, August 31, 2006.
Diallo, Rokhaya. *Ne reste pas à ta place! Comment arriver là où personne ne vous attendait*. Paris: Marabout, 2019.
Diatkine, Anne. "Édouard Louis: 'L'autobiographie est l'une des formes les plus puissantes politiquement.'" *Libération*, September 18, 2020.
Diome, Fatou. *La Préférence nationale, et autres nouvelles*. Paris: Présence Africaine, 2001.
———. *Le Ventre de l'Atlantique*. Paris: Anne Carrière, 2003.
Divry, Sophie. *Cinq mains coupées*. Paris: Seuil, 2020.
———. *La Condition pavillonnaire*. Paris: Noir sur Blanc, 2014.
Dostoevsky, Fyodor. *Crime et Châtiment*. Translated by D. Ergaz. Paris: Gallimard, 1950.
Doubrovsky, Serge, Jacques Lecarme, and Philippe Lejeune, eds. *Autofictions et cie*. Nanterre: Université Paris X-Nanterre, 1993.
Drieu La Rochelle, Pierre. *Rêveuse bourgeoisie*. Paris: Gallimard, 1937.
Drouard, Élodie. "Comment Virginie Despentes a rendu toute une génération accro à son 'Vernon Subutex.'" *France Info*, April 16, 2019.
Dryef, Zineb. "Édouard Louis: Life with His Brothers in Arms and in Spirit." *Le Monde* in English, August 17, 2018.
Dubois, Jacques. *Le Roman de Gilberte Swann: Proust sociologue paradoxal*. Paris: Seuil, 2018.
Dubois, Jacques, Pascal Durand, and Yves Winkin, eds. *Le Symbolique et le Social: La Réception internationale de la pensée de Pierre Bourdieu*. Liège: Editions de l'Université de Liège, 2005.
Dugast-Portes, Francine. *Annie Ernaux: Étude de l'œuvre*. Paris: Bordas, 2008.
Dunn, Mark. "Yale Recognized for Fast Growth of Lower-Income Student Population." *Yale News*, July 7, 2021.
Durrer, Sylvie, and Jérôme Meizoz, eds. "La Littérature se fait dans la bouche." Special issue, *Versants* 30 (1996).
Duteurtre, Benoît. *À nous deux, Paris!* Paris: Fayard, 2012.
Elayoubi, Fatima. *Prière à la lune*. Paris: Bachari, 2016.
Elkharraz, Osman, with Raymond Dikoumé. *Confessions d'un acteur déchu, de L'Esquive à la rue*. Paris: Stock, 2016.
Éribon, Didier. *La Société comme verdict: Classes, identités, trajectoires*. Paris: Fayard, 2013.
———. *Retour à Reims*. Paris: Fayard, 2009.
Ernaux, Annie. *Ce qu'ils disent ou rien*. Paris: Gallimard, 1977.
———. *Écrire la vie*. Paris: Gallimard, 2011.
———. "'J'écrirai pour venger ma race,' le discours de la Prix Nobel de littérature." *Le Monde*, December 7, 2022.
———. *"Je ne suis pas sortie de ma nuit."* Paris: Gallimard, 1997.

———. *Journal du dehors*. Paris: Gallimard, 1993.
———. *La Femme gelée*. Paris: Gallimard, 1981.
———. *La Honte*. Paris: Gallimard, 1997.
———. *La Place*. Paris: Gallimard, 1983.
———. *L'Atelier noir*. Paris: Gallimard, 2021.
———. *L'Autre Fille*. Paris: Nil, 2011.
———. *La Vie extérieure*. Paris: Gallimard, 2000.
———. *L'Écriture comme un couteau: Entretien avec Frédéric-Yves Jeannet*. Paris: Stock, 2003.
———. "Le mouvement MeToo a été pour moi comme une grande lumière, une déflagration." Interview by Léa Salamé, *L'invité de 7h50*, France Inter, November 28, 2019.
———. *Les Armoires vides*. Paris: Gallimard, 1974.
———. *L'Événement*. Paris: Gallimard, 2000.
———. *Le Vrai lieu: Entretiens avec Michelle Porte*. Paris: Gallimard, 2014.
———. "LIRE, souvenirs et notes." Annie Ernaux, Textes. https://www.annie-ernaux.org/fr/lire-souvenirs-et-notes/.
———. *Mémoire de fille*. Paris: Gallimard, 2016.
———. "Mise à distance." *Revue des deux mondes*, July/August 2003.
———. *Monsieur le Président*. Paris: Gallimard, 2022.
———. "Reading, Memories and Notes." Translated by Jo Halliday. Annie Ernaux, Texts. https://www.annie-ernaux.org/reading-memories-and-notes/.
———. *Regarde les lumières, mon amour*. Paris: Seuil, 2014.
———. *Retour à Yvetot*. Paris: Éditions du Mauconduit, 2013.
———. *Une femme*. Paris: Gallimard, 1987.
Etcherelli, Claire. *Elise, ou la vraie vie*. Paris: Denoël, 1967.
Eyers, Tom. *Speculative Formalism: Literature, Theory, and the Critical Present*. Evanston, IL: Northwestern University Press, 2016.
Fanon, Frantz. *The Wretched of the Earth*. Translated by Richard Philcox. New York: Grove Press, 2004.
Fassin, Éric. *Le Sexe politique: Genre et sexualité au miroir transatlantique*. Paris: Éditions de l'École des hautes études en sciences sociales, 2009.
Faure, Guillemette. "'On allait voir les films en VF': Les Transfuges imaginaires." *Le Monde*, October 15, 2022.
Fénelon. *Les Aventures de Télémaque*. Paris: Gallimard, 1995.
Figlerowicz, Marta. *Flat Protagonists: A Theory of Novel Character*. Oxford: Oxford University Press, 2014.
Fischler, Alexander. "Rastignac-Télémaque: The Epic Scale in *Le Père Goriot*." *Modern Language Review* 63, no. 4 (October 1968): 840–48. https://doi.org/10.2307/3723742.
Fitzgerald, F. Scott. *The Great Gatsby*. New York: W. W. Norton, 2022.
Flahaut, Thomas. *Les Nuits d'été*. Paris: Éditions de l'Olivier, 2020.

Flaubert, Gustave. *Œuvres*. Vol. 2. Paris: Gallimard, 1952.
———. *Œuvres complètes*. Vol. 3, *1851–1862*. Paris: Gallimard, 2013.
———. *Œuvres complètes*. Vol. 4, *1863–1874*. Paris: Gallimard, 2021.
Fontaine, Anne, dir. *Marvin ou la belle éducation*. 2017; Paris: TF1 Studio, 2018.
Fort, Pierre-Louis, ed. *Annie Ernaux*. Paris: Herne, 2022.
Fortems, David. *Louis veut partir*. Paris: Laffont, 2020.
Foucault, Michel. *Dits et Écrits: 1954–1988*. Vol. 3, *1976–1979*. Paris: Gallimard, 1994.
Fraisse, Geneviève. *Service ou Servitude: Essai sur les femmes toutes mains*. Lormont: Le Bord de l'eau, 2009.
France, Peter, ed. *The New Oxford Companion to Literature in French*. Oxford: Clarendon Press, 1985.
Freed-Thall, Hannah. *Spoiled Distinctions: Aesthetics and the Ordinary in French Modernism*. New York: Oxford University Press, 2015.
Freud, Sigmund. *The Uncanny*. Translated by David McLintock. London: Penguin Books, 2003.
Gallo, Max. "Rastignac est parmi nous." *Le Monde*, September 11, 2008.
Garelick, Rhonda. "The Cinderella Myth We Can't Quit." *New York Times*, November 10, 2021.
Gaulejac, Vincent de. *La Névrose de classe: Trajectoire sociale et conflits d'identité*. Paris: Hommes & groupes, 1987.
Gautier, Théophile. *Romans, contes et nouvelles*. Vol. 2. Paris: Gallimard, 2002.
Genet, Jean. *L'Ennemi déclaré: Textes et entretiens*. Paris: Gallimard, 1991.
———. *Theâtre complet*. Paris: Gallimard, 2002.
"'Gilets jaunes': l'ONU demande à la France d'enquêter sur 'l'usage excessif de la force.'" *Le Monde* and AFP, March 6, 2019.
"Gilets jaunes: Nous ne sommes pas dupes!" *Libération*, May 4, 2019.
"Gilets jaunes, verts, rouges, roses, convergeons!" *Libération*, December 4, 2018.
Ginsburg, Michal Peled, ed. *Approaches to Teaching Balzac's "Old Goriot."* New York: Modern Language Association of America, 2000.
Giraud, Frédérique. *Émile Zola, le déclassement et la lutte des places: Les Rougon-Macquart, condensation littéraire d'un désir d'ascension sociale*. Paris: Champion, 2016.
Gleize, Joëlle. *Honoré de Balzac: Bilan critique*. Paris: Nathan, 1994.
Goblot, Edmond. *La Barrière et le Niveau: Étude sociologique sur la bourgeoisie française moderne*. Paris: Presses Universitaires de France, 1967.
Goldmann, Lucien. *Pour une sociologie du roman*. Paris: Gallimard, 1964.
———. *Structures mentales et création culturelle*. Paris: Anthropos, 1971.
Goncourt, Edmond de. *Germinie Lacerteux*. Paris: Garnier-Flammarion, 1990.
Gracq, Julien. *Œuvres complètes*. 2 vols. Paris: Gallimard, 1989.
Guène, Faïza. *Kiffe kiffe demain*. Paris: Hachette Littératures, 2004.

Guibert, Hervé. *La Photo, inéluctablement: Recueil d'articles sur la photographie 1977–1985*. Paris: Gallimard, 1999.

Guichardet, Jeannine. *Le Père Goriot d'Honoré de Balzac*. Paris: Gallimard, 1993.

Guillory, John. *Cultural Capital: The Problem of Literary Canon Formation*. Chicago: Chicago University Press, 1993.

Guilluy, Christophe. *Le Temps des gens ordinaires*. Paris: Flammarion, 2020.

Hadni, Dounia. "Abdellah Taïa: Paria gagné." *Libération*, January 5, 2017.

Hagan, John. "The Poor Labyrinth: The Theme of Social Injustice in Dickens's 'Great Expectations.'" *Nineteenth-Century Fiction* 9, no. 3 (December 1954): 169–78. https://doi.org/10.2307/3044305.

Hamon, Philippe. *Le Personnel du roman: Le Système des personnages dans les Rougon-Macquart d'Émile Zola*. Genève: Droz, 1998.

Harchi, Kaoutar. *Comme nous existons*. Arles: Actes Sud, 2021.

Heathcote, Owen, and Andrew Watts, eds. *The Cambridge Companion to Balzac*. Cambridge: Cambridge University Press, 2017.

Heinich, Nathalie. *L'Épreuve de la grandeur: Prix littéraires et reconnaissance*. Paris: Découverte, 1999.

Hoggart, Richard. *La Culture du pauvre: Étude sur le style de vie des classes populaires en Angleterre*. Translated by Françoise Garcias, Jean-Claude Garcias, and Jean-Claude Passeron. Paris: Minuit, 1970.

———. *The Uses of Literacy: Changing Patterns in English Mass Culture*. Fair Lawn: Essential Books, 1957.

Hollister, Lucas. *Beyond Return: Genre and Cultural Politics in Contemporary French Fiction*. Liverpool: Liverpool University Press, 2019.

Houellebecq, Michel. "Alain Robbe-Grillet." Translated by Molly Stevens. *Artforum*, September 2008.

———. *Anéantir*. Paris: Flammarion, 2022.

———. *Extension du domaine de la lutte*. Paris: Nadeau, 1994.

———. "The Joy of Supermarkets." *Guardian*, September 16, 2005.

———. *La Carte et le Territoire*. Paris: Flammarion, 2010.

———. *La Possibilité d'une île*. Paris: Fayard, 2005.

———. *Les Particules élémentaires*. Paris: Flammarion, 1998.

———. *Non réconcilié: Anthologie personnelle 1991–2013*. Paris: Gallimard, 2014.

———. *Plateforme*. Paris: Flammarion, 2001.

———. *Sérotonine*. Paris: Flammarion, 2019.

———. *Soumission*. Paris: Flammarion, 2015.

Houellebecq, Michel, and Bernard-Henry Lévy. *Ennemis publics*. Paris: Flammarion et Grasset, 2008.

Hughes, Edward J. *Egalitarian Strangeness: On Class Disturbance and Levelling in Modern and Contemporary French Narrative*. Liverpool: Liverpool University Press, 2021.

———. *Proust, Class, and Nation*. Oxford: Oxford University Press, 2011.

Hugo, Victor. *Les Misérables*. Paris: Gallimard, 1951.
Hugueny-Léger, Elise. *Annie Ernaux, une poétique de la transgression*. Oxford: Peter Lang, 2009.
Hunkeler, Thomas, and Marc-Henry Soulet, eds. *Annie Ernaux: Se mettre en gage pour dire le monde*. Genève: Métis Presses, 2012.
Idier, Antoine. "'Sortir de la peur': Construire une identité homosexuelle arabe dans un monde postcolonial; Entretien avec Abdellah Taïa." *Fixxion* 12 (2017): 197–207. http://www.revue-critique-de-fixxion-francaise-contemporaine.org/rcffc/article/view/fx12.19/1016.
Isenberg, Nancy. *White Trash: The 400-Year Untold History of Class in America*. New York: Viking, 2016.
Jablonka, Ivan. *L'Histoire est une littérature contemporaine: Manifeste pour les sciences sociales*. Paris: Seuil, 2014.
Jacquot, Benoît, dir. *Journal d'une femme de chambre*. Translated as *Diary of a Chambermaid*. 2015; San Francisco: Kanopy Streaming, 2019.
———. *La Fausse suivante*. 2000; Paris: Éditions Montparnasse, 2002.
———. *Les Adieux à la reine*. Translated as *Farewell, My Queen*. New York: Cohen Media Group, 2012.
Jameson, Fredric. *The Political Unconscious: Narrative as a Socially Symbolic Act*. Ithaca, NY: Cornell University Press, 1981.
Jansen, Yolande. "Stuck in a Revolving Door: Metaphor and Cultural Memory in Proust's *in Search of Lost Time*." *Marcel Proust aujourd'hui* 1 (2003): 81–90. https://www.jstor.org/stable/44869640.
Jaquet, Chantal. *Les Transclasses ou la non-reproduction*. Paris: Presses Universitaires de France, 2014.
Jaquet, Chantal, and Gérard Bras, eds. *La Fabrique des transclasses*. Paris: Presses Universitaires de France, 2018.
Joon-Ho, Bong, dir. *Parasite*. 2019; New York: Criterion Collection, 2020.
Jordan, David. *Transforming Paris: The Life and Labors of Baron Haussmann*. New York: Free Press, 1995.
Jordan, Shirley. *Contemporary French Women's Writing*. Oxford: Peter Lang, 2004.
Kahn, Robert, Laurence Macé, and Françoise Simonet-Tenant, eds. *Annie Ernaux: L'Intertextualité*. Mont-Saint-Aignan: Presses Universitaires de Rouen et du Havre, 2015.
Kaplan, Leslie. *L'Excès-l'usine*. Paris: Hachette POL, 1982.
Kapriélian, Nelly. "Aurélien Bellanger: 'La droitisation du monde nous plonge dans une situation folle.'" *Les Inrockuptibles*, January 12, 2017.
Kaurismäki, Aki, dir. *Le Havre*. 2011; New York: Criterion Collection, 2012.
Kechiche, Abdellatif, dir. *La Vie d'Adèle*. Translated as *Blue Is the Warmest Color*. 2013; New York: Criterion Collection, 2017.
———, dir. *L'Esquive*. Translated as *Games of Love and Chance*. 2003; New York: New Yorker Video, 2006.

Kerangal, Maylis de. *Corniche Kennedy*. Paris: Verticales, 2008.
Kim, Annabel. *Unbecoming Language: Anti-identitarian French Feminist Fictions*. Columbus: Ohio State University Press, 2018.
Kleinman, Julie. *Adventure Capital: Migration and the Making of an African Hub in Paris*. Oakland: University of California Press, 2019.
Kornbluh, Anna. *Realizing Capital: Financial and Psychic Economies in Victorian Form*. New York: Fordham University Press, 2014.
Kritzman, Lawrence, ed. *The Columbia History of Twentieth-Century French Thought*. New York: Columbia University Press, 2006.
Krueger, Alan B. "The Rise and Consequences of Inequality in the United States." Center for American Progress, January 12, 2012. http://cdn.americanprogress.org/wp-content/uploads/events/2012/01/pdf/krueger.pdf?_ga=2.101197897.994889909.1671597872-54049818.1671597872.
Laacher, Smaïn. "Annie Ernaux ou l'inaccessible quiétude: Entretien avec Annie Ernaux précédé d'une présentation de Smaïn Laacher." *Politix* 4, no. 14 (1991): 73–78. https://www.persee.fr/doc/polix_0295-2319_1991_num_4_14_1454.
Lacourt, Chloé. "Xavier Dolan et Léa Seydoux: On vient tous les deux de l'école de la vie." *Madame Figaro*, May 13, 2016.
Lafon, Marie-Hélène. *Les Pays*. Paris: Buchet-Chastel, 2012.
Lagrave, Rose-Marie. *Se ressaisir: Enquête autobiographique d'une transfuge de classe féministe*. Paris: La Découverte, 2021.
Lahire, Bernard, ed. *Ce qu'ils vivent, ce qu'ils écrivent: Mises en scène littéraires du social et expériences socialisatrices des écrivains*. Paris: Archives contemporaines, 2011.
La Rédaction. "Qui est Mathieu Gallet, l'homme à qui on prête une relation avec Emmanuel Macron?" *Voici*, February 7, 2017.
Lascar, Alex. "De la boue balzacienne." *L'Année balzacienne* 10, no. 1 (2009): 105–25. https://doi.org/10.3917/balz.010.0105.
Le Clerc, Xavier. *Un homme sans titre*. Paris: Gallimard, 2022.
Leibovici, Martine. *Autobiographies de transfuges: Karl Philipp Moritz, Richard Wright, Assia Djebar*. Paris: Le Manuscrit, 2013.
———. "Le verstehen narratif du transfuge: Incursions chez Richard Wright, Albert Memmi et Assia Djebar." *Tumultes* 36, no. 1 (2011): 91–109. https://doi.org/10.3917/tumu.036.0091.
"Leila Slimani: By the Book." *New York Times*, January 17, 2019.
Leprince, Chloé. "Un fils de cordonnier à l'Académie française, avant la berceuse transclasse et Bernard Tapie." *France Culture*, November 4, 2021.
Les gilets noirs en lutte, La Chapelle debout and Droit devant!! "Gilets noirs cherchent Premier ministre." *Libération*, June 27, 2019.
Levi, Célia. *La Tannerie*. Auch: Tristram, 2020.
Levine, Caroline. *Forms: Whole, Rhythm, Hierarchy, Network*. Princeton, NJ: Princeton University Press, 2015.

Levine, Caroline, and Mario Ortiz-Robles, eds. *Narrative Middles: Navigating the Nineteenth-Century British Novel.* Columbus: Ohio State University Press, 2011.

Leyris, Raphaëlle. "'Changer: Méthode,' d'Édouard Louis: L'Art du retour sur soi." *Le Monde,* September 25, 2021.

Lichtlé, Michel. "Balzac, une référence pour le XXe siècle?" *L'Année balzacienne* 16, no. 1 (2015): 41–46. https://doi.org/10.3917/balz.016.0041.

Linhart, Robert. *L'Établi.* Paris: Minuit, 1978.

Lob, Jacques, and Jean-Marc Rochette. *Le Transperceneige.* Tournai: Casterman, 1999–2000.

London, Jack. *Martin Eden.* New York: Penguin Books, 1993.

———. *Martin Eden.* Translated by Francis Kerline. Preface by Linda Lê. Paris: Phébus, 2001.

Lopez, David. *Fief.* Paris: Seuil, 2017.

Louis, Édouard. "Can the Yellow Vests Speak?" Translated by David Broder. *Jacobin,* December 8, 2018.

———. *Changer: Méthode.* Paris: Seuil, 2021.

———. *Combats et métamorphoses d'une femme.* Paris: Seuil, 2021.

———. *The End of Eddy.* Translated by Michael Lucey. New York: Farrar, Straus and Giroux, 2017.

———. *En finir avec Eddy Bellegueule.* Paris: Seuil, 2014.

———. *Histoire de la violence.* Paris: Seuil, 2016.

———. *History of Violence.* Translated by Lorin Stein. New York: Farrar, Straus and Giroux, 2018.

———, ed. *Pierre Bourdieu: L'Insoumission en héritage.* Paris: Presses Universitaires de France, 2013.

———. *Qui a tué mon père.* Paris: Seuil, 2018.

Louis, Édouard, and Thomas Ostermeier. *Au Cœur de la violence: Théâtre.* Paris: Seuil, 2019.

Loyer, François. *Paris XIXe siècle: L'Immeuble et la rue.* Paris: Hazan, 1987.

Lucey, Michael. *The Misfit of the Family: Balzac and the Social Forms of Sexuality.* Durham, NC: Duke University Press, 2003.

———. *Someone: The Pragmatics of Misfit Sexualities, from Colette to Hervé Guibert.* Chicago: University of Chicago Press, 2019.

Lukács, Georg. *Marxism and Human Liberation: Essays on History, Culture and Revolution.* New York: Dell, 1973.

Lyon-Caen, Judith. *La Lecture et la Vie: Les Usages du roman au temps de Balzac.* Paris: Tallandier, 2006.

Macé, Marielle. *Styles: Critique de nos formes de vie.* Paris: Gallimard, 2016.

———. "Ways of Reading, Modes of Being." Translated by Marlon Jones. *New Literary History* 44, no. 2 (Spring 2013): 213–29. https://www.jstor.org/stable/24542592.

Macron, Emmanuel. *Révolution.* Paris: Pocket, 2017.

Madjidi, Maryam. *Pour que je m'aime encore*. Paris: Le Nouvel Attila, 2021.
Marceau, Félicien. *Balzac et son monde*. Paris: Gallimard, 1986.
Marcus, Sharon. *Apartment Stories: City and Home in Nineteenth-Century Paris and London*. Berkeley: University of California Press, 1999.
Marivaux. *Romans*. Paris: Gallimard, 1949.
Maris, Bernard. *Houellebecq économiste*. Paris: Flammarion, 2014.
Martin, Jean-Pierre, ed. *Bourdieu et la littérature*. Nantes: Cécile Defaut, 2010.
Marx, Karl, and Frederick Engels. *Collected Works*. Vol. 48, *Engels: 1887–1890*. London: Lawrence & Wishart, 2001.
———. *The Holy Family, or Critique of Critical Critique*. Moscow: Foreign Languages Publishing House, 1956.
Maspero, François, and Anaïk Frantz. *Les Passagers du Roissy-Express*. Paris: Seuil, 1990.
Massol, Chantal, ed. *Balzac contemporain*. Paris: Classiques Garnier, 2018.
Mathieu, Nicolas. *Connemara*. Arles: Actes Sud, 2022.
———. *Leurs enfants après eux*. Arles: Actes Sud, 2018.
Matzat, Wolfgang. "L'image de la ville et sa fonction dans 'Le Père Goriot.'" *L'Année balzacienne* 5, no. 1 (2004): 303–15. https://doi.org/10.3917/balz.005.0303.
Mauger, Gérard, ed. *Rencontres avec Pierre Bourdieu*. Bellecombes-en-Bauges: Croquant, 2005.
Maupassant, Guy de. *Bel-Ami*. In *Romans*. Paris: Gallimard, 1987.
———. *Une vie*. Preface by Annie Ernaux. Paris: Garnier-Flammarion, 2016.
Maza, Sarah. *Servants and Masters in Eighteenth-Century France: The Uses of Loyalty*. Princeton, NJ: Princeton University Press, 1983.
Meizoz, Jérôme. *L'Œil sociologue et la littérature*. Genève: Slatkine, 2004.
Memmi, Dominique, Dominique Guillo, and Olivier Martin, eds. *La Tentation du corps: corporéité et sciences sociales*. Paris: Éditions de l'École des hautes études en sciences sociales, 2009.
Méra, Brigitte. *La Méthode Rastignac: La Comédie humaine, une culture d'entreprise*. Paris: Tallandier, 2009.
Mercier, Louis-Sébastien. *Tableau de Paris 1*. Paris: Mercure de France, 1994.
Merllié, Dominique. *Les Enquêtes de mobilité sociale*. Paris: Presses Universitaires de France, 1994.
Merriman, John, ed. *French Cities in the Nineteenth Century*. New York: Holmes & Meier, 1981.
Miller, Michael B. *The Bon Marché: Bourgeois Culture and the Department Store, 1869–1920*. Princeton, NJ: Princeton University Press, 1981.
Mirbeau, Octave. "Le Comédien." *Le Figaro*, October 26, 1882.
———. *Le Journal d'une femme de chambre*. Paris: Garnier-Flammarion, 1983.
———. "Revue des théâtres." *L'Ordre de Paris*, August 31, 1875.
Molière. *Œuvres complètes*. 2 vols. Paris: Gallimard, 1956.

Moretti, Franco. *The Way of the World: The Bildungsroman in European Culture.* New York: Verso, 2000.

Morson, Gary Saul, and Morton Schapiro. *Cents and Sensibility: What Economics Can Learn from the Humanities.* Princeton, NJ: Princeton University Press, 2017.

Morton, Jennifer M. *Moving Up without Losing Your Way: The Ethical Costs of Upward Mobility.* Princeton, NJ: Princeton University Press, 2019.

Moudileno, Lydie. "Marie NDiaye's Discombobulated Subject." *Substance* 35, no. 3 (2006): 83–94. https://www.jstor.org/stable/4152871.

Mura-Brunel, Aline. *Silences du roman: Balzac et le romanesque contemporain.* Amsterdam: Rodopi, 2004.

Murat, Laure. *Flaubert à la Motte-Picquet.* Paris: Flammarion, 2015.

Naselli, Adrien. *Et tes parents, ils font quoi? Enquête sur les transfuges de classe et leurs parents.* Paris: Lattès, 2021.

Naudet, Jules. *Grand patron, fils d'ouvrier.* Paris: Seuil, 2014.

———. "L'expérience de la mobilité sociale: Plaidoyer pour une approche par le discours." *Bulletin de méthodologie sociologique* 112 (October 2011): 43–62. https://www.jstor.org/stable/23891865.

———. "Mobilité sociale et explications de la réussite en France, aux États-Unis et en Inde." *Sociologie* 3, no. 1 (2012): 39–59.

NDiaye, Marie. *Hilda.* Paris: Minuit, 1999.

———. *La Cheffe: Roman d'une cuisinière.* Paris: Gallimard, 2016.

———. *Ladivine.* Paris: Gallimard, 2013.

———. *La Vengeance m'appartient.* Paris: Gallimard, 2021.

———. *Mon cœur à l'étroit.* Paris: Gallimard, 2007.

Nizan, Paul. *Antoine Bloyé.* Paris: Grasset, 1933.

Noguez, Dominique. *Houellebecq, en fait.* Paris: Fayard, 2003.

Noiriel, Gérard. *Penser avec, penser contre: Itinéraire d'un historien.* Paris: Belin, 2003.

Nord, Philip G. *Paris Shopkeepers and the Politics of Resentment.* Princeton, NJ: Princeton University Press, 1986.

Novak-Lechevalier, Agathe. "Michel Houellebecq, la possibilité d'un dix-neuvième siècle." *Le Magasin du XIXe siècle* 1 (2011): 7–21.

Paine, Jonathan. *Selling the Story: Transaction and Narrative Value in Balzac, Dostoevsky, and Zola.* Cambridge, MA: Harvard University Press, 2019.

Paraschas, Sotirios. *Reappearing Characters in Nineteenth-Century French Literature: Authorship, Originality, and Intellectual Property.* London: Palgrave Macmillan, 2018.

Pasquali, Paul. *Héritocratie: Les Élites, les grandes écoles et les mésaventures du mérite, 1870–2020.* Paris: La Découverte, 2021.

———. *Passer les frontières sociales: Comment les filières d'élite entrouvrent leurs portes.* Paris: Fayard, 2014.

Perec, Georges. *L.G.: Une aventure des années soixante*. Paris: Seuil, 1992.
———. *Œuvres*. 2 vols. Paris: Gallimard, 2017.
Phillips, Caryl. *A Distant Shore*. New York: Knopf, 2003.
Pierron, Sylvie. "La 'langue Françoise' dans *À la recherche du temps perdu* de Marcel Proust." *Littérature* 116 (1999): 47–58. https://doi.org/10.3406/litt.1999.1644.
Piketty, Thomas. *Capital et Idéologie*. Paris: Seuil, 2019.
———. *Le Capital au XXIe siècle*. Paris: Seuil, 2013.
Pinçonnat, Crystel, Thomas Serrier, and Régis Tettamanzi. *Échos picaresques dans le roman du XXe siècle*. Neuilly: Atlande, 2003.
Pommier, Jean. "Naissance d'un héros: Rastignac." *Revue d'histoire littéraire de la France* 50, no. 2 (1950): 192–209. https://www.jstor.org/stable/40520816.
Pourchet, Maria. *Feu*. Paris: Fayard, 2021.
Preciado, Paul B. *Je suis un monstre qui vous parle: Rapport pour une académie de psychanalystes*. Paris: Grasset, 2020.
Prendergast, Christopher. *Paris and the Nineteenth Century*. Cambridge: Blackwell, 1992.
Prince, Gerald, and Debarati Sanyal. "Incipit: The Twentieth and Twenty-First Centuries (Mis)Reading the Nineteenth." *Nineteenth-Century French Studies* 46, no. 3/4 (Spring/Summer 2018): 199–224. https://www.jstor.org/stable/26539509.
Proulx, François. "'À nous deux,' Balzac: Barrès's *Les Déracinés*, and the Ghosts of *La Comédie humaine*." *Nineteenth-Century French Studies* 42, no. 3/4 (Spring/Summer 2014): 235–49. https://www.jstor.org/stable/44122762.
Proust, Marcel. *À la recherche du temps perdu*. Paris: Gallimard, 1999.
———. *Correspondance*. 21 vols. Paris: Plon, 1991.
Provencher, Denis. *Queer Maghrebi French: Language, Temporalities, Transfiliations*. Liverpool: Liverpool University Press, 2018.
Py, Olivier. *Les Parisiens*. Arles: Actes Sud, 2016.
Quintane, Nathalie. "Partage de l'insolence." *Nineteenth-Century French Studies* 49, no. 3 (2021): 415–26. https://doi:10.1353/ncf.2021.0017.
Rambaud, Patrick. *Emmanuel Le Magnifique: Chronique d'un règne*. Paris: Grasset, 2019.
Rancière, Jacques. *La Parole muette: Essai sur les contradictions de la littérature*. Paris: Hachette, 1998.
———. *Le Maître ignorant: Cinq leçons sur l'émancipation intellectuelle*. Paris: Fayard, 1987.
———. *Les Bords de la fiction*. Paris: Seuil, 2017.
Ravindranathan, Thangam. *Behold an Animal: Four Exorbitant Readings*. Evanston, IL: Northwestern University Press, 2020.
Redfield, Marc. *Phantom Formations: Aesthetic Ideology and the Bildungsroman*. Ithaca, NY: Cornell University Press, 1996.

———. *Theory at Yale: The Strange Case of Deconstruction in America*. New York: Fordham University Press, 2016.
Renoir, Jean, dir. *Diary of a Chambermaid*. 1946; Chicago: Olive Films, 2013.
Richard, Emmanuelle. *Désintégration*. Paris: Éditions de l'Olivier, 2018.
Riché, Pascal. "Alexandre Benalla est 'une espèce de Rastignac moderne.'" *France Info*, July 26, 2018.
Robbe-Grillet, Alain. *La Jalousie*. Paris: Minuit, 1957.
———. *Le Miroir qui revient*. Paris: Minuit, 1984.
———. *Pour un nouveau roman*. Paris: Minuit, 1963.
Robbins, Bruce. *The Servant's Hand: English Fiction from Below*. Durham, NC: Duke University Press, 1993.
———. *Upward Mobility and the Common Good: Toward a Literary History of the Welfare State*. Princeton, NJ: Princeton University Press, 2007.
Rosanvallon, Pierre. *Le Peuple introuvable: Histoire de la représentation démocratique en France*. Paris: Gallimard, 1998.
Ross, Kristin. *Fast Cars, Clean Bodies: Decolonization and the Reordering of French Culture*. Cambridge, MA: MIT Press, 1995.
———. "Polar Chaos." *Nineteenth-Century French Studies* 49, no. 3 (2021): 218–29.
Rushdie, Salman. *Imaginary Homelands: Essays and Criticism, 1981–1991*. London: Granta, 1991.
Sagnes, Guy. "Tentations balzaciennes dans le manuscrit de 'L'Éducation sentimentale.'" *L'Année balzacienne* 2 (1981): 53–64.
Saint-Gelais, Richard. *Fictions transfuges: La Transfictionnalité et ses enjeux*. Paris: Seuil, 2011.
Sallenave, Danièle. *Jojo, le Gilet jaune*. Paris: Gallimard, 2019.
Sand, George. *Romans*. 2 vols. Paris: Gallimard, 2019.
Sapiro, Gisèle, ed. *Dictionnaire international Bourdieu*. Paris: CNRS éditions, 2020.
Sarraute, Nathalie. *L'Ère du soupçon: Essais sur le roman*. Paris: Gallimard, 1956.
Sartre, Jean-Paul. *Saint Genet, comédien et martyr*. Paris: Gallimard, 1952.
———. *Situations*. Vol. 1. Paris: Gallimard, 1947.
———. *Situations*. Vol. 4. Paris: Gallimard, 1964.
Sasson, Sarah. *Longing to Belong: The Parvenu in Nineteenth-Century French and German Literature*. New York: Palgrave Macmillan, 2012.
Sayad, Abdelmalek. *L'Immigration, ou Les Paradoxes de l'altérité*. Vol. 1, *L'Illusion du provisoire*. Paris: Raisons d'agir, 2006.
Schaal, Michèle. "Whatever Became of 'Génération Mitterrand'? Virginie Despentes's *Vernon Subutex*." *French Review* 90, no. 3 (2017): 86–99.
Schor, Naomi. *Reading in Detail: Aesthetics and the Feminine*. New York: Methuen, 1987.
Schwartz, Alexandra. "To Exist in the Eyes of Others: An Interview with the Novelist Édouard Louis on the Gilets Jaunes Movement." *New Yorker*, December 14, 2018.

Sebbar, Leïla. *Métro: Instantanés*. Monaco: Rocher, 2007.
Sedira, Samira. *L'Odeur des planches*. Arles: Rouergue, 2013.
Segaunes, Nathalie. "'Qui a tué mon père,' d'Edouard Louis: Le Brûlot qui fait cogiter l'Élysée." *L'Opinion*, June 6, 2018.
Senior, Jennifer. "'The End of Eddy' Captures a Savage Childhood and a Global Movement." *New York Times*, May 17, 2017.
Senni, Aziz, and Jean-Marc Pitte. *L'Ascenseur social est en panne, j'ai pris l'escalier!* Paris: Archipel, 2005.
Shaviro, Daniel. *Literature and Inequality: Nine Perspectives from the Napoleonic Era through the First Gilded Age*. New York: Anthem Press, 2020.
Shea, Louisa. "Exit Voltaire, Enter Marivaux: Abdellatif Kechiche on the Legacy of the Enlightenment." *French Review* 85, no. 6 (May 2012): 1136–48.
Shiller, Robert. *Narrative Economics: How Stories Go Viral and Drive Major Economic Events*. Princeton, NJ: Princeton University Press, 2019.
Sijie, Dai. *Balzac et la petite tailleuse chinoise*. Paris: Gallimard, 2000.
Slaoui, Nesrine. *Illégitimes*. Paris: Fayard, 2021.
Slimani, Leïla. *Chanson douce*. Paris: Gallimard, 2016.
Smith, Sidonie, and Julia Watson, eds. *De/colonizing the Subject: The Politics of Gender in Women's Autobiography*. Minneapolis: University of Minnesota Press, 1992.
Smith, Timothy B. *France in Crisis: Welfare, Inequality, and Globalization since 1980*. Cambridge, MA: Cambridge University Press, 2004.
Somers, Erin. "Künstlermania." *Gawker*, April 8, 2022.
Sprinker, Michael. *History and Ideology in Proust: "À la recherche du temps perdu" and the Third French Republic*. Cambridge: Cambridge University Press, 1994.
Stendhal. *Œuvres intimes*. Paris: Gallimard, 1955.
———. *Œuvres romanesques complètes*. Vol. 1. Paris: Gallimard, 2005.
Sy, Hapsatou. *Partie de rien*. Paris: Dunod, 2017.
Taïa, Abdellah. *L'Armée du salut*. Paris: Seuil, 2006.
———. *La Vie lente*. Paris: Seuil, 2019.
Tasma, Alain, dir. *Rastignac ou les ambitieux*. Paris: France Télévision, 2001.
Tessé, Jean-Philippe. "Chiens battus." *Les Cahiers du cinéma*, no. 714 (September 2015): 14–16.
Thérenty, Marie-Ève. "'Débusquer la part la plus nocturne et la plus quotidienne de l'existence.' Du roman réaliste à *Raconter la vie*." *Autour de Vallès* 48 (2018): 179–95.
Thomas, Chantal. *Les Adieux à la reine*. Paris: Seuil, 2002.
Thomas, Lyn. *Annie Ernaux: An Introduction to the Writer and Her Audience*. Oxford: Berg, 1999.
Thumerel, Fabrice, ed. *Annie Ernaux, une œuvre de l'entre-deux*. Arras: Artois Presses Université, 2004.
Todd, Emmanuel. *Les Luttes de classes en France au XXIe siècle*. Paris: Seuil, 2020.

Triaire, Sylvie, Jean-Pierre Bertrand, and Benoît Denis, eds. *Sociologie de la littérature: La Question de l'illégitime*. Montpellier: Presses Universitaires de la Méditerranée, 2002.
Valance, Georges. *Thiers: Bourgeois et révolutionnaire*. Paris: Flammarion, 2007.
Vallès, Jules. *Œuvres*. Vol. 1. Paris: Gallimard, 1975.
———. *Œuvres*. Vol. 2. Paris: Gallimard, 1990.
Vance, James David. *Hillbilly Elegy: A Memoir of a Family and Culture in Crisis*. New York: Harper, 2016.
Viala, Alain. "Stylistique et sociologie: Classe de postures." *Revue belge de philologie et d'histoire* 71, no. 3 (1993): 615–24. https://doi.org/10.3406/rbph.1993.3893.
Vincent, Catherine. "Édouard Louis: 'Trump et le FN sont le produit de l'exclusion.'" *Le Monde*, December 11, 2016.
Voltaire. *Lettres philosophiques*. Paris: Garnier-Flammarion, 1964.
Wampole, Christy. *Degenerative Realism: Novel and Nation in Twenty-First-Century France*. New York: Columbia University Press, 2020.
Westover, Tara. *Educated: A Memoir*. New York: Random House, 2018.
Willging, Jennifer. *Telling Anxiety: Anxious Narration in the Work of Marguerite Duras, Annie Ernaux, Nathalie Sarraute, and Anne Hébert*. Toronto: University of Toronto Press, 2007.
Williams, Raymond. *Border Country*. Cardigan: Parthian Books, 2010.
Wittig, Monique. *The Straight Mind, and Other Essays*. Boston: Beacon Press, 1992.
Wolfe, Tom. "Stalking the Billion-Footed Beast: A Literary Manifesto for the New Social Novel." *Harper's Magazine*, November 1989.
Woloch, Alex. *The One vs. The Many: Minor Characters and the Space of the Protagonist in the Novel*. Princeton, NJ: Princeton University Press, 2003.
Wright, Richard. *Le Transfuge*. Translated by Guy de Montlaur. Paris: Gallimard, 1955.
Yee, Jennifer. *The Colonial Comedy: Imperialism in the French Realist Novel*. New York: Oxford University Press, 2016.
Zerofsky, Elisabeth. "'I Always Write with a Sense of Shame': How Édouard Louis, a Working-Class Gay Man from the Provinces, Became France's Latest Literary Sensation—And Its Political Conscience." *New York Times Magazine*, March 31, 2020.
Zink, Michel, ed. *L'Œuvre et son ombre: Que peut la littérature secondaire?* Paris: Fallois, 2002.
Zola, Émile. *Les Rougon-Macquart*. 5 vols. Paris: Gallimard, 1960–67.
———. *Thérèse Raquin*. Paris: Gallimard, 2001.

# Index

Page numbers in italics refer to figures.

actors and actresses: as domestics, 274n75; downward mobility of, 46; as lower class by "playing the maid," 46; socially mobile, 146; upward mobility of, 46; wealthy social class of, 46
Adams, Lorraine, 211–12
*Aden Arabie* (Nizan), 74
Adorno, Theodor, 3
*Adventure Capital* (Kleinman), 189, 204
Aït-Taleb, Hamid. *See* Le Clerc, Xavier.
*À la recherche du temps perdu* (*In Search of Lost Time*) (Proust), 130, 134, 197–200, 205–6, 272n41
Albaret, Céleste, 134, 144, 274n87
*Albertine disparue* (*Albertine Gone*) (Proust), 197, 200
Algalarrondo, Hervé, 62
Alger, Horatio, 97
allegory, 98, 216
Alvarez, Julia, 186–87
ambition, 21, 26; and anguish, 92; of climbers, 5; and determination, 68; of maids, 131; metaphors for, 80; and muddy parvenants, 80–82, 87–88; and nonreproduction, 75; of opportunists, 61; provides "dominant dynamic of plot," 81–82; and Rastignac, 49–77, 87, 91–92, 198, 224, 229–30, 259n58; and travel class, 193, 207–9
ambivalence, 3, 15, 26, 45, 128, 164
*American Dirt* (Cummins), 186–87, 196, 281n5
American Dream, 5, 186
American Talent Initiative, 26
*Amour impossible, Un* (*Impossible Love, An*) (Angot), 47, 173–74, 177–79, 184, 195
anadiplosis, and chiasmus, 54
anarchists, 74, 262n134
*Anéantir* (*Annihilate*) (Houellebecq), 223
Angot, Christine: autobiographies, 173; and bourgeois, 174; and class distance, 184; doors in, 47, 156, 173–79, 181, 184; editorial strategy in, 195; and Ernaux, 178–79, 202, 280n100; father (Pierre Angot), 31, 47, 173–74, 177–78, 184, 195; and Houellebecq, 13; and imperfect verb tense, 47, 173–79, 200; and incest, 47, 173–74, 178, 184, 279n94; and interclass, 47; and kinship, 47; and Louis, 181;

Angot, Christine (*continued*)
mother (Rachel Schwartz), 47, 173–74, 178, 184, 195; name change, 31–32; parents, 173–74; and performative texts, 175–76; poetics of, 195; and romance, 47; sexual abuse by father, 47, 173–74, 195; sexuality as social reality in, 13; shame in, 280n100; and social class, 109, 173; and social mobility, 174–75, 178, 202; and social trajectory, 195; and sociology, 13; and swinging door as social mobility, 184; tangible doors in, 156; and texts as performative, 175–76; and trains, 200, 204–6; and trance of transclass, 109; and transclass, 47, 195, 200; and transrace, 47; and travel class, 195, 200; as underclass, 179; and upward mobility, 7; working-class roots, 32
*Années, Les* (*Years, The*) (Ernaux), 22–23, 134, 181, 203, 272n38
"Annie Ernaux, une politique de la forme" (Meizoz essay), 18, 279n77
*Annihilate* (*Anéantir*) (Houellebecq), 223
antagonism, 3–4, 8, 11, 26
antiformalism, 18
*Antoine Bloyé* (Nizan), 206–7
antonomasia (to rename), 49, 256n1
apprenant, parvenant as, 38
aristocracy: and equality, 198; and name changes, 32; and race, 111; and upward mobility, 174
*Armée du salut* (*Salvation Army, The*) (Taïa), 204–5, 211
*Armoires vides, Les* (*Empty Cupboards, The*) (Ernaux), 21, 73, 93, 111–16, 166, 202, 227–28, 262n132
arrival, narratives of, 35, 255n142
arrivisme, 45, 49, 59
arrivistes, 5, 32, 49–53, 192–93; Rastignac as, 43
arrogance, of transfuges, 121

art: and form(s), 40; hybrid forms of, 28; and life, 28; and social class, 200; and social mobility, 242
*As We Exist* (*Comme nous existons*) (Harchi), 47, 181–84
*Atelier noir, L'* (*Dark Workshop, The*) (Ernaux diary), 116, 171–72, 181
Aubenas, Florence: and history, 16; and lower class, 153; on precarity and recession, 142; and social demotion, voluntary, 46, 143–44
*Au Bonheur des dames* (*The Ladies' Delight* or *The Ladies' Paradise*) (Zola), 73, 88, 133, 191, 227, 230–32
audience: and characters, 145; and servants, 46
Auerbach, Erich, 58, 257–58n16, 270n9
Austen, Jane, 9, 65–66, 87–88; and Balzac, 70
authenticity: and purity, 81; and textuality, 21
authors: bourgeoisie, 179; class mobility of, 21, 44; class struggle of, 8; and contemporary French literary scene, 173; and critical skills, 38; as domestics, 274n75; as lower class, 46, 153; marginalized, 19–20; and mud (literary), 82; multiclass, 2; and narrators, 28, 30, 36; "outsider," 19; parvenu/parvenant, 6, 30, 45, 104, 124; and performance, 243; and political unconscious, 8; postcolonial francophone, 19–20; and readers, 13; as readers, 1–2; realist, 5, 99, 218; and recognition, 243; servant and writer, compared, 273n65; and social affiliation, 41; and social class, 38; and social climbing, 242; and social mobility, 1–2, 8, 12, 14, 17–18, 23, 63, 78–79, 107–9, 117, 153, 155, 237, 242; and social skills, 38; social topics in news, and comments on, 154; upwardly mobile, 2; and upward mobility, 2

autobiographical dictionaries, 50
autobiographical novels, 28, 71, 78, 97, 101, 122, 139, 144, 192
autobiographies, 4–5, 11–13, 15, 22, 27–30, 77, 101, 113–14, 181, 210–11, 230, 234, 241–42; and autobiographical narratives, 21, 30, 75, 113, 116, 122, 162, 210, 241; and autofiction, 5, 173, 210; and character study, 150; and essays, 63; intellectual, 30; and nonfiction, 7, 210; and "out-law genre," 30; social, 11, 21, 30; and social sciences, 12; and social world, 22; and sociology, 12–13; of success, 48; upward mobility in, 7, 210. *See also* memoirs
autodidacts, 32
*Autofictif père et fils, L'* (*Autofictional Father and Son, The*) (Chevillard), 50
autofiction, and autobiographies, 5, 173, 210
autonomy, 9, 98, 106, 160, 170
"auto-socio-biography," 22–23, 32, 75
*Autre Fille, L'* (Ernaux), epistolary format in, 278n63
avant-garde, 213
Azzeddine, Saphia, 273n70

Bachelard, Gaston, 80
*Bachelier, Le* (*High School Graduate, The*) (Vallès), 89–92, 100, 262n134, 265n62
*Bad Dream, A* (*Un Mauvais rêve*) (Bernanos), 52
Baglin, Claire, 239–40
Bailly, Jean-Christophe, 285n12
Bakhtin, Mikhail: "hybrid construction" of voices, 279n77; and Moretti, 131
Balbec, France (fictional town): and Barthes, 48; church in, 199; and class, 198; hotel lift in, 198; omnibus in, 198; trains in, 48, 197–200
Baldwin, James, 28

Balzac, Honoré de, 5–12, 17, 43–44, 48–51, 76, 214, 224, 241, 259n63, 278n63; and allegory, 216; and *ambitieux*, 51; and Austen, 70; biography of, 5; and Bourdieu, 258n47; as bourgeoisie, 217; on bric-à-brac, 257n9; characters of, 64, 259n64; characters of, recurring, 49, 65; and class mobility, 77; comeback of, 50, 210; and dandies, 264n37; dandyism and distinction, 24; and Deck, 217; and Despentes, 287–88n83; and doors, 155; and Dostoevsky, 266n87, 285n18; and economic criticism, 9–11, 260n92; and Ernaux, 70–71, 73, 179; father (Bernard-François Balssa), 31–32; and Flaubert, 53, 72, 185; and heroes, 257–58n16; heterogeneous narrative registers, 170; and horizontalization, 198; and Houellebecq, 220, 230; and household workers, 127; literal and metaphorical uses of ductile materials, 44; *medium-light*, 217–23; and mud (literary), 78, 82–84, 88–93, 96–100; name change, 31–32; and NDiaye, 72; and New Novels, 78, 96, 214–17; and novels of manners, 72; opportunists of, 61; as painter of society, 51; *parvenir* in works of, 97; poetics of, 51, 219; and politics, 60; and Proust, 11–12, 51; and -rama suffix, 264n21; Rastignac invented by, in 1830s, 43; reading of and upward mobility, 261n117; as realist, 11; recurring characters, 49, 65; rhetorical strategy, 71; and Romanesque, 210; and roman numerals, 232; and sentimental novels, 73; and social class, 72; social climbers, 48, 91–92; and social demotion, 215; and social mobility, 70–75, 179; and sociology, 12, 15; and Stendhal, 9–10, 44, 73, 98; and syntactic parallelism, 84;

Balzac, Honoré de (*continued*)
and travel class, 197–99; upward mobility and reading of, 261n117; and urban itinerary and social trajectory, 86–87; and urban settings, 77; and Vallès, 78, 88–92, 97–100; and Zola, 12
*Balzac et la petite tailleuse chinoise* (*Balzac and the Little Chinese Seamstress*) (Sijie), 74–75
*Balzac's Lives* (Brooks), 49
Barrès, Maurice, 43, 50, 74–75, 262n134
*Barrière et le Niveau, La* (*Barrier and the Level, The*) (Goblot), 185–86
Barthes, Roland, 16–19, 21; and blank writing, 46, 167; and doors, 167; and Ernaux, 46; and muddy parvenants, 78; and New Novels, 78; on Rastignac, 52; and trains, 48; and travel class, 199–200
*Battles and Metamorphoses of a Woman* (*Combats et métamorphoses d'une femme*) (Louis), 136, 163.
Baudelaire, Charles, 64, 224, 264n20; and mud (literary), 263–64n13
Baudu, Denise (fictional character), 73, 88, 191, 227, 230
"Beaches and Ports" (Freed-Thall and Cadieu, eds.), 284n9
Beaubatie, Emmanuel, 34
Beaumarchais, Pierre, 127
Beaumont, Madame Leprince de, 146
*beau ténébreux, Un* (*Beautiful Dark One, A*) (Gracq), 76
Beauvoir, Simone de, 22, 43, 60, 161–62; author's name in upward mobility, and power of, 258n26; and parallelism, 124
Bécassine (fictional character), 164–65, 277n43
Beckett, Samuel, 213
*Bel-Ami* (Maupassant), 6–7, 52, 122, 190, 223–24, 271n24, 281n16
Belattar, Yassine, 54

Belenky, Masha, 188
Belgrand, Alexandre (fictional character), 238–39
Bell, David, 85
Bellanger, Aurélien, 41, 43, 104–5, 219–20; and Houellebecq, 238; realist novels of, 220; transclass character of, 289n8; and upward mobility, 239
Bellegueule, Eddy (fictional character), 11, 27, 30–31, 62, 64, 94–96, 105, 117, 119, 121, 123, 156, 160–63, 194
Bellos, David, 80
*Belly of the Atlantic, The* (*Ventre de l'Atlantique, Le*) (Diome), 155
Belmont, Georges, 144
*Beloved* (Morrison), 28
Benalla, Alexandre, 62
Benjamin, Walter, 197
Benlaala, Omar, 162
Bensmaïa, Réda, 19–20
bequests, 214–15, 285n16. *See also* inheritance
Bergounioux, Pierre, 15
Berlant, Lauren, 47–48, 192, 208–9, 274n91
Bernanos, Georges, 52, 71
Besson, Philippe, 61–62
Best, Stephen, 228–29
*Bête humaine, La* (*Human Beast, The*) (Zola), 55, 189–90, 209, 281n4
betrayal, 4; and social mobility, 32; and transfuge, 33, 35
*Between the Walls* (*Entre les murs*) (Cantet), 127
*Beyond Return* (Hollister), 17
Bhabha, Homi, 28
Bianchon, Horace (fictional character), 51, 72, 86
*Big Boss, Son of a Worker* (*Grand patron, fils d'ouvrier*) (Naudet), 242
bildungsroman, 12, 18, 35–36, 52–53, 56–57, 61–62, 75–77, 108–9, 121–22, 131, 173, 210–12, 233, 238, 241–42; autobiographical, 192; and class

Index  313

mobility, 5; and contemporary social novels, 209; corporeal, 108–9; death of, 241; founding, 271n20; and *Künstlerroman*, 5, 41, 43, 210, 241; and mud (literary), 78; and muddy parvenants, 77–81, 88–89, 93; and novels, 230–35; and picaresque novels, 48, 230–35; and social climbing, 122; and social immobility, 7; and social trajectories, 9; as textbook, 75; and travel class, 186–87, 192, 195–96, 198, 201, 204–9, 211; and upward mobility, 7
*Birthday* (Tanning), 179–82, *180*
black bodies, 104–5
Black Vests (Gilets noirs), 104
body. *See* embodiment
*Body of Others, The (Corps des autres, Le)* (Jablonka), 16
Boltanski, Luc, 117
Bond, James, 46
*Bonheur des dames, Au (Ladies' Delight, The,* or *Ladies' Paradise, The)* (Zola), 73, 88, 133, 191, 227, 230–32
*Bonnes, Les (Maids, The)* (Genet), 130–31, 137, 142, 145
Bordeaux: advertising branch in, 207; as harbor city, 210–11; restaurant in, 139; as slave-trading port, 285n11; train station, 202, 207, 235
*Border Country* (Williams), 192, 281n24
*Bords de la fiction, Les (Edges of Fiction, The)* (Rancière), 155, 276n5
botanical middle, 288n99
Bourdieu, Pierre, 21, 25–26, 30, 46–47, 58, 181, 214, 278n60, 281n23; "autosocio-biography" of, 32; and Balzac, 258n47; body in, 269n59; and class mobility, 11; "come back," 251n42; death of, 12; and Éribon, 11–12, 76–77, 109; and Ernaux, 11–13, 23, 26, 36, 76–77, 115, 123, 164, 251n41, 255n139, 263n149, 278n60; and forms, 252n61; and Hoggart, 24; and Louis, 11–12, 76–77, 115; and Memmi, 198, 269n59; parvenus' "discordance" in, 269n59; "porte-à-faux" in, 276n4; and Proust, 251n44; and Rastignac, 263n149; on Rastignacian ambition, 77; and social climbing, 137; and social mobility, 12, 23–24, 162; and sociology, 13–14, 23–24; and Spinoza, 75, 137; as transfuge, 164; and travel class, 202; and upward mobility, 11, 198; and Zola, 12
*Bourdieu International Dictionary (Dictionnaire international Bourdieu)*, 11
bourgeoisie, 5, 21, 75, 255n146; authors, 179; Balzac as, 217; bodily knowledge of, 120; city-dwellers, 115; as commuter (bus), 203–4; as constituted or centered subject, 170; courting, 243; and cultivated world, 166; and cultivé, 166; cultural capital of, 237; "destiny," 239; and domestic workers, 136; and doors, 165–66, 173–75; entry into, 31, 36, 166, 202, 206; feminine bodies of intellectual, 119, 121; hatred of, 89; and homosexuality, 119–20; and intellectual elite, 175; living among, 276n2; and maids/servants, 129–30, 141, 153; New Novels as, 217; nineteenth-century, 207; outdated idea of, 96; and *petit commerçant* upbringing, 165–66; petty, 21, 108, 240; from poverty to, 21; and servants, 141; and social ladder, 185–86; and social mobility, 150; and social realization, on train, 201; *Sociological Study of Modern French*, 185–86; and tearing of conscience, 167; tradesman, 54; and travel class, 187; as upstart class, 136; upward mobility that leads to, 207; women, 129, 243; and working class, 3, 36, 115, 134, 149–50, 276n2

Bovary, Emma (fictional character), 51, 71–72
Brizé, Stéphane, 148
Brontë, Charlotte, 21
Brooks, Peter, 49, 81, 198
Brudner Memorial Prize, James Robert, 254n118
Buckley, Jerome Hamilton, 5
Bui, Véronique, 53
Buñuel, Luis, 193
Burton, Charles, 192
buskins, 90–91
Butler, Judith, 75–76

Cagnati, Inès, 93
Calle, Sophie, 46, 142–44, 153
*Cambridge Companion to Balzac* (Jourdan), 76
Camus, Albert, 75, 224; and bourgeoisie, 167; and domestic workers, 153; and Éribon, 273n69; and Ernaux, 273n71; mother as house cleaner/maid, 139–42, 153; and perfect tense, 179; postcolonial rewrite of, 163; and school and service, intersection of, 139–40; as transclass writer, 60; and upper class, 45, 153
Cantet, Laurent, 47–48, 127, 192–93, 208–9
*Capitaine Fracasse* (Gautier), 55
capital: and class, 17; cultural, 44, 89, 98, 161, 178, 237; as fictitious, 20; formal logic of, 17; in realism, 17
*Capital and Ideology* (*Capital et idéologie*) (Piketty), 67
*Capital au XXIe siècle, Le* (*Capital in the Twenty-First Century*) (Piketty), 2–3, 10, 43, 57, 65–66
capitalism: and cynicism, 51; and economic liberalism, 11; fictitiousness of, 17; late, 11, 231; management in late- era, 209; and mud (literary), 100; precarity of, 231
Carbonnier, Clément, 127, 274n72

careerists, 32
caretakers. *See* domestics
Carrère, Emmanuel, 142, 148
*Carte et le Territoire, La* (*Map and the Territory, The*) (Houellebecq), 219, 221, 224
causality, 36–37, 117, 120
Center for American Progress, 67
*Cents and Sensibility* (Morson and Schapiro), 9–10, 250n36
*Ce qu'ils disent ou rien* (*What They Say or Nothing*) (Ernaux), 70, 279n77
*Ce qu'ils vivent, ce qu'ils écrivent* (*What They Live, What They Write*) (Lahire), 13–14
Certeau, Michel de, 24, 48, 199
*César Birotteau* (Balzac), 84
Chabrol, Claude, 216
chambermaids. *See* maids
Chamoiseau, Patrick, 103
Chandernagor, Françoise, 259n64
*Changer* (*Change*) (Louis), 62, 100–101, 122–23, 157, 194, 256n164
*Chanson douce* (*Perfect Nanny, The*, or *Lullaby*) (Slimani), 126
*Character from a Novel, A* (*Personnage de roman, Un*) (Besson), 61
characterization, 52, 60, 87, 214, 221, 230
characters: and aesthetic disorientation, 25; afterlives in literature and society, 75; and audience, 145; classical, 56; of class mobility, 20, 31–41, 237; in contemporary French literature, 257n12; decontextualization of, 98; demoted, 238; downgraded, 215; fourth wall, capacity to break, 257n12; gender of, 230; immobilization of, 48, 209–35; and literary reminiscences, 77; and name-dropping, 76; names as book titles, 71; precarious, 48, 215–16; precarity of, after New Novels, 211–17; reading books, 275n98; and real-

life persons, permeability between, 51; recurring, 49, 52, 65, 230–31; and romantic realism, 100; as "sealed social vessels," micro and macro, 205–6; sexuality of, 283n68; shape-shifting, 53; and social demotion, 44–45; and social mobility, 6, 37, 44, 69, 76, 80–82, 137, 139, 153, 200, 211, 220, 237, 242–43; sociological, 32, 255n138; of twenty-first-century France, 230–31; and undecidability, 215–16; upward mobility of, 31, 46, 215–16; wealthy, 65–66, 146. *See also* domestics; heroes; maids; parvenants; protagonists; servants; *and specific characters*

*Chartreuse de Parme, La* (*Charterhouse of Parma, The*) (Stendhal), 155

Chatiliez, Étienne, 120

*Cheffe, La* (*Cheffe, The*) (NDiaye), 139, 242

Chevillard, Éric, 50, 53

chiasmus: and anadiplosis, 54; and immobilization, 220–21; and threshold, 84; trajectories, 113

*Chiffonniers de Paris, Les* (*Rag-Pickers of Paris, The*) (Compagnon), 80, 92–93, 263n13

*Child, The* (*Enfant, L'*) (Vallès), 89–91, 100

cholera pandemic (1832), 79

*Choses, Les* (*Things*) (Perec), 207, 239–40

*Chouans, Les* (*Chouans, The*) (Balzac), 85

Choukri, Mohamed, 205

cinema, and literature, 41, 45, 121, 126, 150–51, 205. *See also* film

*Cinq mains coupées* (*Five Severed Hands*) (Divry), 104

class, 8, 15, 211; affiliations, 203; borders, 174; boundaries, 57, 242; ceiling, 185, 280n1; "closet," 162; distance, 47, 184, 201; division, 185; and family culture, 28; and former French empire, 189; and gender, 115–17; heritage, 47, 242; inclusiveness, 188; inter-, 47, 229; issues, 8–9, 72; and lifestyle, 222; past, 188; and places, 193; precarity of, 209; "professional-managerial," 237; and race, 38, 45–46, 111, 137–38, 175, 271n29; and relatives, 188; rigidity of, 174, 209; and social ladder, 113; and strata, 186; and upward mobility, 7, 32. *See also* class mobility; social classes; *and specific classes*

classism, 30, 120, 171, 174, 181, 189

class mobility, 13, 15, 47, 211, 253n100, 264n20; and apology for literature, 24; characters of, 20, 31–41; and collectivity, 4; conflicted embodiment of, 101; contemporary, 5, 23, 35, 264n20; corporeal tension at core of, 45; decline of, 4; domestic, 212; and doors, 156, 164, 169, 172, 181; and form, 154; and grammar of advancement, 199; and instability, 197; lack of, 102; landmark narrative of, 72; leading literary voices of, 11–12; and literature, 4–5, 24, 237, 242, 264n20; and muddy parvenants, 78; and names/naming, 31–32; narratives of, as pocket-size panorama of society, 4; and parvenu, 35; poetics of, 23; and political moments, 4; representation of, 50; shapeshifting signifier of, train as, 196; and social climbing, 12, 35–36; and social ladder, 47; and social mobility, 12, 14, 242, 253n100; spatial imagery to describe, 47; successful stories of, 209; and trans trajectories, 34; and travel class, 185, 191; and universalism, 4; unmooring of, 117; unwanted, 47; and upward mobility, 31; and vocabulary, 112. *See also* social mobility; upward mobility

class struggle, 2–4, 8, 48, 190, 243
*Class Struggles in France in the Twenty-First Century, The* (*Luttes de classes en France au XXIe siècle, Les*) (Todd), 2–3
cleaners and cleaning ladies. *See* domestics
*Coal Train in the Rhondda* (Burton painting), 192
coastal cities, 205, 211–13, 284–85nn11–12; and slavery, 284–85n11. *See also* harbor cities; seaside
coastal etymologies, and social vulnerability, 212–13
*cœur simple, Un* (*Simple Heart, A*) (Flaubert), 128–29
Cohen, Margaret, 7, 43, 52, 72–73, 198
collectivity: and class mobility, 4; through individual trajectories, 167
colonialism, 162–63, 266n87, 267n14. *See also* decolonization; postcolonialism
*Combats et métamorphoses d'une femme* (*Battles and Metamorphoses of a Woman*) (Louis), 136, 163
*Comédie humaine, La* (*Human Comedy, The*) (Balzac), 49–52, 54, 58, 60–61, 64, 89, 92, 99, 197, 207, 219, 230, 232, 259n64
coming-of-age stories, 4, 29, 63, 241; books in, importance of, 261n117
*Comme nous existons* (*As We Exist*) (Harchi), 47, 181–84
Communism, 34
commuters, 47, 188, 196–97, 209
Compagnon, Antoine, 80, 92–93, 230, 263n13
compartmentalization, 47, 111, 189
Condé, Maryse, 273n66; on maids, 132–33, 137–40, 142; and NDiaye, 139; and upper class, 153; and upward class/mobility, 7, 45, 138
*Condition pavillonnaire, La* (*Suburban Condition, The*, or *Madame Bovary of the Suburbs*) (Divry), 104, 240–41
Congo, 256n167
*Connemara* (Mathieu), 238
consciousness, 171; class, 3; collective, 14; self-, 2, 213
constructivism, and essentialism, 45
consumerism: and class, 37, 48, 224, 229; and cleanliness, 78; and harbor city wanderer, 212–13; and leisure, 228; postwar, 209; and social trajectory, 229; and supermarkets, 37, 48; and women, 230; and writing, 228
"Contagion des Rastignac, La" ("Contagion of Rastignacs, The") (Barrès article), 73–74
contemporary French literature, 2, 5–7, 9, 17, 19, 23, 30, 70–75, 105, 133, 173, 237, 242–43, 257n12
contextualization, 18, 25–26; of social tropes, 78–79; and textuality, 12. *See also* decontextualization
contradictions, 122, 165; of parvenant writers, 45; social, 8; and wisdom, 269n74
Corbin, Alain, 44, 80, 92–93
Cormery, Jacques (fictional character), 139–40, 153
coronavirus pandemic, and "Jean Valjean tax" on patrimony, 275n103
*Corps des autres, Le* (*Body of Others, The*) (Jablonka), 16
Courant, Pierre, 217
COVID-19 pandemic, 102
Coward, David, 224
*Crime and Punishment* (Dostoevsky), 55, 97
cross class, 37; body, 105; and class mobility, 31; conversations, 237; and education and schooling, 237; encounters, 47; and homosexuality, 45; interactions, 189; marriage arrangements, 282n35; and naming/renaming, 31–32; romance, 19;

trajectories, 2, 21, 28–29, 31, 45; and transportation, 47; and travel class, 189–90
*Crossing Social Frontiers* (*Passer les frontières sociales*) (Pasquali), 14, 280n1
*Cruel Optimism* (Berlant), 192, 208
Cruickshank, Ruth, 218
cubism, 34
cultural capital: acquisition of, 44, 98, 178; of bourgeoisie, 237; and complicity, 161; and literary canon formation, 237; of "old bourgeoisie," 237; of poet, 89; and working class, 237
*Cultural Capital* (Guillory), 237
cultural-political left, 63
cultural studies, 19, 192; and forms, 14; and sociology, 14
culture: and class, 28; and education, 71, 77, 97; and social mobility, 75–77; "somatic," of social group, 117; and upward mobility, 97
Cummins, Jeannine, 186–87, 281n5
*Curée, La* (*Mad Rush, The*) (Zola), 54–55, 223–24

dandies and dandyism, 264n37; and distinction of Balzac, 24; and harbor city wanderer, 212–13; postmodern nihilo-, 16
Danius, Sara, 206
*Dark Workshop, The* (*Atelier noir, L'*) (Ernaux), 116, 171–72, 181
Dati, Rachida, 60
Deck, Julia, 211–17, 234, 238, 284n6, 284–85nn10–13; and Balzac, 217; and formalism, 48; and social climbing, 217; and social immobility, 7
*déclassement*, 12; and pedagogical reforms in 1880s and 1890s, 262n134
decolonization, 78. *See also* colonialism
deconstruction, 20, 25, 106, 117

decontextualization, 12, 26; of characters, 98; and mobility, 63; and mud (literary), 44, 92, 98; of Rastignac, 69; and upward movement, 38–40. *See also* contextualization
defectors: class, 28–29, 80; transfuges as, 34
*Degenerative Realism* (Wampole), 210, 220
*Degré zéro de l'écriture, Le* (*Degree Zero of Writing, The*) (Barthes), 167
Deleuze, Gilles, 200
Delphy, Christine, 132
Delsaux, Aurélien, 104
de Man, Paul, 16–17, 25
demotion, social. *See* social demotion
Denis, Claire, 279n83
Déon, Michel, 43, 63
departure, narratives of, 35, 117, 242, 255n142
*Déracinés, Les* (*Uprooted Ones, The*) (Barrès), 74
Derrida, Jacques, 16–17, 25
*Désaxés, Les* (*Unbalanced Ones, The*) (Angot), 176
deserters: social climbers as, 3; transfuges as, 35
*Désintégration* (*Disintegration*) (Richard), 239
*Désorientale* (Djavadi), as migration novel, 282n54
Despentes, Virginie, 43, 48, 59, 76, 211, 230–35, 238; and Balzac, 230, 287–88n83; and social immobility, 7; and social mobility, 231
Desplechin, Arnaud, 146
determinism, 88, 94, 114, 120, 140, 155, 165, 183, 196, 218, 228, 239–40; and emancipation, 88, 140
detour, and digression, 277n32
*Deuxième Sexe, Le* (*Second Sex, The*) (Beauvoir), 124
*Deux jeunesses françaises* (*Two French Youths*) (Algalarrondo), 62

Diallo, Nafissatou, 132
Diallo, Rokhaya, 30
diaries, 22, 70. *See also* memoirs
*Diary of a Chambermaid, The* (*Journal d'une femme de chambre, Le*) (Mirbeau), 46, 94, 129–30, 143–51, 193, 275n104
*Diary of the Outside* (*Journal du dehors*) (Ernaux), v, 189, 237, 282n54, 287n62
Dickens, Charles, 253n100; mess, waste, and stains in, 266n87; mudbanks in, literal and figurative, 97; servants in, 274n88
*Dictionnaire Balzac*, 49
*Dictionnaire des personnages populaires* (*Dictionary of Popular Characters*), 50
*Dictionnaire international Bourdieu* (*Bourdieu International Dictionary*), 11
digression, 159–60, 277n32
Diome, Fatou, 45, 141–42, 153, 155, 274n74
dirt. *See* mud (literary)
*Disappearing Act, New York* (Kertész), 38–40, 39
discontinuities, 8, 122, 269n73
Disegni, Sylvia, 99
*Disintegration* (*Désintégration*) (Richard), 239
disloyalty, and transfuges, 32–33
disorientation, 25, 36, 40
displacement, 40, 44, 80–81, 91, 94, 123, 197
"Dissenting Child, The" (Éribon lecture), 26, 254n118
*Distinction, La* (*Distinction, The*) (Bourdieu), 115
Divry, Sophie, 41, 43, 101, 104, 240–41, 289n15
Djavadi, Négar, 282n54
Djebar, Assia, 13; as class renegade, 13
Doisnel, Antoine, 76

Dolan, Xavier, 146
domestics, 37, 274n81; and bourgeoisie, 136; as "class apart," 128; class mobility of, 127–28, 212; cleaning and marrying, as "domestic" service, 137; and complexion particular to condition, 137; contemporary French, 45; and education, 139; and exploitation, 138; fate of, 142; and importance of giving visibility to race of workers, 274n72; in-betweenness of, 130; and international migration, 212; liminal position of, 132, 153; "limits of their caste," 130; in literature, 127; and lower class, 153; and mobility, 131; as "monstrous human hybrid," 129; "monstruous strangeness" of, 130; motherhood as domestic labor, 136; as precarious, liminal, and "aggressively vestigial," 132; race and class when representing, labor in literature, 137; and racial/social hierarchies, 138; return of, 45, 127; sameness of, 127; and social class, 153; social mobility of, 45–46, 125–53; and social rank, 140; theatrical, and audience, 274n94; union for, 142; and upper class, 45, 133; and upward trajectories, 132; and visibility, 274n72; women as, 274n72. *See also* maids; servants
*Don't Stay in Your Place!* (*Ne reste pas à ta place!*) (Diallo), 30
doors: behind, 168–69, 276n5; and bourgeoisie, 173–75; and class, 46; and class distance, 47, 184; and class mobility, 156, 164, 169, 172, 181; as class rigidity, 174; concrete, 155, 181, 184; crossing, 155; and emancipation, 155–56, 165, 170; and formal mobility, 156; and gates, 156–63, 184; and immigrants, 155; intangible, 156; and liminality, 155, 276n2; and

Index   319

liminal social statuses, 276n2; as liminal space, 155; as literary object, 276n4; metaphor of, 155, 157, 166, 171, 174, 184; and mobility, 156; and mud (literary), 156; as narratological entryways, 155; and polyphony, 156; and reading, 184; representation of, 155; and reproduction, 156; revolving, 46, 130–31, 198; and rites of passages, 19, 174; and secondary characters, 276n5; and social climbing, 46; and social ladder, 155–56; and social mobility, 41, 46–47, 154–84; as social mobility, 174; and social polyphony, 156; space behind, 168–69, 276n5; swinging, 8–9, 175, 184; symbolism of, 37, 46, 155, 181; tangible, 156; as thresholds, 155–56, 165–67, 174, 184; and transclass, 156; as transit zones, 37, 46, 155; and transmission, 155–56; unsaid, 155; and violence, 184; and writing, 184
Dostoevsky, Fyodor, 9–10, 55, 97; and Balzac, 266n87, 285n18
downgrading, 34, 36; and amnesiac, 215; family, abuse as, 174; of genres, 56–57; of parvenu, 241; and realism, 211; and social immobility, 48, 232
downward mobility, 32, 35–36, 46, 65, 105–7, 186
*Dreamy Bourgeoisie* (*Rêveuse Bourgeoisie*) (Drieu La Rochelle), 75
Drieu La Rochelle, Pierre, 75
*Drinking Den, The* (Zola), 73
Duchesne, Annie. *See* Ernaux, Annie
Duras, Marguerite, 213, 285n12
*Du soleil à cinq heures* (*Sun at Five O'clock*) (Ernaux), 25
Duteurtre, Benoît, 53

Echenoz, Jean, 50
École nationale d'administration (ENA) (National School of Administration), 60–61

economics: and domestic workers, 127; of Gatsby, 65–70; and kinship, 12; and literature, 9–11, 16, 67–68; macro-, 10; micro-, 10; narrative, 9–10; and politics, 19; of Rastignac, 65–70. *See also* socioeconomics
*Écriture comme un couteau, L'* (*Writing as a Knife*) (Ernaux), 35
Eden, Martin (fictional character), 242–43
*Edges of Fiction, The* (*Bords de la fiction, Les*) (Rancière), 155, 276n5
editorial strategies, 19, 48, 195
*Educated* (Westover), 7–8, 29, 191
education and schooling, 262n134; baccalaureate as "gate" between classes, 281n3; and cross class, 237; and culture, 71, 77, 97; and emancipation, 138; *grandes écoles*, 14; and labor, 74; and literature, 23, 237–38; novels of, 241; and reading, 24, 205; and service, 139; and social climbing, 77; and social ladder, 24, 26, 237–38; and social mobility, 26, 43–44, 73–77, 262n119; and upward mobility, 77, 97; and writing, 181. *See also* learning; meritocracy; teaching
*Éducation sentimentale, L'* (*Sentimental Education, The*) (Flaubert), 14, 52–53, 121, 185, 193, 198, 240–41
*Egalitarian Strangeness* (Hughes), 242
egotism, 22, 224
Elayoubi, Fatima, 151, 153
*Elementary Particles, The* (*Particules élémentaires, Les*) (Houellebecq), 218, 221–22, 224
*Éléments pour une ethnologie familiale* (*Towards a Familial Ethnology*) (Ernaux), 13
Eliot, George, 9
*Élise, ou la vraie vie* (*Élise, or Real Life*) (Etcherelli), 107
elitism, Republican, 259n63

Elkharraz, Osman, 152–53
emancipation, 56–57, 62, 70, 230; and characters, 43–44; and class mobility, 23; contemporary routes of, 23; and determinism, 88, 140; and doors, 155–56, 165, 170; and education, 23; and education and schooling, 138; and literature, 23; and maids, 135, 138, 140, 150; meaning of, 43; metaphors for, 135; and mobility, 155; and muddy parvenants, 82, 85, 88, 92–93; positive tales of, 48; and racial passing, 45; social, 43–44, 57, 92, 160, 195, 230; and social climbers, 19, 46; and social climbing, 19; of social group, 249n9; and transclass, 114; and violence, 156–57
embodiment, 267n6; and being/becoming, 117–25; and class, 33, 45, 111, 115, 117; of class mobility, 101, 117, 125; of maids, 125; of oppressors, 34; of parvenants, 41, 101, 125; of poverty, 147–48; and social class, 117–18, 268n37; and social climbing, 45, 116; and social demotion, 44–45; and social mobility, 107–8, 112–13; of transclass, 41, 44–45, 102–25; and upward mobility, 44–45
*Émile Zola, le déclassement et la lutte des places* (*Émile Zola, Demotion, and Place Struggle*) (Giraud), 12
*Emmanuel Le Magnifique* (*Emmanuel The Magnificent*) (Rambaud), 62
*Emploi du temps, L'* (*Time Out*) (Cantet), 208–9
employment discrimination, 31
*Empty Cupboards, The* (*Armoires vides, Les*) (Ernaux), 21, 73, 93, 111–16, 166, 202, 227–28, 262n132
ENA. *See* École nationale d'administration (ENA) (National School of Administration)
*Ending Eddy Bellegueule* (*En finir avec Eddy Bellegueule*) (Louis), 11–12, 27–28, 30–31, 62, 64, 94–95, 105, 117, 119–21, 123, 156, 160–63, 194, 269n70
*Enfant, L'* (*Child, The*) (Vallès), 89–91, 100
"Enfin Balzac a vieilli" ("Finally Balzac Has Aged") (Barrès article), 74
*En finir avec Eddy Bellegueule* (*Ending Eddy Bellegueule*) (Louis), 11–12, 27–28, 30–31, 62, 64, 94–95, 105, 117, 119–21, 123, 156, 160–63, 194, 269n70
Engels, Friedrich, 69
*Engine of Modernity* (Belenky), 188
*En salle* (*In the Dining Room*) (Baglin), 239–40
*Entre les murs* (*Between the Walls*) (Cantet), 127
epistolary format/genre, 5, 167–68, 278n63
*Ère du Soupçon, L'* (*Era of Suspicion, The*) (Sarraute), 214
Éribon, Didier, 14, 26, 28, 31–32, 256n161, 260n83, 281n23; autobiographical bildungsroman of, 192; "auto-socio-biography" of, 32, 75; *Border Country*'s train, and brief mention of, 281n24; and Bourdieu, 11–12, 76–77, 109; and Camus, 273n69; and class mobility, 11, 20–21; and doors, 154, 156–57; and Ernaux, 11, 75, 117; and history, 16; and Louis, 11, 162; and mother, 20; parvenant peers, 109; and *parvenir*, 36; on Rastignac, 63–64; return, narratives of, 117; as socially mobile author of cultural-political left, 63; and social mobility, 63–64, 107–8, 162; and Sorel, 75; and transclass, 107–9; and travel class, 192, 194; and upward mobility, 7; and working class, 107–8
Ernaux, Annie, v, 18–19, 28, 30, 75–76, 217, 237, 261n117, 278n56, 283n63; and Angot, 178–79, 202, 280n100; autobiographical writings of, 6, 22,

181, 241; "auto-socio-biography" of, 22–23, 32, 75; and backstreet abortion, 45; and Balzac, 70–71, 73–74, 179; and Barthes, 46; biography of, 114; and body (*corps*), 268n37, 270n80; and Bourdieu, 11–13, 23, 26, 36, 76–77, 115, 123, 164, 251n41, 255n139, 263n149, 278n60; as bourgeoisie, 5, 108, 165–66; and Bovarysm, 72; and bus as opposite of train, 283n63; and Camus, 273n71; and Chamoiseau, 103; and class affiliations, 203; and class arrival, 166–67; and class inequality, 154; and class mobility, 11, 21, 170–71; and cross-class body, 105; and cross-class trajectory, 21; and degree of generality, 22; and destiny, 184; diaries of, 22–23; displaced affects of, 29; and doors, 156, 163–74, 184; embodied reactions of, 123–24; and epistolary format, 167–68, 278n63; and Éribon, 11, 75, 117; and ethnology, 13; and family, 169; and father, 22, 108, 123–24, 133, 163, 172, 201, 253n93; through "feminist hermeneutics," analysis of, 270n86; first book, 21, 25; flat writing, 46–47, 123–24, 163–73, 228–29, 278n56; geosocial trajectories of, 75; and Harchi, 181; and heart (*cœur*), 270n80; and history, 16; and homecoming, 166; and Houellebecq, 224, 226, 229–30; in-betweenness in, 278n75; on inheritance, 277n47; and interdisciplinarity, 70; and intertextuality, 135, 230, 262n132; and Kerangal, 229; as learner, 38; and Lejeune, 253n94; on life and interpretation through reading, 20–21; and Linhart, 116; and literary realism, 266n76; and Louis, 44, 78–79, 97, 105, 123–24, 150, 154, 171–72, 174; maiden name (Duchesne), 228; on maids, 132–35; and Marivaux, 151; and Maupassant, 135; metacommentaries in, 21, 253n91; and middle of tracks, 37; and mobility, bodily consequences of, 115; and mother, 4, 70–71, 73, 133–35, 164, 167–72, 226; mud in, 44, 78–79, 93; name change, 31–32, 228; as "narrator-prof-transfuge," 36; and nature, 25; and NDiaye, 113, 139; and New Novels, 25, 253n113; on Nizan, 283n74; Nobel lecture, 184; and nonfiction, 124, 230; and orality and patois, 18; and parents, 71, 168, 202; and parents-in-law, 178; parents of, as transfuges, 164; and parvenants, 36–37, 97, 113; *parvenir* in works of, 97; and past participle, 179; and Perec, 283n76; and Piketty, 70; polyphony in, 279n77; and Proust, 22, 24–25, 228, 272n38; quoted across fields, 251n39; and Rastignac, 263n149; on reading, 20–25, 71–73, 243, 253n99; and Renaudot prize, 263n140; return, and narratives of, 117; rhetorical strategy of, 71; and Richard, 239; and Sallenave, 24; as "schizo-prof," 36; and self-confrontation, 171; and sentimental novels, 73; and servants, 272n36; shame in, 280n100; sister of, 278n63; and social class, 24–25, 46–47, 97, 166–67, 173; and social climbing, 40, 111; and social estrangement, 163; and social inclusiveness, 229; and social inequality, 189; and social ladder, 113; and social mobility, 25, 35, 46, 70–71, 78–79, 107–8, 150, 154, 179, 202; and social mobility through form and train, 202; and social novels, 27; and social rigidity, 174; social trajectory of, 25, 73, 135; and sociological characters, 255n138; and sociology, 13–14, 23; and Sorel, 75; as spectator

Ernaux, Annie (*continued*)
of self, 13; and Steedman, 251n41; and supermarkets, 16, 26, 226–29, 287n62; and symbolic servants, 142; and Tanning, 179, 181, 280n107; on temporality, 36; and trains, 200–201, 203–6; and transclass, 104, 111–16, 166, 170, 202–3; transformation in, 116; and transfuges, 35, 164; trauma and shame in, 255n139; and travel class, 200–201, 203–6; underprivileged upbringing in countryside of, 4, 97; and upper class, 45, 153, 226; and upward mobility, 7, 34, 70, 163, 165, 227; and Westover, 29; and Wittig, 255n144; word choice, and attention to, 253n90; and working class, 32, 103, 107–8, 118–19; and Zola, 73, 230
escalators, subway, and social ladder, 282n54
*Escalier rouge à Cagnes, L'* (Soutine painting), 203
escapees, transfuges as, 33, 35
*Esquisse pour une auto-analyse* (*Sketch for a Self-Analysis*) (Bourdieu), 12, 25–26, 30, 162, 164, 278n60
essentialism: and class identities, 124; and constructivism, 45; and feminism, 124; feminist, 124; and upward mobility, 116
estrangement. *See* social estrangement
*Établi, L'* (Linhart), 105–6, 116, 124, 199
Etcherelli, Claire, 107
ethnology, and sociology, 13
*Étranger, L'* (*Stranger, The*) (Camus), 163, 167
etymology, 21, 48, 53, 199, 284n9; coastal, 213
*Eugénie Grandet* (Balzac), 214–16, 259n64, 261n117, 266n87, 285n18
Eurydice, 283n63
*Événement, L'* (*Event, The*) (Ernaux), 113–14

*Excès-l'usine, L'* (*Excess-The Factory, The*) (Kaplan), 107
exhibitionism, 22
Existentialism, 34
*Experimental Nations* (Bensmaïa), 19–20
exploitation, class, 138
*Extension du domaine de la lutte* (*Extension of the Domain of Struggle*) (Houellebecq), 219, 229
*External Life, The* (*Vie extérieure, La*) (Ernaux), 36, 189, 227
extratextual, 134
Eyers, Tom, 20–21

*Fables* (La Fontaine), 72
*False Servant, The* (*Fausse Suivante, La*) (Marivaux), 151
Fanon, Frantz, 105, 137
Farès, Nabil, 20
Fassin, Éric, 13
*Fast Cars, Clean Bodies* (Ross), 78, 207, 216
*Fatima* (Faucon film), 151
Faucon, Philippe, 151
Faulkner, William, 28, 157–58, 276n14, 276n16
*Fausse Suivante, La* (*False Servant, The*) (Marivaux), 151
feminist: "class ceiling," 185; essentialism as key for, identities, 124; "hermeneutics," 270n86; mobility, 185; studies, 134
*femme, Une* (*Woman, A*) (Ernaux), 22, 70–71, 164, 166–67, 172, 253n90
*Femme de trente ans* (*Woman of Thirty*) (Balzac), 61
*Femme gelée, La* (*Frozen Woman, The*) (Ernaux), 21, 71–72, 133–34, 165, 178
Fénelon (François de Salignac), 56–57
*Feu* (*Fire*) (Pourchet), 241
fiction: as interpretation, 38; and precarity, 285n9; and quantitative research, 9–10; realist, 5, 211; and

reality, 148, 151; and social entities, 16; of social ladders, 155–56; and testimony, 20; transfuge, 35; of upward mobility, 31, 105; and upward success, 31. *See also* autofiction, and autobiographies; nonfiction; novels
*Fief* (Lopez), 238
*Figaro Le* (newspaper), 59, 63, 149
Figlerowicz, Marta, 52
Filippetti, Aurélie, 281n11
*Fille aux yeux d'or, La* (*Girl with the Golden Eyes, The*) (Balzac), 83–84 film, 76, 127, 211–13, 215–16; adaptations, 8, 46, 126, 132, 142, 144–46, 149–51, 190, 193, 195, 269n70; afterlives of literary protagonists and tropes in, 8; literary, 275n98; locations (France), 211; social mobility in, 8; and travel class, 47–48, 187–88, 192–93. *See also* cinema, and literature
"Finally Balzac Has Aged" ("Enfin Balzac a vieilli") (Barrès article), 74
*Fire Escape* (Rodchenko), 41–42, 42
*Fire* (*Feu*) (Pourchet), 241
*First Man, The* (*Premier Homme, Le*) (Camus), 139–40, 223–24
first-person narrative, 5–6, 10, 16, 101, 142, 151, 171, 173
Fischler, Alexander, 55–56
Fitzgerald, F. Scott, 67–69
*Five Severed Hands* (*Cinq mains coupées*) (Divry), 104
Flahaut, Thomas, 41, 43, 240
*flâneuse*, 212
Flaubert, Gustave, 8, 23, 43, 46–47, 52–53, 64, 127–31, 135, 240–41; and Balzac, 53, 72, 185; and bourgeoisie, 167; and Bovarysm, 72; class and race in, 271n29; correspondence, sociology *versus* textuality in, 252n61; and doors, 155–56, 170; and free indirect style, 170; and heroes, 257–58n16; and household workers, 127;

and mud (literary), 88, 264n13; and NDiaye, 72; and novels of manners, 72; and sociology, 14–15; speech, and forms of, 170–71; and travel class, 185, 193, 196–98
Fontaine, Anne, 194, 269n70
*For a Sociology of the Novel* (*Pour une sociologie du roman*) (Goldmann), 12, 14
formalism: anti-, 18; financial, 17; and history, 17; and poetics, 19; and precarious characters, 48; and seaside, 285n12; and social sciences, 242; and sociology, 14
forms, 18–19; and art, 40; and Bourdieu, 252n61; and class mobility, 154; and details, 6, 23; of discourses, 46; and genre, 98–99; and ideology, 251n59; impersonal, 22; and life, 22, 181; literary, 21–22, 26, 30, 116, 178, 197, 214; and mediation, 20; and novels, 21; and prestigious genres, 26; and reading, 237; and social mobility, 202; and social realities, 41; and sociopolitical experience, 24; and textuality, 24; and trains, 202; and transmission, 46; transpersonal, 22; as transposition of social content, 20; and words, 37
*Forms* (Levine), 24
Fort, Pierre-Louis, 252n87, 261n117, 262n123, 271n33, 277n42, 277n49, 278n56, 278n67, 280n117, 283n63, 287n62
Fortems, David, 163
Foucault, Michel, 4
*400 Coups, Les* (Truffaut film), 76
Fraisse, Geneviève, 127
*France #002* (Houellebecq), 225
*France Hasn't Said Its Last Word* (*France n'a pas dit son dernier mot, La*) (Zemmour), 65
Frantz, Anaïk, 188
Freed-Thall, Hannah, 24–25, 214, 284n9

*French Suicide, The* (*Suicide français, Le*) (Zemmour), 65
Freud, Sigmund, 37, 94
*Frozen Woman, The* (*Femme gelée, La*) (Ernaux), 21, 71–72, 133–34, 165, 178

Gallet, Mathieu, 64
Gallo, Max, 61
Gans, Christophe, 146
Garelick, Rhonda, 147–48
Garréta, Anne, 34
Gates, Bill, 221–22
Gatsby, Jay (fictional character): economics of, 65–70; neo-, 76
Gautier, Théophile, 55
gender: and bodily transformation, 116; and characters, 230; and class, 115–17; identity, 33, 143–44; and nationality, 134; normativity, 117; and race, 117; and sex, 111–12; and sexuality, 119–20; and social class, 119–20
Genet, Jean, 35, 45, 127, 130–31, 137, 142, 145, 169, 259n64, 273n52
Genette, Gérard, 16–17, 50
genres: and class, 7, 150; downgrading of, 56–57; and form, 98–99; partition and social potency of, 43; and parvenants, 43; prestigious, 26; and realism, degenerating, 210; and social class, 150; and social knowledge, 43; and socially mobile body in transit, 150; and social mobility, 238; and writer's body, 124. *See also specific genres*
geosocial trajectories, 75
Gerald, Casey, 26
*Germinie Lacerteux* (Goncourt), 128, 270n9
*Getting Lost* (*Se perdre*) (Ernaux), 22
Gide, André, 76, 160
Gilets jaunes (Yellow Vests) movement and protests, 2–3, 7, 9, 98, 102–5, 154, 267nn6–7

"Gilets jaunes, verts, rouges, roses, convergeons!" ("Yellow, Green, Red, and Pink Vests—Unite!"), 103
Gilets noirs (Black Vests), 104
Girardin, Delphine de, 53
Giraud, Frédérique, 12
*Girl's Memory* (*Mémoire de fille*) (Ernaux), 115–16, 133, 171, 278n63
*Girl with the Golden Eyes, The* (*Fille aux yeux d'or, La*) (Balzac), 83–84
Giroud, Françoise, 216
*Gloire de mon père, La* (*My Father's Glory*) (Pagnol), 75–76
Goblot, Edmond, 185–86, 281n3
*Gobseck* (Balzac), 89
Goethe, Johann Wolfgang von, 120–21, 271n20
Goldmann, Lucien, 12, 14–15, 18–19, 21
Goncourt, Edmond and Jules de, 128, 131, 270n9, 270–71n12
Goncourt prize, 9, 35, 126, 139, 273n63
*Gone with the Wind* (Mitchell), 28, 181
Gozlan, Léon, 53
Gracq, Julien, 76
grammar, 135, 171, 199. *See also* language
*grandes écoles*, French elite system of higher education, 14
Grandet, Eugénie (fictional character), 214–16, 259n64, 261n117, 266n87, 285n18
*Grand Paris, Le* (Bellanger), 238–39
*Grand patron, fils d'ouvrier* (*Big Boss, Son of a Worker*) (Naudet), 242
*Great Expectations* (Dickens), 97
*Great Gatsby, The* (Fitzgerald), 68–69
"Great Gatsby Curve" (Krueger), 7, 43, 67–69
*grève*, 213; etymology of, 284n9
Guène, Faïza, 45, 141–42, 153
Guibert, Hervé, 40–41
Guichardet, Jeannine, 58
Guillory, John, 237–38
Guilluy, Christophe, 3, 28, 249n10

habitus, 15, 58, 115, 119, 137, 163
Haiti, 256n167; *négritude* in, 273n59
Hamon, Philippe, 55
harbor cities, 48, 210–13, 243, 284n4, 284n10. *See also* coastal cities; industrial harbors, as site of creativity; seaside; *and specific cities*
Harchi, Kaoutar: and class distance, 184; and doors, 156, 179–84; and Ernaux, 181; and immigrant family, 47, 181–82; "postcolonial and proletarian existences," 47; and present participle, 179–84; and transclass, 182; and upward mobility, 7
Hauts-de-Seine, 238–39
hawthorns, 24–25
Heinich, Nathalie, 203
heredity: and reinvention, 136; and social determinism, 228; and trains, 209. *See also* inheritance
hermeneutics, feminist, 270n86
heroes: audacity and genius of, 100; characters as, 32, 52, 100, 257–58n16; and "halo of political glory and a gleam of great life," 100; problematic, 32; sentimental, 52. *See also* characters
heterogeneity, 8, 81, 109, 145, 170. *See also* homogeneity
hexis, 115
*High School Graduate, The (Bachelier, Le)* (Vallès), 89–92, 100, 262n134, 265n62
*Hilda* (NDiaye), 136–39, 211
*Hillbilly Elegy* (Vance), 5, 7–8, 26–27, 195–96, 269n74; as memoir, 27, 105
*Histoire de la Révolution* (Thiers), 60
*Histoire de la violence (History of Violence)* (Louis), 77, 95–97, 156–63, 184, 276n16
*Histoire est une littérature contemporaine, L' (History Is a Contemporary Literature)* (Jablonka), 16
historicity, contemporary, 274n91

historicization: of "French novel's transformation from polite entertainment into ambitious social analysis," 72; of social issues, 44, 97–98; of social tropes, 78–79; of social unveiling through nature, 25; of upward mobility, 44
history, 11, 70, 217; and age of return, 17; *"creative,"* 16; and "democratization," 16; as "discursive construction," 16–17; and first-person narrative, 16; and "formalism," 17; and interdisciplinarity, 16; and literature, 9, 16–17, 274n81; and "literature of the real," 16; and "narrating," 16; and "postrealism," 16; and return, 17; and "text-investigation," 16
*History and Ideology in Proust* (Sprinker), 74, 251n59
*History Is a Contemporary Literature (Histoire est une littérature contemporaine, L')* (Jablonka), 16
*History of Violence (Histoire de la violence)* (Louis), 77, 95–97, 156–63, 184, 276n16
Hobbs, Jeff, 26
Hoggart, Richard, 2; and Bourdieu, 24; and history, 16; and sociology, 24; and transclass, 33; and upward mobility, 11; on working class and social mobility, 14
Hollande, François, 60–61
Hollister, Lucas, 17
Holmes, Sherlock, 98, 266n88
*Holy Family, The* (Marx and Engels), 69
home helpers. *See* domestics
Homer, 55–56
*Homme sans titre, Un (Man without a Title, A)* (Le Clerc), 31
homogeneity, 11, 141, 167. *See also* heterogeneity
homology, 14
homophobia, 27, 64

homosexuality, 27, 64; and bourgeoisie, 119–20; and class mobility, 45, 96; and cross-class trajectory, 45, 282n35; and upper class, 120
Honoré, Christophe, 146, 275n98
*Honte, La* (*Shame, The*) (Ernaux), 13
horizontalization, and trains, 187, 198
Houellebecq, Michel, 210–11; and Angot, 13; and Balzac, 220, 230; and Bellanger, 238; biography of, 223; contrapuntal example of, 229; and economics, 10–11; and Ernaux, 224, 226, 229–30; and middle class, 48, 217–23, 234; and realism, 210; and social class, 218, 223; and social immobility, 7, 220; and social ladder, 220; and sociology, 13
*Houellebecq économiste* (*Houellebecq Economist*) (Maris), 10–11
housekeepers/household workers. *See* domestics
housework, 127, 133, 139–40. *See also* domestics
*How the Garcia Girls Lost Their Accents* (Alvarez), 186–87
Hughes, Edward, 242, 271n15, 277n32, 282n35
Hugo, Victor, 93, 155
*Human Beast, The* (*Bête humaine, La*) (Zola), 55, 189–90, 209, 281n4
*Human Comedy, The* (*Comédie humaine, La*) (Balzac), 49–52, 54, 58, 60–61, 64, 89, 92, 99, 197, 207, 219, 230, 232, 259n64
humanities, 9, 127
*Human Resources* (*Ressources humaines*) (Cantet film), 192–93, 208
Huysmans, Joris-Karl, 230

identities: defined by trajectories, 4; and essentialism, 124; and gender, 143–44; self-identification, 71–72, 136; sexual, 120; social class, as paper, 37; and social mobility, 33; and "unbecoming," 34; and voice, 6
ideologeme: of cleanliness, 78; and social class, 8
ideology, and forms, 251n59
*Ignorant Schoolmaster, The* (*Maître ignorant, Le*) (Rancière), 56
"I Have Not Emerged from My Night" (*"Je ne suis pas sortie de ma nuit"*) (Ernaux), 22
*Illégitimes* (*Illegitimate*) (Slaoui), 33–34, 191, 255n146
*Illusions perdues* (*Lost Illusions*) (Balzac), 51, 70, 84, 86, 89–90, 93, 121, 179, 197, 216, 223–24, 264n37
imagination: and reality, 41, 130–31; and social realities, 41; and testimony, 219
IMEC. *See* Institute for Contemporary Publishing Archives (IMEC)
imitation, 75, 128, 130, 260n87
immigrants: and citizens, 40; and doors, 155; as "émigrés-immigrés," 182; from former French colonies, 243; "from the inside," 36; and maids, 151; Moroccan, 47, 181–82, 190–91; and parvenants, 243; and social class, 38; and solidarity, 126; as transfuges, 182; and workers, 190; and working class, 212. *See also* migrants
immigration, 151, 203, 249n3. *See also* migration
immobilization: and chiasmus, 220–21; of fictional characters, 48, 209–35; and mobility, 78; and railroad metaphor, 209; of Rastignac, 48, 210–35; of Subutex, 48, 210–35. *See also* social immobility
*Impossible Love, An* (*Amour impossible, Un*) (Angot), 47, 173–74, 177–79, 184, 195
in-betweenness, 28, 33–34, 226; and doors, 165, 181, 183; in Ernaux,

278n75; and maids, 130; of parvenants, 40–41; and social ladder, 40; and suspension, 40; of transclass, 41; and travel class, 198; and upward mobility, 40
incest: in Angot, 47, 173–74, 178, 184, 279n94; and the imperfect, 279n94; in social terms, 173
*Inceste, Le* (*Incest, The*) (Angot), 173
*Indiana* (Sand), 128
individualism, and social mobility, 3
industrial harbors, as site of creativity, 285n12. *See also* harbor cities
industrialization, and mobility, 206. *See also* postindustrialism
inequality: and class mobility, 102; and class struggle, 3–4; and housework, 127; and immigration, 249n3; of income dispersion, 67–68; pleas against, 9; and precarity, 249n5; social, 102, 189, 250n37; and social climbing, 232; and social mobility, 2–3, 154; and voting, 154
inheritance, 65–69, 138, 166, 215, 217, 223, 233, 238–39, 277n47; social issues linked with, 250n37; and travel class, 207. *See also* bequests; heredity
ink, and mud (literary), 90
*Inrockuptibles, Les*, Louis essay in, 103
*In Search of Lost Time* (*À la recherche du temps perdu*) (Proust), 130, 134, 197–200, 205–6, 272n41
inspiration, 243
instability: and class mobility, 197; and discontinuity, 122, 269n73; of mud, 80; and social mobility, 269n73
Institute for Contemporary Publishing Archives (IMEC), 177
*Insurgé, L'*(*Insurgent, The*) (Vallès), 89, 92, 98–100, 262n134
interclass, 47, 229
interdisciplinarity, and disciplinary readings, 8–17; and history, 16; and social mobility, 17–18, 70; and textual details, 28; and upward mobility, 2; and writings, 8–17
International Monetary Fund, 132
International Organization of La Francophonie, 126
interpretant, parvenant as, 38
interpretation: as fiction, 38; and social climbers, 38; and social realities, 41
intersections and intersectionality, 119; and class boundaries, 242; and domestic service, 137; of housework, 137; and maids, 45–46, 132–42
intertexts and intertextuality, 19; in Ernaux, 135, 230, 262n132; and lexical field, 71; and mud (literary), 101; and one dimensional, 40; and punctuation, 20; and rewriting, 35; and rhetorical device, 48; and social knowledge, 43; and social trajectory, 75; and speech, 162; and trains, 48, 197
*In the Dining Room* (*En salle*) (Baglin), 239–40
introspection, 11–12, 206
intuition, in critical context, 253n97
Isaure (pseudonym), 274n81
italics, 55, 71, 144, 159, 161, 171–72, 218–19; and asterisks, 30; and cosplaying, 97; and polyphonics, 29; and quotation marks, 37, 46, 172; and social mobility, 119–20
*Ixtepec, Mexico* (Verdugo), 187

Jablonka, Ivan, 16–17
Jacotot, Joseph, 56, 156
Jacquot, Benoît, 46, 143–53
James, Henry, 38
Jameson, Fredric, 8, 11, 14, 21, 46–47, 170
*Jane Eyre* (Brontë), 21, 28, 181
Jansen, Yolande, 198

Jaquet, Chantal, 32, 37, 75, 137, 155, 164, 185–86, 249n8, 255n140, 264n20, 273n69
"Je ne suis pas sortie de ma nuit" ("I Have Not Emerged from My Night") (Ernaux), 22
*Jojo, le Gilet jaune* (Sallenave), 102
*Jolies Choses, Les* (*Pretty Things*) (Despentes), 59, 234–35
Joon-Ho, Bong, 126–27, 190
Jordan, Shirley, 59, 272n47
Jourdan, Éric, 76
*Journal du dehors* (*Diary of the Outside*) (Ernaux), v, 189, 237, 282n54, 287n62
*Journal d'une femme de chambre, Le* (*Diary of a Chambermaid, The*) (Mirbeau), 46, 94, 129–30, 143–51, 193, 275n104
*Journey to the East, The* (*Voyage dans l'Est, Le*) (Angot), 174
July Monarchy (1830–48), and "truth" in literature, 67
*Juste la fin du monde* (*Just the End of the World*) (Lagarce), 31, 146

Kafka, Franz, 38, 53, 184, 260n83, 276n5
Kaplan, Caren, 30
Kaplan, Leslie, 74, 107, 262n137, 267n6
Kaurismäki, Aki, 212
Kechiche, Abdellatif, 46, 127, 146, 151–53
Keke, Rachel, 127–28
Kerangal, Maylis de, 229
Kertész, André, 38–41, 183
Kim, Annabel, 34
kinship, 47; and economics, 12; and family, 174; and labor, 136
*Kipps* (Wells), 186
Kleinman, Julie, 189, 204
knowledge: bodily, of bourgeoisie, 120; bodily, of transfuges, 105; and books, 97; and class mobility, 112, 260n79; and language, 44, 78, 112; and mud (literary), 44, 78, 91; and school, 91; social, 43; and vocabulary, 112
Kornbluh, Anna, 17, 20
Krueger, Alan, 7, 43, 67–69
"Künstlermania" (Somers), 241
*Künstlerroman*, 5, 41, 43, 210, 241

labor and laborers, 148, 192; agricultural, 139; and class, 117; and education, 74; farm, 102; and harbor city wanderer, 212–13; international division of, 211; and kinship, 136; manual, 63, 105–7, 114, 138, 140, 143, 206–7, 239–40, 242–43; as "mudsills," American, 266n87; and peasants, 150, 172; professional, 106; and race, 126; social fate of, 124. *See also* working class
*Ladies' Delight, The* or *Ladies' Paradise, The* (*Au Bonheur des dames*) (Zola), 73, 88, 133, 191, 227, 230–32
*Ladivine* (NDiaye), 31, 110–11, 113, 135–36, 200, 211
Lafayette, Madame de, 146
Lafon, Marie-Hélène, and train, for social mobility, 201–2, 205–6
La Fontaine, Jean de, 72
*La France n'a pas dit son dernier mot* (*France Hasn't Said Its Last Word*) (Zemmour), 65
Lagarce, Jean-Luc, 31, 146
Lagasnerie, Geoffroy de, 157
Lagrave, Rose-Marie, 28–29, 185
Lahire, Bernard, 13–14
Lamartine, Alphonse de, 270–71n12
language: in diaries, 22; diversity of, 278–79n76; ecstasy (*jouissance*) of, 202; and knowledge, 44, 78, 112; and literature, 4, 9, 17, 138, 168; and mud (literary), 44, 78; stimulating postwar care for, 17; and topography, 285n12; vernacular, 21. *See also* grammar; vocabulary

Larsen, Nella, 137
Lascar, Alex, 82–83, 85, 89
laughs and laughing, practicing new, 121, 270n76
Lê, Linda, 243
learning, 38, 100; and social climbing, 38. *See also* education and schooling
*Leave the City* (*Quitter la ville*) (Angot), 173
Le Clerc, Xavier, 31–32
Le Clézio, Jean-Marie Gustave, 15
*Lecture et la Vie, La* (*Reading and Life*) (Lyon-Caen), 67
Lefebvre, Marie-Line, 149
*Le Havre* (Kaurismäki film), 212
Le Havre, as harbor city destroyed during WW II, 212; as "mud city," 285n12; rebuilt, with grid street plan (now UNESCO World Heritage Site), 212, 217
Leibovici, Martine, 13
*Le Monde* (newspaper), 121, 259n64
Le Pen, Marine, 60
Lesur, Denise (fictional character), 73, 112, 227–28
*Lettre à un jeune Rastignac* (*Letter to a Young Rastignac*) (Déon), 63
*Leurs enfants après eux* (*Their Children after Them*) (Mathieu), 9, 35, 238
Levi, Célia, 41, 43, 240, 241
Levine, Caroline, 24, 221, 253n100
*L'Express* (magazine), 59, 63
*Libération* (newspaper), 59, 103–4, 109, 147, 154
*Life, A* (*Vie, Une*) (Maupassant), 134–35, 272n42
*Life Is a Long Quiet River* (*Vie est un long fleuve tranquille, La*) (Chatiliez film), 120
*Life of Adèle, The* (*Vie d'Adèle, La*) (Kechiche), 127, 146, 151
life stories, 15–16
*Lily in the Valley, The* (*Lys dans la vallée, Le*) (Balzac), 5

liminality: and domestics/maids, 125, 132, 153, 155; and doors, 155, 276n2; and muddy parvenants, 96; parvenants, and estrangement of, 153; as positive, 153; and social climbing, 40; and social status, 102–3, 276n2
Lindon, Jérôme, 148
Lindon, Vincent, 148–50; and "Jean Valjean tax" on patrimony during coronavirus pandemic, 275n103
linguistics, 21, 164; and class, 134; and maids, 137; and social code, 4
Linhart, Robert, 105–7, 116, 124, 199
literary criticism and critics, 1–2, 5, 8, 11, 18, 24, 32, 67, 251n39; "character turn" in, 50; and social sciences, 1; and sociology, 13–14; and travel class, 199
literary history: backdrop of, 149; canonical, 132; French, 235; and reflexive novels, 215; and social knowledge, 43; and travel class, 198
"Literary Manifesto for the New Social Novel" (Wolfe), 229–30
literary studies, 24
literature: and cinema, 41, 45, 121, 126, 150–51, 205; and class, 242; and class issues, 8–9; and class mobility, 4–5, 12, 15, 24, 47, 237, 242; and cultural capital of old bourgeoisie, 237; and economics, 9–11, 16, 67–68; and education, 23, 237–38; as factory of words and archetypes, 49; foreign, 28; and friendship, 31; gazing in, 188; historical and testimonial, 104; and history, 9, 16–17, 274n81; hybridity of, 17; imaginative and testimonial, 219; and language, 4, 9, 17, 138, 168; and life, 31; and parvenants, 43, 241–42; and politics, 62–63; post-WWI, 65; publishing business of, 10; Rastignac's social class in, 57–65; and reality, v, 20, 22, 237; self

literature (continued)
in, 252n74; social, 9, 15–17, 43, 100; and social analysis, 67; and social class, 43, 71; and social climbing, 242; as social field, 17; and social knowledge, 43; and social ladder, 237–38; and social mobility, 28, 43, 242; and social questions/topics, 154; and social sciences, 8–12, 16–18, 23, 47–48, 185; and social world understanding, 9; and sociology, 9, 11–16, 18–19, 23–24, 36; testimonial, 104, 219; and "transfleeing" body, 105; truth in, 67; as unfiltered data, 43, 67; and upward mobility, 44; as user's manual, 252n86

*Literature and Inequality* (Shaviro), 9–10, 131

"Littérature sociale, La" ("Social Literature") (Vallès), 100

*Little Ones, The* (*Petits, Les*) (Angot), 173

living standards, 66

Lob, Jacques, 190

*L'Obs* (magazine), 62, 63

London, Jack, 14, 75, 242–43

*Look at the Lights, My Love* (*Regarde les lumières, mon amour*) (Ernaux), 16, 230, 262n132

Lopez, David, 238

*Lost Illusions* (*Illusions perdues*) (Balzac), 51, 70, 84, 86, 89–90, 93, 121, 179, 197, 216, 223–24, 264n37

Louis, Édouard, 8, 28–30, 33, 64, 120–22, 254n131, 269n70, 276n16, 277n34; and Angot, 181; and Bourdieu, 11–12, 76–77, 115; and class inequality, 154; and class mobility, 11, 156; and cross-class body, 105; and cross-class trajectory, 45; and doors, 156–63, 174, 184; emancipation and violence, and intersection of, 156–57; embodied reactions, 123–24; and Éribon, 11, 162; and Ernaux, 44, 78–79, 97, 105, 123–24, 150, 154, 171–72, 174; and father, 62, 120, 161; and Faulkner, 157–58; first novel of, 27, 62; and homosexuality, 45; and Macron, 43; as militant writer, 44; and mother, 101, 121–22, 136, 160–61, 163, 169; mud in, 44, 78–79, 94–97; name change, 27, 31–32; as parvenant, 97; *parvenir* in works of, 97; and social class, 97; and social mobility, 11–12, 78–79, 107–8, 150, 154; and social rigidity, 174; social trajectory of, 163; solidarity with servant, 272n46; speech and voices in, 46; and transclass, 94, 103–5, 134; as transfuge, 62; and travel class, 194; underprivileged upbringing in countryside of, 97; and upward mobility, 7, 30–31, 94; and Vallès, 44, 101; and Vance, 27–29; voices and speech in, 46; and Westover, 29; and working class, 32, 107–8, 117–19

love affairs, and social ladder, 81. *See also* romance

*Lovers Market* (*Marché des amants, Le*) (Angot), 47, 174–79, 200, 279n83

lower classes, 46; and domestics, 153; and muddy parvenants, 82, 92; precarity of, 79; stylistic strength of, 24. *See also* middle class; working class

Lucey, Michael, 11–12, 33, 64, 162, 251n44, 260n87

*Lullaby* or *The Perfect Nanny* (*Chanson douce*) (Slimani), 126

*Luttes de classes en France au XXIe siècle, Les* (*Class Struggles in France in the Twenty-First Century, The*) (Todd), 2–3

Lyon-Caen, Judith, 67, 257n9

lyric poetry, as prestigious genre, 26

*Lys dans la vallée, Le* (*Lily in the Valley, The*) (Balzac), 5

Macé, Marielle, 24
Macron, Emmanuel, 43, 60–64, 102, 126, 150, 189, 259n63, 260nn78–79, 263n142, 281n11
*Madame Bovary* (Flaubert), 88, 134, 156, 241
*Madame Bovary of the Suburbs* or *Suburban Condition, The* (*Condition pavillonnaire, La*) (Divry), 104, 240–41
*Madame Figaro* (magazine), 147
Madelin, Alain, 36–37
Madjidi, Maryam, 198
*Mad Rush, The* (*Curée, La*) (Zola), 54–55, 223–24
Mahfouz, Naguib, 65
maids, 211, 271n20, 271n24; ambition of, 131; and bourgeoisie, 129–30, 153; and class, race, 271n29; and class mobility, 125, 127–28, 141; in contemporary literature, 45–46; and downward mobility, 124–25; and emancipation, 135, 138, 140, 150; embodiment of, 125; employers point of view of, 274n76; French, as eroticized and flirtatious, 132; function of, 134; imitative, 128; and immigrants, 151; as intersectional, 45–46, 132–42; and liminality, 125, 155; and linguistics, 137; in literature, 153; as lower class, 46; metaphor of, 134; and migration, 132–42; as "most extraordinary example of revolving doors of being and appearance, of imagination and reality," 130–31; naming in literature, 272n50; on-screen (Marivaux), 151–53; and parvenants, 128–32, 141, 150; and parvenus, 45; playing roles of, 46, 142–51; precarity of, 45, 128, 132–33, 142–43; and returns, 37; self-, 45; signifier, and social mobility, 136; and social change, 275n104; and social class, 135, 150, 275n104; and social climbing, 37, 137; and social demotion, 143–44; and social ladder, 124–25, 153; and social migrations, 132–42; social mobility of, 41, 45–46, 125–53, 193–94; social status of, 45; as transclass, 37; as transfuges, 155; transient, 128; as transitional archetypes, 141; as transitional position, 153; and upward mobility, 46, 124–25, 128, 148. *See also* domestics; servants
*Maids, The* (*Bonnes, Les*) (Genet), 130–31, 137, 142, 145*Maison Nucingen, La* (*Nucingen House, The*) (Balzac), 51, 185
*Maître ignorant, Le* (*Ignorant Schoolmaster, The*) Rancière), 56
*Mandarins, Les* (*Mandarins, The*) (Beauvoir), 22, 60
*Man without a Title, A* (*Homme sans titre, Un*) (Le Clerc), 31
*Map and the Territory, The* (*Carte et le Territoire, La*) (Houellebecq), 219, 221, 224
Marbouty, Caroline, 53
Marceau, Félicien, 257n11, 279n76
*Marché des amants, Le* / *Lovers Market* (Angot), 47, 174–79, 200, 279n83
Marcus, Sharon, 198, 228–29
marginalization, 19–20, 33, 129, 237
Maris, Bernard, 10–11, 223–24
Marivaux, Pierre de, 5–6, 8, 46, 133, 275n112; and maids on-screen, 151–53
Markovits, Daniel, 254n117
Maroh, Jul, 146
marriage: and cleaning, 137; and cross-class arrangements, 282n35; "morganatic," 26; and prosperous class, 65–66; and social ladder, 73; and wealth, 65–67. *See also* patrimony
Marseille, as harbor city destroyed during WW II, 212
Martin, Jed (fictional character), 219
*Martin Eden* (London), 242–43

Marx, Karl, 43, 67, 69
Marxism, 3, 14
Maspero, François: and history, 16; and transportation/travel, 47, 188
materiality, and textuality, 37, 156, 183
Mathieu, Nicolas, 9, 35, 41, 43, 238
Matzat, Wolfgang, 83
Maupassant, Guy de, 6–7, 52, 70, 93, 134–35, 155, 190–91, 224, 230, 271n24; and Ernaux, 135
*mauvais rêve, Un* (*Bad Dream, A*) (Bernanos), 52
May 68 intellectuals, 43–45, 74, 105
Maza, Sarah, 128
Mecke, Jochen, 11
media studies, 19
mediation, 18, 20; and social climbing, 20
Meizoz, Jérôme, 18, 252n61, 279n77
Mélenchon, Jean-Luc, 60
Memmi, Albert, 13; as class renegade, 13
Memmi, Dominique, and Bourdieu, 198, 269n59
*Mémoire de fille* (*Girl's Memory*) (Ernaux), 115–16, 133, 171, 278n63
memoirs: and class mobility/travel class, 209; and novels, 26–29. *See also* autobiographies; diaries
memory: conflicting, 30; and supermarkets, 287n62; topography of, 25, 212; and writing, 40
Méra, Brigitte, 54
Mercier, Louis-Sébastien, 79
meritocracy, 4, 64–65, 76–77, 147, 154, 208–9, 238, 262n134. *See also* education and schooling
*Meritocracy Trap, The* (Markovits), 254n117
Mesrine, Jacques, 259n64
metacommentary, 18, 21, 149, 242, 253n91
metaphors: for ambition, 80; for circular movement, 3; for class mobility, 114, 185, 190, 196, 198, 200–201; for emancipation, 135; for flat writing (Ernaux), 123–24; for flitting between classes, 198; for language and knowledge, 44, 78; for literary characters, 215; moral connotation of, 186; and "plottedness," 81; and precarity, 56; Proustian, 198; for social climbing, 84; for social distance, 159; for social immobility, 158; for social ladder, 19, 166; for social mobility, 46–48, 190, 200, 223; spatial, 159, 185, 222–23; for transclass romance, 200; and transportation, 48; for upward mobility and trajectories, 47, 187, 190. *See also* doors; trains; *and specific metaphors*
*Méthode Rastignac, La* (*Rastignac Method, The*), 54, 60–61
metonymy, 25–26; and mud, 91; in parvenant biography, 191; of poverty, 80; of school and knowledge, of reading books and writing articles, 91; for socially mixed characters, 80; of social mobility, 131
Metzler, Molly Smith, 148
*Miasma and the Daffodil, The* (*Miasme et la Jonquille, La*) (Corbin), 92–93
Michelet, Jules, 75, 185, 242
Michelis, Denis, 104
microreadings, 45
middle class, 40, 48, 72, 217–23, 226, 239; melancholy, 104; poetics of, 222; precarity of, 104, 238; and transclass, 102; and upper class, 224. *See also* lower classes; middleness; working class
middleness: emphasis on, 219–20; experience of, 221; and flatness, 229; instances of, 234; poetics of, 234; redoubled, 226; of setting, 222; and upper class, 224. *See also* middle class

migrants: and doors, 155; and freight train travel, 186; parvenants as, 38; and railroad infrastructures, 204; social, 155; and social class, 38; and social mobility, 187; subaltern, 271n29; and workers, 4. *See also* immigrants
migration, 282n54; class, 2, 122; class, as social issue, 2; of maids, 132–42; and mobility, 45–47, 141–42, 181–82, 204; social, of maids, 132–42; and social mobility, 38, 45–47, 141, 181–82, 186–87. *See also* immigration
Miller, D. A., 64
Mirbeau, Octave, 8, 46, 53, 94, 129–31, 143–46, 149–50, 153, 193–94, 270–71n12, 275n104
*Misfit of the Family, The* (Lucey), 12, 64
misfits, 12, 33, 64
misogyny, 59, 181
mobility: bodily consequences of, 115; and class, 185, 253n100; crisis, 3; and dirtiness, 78; and doors, 156; and emancipation, 155; feminist, 185; formal, 156; and industrialization, 206; lateral, 47–48, 186–87, 196, 209, 221; and migration, 45–47, 141–42, 181–82, 204; and service, 131; sideways, 47–48, 209; and social class, 253n100; and social climbers, 46; and socioeconomics, 3; and stability and continuity, 269n73. *See also* class mobility; social mobility; upward mobility
*Modeste Mignon* (Balzac), 217
Molière, 49, 54, 149
*Mon cœur à l'étroit* (*My Heart Hemmed In*) (NDiaye), 114
money: and class, 131; and literature/novel, 250n37, 261n111; and mud (literary), 89; and networks, 44; novels on, 223–24. *See also* wealth
*Mon père est femme de ménage* (Azzeddine), cleaning and word choice in, 273n70

*Monsieur Ouine* (Bernanos), 52
Montlaur, Guy de, 34
Moreau, Frédéric (fictional character), 52, 61, 121, 240
Moreau, Jeanne, 193
Morel, Nathalie, 127, 274n72
Moretti, Franco, 45, 88, 93, 121, 123, 131, 241
Morrison, Toni, 28
Morson, Gary Saul, 9–10, 250n36
Morton, Jennifer, 4
*Mort très douce, Une* (*Very Gentle Death, A*) (Beauvoir), 161–62
Moudileno, Lydie, 72
Mouvement des gilets jaunes. *See* Gilets jaunes (Yellow Vests) movement and protests
*Moving Up without Losing Your Way* (Morton), 4
mud (literary), 37, 44, 78–101, 265n62; and allegory, 98; and America as "vacuous muck," 266n87; and blood, 100; and capitalism, 100; and class mobility, 44, 81–85, 88, 98; and cleanliness, 78, 81; communal, 98–101; connotation of, 263n11; in contemporary literature, 92–98; and cultural capital, 44; and decontextualization, 44, 98; and dirt, 44, 83, 88, 91, 94–95, 130, 263n11; and doors, 156; and earth, 44, 95, 265n61; of Flaubert, 264n13; heteroclite nature of, 80; and ink, 90; as interpretive category, 263n11; and intertextuality, 101; and knowledge, 44, 91; and language, 44; and lower classes, 92; metaphors of, 44, 80, 83, 88, 91, 98; and mobility, 78, 98; and money, 89; and moral turpitude, 80; and Paris, 79–80, 83–85, 95, 97–98; pliability of, 80; plots of, 79–82; and poverty, 80; and sand, 95; semiotic study of, 78; and social class, 98; and social climbing,

mud (literary) (*continued*)
78; and social issues, 97–98; social meaning of, 44; and social mobility, 44, 78–88, 93, 96–97; and sociohistorical contexts, 44; and struggles, 99; as symbolic, 85; as *terre meuble*, 98; and threshold between lower and upper classes, 156; and topographies, 83–85; trope of, 77; and uncleanliness, 78, 263n11; and unequal conditions, 79; and upper class, 87; and upward mobility, 80, 94, 98

muddy parvenants, 37, 41, 77–101; and bildungsroman, 77–81, 88–89, 93; and class mobility, 78; and emancipation, 82, 85, 88, 92–93; and social climbing, 44; term, usage, 97

Murat, Laure, 196–97, 202

*Muse du département, La* (*Muse of the Department, The*) (Balzac), 51

music industry, 231, 234–35

*My Father's Glory* (*Gloire de mon père, La*) (Pagnol), 75–76

*My Heart Hemmed In* (*Mon cœur à l'étroit*) (NDiaye), 114

*Mystères de Paris, Les* (*Mysteries of Paris, The*) (Sue), 69

myth, and reality, 181

*Naked Bread, The* (*Pain nu, Le*) (Choukri), 205

Napoleon, 75, 263n142

Napoleonic Civil Code, 12

*Narrative Economics* (Shiller), 10

*Narrative Middles* (Levine and Ortiz-Robles), 221

Naselli, Adrien, 60

National Assembly (France), 128

nationality, and gender, 134

National School of Administration (École nationale d'administration) (ENA), 60–61

Naudet, Jules, 15, 122, 242, 255n138, 269n73

*Nausea, The* (*Nausée, La*) (Sartre), 76, 181

NDiaye, Marie, 31, 181–82, 238; and Balzac, 72; biography of, 139; and Condé, 139; and Ernaux, 113, 139; and Flaubert, 72; and Genet, 273n52; lower-middle-class characters, 72; and magic, 211; on maids, 132–33, 135–39, 142; and novels of manners, 72; parvenants/parvenus, and transition of, 45, 113; and social climbing/ladder, 113, 210–11; and social immobility, 7, 210–11; and social mobility, 210–11; thresholds in, 272n47; and trains, 204–6; and transclass, 110–11, 113–14, 116, 200; and upper class, 45, 153

Nelson, Maggie, 213

neoliberalism, 9, 33, 288n88

neologisms, 35, 50

*Ne reste pas à ta place!* (*Don't Stay in Your Place!*) (Diallo), 30

New Novels, 176; and avant-garde, 213; and Balzac, 78, 96, 216; and Barthes, 78; and Ernaux, 25, 253n113; legacy of, 48; precarity of characters after, 48, 211–17; and Proust, 275n98; textuality extolled by, 9; topography of, 215

New Wave: films, 50, 213; first film of, 284n10; novels, 213

*New Yorker*, 103–4

*New York Times*, 26–27, 126, 147–48

*New York v. Strauss-Kahn* ("L'affaire DSK"), 132

Nietzsche, Friedrich, 95–96

*Night of the Proletarian, The* (*Nuit des prolétaires, La*) (Rancière), 156

Nizan, Paul, 14, 43, 47, 74–75, 206–9, 242, 283n74

Noguez, Dominique, 224

noirisme/noiristes, 138, 273n59

nonfiction: and autobiographies, 7, 210; and fiction, 36, 43, 122, 134;

hybrid forms of, 16; polyphonic form of, testimony, 104; self and metacommentary as, 242; social and textual as, 242; social climbing in, 242–43; of testimony, 104; and upward mobility, 7, 210. *See also* fiction; history
Nora, Olivier, 233
*nouveau riche*, 32
novels: airport, 202; anglophone refugee, 211–12; contemporary social, and bildungsroman, 209; and data, 250n37; deformed, 104; as demoted, 238; didactic, 57; and downgrading, 48; and forms, 21; great occidental, 219; of manners, 72; and memoirs, 26–29; as "mirror going along a muddy road," 44; and money, 250n37, 261n111; name changes in, 31–32; naturalist, 79; New Wave, 213; picaresque, and bildungsroman, 48, 230–35; rage of, 67; railroad, 192; realist, 5, 9–10, 79, 97, 209–10, 217, 220, 232; reflexive, 213, 215; sentimental, 73; social, 27, 48, 209, 242; as social analysis, 67, 72–73; and social immobility, 48; and social inequality, 250n37; and social milieu, 14; and social mobility, 238; sociology of, 12; special status of, 261–62n119; as subtitle, 27; teaching of, in education programs, 261–62n119; over theater, power of, 266n94; third-person, 6; train station, 202; of transfictionality, 35; trapped in settings of, 217; unrealistic, 211; and upward mobility, 7, 48; of upward mobility, 15. *See also* fiction
*NRF* (magazine), 61
*Nucingen House, The* (*Maison Nucingen, La*) (Balzac), 51, 185
Nuit Debout, social protest movement, 98, 240

*Nuit des prolétaires, La* (*Night of the Proletarian, The*) (Rancière), 156
*Nuits d'été, Les* (*Summer Nights, The*) (Flahaut), 240

observation, 12–13, 205–6
*Odyssey* (Homer), 55–57
*Old Man Goriot* (*Père Goriot, Le*) (Balzac), 43–44, 49–60, 62, 65–75, 131, 168, 171, 179, 198, 216, 232, 240–41, 264n21, 278n63; and mud (literary), 80–87, 91–92; and recurring characters, 49; as textbook, 44, 72–73, 75
omnibus, 47, 188–89, 198
*One vs. The Many, The* (Woloch), 52
Onfray, Michel, 60
"On ne naît pas femme" ("One Is Not Born a Woman") (Wittig essay), 124
opportunists, 32, 61
oppression, 101
oppressors, embodiment of, 34
orality, and patois, 18
ordinary people: cultural renaissance of, 3; Orwell's, 249n4
Organization for Economic Co-Operation, 102
orphanhood, and social mobility, 269n65
Orpheus, 283n63
Ortiz-Robles, Mario, 221
Orwell, George, 249n4
Ostermeier, Thomas, 276n16
*Ouistreham* (Carrère film), 142
*Outsider, The* (Wright), 34
outsiders, 19, 32, 61, 63

Pagnol, Marcel, 75–76
Paine, Jonathan, 10, 260n92
*Pain nu, Le* (*Naked Bread, The*) (Choukri), 205
Palme d'Or, 126–27
Pamuk, Orhan, 65
*Panorama of Paris* (*Tableau de Paris*) (Mercier), 79

parallelism, 84, 124
paraphrases and paraphrasing, 2, 18, 30
*Parasite* (Joon-Ho film), 126–27, 190
*Paris and the Nineteenth Century* (Prendergast), 80
Paris Commune, 44, 98, 100
*Parisians, The* (*Parisiens, Les*) (Py), 59
*Particules élémentaires, Les* (*Elementary Particles, The*) (Houellebecq), 218, 221–22, 224
*Partie de rien* (*Starting from Nothing*) (Sy), 242
parvenants, 1–48, 52–53, 211, 237, 242–43, 265n62; and anglophone literature, 28; as *apprenant*, 38; and arrivals, 36, 40; ascension of, 242; aspiring, 89, 141; and "autobiographical out-law genre," 30; background of, 40; biography of, 191; body of, 101, 105; and class mobility, 35–36, 211, 237; degenerated, 211; and departures, 37; "discordance" in Bourdieu of, 269n59; and downward mobility, 105–7; embodiment of, 101, 125; as entryway into French landscape and literary field, 35; estrangement of, 153; and form, 17; from French provinces, 243; and genres, 43; and immigrants, 243; in-betweenness of, 40–41; as interpretant, 38; and learning, 38; and liminality, 153; and literature, 43, 241–42; as migrant, 38; and partition and social potency of genres, 43; vs. parvenus, 36; as passant, 37; as passenger, 37; as passerby, 37; precarity of, 7; as protagonist, 38; and returns, 36–38, 238; as revenant, 37–38, 40; as servant, 37; singular position of, 276n4; and social affiliation, 41; and social class, 97; and social climbing, 40, 210; and social ladder, 36, 40; as socially uncanny, 37; social mobility of, 7, 35–36, 136; as storyteller, 35; term, usage, 35; and textuality, 35; transclass, 105; transition of, 113; working-class family cohabiting with, 141. *See also* muddy parvenants

*parvenir*, 36, 97, 158, 183
*Parvenu Peasant, The* (*Paysan parvenu, Le*) (Marivaux), 5–6
parvenus, 60; in anglophone literature, 28; and arrivistes, 52–53; and cross-class trajectories, 31; downgrading of, 241; and maids, 45; vs. parvenants, 36; and "porte-à-faux," 276n4; and provincials, 131; and social climbing, 48, 210; and social status, 215; and upward trajectories, 5
Pasquali, Paul, 14, 238, 262n119, 280n1
passant, parvenant as, 37
*Passer les frontières sociales* (*Crossing Social Frontiers*) (Pasquali), 14, 280n1
Passeron, Jean-Claude, 14
passing: class, 32; on social mobility, 41, 46–47, 154–84. *See also* racial passing
*Passion simple* (*Simple Passion*) (Ernaux), 22, 272n36
patois, 18, 93, 130
patrimony: and income, 65, 68; pandemic tax, 275n103; violent struggles over, 207; and work, 66–67. *See also* marriage
patronyms, 53, 55
*Paysan parvenu, Le* (*Parvenu Peasant, The*) (Marivaux), 5–6
*Paysans, Les* (*Peasants, The*) (Balzac), 83
peasants, 5, 150, 172
*Peasants, The* (*Paysans, Les*) (Balzac), 83
*Peau de chagrin, La* (*Shagreen, The*) (Balzac), 58, 63, 92, 257n11
pedagogues, 56, 156
pedagogy, 38, 56, 72, 156, 262n134

Index    337

Penser/Classer (Thinking/Classifying) (Perec), 197
Père Goriot, Le (Old Man Goriot) (Balzac), 43–44, 49–60, 62, 65–75, 131, 168, 171, 179, 198, 216, 232, 240–41, 264n21, 278n63; and mud (literary), 80–87, 91–92; and recurring characters, 49; as textbook, 44, 72–73, 75
Perec, Georges, 16, 47, 76, 197, 207–9, 217, 239, 283n76, 285n12
Perfect Nanny, The or Lullaby (Chanson douce) (Slimani), 126
Perret, Auguste, 212, 217
Personnage de roman, Un (Character from a Novel, A) (Besson), 61
Petits, Les (Little Ones, The) (Angot), 173
Phantom Formations (Redfield), 241
Phillips, Caryl, 211–12
phonemes, 55, 61
photography, and life, 40
picaresque, 155–56; and bildungsroman, 48, 230–35
Piketty, Thomas, 2–3, 10, 43, 57, 65–71; and Ernaux, 70; and interdisciplinarity, 70; and literature as unfiltered data, 67; on money and literature, 261n111; on money and novel, 250n37
Place, La (Place, The) (Ernaux), 5, 70–75, 93, 108, 123, 134, 163–73, 179, 200–203, 253n93, 277n43; as scholarship student's textbook (Renaudot prize), 263n140; as social mobility narrative, 35
Plateforme (Platform) (Houellebecq), 218–19, 221, 229
plurality, 34, 159
poetics: of Angot, 195; and Balzac, 51, 219; of class mobility, 23; and formalism, 19; of middle class, 222; of middleness, 234; of social mobility, 17–26, 35; socio-, 14–15

Political Sex, The (Sexe politique, Le) (Fassin), 13
Political Unconscious, The (Jameson), 8, 14, 170
politics: and economics, 19; and literature, 62–63; Rastignac's social class in, 57–65; and revolution, 99; and social climbing, 71, 91; and social mobility, 91; socio-, 6, 24, 51
polyphonics, 29, 46, 104, 156, 160, 162–63, 171–72, 233, 279n77
polysemy, 81, 84, 86, 96, 130, 213, 229
Pommier, Jean, 58
Ponge, Francis, 24
Porte, Michelle, 228
"porte-à-faux," to support or to carry, 276n4
portière, 276n2
Possibility of an Island, The (Possibilité d'une île, La) (Houellebecq), 218–21, 224
postcolonialism, 19–20, 47, 163, 182, 205. See also colonialism
postindustrialism, 238, 240. See also industrialization
postmodernism, 16, 59, 233
postrealism, and history, 16
"Posture de l'auteure en sociologue" (Meizoz essay), 18
postwar reconstruction, 215, 284n6
Pourchet, Maria, 241
Pour une sociologie du roman (For a Sociology of the Novel) (Goldmann), 12, 14
poverty: and bourgeoisie, 21; distinguishing features of, 27; embodiment of, 147–48; getting out of, 153; literature as symptom of, and fleeing of milieu, 21; metonymy of, 80; and mud (literary), 80; places of, 27; transmission of, 113
Prayer to the Moon (Prière à la lune) (Elayoubi), 151

precarity, 3, 15, 30–31, 231–32; of characters after New Novel, 211–17; of class, 209; and class mobility, 102; and French fiction, 284n9, 285n9; and global economy, 208; and homophobia, 27; and inequality, 249n5; of late capitalism, 231; of lower classes, 79; of maids, 45, 128, 132–33, 142–43; and metaphors, 56; and middle class, 104, 238; of middle class, 104, 238; and middle-class melancholy, 104; and mud (literary), 84; of parvenu, 7; and recession, 142; social, and return of, 102; and social class, 146; and social immobility, 7; and socioeconomics, 3; and stagnation, 235, 238; of transclass, 104; transition from prosperity to, 235; of travel class, 208–9

Preciado, Paul B., 34

preciosity, and patois, 130

*Premier Homme, Le* (*First Man, The*) (Camus), 139–40, 223–24

Prendergast, Christopher, 71, 80

*Pretty Things* (*Jolies Choses, Les*) (Despentes), 59, 234–35

pride, and snobbery, 146

*Pride and Prejudice* (Austen), 87–88

*Prière à la lune* (*Prayer to the Moon*) (Elayoubi), 151

Prince, Gerald, 171

prosody, 53, 227, 229

prosperity, 215, 235

protagonists, 32; and class, 243; and downward mobility, 238; in film, afterlives of, 8; flat, 51; mysterious, 53; parvenants as, 38; precarious, 214; Rastignac as, 49; single-use, 230–31; stagnant and demoted, 238; and upward mobility, 238. *See also* characters

Proulx, François, 74

Proust, Marcel, 38, 51, 64, 73, 74, 214; and Albaret (housekeeper), 134, 144, 274n87; and Balzac, 11–12, 51; and Bourdieu, 251n44; and close reading, 24; and doors, 155; and Ernaux, 22, 24–25, 228, 272n38; and Genet, 45; and household workers, 127, 130–31, 134–35, 137; "implausible train route," 282n34; and New Novels, 275n98; "sadistic dismissal" in, 271n15; and trains, 48, 197–200, 205–6, 283n72

Provencher, Denis, 205, 283n62, 283n68

psyche, and physical reactions, 267n14

*Pulling Oneself Together* (*Se ressaisir*) (Lagrave), 28–29

punctuation, 19, 20, 48, 73, 168, 204. *See also specific punctuation marks*

Py, Olivier, 59, 64

*Quai de Ouistreham, Le* (Aubenas), 142, 148

Queneau, Raymond, 23

*Qui a tué mon père* (*Who Killed My Father*) (Louis), 62, 101, 161

Quintane, Nathalie, 98, 266n89

*Quitter la ville* (*Leave the City*) (Angot), 173

quotation marks, 37, 46, 73, 112, 159, 161–62, 169–73, 200–201, 223

*Rabouilleuse, La* (Balzac), 258n19

race: and aristocracy, 111; and class, 38, 45–46, 111, 137–38, 175, 271n29; and gender, 117; and identity, 33; and labor, 126; trans-, 47; of workers, 274n72

racial passing: and class mobility, 45; and emancipation, 45; and social mobility, 111; and transclass, 32

Racine, Jean, 213

racism, 141, 181

"Raconter la Vie" (Rosanvallon), 16

Radio France, 64

*Ragged Dick* (Alger), 97

Rag-Pickers of Paris, The (Chiffonniers de Paris, Les) (Compagnon), 80, 92–93, 263n13
rags to riches narratives, 19, 148, 187, 243
railcars, railroads, railways, 48, 234–35; and class demarcations, 190; and class mobility, 47–48, 190; commuter, 47, 188, 204; compartmentalization, 189; and daily grind, 209; and immobilization, 209; middleness, and poetics of, 234; and migrants, 204; and reading, 197; as setting or shuttle, 187; and social climbing, 47, 188; and social estrangement, 47; and social ladder, 186, 209; and social mixing, 188; and social mobility, 48, 188, 190–91, 200; speculative, 207; and transitional class, 207–8; as transit zone, 187; and transversality, 200; and travel class, 186, 188, 192–93, 195, 202; and upward trajectory, 187. *See also* trains
Rambaud, Patrick, 62
Rancière, Jacques, 24, 46–47, 56–57, 155–56, 170, 242, 275n95, 276n5, 276n8
rascals, 102
Raskolnikov (fictional character), and Rastignac, 55, 97, 266n87
Rastignac, Eugène de (fictional character), 259n63, 263n142, 263n149, 266n87; as alive in contemporary France, 250n64; and ambition, 49–77, 87, 91–92, 198, 224, 229–30, 259n58; arrival of, 239; and arrivisme, 49, 59; as arriviste, 49; as banker, 44, 49, 241; as bookend, 41; as cabinet minister, 49; and carriage travel, 86–87; and class issues, 72; and class mobility, 77; in conservative press, 43; as dandy, 264n37; decontextualization of, 69; as demoted, 48; dilemma of, 66; and doors, 173; downgraded, 211, 220; and dual social class, 43; economics of, 65–70; and education, 50, 74–75, 77, 210; elasticity of, 63; and emancipation, 57; as flat protagonist, 51; homophobia of, 64; and horizontalization, 198; and ideological conflicts, 74–75; immobilization of, 48, 210–35; impoverished background of, 57; invented by Balzac in 1830s, 43; and language, 279n76; as literary archetype of social mobility, 49; literary function, 51; literary life and afterlives of, 43–44; meta-, 62; models for, 51; and mud (literary), 78–79, 92, 97; multiplicity of, 257n11; name, 53–55; name-dropping of, 43, 50, 60, 63–64, 76; as narrator of nonfiction, 241; neo-, 76; as outcast, 210; in Paris, 239; phoneme, 61; as politician, 44; posterity of, 50; postmodern, 59; privileged background, 57; as provincial who wants to make it in Paris, 49; return of, 7, 10, 37, 43–44, 48–77, 243; as serial protagonist par excellence, 49; as shapeshifting archetype endowed with dual social class, 43; social class of, 43, 57–65; as social climber, 49–51, 54–55, 60–62, 69, 198, 210–11, 256n2; social emancipation of, 57; as socialite, 44; and social ladder, 69; and social mobility, 43–44, 48, 49, 57–59, 64, 71, 77, 150, 171, 243; as student, 44, 49, 74–77; as studious, 75–77; and Subutex, 210–35; term, usage, 256n2; and transclass, 51, 289n8; and travel by carriage, 86–87; and upper class, 57; and upward mobility, 43, 49–50, 60, 76, 210, 220, 239; and urban settings, 77; and values, 74–75; as writer, 241

"Rastignac Is among Us" ("Rastignac est parmi nous") (Gallo article), 61
*Rastignac Method, The (Méthode Rastignac, La)* (Méra), 54, 60–61
*Rastignac ou les ambitieux (Rastignac or the Ambitious Ones)* (miniseries), 59–60
Ravindranathan, Thangam, 110
"Reading, Memories and Notes" (Ernaux), 253n99
*Reading and Life (Lecture et la Vie, La)* (Lyon-Caen), 67
reading and readers: and authors, 13; authors as, 1–2; by characters, 275n98; and class mobility, 21; as decoding, 20, 256n164; and doors, 184; and education, 24, 205; forms, and rejuvenated and socially conscious reading of, 18; and identification, 237; interpretative, 26; and learning, 100; of marginalized authors, 19–20; as momentarily separated from oneself, 253n99; "morganatic," 26; quotidian, 202; of railroad novel, 192; and riding train or subway, 196–97; and social climbing, 20, 24; and social ladder, 20, 24; and social mobility, 71, 73–74; too-close, 24; and trains/subways/rails, 196–97, 199; and transportation, 197; and writing, 91, 184, 201, 243
*Reading for the Plot* (Brooks), 81
*Reading in Detail* (Schor), 38
realism: capital in, 17; and characters, 43, 285n16; and class mobility, 81–82, 209; degenerating, 210; and downgrading, 211; history of, 43; Kmart, 230, 287n78; literary, in Ernaux novels, 266n76; post-, 16; romantic, 100; and social mobility, 210
realist: authors, 5, 99, 218; characters, 75, 218, 285n16; fiction, 5, 211. *See also* novels: realist

reality: falsification of, 176; and fiction, 148, 151; human beings as reflecting surfaces of, 101; and imagination, 41, 130–31; and literature, v, 20, 22, 237; and myth, 181; social, 13, 41, 218. *See also* unreality, and transfuges
*Realizing Capital* (Kornbluh), 17
recognition, 173–74, 178, 243
reconstruction, postwar, 215, 284n6
*Red and the Black, The (Rouge et le Noir, Le)* (Stendhal), 31, 52, 61, 81–82, 122, 131–32, 240, 264n20, 269n72
Redfield, Marc, 25–26, 241
*Réfractaires, Les (Resistors, The)* (Vallès), 99–100
refugees, 211–12, 282n54
*Regarde les lumières, mon amour (Look at the Lights, My Love)* (Ernaux), 16, 230, 262n132
*Règles de l'art, Les (Rules of Art, The)* (Bourdieu), 14, 23–24, 170
reinvention, 2, 31, 80, 136, 161, 194, 228
Renaudot prize, 70, 163, 203, 263n140
renegades: class, 13, 96, 150; transfuges as, 35
Renoir, Jean, 144, 150, 193–94
reported speech. *See* speech, reported
Republican elitism, 259n63
*Resistors, The (Réfractaires, Les)* (Vallès), 99–100
Resnais, Alain, 213
*Ressources humaines (Human Resources)* (Cantet film), 192–93, 208
*Retour à Reims (Return to Reims)* (Éribon), 20, 26, 36, 63–64, 108–9, 162, 192, 254n118, 256n161, 273n69, 277n32
*Retour des domestiques, Le* (Carbonnier and Morel), 127
return: discourse of, 17; narratives of, 35–38, 117, 242; of parvenants, 37–38, 238; and trains, 37–38, 47
"Réussir sa vie" (Making It in Life) (Tapie song), 62

revenants, 37–38, 40
*Rêveuse Bourgeoisie* (*Dreamy Bourgeoisie*) (Drieu La Rochelle), 75
*Révolution* (Macron), 61
revolution, and politics, 99
Richard, Emmanuelle, 41, 43, 239
"Rise and Consequences of Inequality in the US, The" (Krueger speech), 67–68
Robbe-Grillet, Alain, 15, 48, 176, 213–18, 285n16
Robbins, Bruce, 5–6, 45, 68, 127, 137, 145, 186, 211, 269n65, 274n88
Robcis, Camille, 75–76, 263n144
Rochette, Jean-Marc, 190
Rodchenko, Alexander, 41–42
Rolin, Jean, 284n4, 284n6
Romains, Jules, 198
romance, 19, 47, 127, 175, 200, 281n11. *See also* love affairs, and social ladder
Romanesque, and Balzac, 210
Roméo, Patrick, 242
Rosanvallon, Pierre, 16
*Rosie Carpe* (NDiaye), 72
Ross, Kristin, 44, 78, 98, 207, 216–17, 266n89
*Rouge et le Noir, Le* (*Red and the Black, The*) (Stendhal), 31, 52, 61, 81–82, 122, 131–32, 240, 264n20, 269n72
Rousseau, Jean-Jacques, 91
Rubempré, Lucien de (fictional character), 51–52, 57–65, 75–76, 88–92, 121, 197, 216, 259n64, 260n87
*Rules of Art, The* (*Règles de l'art, Les*) (Bourdieu) 14, 23–24, 170
rurality, 15, 27
Rushdie, Salman, 38

Saint-Gelais, Richard, 35
*Saint Genet, comédien et martyr* (*Saint Genet, Actor and Martyr*) (Sartre), 130–31
Saint-Nazaire, as harbor city destroyed during WW II, 212

Sallenave, Danièle, 23–24, 102
Salvation Army, The (*Armée du salut, L'*) (Taïa), 204–5, 211
*Sanctuary* (Faulkner), 157–58
sand. *See* mud (literary)
Sand, George, 128, 131, 137, 197–98, 265n62
San Francisco, as harbor city, 243
Sapiro, Gisèle, 11, 251n39, 269n59, 281n23
Sarkozy, Nicolas, 60, 66, 238
Sarraute, Nathalie, 15, 24–25, 34, 48, 214–17, 285n18
Sartre, Jean-Paul, 43, 74–76, 130–31, 137, 145, 179, 285n12; author's name in upward mobility, and power of, 258n26
Sasson, Sarah, 81
Sayad, Abdelmalek, 181–83
"scallywag," 102
Schapiro, Morton, 9–10, 250n36
schooling. *See* education and schooling
Schor, Naomi, 38
Schultheis, Franz, 251n41, 263n149
Schwartz, Christine. *See* Angot, Christine
Schwartz, Vanessa, 198
Scott, Sir Walter, servants in, 274n88
seaside, 214, 285n12. *See also* coastal cities; harbor cities
Sebald, W. G., 155
Sebbar, Leïla, 47, 188–89
*Second Sex, The* (*Deuxième Sexe, Le*) (Beauvoir), 124
security guards: as job in supermarket, 148; as socially intermediary figures, 275n102
Sedira, Samira, 274n75
Seine-Saint-Denis, 238–39
self, and metacommentary, 242
self, narratives of, 7;
self, return of, in literature, 252n74;
self, social, 45
self-analysis, 1, 12, 14, 162

self-centered, 173
self-coherent, 269n73
self-consciousness, 2, 213
self-fashioning, 6, 68, 80, 111, 206
self-identification, 71–72, 136
self-invention, 29
self-made stories, 10, 35, 45, 68, 130, 140, 242
self-referential, 9
*Selling the Story* (Paine), 10, 260n92
*Semaine de vacances, Une* (*Week's Vacation, A*) (Angot), 195
Sembène, Ousmane, 284n4, 285n11
semiology, 21, 196–97
semiotics, 44, 78, 98
Senior, Jennifer, 27–28
Senni, Aziz, 190–91
*Sentimental Education, The* (*Éducation sentimentale, L'*) (Flaubert), 14, 52–53, 121, 185, 193, 198, 240–41
*Sentimental Education of the Novel, The* (Cohen), 7, 52, 72–73
*Se perdre* (*Getting Lost*) (Ernaux), 22
*Se ressaisir* (*Pulling Oneself Together*) (Lagrave), 28–29
*Sérotonine* (*Serotonin*) (Houellebecq), 219, 223, 234
servants, 272n36, 276n2; and audience, 46; author and teacher identify with, 134; authors and actors who play, 150; black, 271n29; bourgeois household living with, 141; canonical, brief survey of, 45; and class, race, 271n29; in Elizabethan drama, 274n88; French railroad employees as, 190; fulfill analogous functions in novels, 131; as halfway between provincial and parvenu, 131; as happy, 130; in-betweenness of, 130; "limits of their caste," 130; parvenants as, 37; parvenus, roles as foils to characters of, 45; and peasants, 5; as phantom rung of an upward trajectory, 46; place of, 135; *portière*, worked as, 276n2; prone to breaking referential illusion by talking to audience, 46; rape of, 132; sameness of, 127; social condition of, 153; and social journey, 138; social mobility of, 5–6, 41, 45–46, 125–53; solidarity with, 272n46; stands between kinship and labor, 136; subordination of, 135; symbolic, 142; as theatrical characters, 144; and upward trajectory, 46; and writers/authors, comparison, 273n65. *See also* domestics; maids
*Servant's Hand, The* (Robbins), 127, 137, 145
*Service ou Servitude* (*Service or Servitude*) (Fraisse), 127
Sète, as harbor city, 284n4, 284n10
Seuil, Le (publishing house), 16, 30, 50
Sévigné, Madame de, 197–98
sex, and gender, 111–12
*Sex Defectors, The* (*Transfuges de sexe, Les*) (Beaubatie), 34
*Sexe et Mensonges* (*Sex and Lies*) (Slimani), 126
*Sexe politique, Le* (*Political Sex, The*) (Fassin), 13
sexual: abuse, 47, 173–74, 195; competition, 218; orientation, 26, 117; violence, 173–74
sexuality: of characters, 283n68; and gender, 119–20; and social class, 119–20; as social reality, 13
sexual orientation, 26, 117
Seydoux, Léa, 46, 146–47, 149–50, 153
*Shagreen, The* (*Peau de chagrin, La*) (Balzac), 58, 63, 92, 257n11
shame, 280n100; of being ashamed, 140; social, 239; and trauma, 255n139
*Shame, The* (*Honte, La*) (Ernaux), 13
shapeshifting, 41, 43, 53, 196
Shaviro, Daniel, 9–10, 131

Index   343

Shiller, Robert, 10
*Short and Tragic Life of Robert Peace, The* (Hobbs), 26
*Sigma* (Deck), 285n12
Sijie, Dai, 43–44, 74–76
Simenon, Georges, 50
Simon, Claude, 95–96
*Simple Heart, A* (*Un cœur simple*) (Flaubert), 128–29
*Simple Passion* (*Passion simple*) (Ernaux), 22, 272n36
*Sketch for a Self-Analysis* (*Esquisse pour une auto-analyse*) (Bourdieu), 12, 25–26, 30, 162, 164, 278n60
Slaoui, Nesrine, 33–34, 191–92, 255n146
slavery, and coastal cities, 284–85n11
Slimani, Leïla, 126–27, 243
*Slow Life, The* (*Vie lente, La*) (Taïa), 203, 205
Smith, Zadie, 28
snobbery, 146
social: affiliation, 41; analysis, 67, 72–73; appropriation, 149–50; "closet," 162; cohabitation, 189, 199; contradiction, 8; conversion, 6, 116; difference, 134–35, 190; disparities, 127, 138; distance, 159, 174, 200–201; frontiers, 14, 280n1; identity, 143–44; inclusiveness, 229; influence, 163; interfaces, 48; issues, 2, 44, 48, 97–98, 243, 250n37; knowledge, 43; in literature, return of, 9; manners, 24, 118; mixing, 188; negotiation, 47, 188; order, and class identity, 34; order, and social mobility, 275n112; realities, 13, 41, 218; realization, 201; reproduction, 77, 94, 114, 116, 163; shame, 239; spheres, travel between, 211; split, 194; status, 26, 45, 53, 57, 82, 102–3, 108, 110, 148, 157–58, 164, 174, 194, 215, 224, 241, 276n2; swerves, 160; symbolism, 155; tropes, 78–79, 237; unveiling through nature, 25; visualization, 186; vulnerability, and coastal etymologies, 212–13
social classes, 2, 8, 19, 56, 213; dangling, 207; and financial crisis, 2; and precarity, 146; women as, 124. *See also* class; social mobility
social climbing, 2–5, 19–20, 28–32, 35–40, 44–48, 238–43; and class mobility, 12, 35–36; as compelling entryway into intricate coordinates of contemporary social field and literary landscape, 2; and foreign literature, 28; and inequality, 232; and name changes, 31–32; and naming climbers, 240, 255n138; in nonfiction, 242–43; and Paris, 211; and policy change, 4; and social groups, 12; and social mobility, 3, 12, 155; Spinoza-infused philosophical reflection on affects of, 32; trance of, 45; and upward mobility, 5; and vertical imagery of "lead climbers," 281n11. *See also* social ladder
social demotion, 3, 41, 43, 48, 73, 214–15, 238, 240–41; anxiety and fear of, 74; and arrested trains, 209; and characters, 44–45; and class, 209; and decline, 65; and nonnational workers, 133; and school reforms, 74; and upward mobility, 36, 58, 133; voluntary, 44–46, 74, 105, 143–44
social determinism. *See* determinism
social elevator (*l'ascenseur social*), 221; and class, 198; and class mobility, 47; idiom of, 47; and subway escalator, 282n54; and travel class, 185–86; and upward mobility, 47, 185. *See also* social ladder
social emancipation. *See* emancipation
social estrangement, 4; and doors, 163, 167, 169, 179; mitigated, 188; of parvenants, 153; and railroads, 47; and transclass, 124; and writing, 167

social immobility, 7, 48, 125, 210–11, 232. *See also* immobilization; social mobility
socialism, paternalist, 69
socialites, 44, 72
social ladder, 38–40, 288n88; American, 185; and class, 113, 198; and class mobility, 47; and class struggle, 190; climbing, 5–6, 20, 24, 26, 32, 38–41, 46, 48, 53, 58, 66, 69, 113, 132, 153, 155–56, 166, 185–86, 199, 220; and escalators, 282n54; fiction of, 155–56; and hierarchies, 167; idiom of, 41, 47; and love affairs, 81; as metaphor, 19; phantom, 40; railway/train as metaphor for, 37–38, 41, 209; and subway escalators, 282n54; and trains, 37–38, 41, 185–209; and traitors, 35; and transclass, 124–25; and transfuges, 35; as transitional position, 153; and travel class, 41, 47–48, 185–209; and upward mobility, 47; and vertical imagery of "lead climbers," 281n11. *See also* social climbing; social elevator (*l'ascenseur social*)
"Social Literature" ("La Littérature sociale") (Vallès), 100
*Social Mobility* (Sorokin), as first study on social mobility, 249n8
social mobility, 239; American and French, compared, 28, 30; and authors, 242; and body in transit, 150; in books, 7; and class inequality, 154; and class mobility, 12, 14, 242, 253n100; as commonplace but understudied, 2; constraints of, 112; contemporary, 2–8, 9, 30, 37, 70–75, 243; and creativity, 199, 201; "crottorama" of, 82–88; decline of, 249n10; demoted plot of, 41, 43; fictional, 4; first study on, 249n8; formal logic of, 17; French and American, compared, 28, 30; impeded today, 40; lateral, 187; and multigeneric approach, 107–8; narratives of, 17–18; passing on, 154–84; and pendular movements, 47, 187–88; of people in France, 242; plot as commonplace, 2; poetics of, 17–26, 35; postwar, 11; and reproduction, 154–55, 163; social order, and reaffirmation of, 275n112; and social sciences, 17–18; at standstill, 48; trajectory of, 255n142; and transatlantic dialogue, 7–8; and *Une vie*, 272n42; voice and journey conveyed, 155, 242. *See also* class mobility; social classes; social immobility; upward mobility
social sciences: and autobiographies, 12; and class mobility, 3, 11–12, 15, 47; empirical research, 9–10; and formalism, 242; and literary criticism, 1; and literature, 8–12, 16–18, 23, 47, 185; and narrating, 16; research, 3, 9–10; and social mobility, 17–18; and sociology, 12, 15
social trajectories, 9, 30, 32, 77, 113, 206, 208; geosocial, 75
socioanalysis, 14
socioeconomics, 3, 97. *See also* economics
sociology, 2; and autobiographies, 12–13; and class mobility, 12; and cultural studies, 14; and ethnology, 13; and formalism, 14; and forms, 14; and literature, 9, 11–16, 18–19, 23–24, 36; Marxist, 14; and mediation, 18; of novels, 12; and observation, 12–13; and qualitative research, 15; and quantitative research, 15; and social climbing, 15; and social mobility, 12, 17–18, 32, 185; and social sciences, 12, 15; in texts, 181; and textuality, 13–14, 252n61; and upward mobility, 11, 15
sociopoetics, 14–15
sociopolitics, 6, 24, 51

*Sodome et Gomorrhe* (*Sodom and Gomorrah*) (Balzac), 197, 199
solidarity, and immigrants, 126
Somers, Erin, 241
sonority, 20, 53–54, 56, 229
Sorel, Julien (fictional character), 32, 51–52, 61–62, 75–76, 122, 131–32, 134, 240; and Éribon, 75; and Ernaux, 75; geosocial trajectories of, 75; as hero, 257–58n116; and mud (literary), 82
Sorokin, Pitirim, 249n8
*Soumission* (*Submission*) (Houellebecq), 219, 223–24, 230
Soutine, Chaïm, 203
spatialization/spatiality, 186, 190, 217, 221–22, 226, 243
*Speculative Formalism* (Eyers), 20–21
speech, reported, 7, 20, 46, 87, 156, 159–60, 162, 167–72, 184, 200–201, 277n31
Spinoza, Baruch, 32, 75, 137
Spivak, Gayatri, 211
*Splendeurs et misères des courtisanes* (*Splendors and Miseries of Courtesans*) (Balzac), 6–7, 52, 88, 218
*Spoiled Distinctions* (Freed-Thall), 24
Sprinker, Michael, 74–75
stagnation, 235, 238
stairs/stairsteps/stairways, 221–22; and class, 198; Escherian, 84; and mud, 83–84; service, and mobility, 185; and upward mobility, 38–40
*Starting from Nothing* (*Partie de rien*) (Sy), 242
Steedman, Carolyn, 11, 251n41
Stendhal, 31–32, 45, 52, 75, 123, 132, 259n63; and Balzac, 9–10, 44, 73, 98; body in, 269n72; canonical definition of novel as "mirror going along a muddy road," 44; and class division, 185; and "crystallization," 61; and doors, 155; and muddy parvenants, 81–82; and realism, 81–82; and sentimental novels, 73

Stevenson, Robert Louis, 52
*Stranger, The* (*Étranger, L'*) (Camus), 163, 167
Strauss-Kahn, Dominique, 132
structuralism, 9
Sturel, François, 74
style, literary, 24
subalterns, 46, 241, 271n29
*Submission* (*Soumission*) (Houellebecq), 219, 223–24, 230
subtitles, 27–31, 34–35, 54, 101, 123, 127, 139, 144, 187, 196, 219; as marketing strategy, 27
*Suburban Condition, The* or *Madame Bovary of the Suburbs* (*Condition pavillonnaire, La*) (Divry), 104, 240–41
suburbanites, 239
Subutex, Vernon (fictional character), 7; immobilization of, 48, 210–35; as Nicolas Nil, 288n87; and Rastignac, 210–35; and social mobility, 48
subways, 34; as "Babel" of languages, cultures, classes, 188–89; and escalators, 282n54; as metaphor, 202; and railway, 234–35; and reading, 196–97; and social cohabitation, 189; and social ladder, 282n54; and travel class, 194, 205, 209. *See also* trains
success stories, 4, 6, 47; of class mobility, 209; and integration, 239; of travel class, 187–88
Sue, Eugène, 43, 67, 69, 230–31
suicide, 65, 128, 163, 234, 241–43; and social demotion, 243
*Suicide français, Le* (*French Suicide, The*) (Zemmour), 65
Sullivan, Vernon, 231
*Summer Nights, The* (*Nuits d'été, Les*) (Flahaut), 240
supermarkets, 16, 26, 96, 108, 148, 165, 262n132, 286n56; and class, 37, 48; and consumerism, 37, 48; and memory, 287n62; milieus, 223–30

Surrealism, 181
suspension, 40
Swann, Gilberte (fictional character), 197–98, 200, 282n38
Sy, Hapsatou, 242
symbolism: of doors, 37, 46, 155, 181; of mud, 85; social, 155; of trains, 235
symbols, and temporalities, 96

*Tableau de Paris* (*Panorama of Paris*) (Mercier), 79
Taïa, Abdellah, 36, 43–44, 59, 64, 76, 181–812, 211, 261n117, 283n62; and punctuation, 48; and social mobility, 48, 204; and train as formal device and tool, 48, 203–6, 283n68; and transclass, 204; and upward mobility, 7, 36
Tangiers, as coastal city, 205, 211
*Tannerie, La* (*Tannery, The*) (Levi), 240
Tanning, Dorothea, 179–83, *180*; and Ernaux, 179, 181, 280n107
Tapie, Bernard, 62
Tartuffe (fictional character), 49
*Tartuffe* (Molière), 51, 149, 275n107
teaching, 165; and social class, 1–2; and social mobility, 71; and writing, 201. *See also* education and schooling
Telemachus (Télémaque), fictional character in Greek mythology, 55–57, 71, 258n38
*Téléréalité* (Bellanger), 289n8
television, 43, 60, 150, 173, 227–28, 231, 242, 262n121, 277n31
temporality, 36–37, 96, 179, 217
*Temps des gens ordinaires, Le* (*Time of Ordinary People, The*) (Guilluy), 28, 249n4, 249n10
tensions: between classes, 5; of class mobility, 45, 122, 237; resolving, 269n73; social, and alliances, 195; and transclass, 121–22; and trans trajectories, 34

*Terminal Frigo* (Rolin), 284n4, 284n6
testimony, 19–20, 104, 219; and social mobility, 4
textuality: and authenticity, 21; and contextualization, 12; and details, 22; and forms, 24; and interdisciplinarity, 28; and literature, 13–14; and materiality, 37, 156, 183; and New Novels, 9; and parvenants, 35; and social climbing, 19; and sociology, 13–14, 252n61. *See also* intertexts and intertextuality
*Their Children after Them* (*Leurs enfants après eux*) (Mathieu), 9, 35, 238
*Thérèse Raquin* (Zola), 94
*There Will Be No Miracles Here* (Gerald), 26
Thiers, Adolphe, 51, 60, 100–101, 259n63
*Things* (*Choses, Les*) (Perec), 239–40; ends on a train, 207
*Thinking/Classifying* (*Penser/Classer*) (Perec), 197
third culture kids, 32, 255n138
third-person novels, 5–6
Thomas, Chantal, 146
Thomas, Lyn, 202, 251n41, 262n132, 272n36
*Time of Ordinary People, The* (*Temps des gens ordinaires, Le*) (Guilluy), 28, 249n4, 249n10
*Time Out* (*Emploi du temps, L'*) (Cantet), 208–9
*Times Literary Supplement*, 224
Todd, Emmanuel, 2–3
Tolstoy, Leo, 9
topography, 212–15, 240; artificial, 212; and language, 285n12; of memories, 25, 212; and mud, 83–85; of New Novels, 215; nonexistent, 285n12; seaside, 214; social, of "up" and "down," 186
toponyms, 55, 212

*Towards a Familial Ethnology* (*Éléments pour une ethnologie familiale*) (Ernaux), 13

trains: accidents, 190; and arrested mobility, 191, 209; bourgeoisie, as entryway into, 202; broken down, 209; bus as opposite of, 283n63; and class demarcations, 190; of class mobility, 114, 191, 196, 198, 200–201, 209; commuter, 47, 188; and demotion, 209; emergency brake, 188; in endings, 192, 207; as formal device, 196–206; and forms, 202; as framing device, 190–96; freight, and migrants, 186; and heredity, 209; and horizontalization/horizontal travel, 187, 198; implausible routes, 282n34; and intertextuality, 48, 197; of lateral mobility, 187; as metaphor, 37, 41, 47–48, 114, 186–88, 190, 194–95, 199, 200, 206, 209; moving, and new, uprooted milieu, 207–8; and multidirectional social trajectories, 206; as neutral space, in which private and public spheres intertwine, 283n68; as new uprooted milieu, 207; to nowhere, 209; and punctuation, 48, 204; rapid transit, 189, 204, 226; and reading, 196–97, 199; rectilinear, 207–8; and returns, 37–38, 47, 188; as rhetorical device, 48; and round trips, 188; as shape-shifting signifier of class mobility, 196; slow, 48, 199; and snowstorms, 189–90, 209; social, 114; and social class, 190; and social climbing, 189–90, 192; and social cohabitation, 189; and social difference, 190; and social inequality, 189; and social ladder, 37–38, 41, 185–209; as social launching pad, 205; of social mobility, 191–92, 198, 200–202, 281n11, 281n24; and social negotiation, 47, 188; and social realization, 201; as social setting, 188–90, 197; and social split, 194; and social trajectories, 195, 197, 206, 208–9; and social visualization, 186; symbolism of, 235; as topos, 197; transcends nation, 283n68; and transclass, 175, 202; of transitional class, 207–8; and transition from prosperity to precarity and stagnation, 235; and travel class, 41, 47–48, 185–209; as unyielding routes, 206–9; and upward mobility/trajectories, 47, 186–88, 190, 192, 206. *See also* railcars, railroads, railways; subways

traitors, 3, 33, 35

transatlantic dialogue, and social mobility, 7–8

transclass, 31–32, 34–35, 46, 51, 242; affair, 175; and being/becoming, 117–24; characters, 37, 154–55, 289n8; in contemporary prose, 154–55; and doors, 156; and downward mobility, 124–25; and emancipation, 114; embodiment of, 41, 44–45, 102–25; Gilberte character as, 282n38; heritage, 47; in-betweenness of, 41; malaise, 107–17; and middle class, 102; origins of word (*transclasse*), 255n140; and *passe-blanc*, 32; and *passe-classe*, 32–33; precarity of, 104; and racial passing, 32; and Rastignac, 289n8; and reproduction, 154–55; romance, 127, 175, 200, 281n11; and social estrangement, 124; and social mobility, 154–55, 241; temporality of, 36; term, usage (*transclasse*), 32–35; and trade, 242; trajectories of, 154–55; and "transfleeing" body, 105; and transgeneric body, 122; transient body of, 41, 44–45, 102–25; and transition, 255n142; and travel class, 198, 200, 202, 204, 207–8; and upward mobility, 124–25, 154–55. *See also* transfuges

*Transclasses ou la non-reproduction, Les* (*Transclasses or Non-reproduction, The*) (Jaquet), 32, 75, 164, 186
"transcoding," 14
*Transfuge* (magazine), 34–35
*Transfuge, Le* (Montlaur), 34
transfuges: and acculturation, 30; arrogance of, 121; and betrayal, 33, 35; bodily knowledge of, 105; and class, 28–29, 35, 243; and class mobility, 34; continually crossing doorways, 155; as defector, 34; as deserter, 35; and disloyalty, 32–33; as "émigrés-immigrés," 182; Ernaux's parents as, 164; as escapee, 33, 35; fiction, 35; flees but never fully arrives, 33; immigrant, 182; literary spasms of, 105; maids as, 155; and marginalized identities, 33; as renegade, 35; as self-made man, 35; and social ladder, 35; as social traitor who flees, 33; term, usage, 32–35; as traitor, 33, 35; and transclass, 32–33; as "trans-fleeing" body, 105; and transition, 33, 105; as "unbecoming language," 34; and unreality, 30. *See also* transclass
*Transfuges de sexe, Les* (*Sex Defectors, The*) (Beaubatie), 34
transition, and transfuges, 33, 105
*transmettre*, 155
transplants, 32, 113
transportation: and class mobility, 47, 200; clean mode of, 80; and compartmentalization, 47; and cross-class encounters, 47; and metaphors, 48; and reading, 197; and social mobility, 188; and social negotiations, 47. *See also* commuters; omnibus; subways; trains
transsexual, 32, 34
Traoré, Adama, 104
trauma: generations of, 135–36; and shame, 255n139; war, 209

travel class, and bourgeoisie, 187; and class mobility, 185, 191; and cross class, 189–90; and dangerous classes, 189; and evolutions, 186; and inheritance, 207; and social ladder, 41, 47–48, 185–209; and social mobility, 47, 185; and trains, 41, 47–48, 185–209; and transclass, 198, 200, 202, 204, 207–8
*Trial, The* (Kafka), 184, 260n83
*Triangle d'hiver, Le* (*Winter Triangle, The*) (Deck), 212–13, 215, 217, 234, 284n7, 285n13
Trierweiler, Valérie, 60
Trieste industrial harbor, as site of creativity, 285n12
Truffaut, François, 76
*Two French Youths* (*Deux jeunesses françaises*) (Algalarrondo), 62
typography, 37, 159, 161–62, 172, 184, 201

*Unbalanced Ones, The* (*Désaxés, Les*) (Angot), 176
unbecoming, and identity, 34
underclass, 179; white, 27
underprivileged, 37, 57, 127; anxiety about rise of, 43
United Nations, 104
universalism, 4, 29
unreality, and transfuges, 30. *See also* reality
upper class, 45; characters, 135, 153; as enemy, 169; and homosexuality, 120; and middleness, 224; and social mobility, 57
uprooted, 32, 206–7, 215
*Uprooted Ones, The* (*Déracinés, Les*) (Barrès), 74
upstart class, 32, 136
upward mobility, 38–40, 216; and Ancient Egypt, 174; and aristocracy, 174; and authors, 2; authors' names, and power of, 258n26; in autobiog-

raphies, 7, 210; and Balzac, reading of, 261n117; and class, 7, 32; and class mobility, 31, 35–36; contemporary, 45, 105; and cruel optimism, 208–9; decreasing, 6; deserving, 32; and European novel at turn of nineteenth century, 5; exclusiveness of, 154–55; fiction of, 31, 105; generational, 138; historicization of, 44; meanders of trajectory, 5; memoirs of, 7–8; and naming/renaming, 31–32; narratives of, 15, 28; in nonfiction, 7, 210; novels of, 15; plot of, 94; and reading of Balzac, 261n117; and social climbing, 5; and social demotion, 58, 133; social issue of, 44; and social ladder, 47; and social mobility, 241; and success, 30; successful plots of, 7; and suspension, 40; and vertical spatializations, 186; and yuppies, 32, 193. *See also* class mobility; social mobility

*Upward Mobility and the Common Good* (Robbins), 6, 68, 186, 211, 269n65

urbanism, 238

urban itinerary, and social trajectory, 86–87

urban settings, 77, 79

*Uses of Literacy, The* (Hoggart), 14

Vallès, Jules, 73, 262n134; autobiographical novels on class mobility, 78; and Balzac, 78, 88–92, 97–100; and class mobility, 78; and journalism, 44; and Louis, 44, 101; as militant writer, 44; mud in works of, 44, 78, 88–92, 94–95, 97–101, 265n61; and Paris Commune, 44; *parvenir* in works of, 97; on power of novel over theater, 266n94; and supermarkets, 287n62; as transclass writer, 206–7

Vance, J. D. (James David), 5, 7–8, 26–30, 269n74; and Louis, 27–29; and social trajectory, 196; as transclass writer, 105; and travel class, 195–96; and upward mobility, 196; and Westover, 29–30

Vandenesse, Félix de (fictional character), 5

Vautrin (fictional character), 52, 57, 60, 64, 66–69, 83, 259n64

*Vengeance m'appartient, La* (*Vengeance Is Mine, The*) (NDiaye), 210–11

*Ventre de l'Atlantique, Le* (*Belly of the Atlantic, The*) (Diome), 155

verb tenses, 18–19, 47, 170–71, 173–79, 195, 200

Vercors, 213

Verdugo, Eduardo, 187

*Vernon Subutex*, trilogy (Despentes), 48, 230–35

*Very Gentle Death, A* (*Mort très douce, Une*) (Beauvoir), 161–62

Viala, Alain, 14–15

Vian, Boris, 231

Viart, Dominique, 74

"Victimes du livre, Les" ("Victims of the Book, The," 99–100

*Victoire* (Condé), 138

*vie, Une* / *Life, A* (Maupassant), 134–35, 272n42

*Vie d'Adèle, La* (*Life of Adèle, The*) (Kechiche), 127, 146, 151

*Vie est un long fleuve tranquille, La* (*Life Is a Long Quiet River*) (Chatiliez film), 120

*Vie extérieure, La* (*External Life, The*) (Ernaux), 36, 189, 227

*Vie lente, La* (*Slow Life, The*) (Taïa), 203, 205

violence, 27, 104, 156–57, 173–74, 184

Viviane Elizabeth Fauville (Deck), 212, 217

vocabulary, 112. *See also* language

*Voyage dans l'Est, Le* (*Journey to the East, The*) (Angot), 174

Wampole, Christy, 210–11, 220, 288n99
wannabes, 32
*Way of the World, The* (Moretti), 88, 93, 131, 241
wealth, 45, 55, 65–67, 137, 146, 189. *See also* money
*Week's Vacation, A* (*Semaine de vacances*) (Angot), 195
welfare state, 6, 27, 68, 249n10
Wells, H. G., 186
Westover, Tara, 7–8, 191–92; and Ernaux, 29; and Louis, 29; and Vance, 29–30
*What They Live, What They Write* (*Ce qu'ils vivent, ce qu'ils écrivent*) (Lahire), 13–14
*What They Say or Nothing* (*Ce qu'ils disent ou rien*) (Ernaux), 70, 279n77
*Who Killed My Father* (*Qui a tué mon père*) (Louis), 62
Wideman, John Edgar, 28
Wilde, Oscar, 64
*Wilhelm Meister's Apprenticeship* (Goethe), 120–21, 271n20
Williams, Raymond, 11, 192, 281n23
*Winter Triangle, The* (*Triangle d'hiver, Le*) (Deck), 212-13, 215, 217, 234, 284n7, 285n13
Wittig, Monique, 33–34, 124, 255n144, 270n85
Wolfe, Tom, 229–30
Woloch, Alex, 43, 52, 87, 135, 171, 272n41
*Woman, A* (*Femme, Une*) (Ernaux), 22, 70–71, 164, 166–67, 172, 253n90
*Woman of Thirty* (*Femme de trente ans*) (Balzac), 61
women: bourgeoisie, 129, 243; and consumerism, 230; as home helpers, 274n72; and love in Surrealism, 181; as social class, 124; as step ladders for social climbers, 185; working, in France, 127
Woolf, Virginia, and servants, 272n36

WordReference online dictionary, 256n2
working class, 2, 40, 69, 210–11, 223, 239–40; authors, 19, 31–32; black, 138; and bourgeoisie, 3, 36, 115, 134, 149–50, 276n2; children, 117–18; and cultural capital, 237; and immigrants, 212; and labor, 242; and maids, 140–41, 146, 150; roots, 32; and social mobility, 14, 107–8; and strenuousness of jobs, 103; and transclass, 104–9, 115, 118–19; and voting, 28. *See also* labor and laborers; lower classes; middle class
*Wrecker, The* (Stevenson), 52
Wright, Richard, 13, 16, 34
writers. *See* authors
writing: and consumerist leisure, 228; and doors, 184; and education, 181; and housework, 139; and memory, 40; and reading, 91, 184, 201, 243; and social estrangement, 167; and social mobility, 71; and teaching, 201; and transclass, 139
*Writing as a Knife* / (*Écriture comme un couteau, L'*) (Ernaux), 35

Yacine, Kateb, 20
Yale Black Men's Union, 26
Yale Lesbian, Gay, Bisexual, and Transgender Studies, 254n118
Yale University (New Haven, CT), 25–26; Law School, 26, 196, 254n117
"Yellow, Green, Red, and Pink Vests—Unite!" ("Gilets jaunes, verts, rouges, roses, convergeons!"), 103
Yellow Vests. *See* Gilets jaunes (Yellow Vests) movement and protests
yuppies (young upwardly mobile professionals), 32, 193

Zemmour, Éric, 65
Zeroual, Soria, 151

Zola, Émile, 54–55, 133, 172, 224, 227, 229–32, 270n9, 281n4; and Balzac, 12; class and race in, 271n29; and economics, 10; and Ernaux, 73, 230; and mud (literary), 88, 94, 101; and social mobility, 12; and sociology, 12; and transportation, 47; and travel class, 189–92, 209; as tutelary figure for Ernaux, 73; and upward mobility, 12

Zweig, Stefan, 161–62

www.ingramcontent.com/pod-product-compliance
Lightning Source LLC
Chambersburg PA
CBHW022028290426
44109CB00014B/788